John Doyle Lee

JOHN DOYLE LEE
Probably about 1850. From a print in the possession of
Mr. Lee's grandson, Elwood Lee of Virgin City, Utah.

JOHN DOYLE LEE

Zealot, Pioneer Builder, Scapegoat

by

Juanita Brooks

UTAH STATE UNIVERSITY PRESS
LOGAN, UTAH

1992

Books in the Western Experience Series

Quicksand and Cactus: A Memoir of the Southern Mormon Frontier
Juanita Brooks

John Doyle Lee: Zealot, Pioneer Builder, Scapegoat
Juanita Brooks

Emma Lee
Juanita Brooks

Heaven on Horseback: Revivalist Songs and Verse in the Cowboy Tradition
Austin and Alta Fife

Roping the Wind: A Personal History of Cowboys and the Land
Lyman Hafen

Wild Mustangs
Parley J. Paskett

The Roll Away Saloon: Cowboy Tales of the Arizona Strip
Rowland W. Rider as told to Deirdre Murray Paulsen

Cattle in the Cold Desert
James A. Young and B. Abbott Sparks

12 11 10 9 8 7   07 08 09 10 11

Library of Congress Cataloging in Publication Data

Brooks, Juanita, 1898-1989
        John Doyle Lee—zealot, pioneer builder, scapegoat / by Juanita Brooks.
        p. cm.
        Originally published: New ed. with corr. Glendale, CA: A.H. Clark, 1972
        Includes bibliographical references and index.
        ISBN0-87421-162-X
        1. Lee, John Doyle, 1818-1877. 2. Pioneers—Utah—Biography.
3. Mormons—Utah—Biography. 4. Mountain Meadows Massacre, 1857.
5. Utah—History.   I. Title
F826.L4753B76   1992   979.2'02'092—cd20   92-36969
[B]   CIP

Contents

Illustrations

Publisher's Note

Juanita Brooks died in 1989. For a number of years before that, her health had prevented her from actively participating in preparing her books for publication or reprinting. Hence, although *John Doyle Lee: Zealot, Pioneer Builder, Scapegoat* has remained, since its first release, almost continuously in print—in successive editions from Arthur H. Clark, Howe Brothers, and Utah State University Press—it has not been revised or corrected since the 1972 revised edition published by Arthur H. Clark.

Juanita Brooks wrote, as is printed on page 245, "James McKnight.... This man who had been baptized in Australia by Charles W. Wandell, served as bishop of the Minersville ward from 1866 until his excommunication from the church for 'apostasy' on December 19, 1875, soon after the first trial of John D. Lee." There is no evidence in Church of Jesus Christ of Latter-day Saints (LDS) records that the James McKnight who was baptized in Australia by Charles Wandell and served as a Mormon bishop of the Minersville ward was excommunicated from the LDS church. In August 1990, a representative of the LDS Church Historical Department confirmed this in a letter to James C. McKnight, a descendent of Bishop McKnight. A James McKnight of Salt Lake City was excommunicated in 1875. He appears to have been the newspaperman of the same name who was in southern Utah in 1858, and he was probably the man who assisted George A. Smith during the events described herein on pages 242-44. Copies of the letter to James C. McKnight and supporting documents gathered by him are in the possession of the publisher. See also entries for James McKnight in "Journal History of the Church," LDS Church Historical Department, Salt Lake City.

Introduction

Low in the valley, about a mile and a half from the Utah State Highway 18, between St. George and Enterprise, the monument stands, its location clearly pointed by a large sign. The visitor makes a sharp, right-angle turn, winds down the narrow road and through a farm gate to stop at the edge of a gully some fifty feet wide and half as deep. Hanging to the opposite edge is an oblong enclosure surrounded by a thick, rock wall, on the west side of which are steps to the top and a plaque which tells this story:

MOUNTAIN MEADOWS

A FAVORITE RECRUITING PLACE ON
THE OLD SPANISH TRAIL

In this vicinity, September 7-11, 1857, occurred one of the most lamentable tragedies in the annals of the West. A company of about 140 Arkansas and Missouri emigrants led by Captain Charles Fancher, enroute to California, was attacked by white men and Indians. All but 17, being small children, were killed. John D. Lee, who confessed participation as leader, was legally executed here March 23, 1877. Most of the emigrants were buried in their own defense pits.

This monument was reverently dedicated September 10, 1932 by The Utah Pioneer Trails and Landmarks Association and the people of southern Utah

It is difficult to visualize a massacre in this setting. Today's visitor finds peace and absolute quiet here, with only the breeze that sucks through the draw below to ruffle the ancient, pindrop stillness. The wide valley floor is covered with sparse desert vegetation; scrub oak, juniper and stunted cedars dot the higher levels. The lush meadow described with such enthusiasm by early travelers is gone, the stirrup-high grass replaced by this twisting wash. This land, poisoned and contaminated by the blood that was spilled here, has been cursed by God, old-timers say; He washed it clean and decreed that nothing of value should ever again grow upon it. It was only overgrazed, ecologists insist, the sod cut through by the tires of so many wagons that erosion set in and drained off the precious topsoil.

John D. Lee, the only man whose name appears on the plaque, is the subject of this book. He has become one of the most controversial figures in the history of the West, a man around whose name has grown an amazing mass of folklore. In the minds of many he is a fiend incarnate, one who would dash out a child's brains or violate a teen-age girl and then cut her throat. Tales have been told not only of murder, but of a strange Satanic power by which he could win any woman to his evil lust. One legend says that actually he was not killed, but faced a squad whose guns were loaded with blanks, fell back uninjured into his coffin, and was hauled away to escape into Mexico.

His family, on the other hand, picture him as a hero-martyr who died to save the good name of his church and assumed in silence the full disgrace of a group crime for which he was not responsible. They insist that, although he participated in the massacre, he did so on the orders of his ecclesiastical and military superiors and under protest.

Somewhere between, lies the truth. For more than a hundred years the whole subject has been taboo in the Mormon Church, something to skirt around, leave out, or glance at quickly, then look the other way. The story of a massacre by Indians acting under the direction of John D. Lee has been stoutly defended. However, except for his connection with that tragedy, Lee's name has been cut from the records of the church.

It seems time now to bring him out of the shadows and present him in his true light as a zealot, frontiersman, colonizer, and loyal member of his church. That I, who have no blood ties to John D. Lee, should attempt to do this has given rise to so many questions that I shall outline briefly the long chain of events which led to this book.

I must go far back to the winter when, at the age of nineteen, I was teaching school in Mesquite, Nevada. There I became acquainted with Brother Nephi Johnson, a patriarchal old man with a long beard and a kindly face. One afternoon in the spring he entered my schoolroom, walked up the aisle, and seated himself at my desk. Waving his cane at the startled children he said, "Now you go right on with your work. Don't let me disturb you."

As soon as I had dismissed the children, I came to talk to him, never guessing the reason he had come in. He did not leave me long in doubt.

"I want you to do some writing for me," he said. "My eyes have witnessed things that my tongue has never uttered, and before I die, I want them written down. I want you to do it for me."

Why did I not get a pen and paper, settle down right there, and record what he had to say? What a story I might have had! But a girl of nineteen usually is interested more in young men than in old ones,

The Monument at Mountain Meadows
Photograph by Oliver Sigurdson, Los Angeles, California.

and I was no exception. I told him that I would really like to do as he wished, but that evening I had another appointment. I would be very glad to do it, though, sometime soon.

I was so engrossed with the closing-of-school activities, that almost before I knew it, school was out and I was at home, working on my trousseau. Then word came that Brother Johnson was ill and asking for the "little school-teacher."

I went at once to his bedside. He recognized me, but was too weak to talk clearly, too tired to follow a coherent thought. I remained at the home during his last two days. In his delirium he preached in the Indian language, sang, prayed, and exhorted, tossing about and jumbling things together. At one time he opened his eyes wide to the ceiling saying, "Blood! Blood! Blood!!" in a way that made my scalp fairly crawl.

"What troubles him?" I asked one of those present. "He acts as though he is haunted."

"Maybe he is. He was at the Mountain Meadows massacre, you know," was the answer.

No, I certainly had not known. I could not imagine this man connected with violence of any kind. He seemed the epitome of old age at its best, a sheaf of clean wheat, ripe unto the harvest. I tried to visualize him as a young man, tall, strong, handsome, — and honorable.

Too late I guessed what he had wanted me to write.

Life has a way of catching one up to fulfill its own purposes. I became a wife, mother and widow, in the short space of fifteen months. Then I was faced with gathering up my broken plans. I finished college and taught school again. Eventually I remarried and had four additional children. The years passed swiftly by. Only once during that time was I brought into contact with the event at Mountain Meadows. That was when I rode over the ground in a covered wagon, en route from the Truman ranch on the Mogotsu to the town of Enterprise. I had only to study the terrain as we slowly inched off the miles to know that if more than two people ever met at this place it was not by accident. A group would have come only under orders. Whose orders?

In time I became interested in collecting original diaries. Under a WPA project I was put in charge of finding old records, supervising the copying and proofreading of them, and making an index. Whenever the name of John D. Lee appeared, I made a note of it.

Then fate took a hand. In Arlington, Virginia, a man attending a party learned that the Henry E. Huntington Library at San Marino, California, had purchased the original diaries of John D. Lee from the descendants of William Nelson, U.S. Marshall who had charge of Lee's execution. My good friend, Dale L. Morgan, passed the word on to me, and I wrote immediately to verify it and to ask permission to see the diaries.

Dr. Robert G. Cleland invited me to come to San Marino, where under charge of strictest secrecy I was allowed to examine the original documents. The trip resulted in my being appointed a "Field Fellow" to collect original Mormon manuscripts which the Huntington Library photostated for their files. A few years later, under a Rockefeller Foundation grant I was offered a stipend to do work on the Mountain Meadows massacre. This resulted in a book by that name, published by Stanford Press in 1950.

Once again the hand of fate entered in. Among the papers of the Office of Indian Affairs Dale L. Morgan found an original letter dated Crooked Creek, Arkansas, April 27, 1860, and signed by William C. Mitchell, Special Agent, giving the names of the entire company from Arkansas. This is the only list extant of the parents and children who were killed at Mountain Meadows, and it had arrived too late to be included in *Senate Document No. 42*, the official government investigation. This letter was found after my book was finished, but arrived in time to be included as a footnote.

Then came the request from Dr. Cleland to help him edit the original diaries of John D. Lee. As I followed Lee day by day, I became more and more involved emotionally, more eager to learn of his early life and to fill in the missing parts.

For those who know the settings, there can be no substitute for reading Lee's own account as published in *A Mormon Chronicle, The Diaries of John D. Lee*. Despite wide gaps between some entries, he writes more eloquently for himself than anyone else can write for him. Some of his records may be permanently lost; others, though unpublished, are available and have been used in this book; still others are extant but are not available.

It is my hope that the reader will find here an authentic picture of John D. Lee as the loyal, fervent, Mormon convert of the first generation, who was willing to give his full strength and talent to the building up of the kingdom of God upon the earth, according to his understanding of it.

1812-1838
The Convert

The piece of paper pulled over the chimney of the coal oil lamp served as a reflector to throw full light on the pages of the book at the same time that it cast a shadow across the room, on the little form lying so straight and cold under the sheet. It was two o'clock, the low tide of the night, the hour when evil is abroad and darkness reigns. John D. Lee set the open book face down on the table and went to the body, turned back the sheet, and lifted the damp cloth from the face. His little two-year-old, Elizabeth Adoline, a few weeks ago so bright and happy, lay like a marble doll, her hair in damp curls about her face. He dipped the folded cloth into the saltpetre solution on the stand, squeezed out the extra moisture, and fanned it back and forth to cool it. Then after examining the alabaster brow for any sign of discoloration, he touched the cold cheek, replaced the cloth and sheet, and returned to his book.

He had spent his tears for this child during her illness, in the long hours at her bedside, when with all the remedies and prayers he knew, he tried to save her. Now that she was gone, he wondered if ever again a child could be so sweet, so affectionate toward her father. Resigned, he picked up *The Book of Mormon*. He had started it a week ago before little Elizabeth had been taken ill, and during her brief struggle for life had put it aside. Now after reading all night, he neared the end. As he turned the page of Moroni, chapter ten, the fourth verse drew his instant attention:

> And when ye shall receive these things, I would exhort you that ye ask God, the Eternal Father, in the name of Christ if these things are not true; and if ye shall ask with a sincere heart, with real intent, having faith in Christ, he will manifest the truth of it unto you, by the power of the Holy Ghost.

Surely this had been written especially for him, or why had it taken on that lifted, bold, three-dimensional look? Certainly it was clear enough; a condition and a promise. On his knees he asked God to keep that promise.

Suddenly he was filled with a joy that was a mixture of exhilaration and peace. He knew! Beyond all shadow of a doubt, he knew! He knew in such a way that for all the remaining years of his life he never once doubted that God had given him a direct answer. Other men might dissect this book, argue as to its geography, search it for evidences of fraud, compare it with contemporary publications, but Lee brushed all these aside. For him, there was but one answer. The book was true!

Trembling, he rose to his feet. Truly God moves in a mysterious way His wonders to perform, he told himself. He carefully shapes our lives, taking us into the depths of frustration and sorrow that we may breathe more freely the air of spiritual ecstasy. He stretched himself. His body seemed filled with a potential of power waiting to be released, as though head up he stood facing a future bright with new opportunities.

He would not waken Aggatha Ann to tell her. Weary with watching and spent with weeping, she had taken little Sarah Jane to bed early. Dear Aggatha! She was blest to have another little baby girl to love. When their first-born, William Oliver, had died before he was a year old, she had sorrowed for months, and this time she was taking it harder than ever. He would wait until she came in to tell her his experience, hoping that she would share it.

He sat down to resume his reading, but instead leaned back to meditate on what had happened to him. As he relaxed, it seemed as if with the eye of Omniscience, he saw his life pass in review.

John D. Lee was born on September 12, 1812, in Kaskaskia, the capital of the three-year-old territory of Illinois. At that time, it was a busy, important little city with more than a hundred years of history behind it. It lay across the Mississippi River, about a hundred miles south of "The Rock," or the present site of St. Louis, on a peninsula whose rocky promontory jutted out so far into the stream that the village was surrounded on three sides by water. The old Kaskaskia remained essentially a French town, built around the church and the central square; the homes of stone or upright timbers with steep, thatched, overhanging roofs, surrounded by white picket fences that enclosed bright flower gardens. This section of town was a part of the very early life of John D. Lee, for it was to this church that he was taken as a child. Though it was crude, with its upright lumber walls, whitewashed on the inside and decorated with indifferent paintings, still the candles in that dim interior and the priest in his robes filled the little boy with awe.

Outside in the yard was the "Liberty Bell of the West" suspended in its own rock tower, its oft-repeated story well known to all the people. Older than the Liberty Bell in Philadelphia by eleven years, this one was cast in France and presented by King Louis xv in gratitude to the town that had sent 6000 cwt. of wheat by barge to the starving colony at New Orleans. The bell was brought by ship to that point and then transported upstream on a barge pulled along by ropes and cables from the shore, inched along a few miles a day in a three-month's journey. Just two years to the day after the bell at Philadelphia had rung out its declaration of liberty to the world, this one proclaimed that the nation about to be born would extend to the Mississippi River rather than the Allegheny Mountains.

The town had spread out, by 1812, along the river bank to the east, up over the bluffs, and back into the fertile timberland. River trade was brisk, with boats and craft of many kinds moving from Galena on the north to New Orleans on the south. The territorial offices stimulated land trade also, people coming on horseback or with their clumsy, two-wheeled wooden carts to trade and to take care of official business.

This prosperity was to be short lived, for the Cumberland Road started by Thomas Jefferson in 1806 had its route marked out to go through the Cumberland Gap, to Columbus, Ohio, then to Indianapolis, Indiana, and on to Vandalia, Illinois, making that central city the territorial capital. The road was designed to be sixty-two feet wide, surfaced with stone covered with gravel, with stone bridges to span the streams and gentle slopes cut around the hills — an express route for stagecoach and mail as well as a safe route for emigrants.

Also by this time, St. Louis to the north had become the outfitting center for all points west, and quickly overshadowed its downstream rival of earlier days.

Lee's maternal grandfather, John Doyle, was a man of importance in Kaskaskia, having come there first with the army of George Rogers Clark in the daring exploit which wrenched the fort from the British. His grandchildren had heard the story again and again. They knew the very place where the soldiers had remained hidden that afternoon in July, 1778, waiting for nightfall before they made the attack, and how they paddled quietly across the river to the old fort, now replaced by a stockade high on the bluff. Each man was assigned his duty; some to station themselves at strategic points in the town while others went with Clark, intimidated the guards, and dragged the British commander out of bed in his underwear to sign the papers of surrender.

Perhaps an even better story was that of the young redhaired leader going to the dance where the French folks were contesting in reels and jigs. A squatting Indian near the door marked the stranger with a shouted warning; the dance stopped in confusion. Clark called out for them to go on with their fun, but to understand that they were now dancing under the American flag rather than the British. He then reassured the priest, telling him that none would be harmed who returned quietly home and went about their business.

There were many stories of that expedition; of men wading in icy water, sometimes waist deep, to capture Fort Vincennes, and their return to Virginia. John Doyle was one of the group of eight men who first came back to settle in the Kaskaskia area. He was one of the first to get an allotment of 400 acres of land under the grant of 1787, and perhaps the first school teacher in what is now the state of Illinois, certainly the second. He was a linguist, speaking the French and Indian languages as well as English, and a large landholder, but one who did not devote his time to gaining wealth.[1] He married a daughter of Henry Smith, another early settler. Her name has not yet been found, but it seems that she died early, before 1810 according to the census record, and that she left only two children, Elizabeth and Charlotte.

---

[1] Much of the material concerning John Doyle comes to us from *The Combined Histories of Randolph, Monroe, and Perry Counties, Illinois,* published by J. L. McDonough & Company, Philadelphia, 1883. This large volume is the work of many people who have written from first-hand knowledge or have collected from original sources. It has been quoted by many writers. On page 64 it states:

The favorable report of the Illinois country, carried back by the soldiers of Col. Clark, occasioned the first American migration in 1780. Descending the Ohio, and stemming the current of the Mississippi, a colony of settlers reached Kaskaskia, among the members of which were John Montgomery, John Doyle, David Pagan, Joseph Anderson, John Dodge, Minard Asurgus, James Curry, and Levi Teel. . .

John Doyle was one of Clark's soldiers. He resided in and near Kaskaskia. He was a man of some education and taught one of the earliest English schools in the county. He was acquainted with both the French and the Indian languages, and was often employed as an interpreter. He was unambitious, made no endeavor to obtain either wealth or position, but was respected as an honest man.

The above description is quoted verbatim in *The Pioneer History of Illinois* by John Reynolds (Chicago: Fergus, 1887) p. 424.

As to John Doyle's receiving land in payment for service in the army, two sources give evidence. The first is *American State Papers, Public Lands* (Duff Green ed.) v. 2, p. 132, National Archives:

. . . Of these acts . . . one approved March 3, 1791, gave to each "head of a family" who had cultivated or improved land in Illinois prior to and including 1788, the right to four hundred acres. . . Of those claiming under these acts . . . John Doyle. . .

The second comes from a letter written by Mrs. Josephine L. Harper, Manuscripts Librarian, Wisconsin State Historical Society, dated April 3, 1957:

In series κ, Clark Miscellanies, composed primarily of printed materials, volume 4K consists of a document compiled and printed in Virginia in 1833 and containing a list of men who served "in the Illinois Regiment and the Western Army." On this list the name of John Doyle appears with the notation that he was entitled to land for 3 years' service. . .

John D. Lee's mother was Elizabeth. In 1799 she was married to Oliver Reed, a promising young man of that area. For five years they lived together, prosperous and happy. They had two children, Elizabeth Virginia, usually called Eliza, and William Oliver, named for his father.

But tragedy overtook them. One night, following some difficulty over a land claim, a man came into the house and struck the sleeping husband over the head with the iron seat of a loom, killing him instantly. The baby was injured also. When the mother, awakening, called out the man's name, he struck at her and then fled. Later he was apprehended, tried, and hanged for this crime.[2]

The widowed Elizabeth took her two children and went to live with her father. According to family legend, her son died two years later. The official county record shows that she was married to Ralph Lee on February 26, 1811.

Of this man, very little record has been found. The family say that he was of the Lees of Virginia, a second cousin of General Robert E. Lee, and that he served as an apprentice and learned the carpenter's trade in Baltimore, Maryland. The court records of Randolph County show that in 1811 he was administrator of the estate of Isaac Baker; in 1813 he was paid $8.50 by the county for making a coffin; and on January 24, 1813, he registered his brand as RL, with the ear mark a crop off the left and a small fork in the right ear.[3] Trifling as these are, they indicate that the man was responsible, had some skill as a carpenter, and that he owned cattle. His son said he was a master workman who contracted and put up buildings, and erected a fine home for himself. When his wife's health failed so that he knew she could never be well again, he began to drink to excess.

John D. Lee's earliest memories were of a pale and listless mother, and an eleven-year-old sister who dressed, fed, and cared for him. Another item in the court record would seem to bear this out: "May 1815 Ralph Lee and wife Elizabeth Doyle execute a deed of trust to George Fisher of all property to be held in trust for children Elizabeth Reed and John Lee." Did Elizabeth know at the time that she had not

---

[2] Lee tells this story in the opening chapter of every edition of his *Confessions*. Supporting evidence is found in *The Combined Histories*, cited in note 1 above, page 70:

. . . Near the present town of Rockwood, a man by the name of Emsley Jones settled about the year 1804. In a quarrel with a man named Reed, living in the same neighborhood in the Mississippi bottoms, he killed Reed. For this murder he was hung in the commons, south of Kaskaskia. His execution was witnessed by a great concourse of people. This was the second hanging to take place in the county. [The first was an Indian.]

[3] These dates and all those as cited from the Court Records of Randolph County can be identified only by date. The material is chronologically arranged.

long to live? Was the property which was deeded only her share of her father's estate? Was her husband already drinking so heavily that she could not trust the welfare of the children in his hands, especially the daughter by her earlier marriage? She died in November after the court action was taken.

Here again the record is blurred. Lee's *Confessions* say that his sister Elizabeth, then about fourteen years of age, first went to live with her Aunt Charlotte, who was married to James Conner, but was so unhappy there that she left, going to the home of her guardian, Dr. George Fisher, where she remained until she was married. The three-year-old John D., evidently supported by the money from his mother's estate, was put into the hands of a colored nurse who spoke only French. For four years this woman, whose name has not come down to us, cared for the child, evidently teaching him habits of personal cleanliness and instilling into his mind many of the folk ways and superstitions which marked his later life.

The death of his grandfather, John Doyle, on October 20, 1819, changed his way of life. His uncle, James Conner, was appointed administrator of the estate,[4] which meant that John D. Lee became a member of this household.

In later years, Lee wrote bitterly about his life with Uncle Jim and Aunt Charlotte. Instead of being an only child supervised by a nurse, he became one of a family of six children, two girls of whom were older, two other girls and a boy younger than he. Moreover, he spoke only French, while they spoke English. Most important of all, he was made to feel that he was an extra child in a home where there were already too many children. His aunt was an impetuous woman, loud of voice and sharp of tongue; quick to criticize and quicker still to strike. Her husband was easy-going, given to a sociable drink which often ended in complete drunkenness. His wife's anger at him was too often taken out on the children.

Still there must have been some happy times. Certainly there was work — wood to cut and carry; cows to milk; horses, pigs, and chickens to feed; corn meal to grind; pots to scour; weeds to pull. But this work was not drudgery, and there were opportunities for fun and adventure. On the bank of the Mississippi where heavy wooded growth

---

[4] The court records of Randolph County contain two papers signed by J. Clyde Hamilton, County clerk and clerk of the probate court, both dated November 11, 1819. The first is an affidavit from James Conner to the effect that . . . "John Doyle of said county died about the 20th day of October 1819 intestate to the best of the deponant's knowledge and belief. . ." The other is a bond executed by James Conner, Paul Harralson, and George Day, all of Randolph County which binds each of them in the sum of five hundred dollars in the appointment of James Conner as administrator of the estate of John Doyle and in his proper discharge of the duties of that assignment.

filled in all the hollows and creek bottoms like a jungle there might be mosquitoes and woodticks and snakes, but also there was game to hunt — rabbits, squirrels, possums, grouse, and quail. There were berries to gather in the summer and nuts in the fall. Best of all, was the companionship of other children who shared the chores and the excursions.

Though he felt that he had to work hard, John D. Lee had some good training during those nine years under his Uncle Jim and Aunt Charlotte. He developed resourcefulness and independence; he learned the art of fishing and acquired an uncanny accuracy with a gun. He had experience in the use of farm tools and in the repair of farm machinery, all of which stood him in good stead during his later life.

What had become of Ralph Lee in the meantime? His name appears only once more in the records of Randolph County. In 1822, "Ralph Lee, an insolvent, was brought into court and presented a list of his debts. He was discharged from all obligations, and declared bankrupt." Family legend says that he left the area intending to go to Texas, but present day descendants have searched for records of him there without success.

During his sixteenth year John D. Lee determined to leave the Conner home and fend for himself. He thought a young man in good health would do better to be free of all the contention, so slipped away, following a trail shortcut to Kaskaskia, in search of his god-father, William Morrison, a prominent business man there. Failing to contact him, he went to Robert Morrison, brother of William, and secured work as a mail carrier.

His horseback run was from St. Genevieve to Pinkney via Potosi, a distance of about one hundred and twenty-seven miles, and west of the river, which seemed very far indeed from the farm. He was to receive board and clothing and seven dollars a month wages; the horses were furnished and cared for by Mr. Morrison's help stationed at the camps. The first few trips were bitter punishment for the boy, but as he became accustomed to the long hours in the saddle, familiar with the roads, and attached to his mounts, he began to enjoy it. He found interest in the world about him — animals and their signs, birds, the weather — nothing escaped him. It was there that he developed the love and pride he always took in a fine horse.

During the next six months he changed routes twice. The third one took him past the farm, and he could not resist calling. After all, he had been gone for six months and this was the only home he knew. He had done a man's work and had some money in his pocket; he could afford to stop. They all seemed so genuinely glad to see him, especially little Edgar, that it warmed his heart. They urged him to come back and manage the farm himself during the summer. He

could make more than he could riding a mail pony. His Uncle Jim
was at the lead mines in Galena; spring was coming and the crops
should be planted. Before this show of affection, Lee's bitterness
melted. Or was it the smile and unspoken encouragement of the new
girl who had been added to the family — Emily Conner, Uncle Jim's
niece, who like himself was motherless. John D. closed his accounts
with Mr. Morrison and came back to the farm.

That summer he worked hard and conditions were so favorable that
he had a good crop. There was food for the family and for the farm
animals, but little cash for him. He considered leaving to find work
for the winter. When Uncle Jim returned in the late fall, however, he
was so pleased with what had taken place that he insisted John D.
remain and attend school that winter. There would be time for other
employment in the spring. Many years later when Lee wrote in his
Confessions that he had had only three months of formal schooling in
his life, he meant this winter. He went with Emily and the younger
children, and tried to get as much out of his books as he could.

In the spring he helped Uncle Jim make a cart for general use on
the farm. They had both seen the Yankee wagons with their iron tires,
shining paint, and many gadgets and additions too difficult for them
to duplicate. Theirs would be an all wood, two-wheeled cart with a
sturdy box and double shafts, to be pulled by a single horse. Even so,
it required a careful selection of wood for each part, precise fitting,
and firm bolting. When finished, it was sturdy and usable, and a great
satisfaction to its builders. For young John D. Lee the building was
an experience which was of great value later in his life.

Early in 1832 the Black Hawk war broke out in the northern part of
Illinois, and James Conner enlisted. At the first call for men, John D.
Lee offered his services, but since he was still a minor, he must have
the consent of his guardian. This accounts for the entry in the Randolph County records of that year that, "John Lee, a minor over 14
years of age, chooses James Conner as his guardian."

The war was of short duration. The record shows that the Third
Regiment, Second Brigade, of the Illinois Mounted Volunteers were
mustered in on May 15, 1832, and mustered out on August 17, 1832;
Josiah Briggs was captain; John Morrison, first lieutenant. John Lee's
name was number twenty-two in a list of forty-two, and beside it, the
notation, "Horse lost." [5]

When he reached the farm again, weary, ragged, with no horse and
little money, he felt that, though he was just twenty years old, at last
he was a man. He decided to call on Emily, who was now living with
her father and his second wife, declare his love for her, and make a

---

[5] This comes from *The Combined Histories, etc.* p. 204.

proposal of marriage, for she had come to mean more to him than all the world. He found that she returned his feeling. They planned to be married as soon as he could earn enough to set them up in housekeeping. In the meantime, they would write often and would be true to each other.

Where should a young man seeking employment go except up the river to St. Louis, then the center of activity for the far west? Its population of some seven thousand was made up of people from all parts of the globe; its business was not only up and down the river, but came from all points east and fanned out in all directions west. Lee finally got employment on a river boat. As a child he had often dreamed of being an officer on one of those ships.

Through his industry and resourcefulness as a worker on the ship he attracted the attention of a Mr. Boggs who operated a store at the mining town of Galena. Would Lee be interested in a position as clerk in his store? Would he! It was too good to be true!

These mines were among the oldest in the west, having been worked as early as 1719 — more than a hundred years. Now they were entering into a boom period during which the place fairly hummed with activity. Men spilled out of the tunnels, from the mills, and from river boats. There were lumbermen from the forests to the north, builders, contractors, and gamblers. Lee soon learned to recognize many of them by name and most of them by profession. This was a period of much building — mansions of three and four stories rising on the terraced hillside, looking down upon the shacks below. Their stone buttresses and steps matched their walls, while ornate iron fences and trimmings added decoration.

Lee was introduced into a new kind of life. Through his hands, from dock and warehouse, passed freight of all kinds — groceries, drygoods, building materials. In addition to his work as clerk and warehouse attendant, he acted as bartender, serving coffee, beer, or whiskey and making up sandwiches or hot lunches for men on night shifts. Every moment was packed full, and he felt a fierce joy at being a part of all this activity.

Mr. Boggs trusted him, praised him, and advised him, and Lee tried to merit the confidence of his employer by being alert. Mr. Boggs, watching him loan money to a companion for a gambling stake, at once advised against it, insisting that a man who gambled could never build a successful business. He should buy to advantage, sell at whatever the market would bear, but give full value for money taken in, so that satisfied customers would continue to trade. He must be cheerful, honest and accommodating if he wished to succeed.

Lee followed his advice, and true to his promise to Emily, remained sober and frugal, saving his money and working extra hours to make more. Two incidents combined to make him leave earlier than he had planned: a letter from Emily so tender that a surge of longing rose in him that he could hardly resist, and a fight with the camp tough, Shaunce. This fellow often came in to drink and ended by throwing bottles and glasses around until regular customers took his entry as their signal to leave. One night Lee opposed him and instantly was grasped in a twisting, straining clasp that it seemed would crush out his life. Then in some way he got the thumb of the bully between his teeth, and held on until the terror of the camp was brought begging to his knees. After this he decided that his life might not be safe there any longer.

Taking no time for regrets, Lee collected his final pay, purchased a fine dress suit, bought some trinkets for Emily, and started back to Kaskaskia with five hundred dollars in his pocket. He found Emily employed at a small tavern owned by a brother-in-law and determined to stay on for the season. Therefore, with time on his hands he began playing cards with some Frenchmen who frequented the place, professionals who let him win just often enough to keep him encouraged. Emily grew worried as she watched his money melt away; perhaps because of this she would not accept his offer for an immediate marriage. He knew well that she wanted him to say that he would stop gambling, but he wanted her to love and trust him as he was. He expected to stop, but resented being told to. This proud, perverse streak in his nature kept him from making any concession, so although it hurt him bitterly, he left.

Smarting under hurt pride and the loss of most of his money, he set out for Vandalia where his sister Eliza lived. There he became acquainted with the Woolsey family, a large, sociable group who welcomed him and looked upon him as a very remarkable young man. The eldest of five sisters, Aggatha Ann, appealed to him, and after a brief courtship they were married on July 24, 1833.

Now, five years later, he was twenty-six years old, married, and established in a good home of his own; part of his success due to his own industry and part to the small legacy which he had received from his grandmother Doyle.[6] He had fathered three children, one now in

---

[6] *The Combined Histories*, page 65, says that "Settlements were also made in the year 1780 by John Hilterbrand, Henry and Elijah Smith, and Haydon Wells, on the east side of the Kaskaskia River, above the mouth of Nine Mile Creek." The court record for 1834 shows that:

John Lee and his sister, Eliza, otherwise Elizabeth, Reed, are legal heirs of Elizabeth Doyle, late wife of Ralph Lee, said Elizabeth being a descendant of Henry Smith, Deceased, do declare settlement has been made of their mother's estate.

the cemetery, a second to be placed there tomorrow, the third asleep in her mother's arms. Sitting with death, he was facing a new life.

Though he might remember himself as an unwanted child in Aunt Charlotte's home, or a boy riding a mail pony through winter sleet, or a young man serving at a bar in a mining town, Lee knew that the most important event of his life to date was his meeting with Elder King. When that young missionary had called at his door the previous fall, Lee invited him in, and gave him food and lodging, but told him frankly not to preach religion. That line was good for some folks, but not for John D., whose creed was to live uprightly before God, to deal honestly with his fellow men, and to get on in the world. If a man wanted to spend his time walking from place to place preaching, that was his own business; as for Lee, he had never turned a beggar away hungry. He saw no reason to close his door to a self-appointed minister.

He was attracted, however, by the sincerity of Elder King. Also, the fact that all the ministers of the area attacked him so viciously was all in his favor. Lee wondered why were they so bitter if they were not afraid of the message King carried?

Then within a few weeks Levi Stewart, his neighbor and friend, called to tell of two other Mormon missionaries who were preaching in the neighborhood. Although his wife had been quickly converted, Stewart wanted to learn more of this strange, new sect, and like a doubting Thomas, went to see for himself. He brought back with him a copy of *The Book of Mormon*, the book which presently had brought about a miracle. Lee knew that all other plans must be set aside that he might gather with the saints and lend his strength to the building of the kingdom.

When he related his experience to Aggatha the next morning, she shared his enthusiasm. They began at once to put their affairs into shape to move westward.

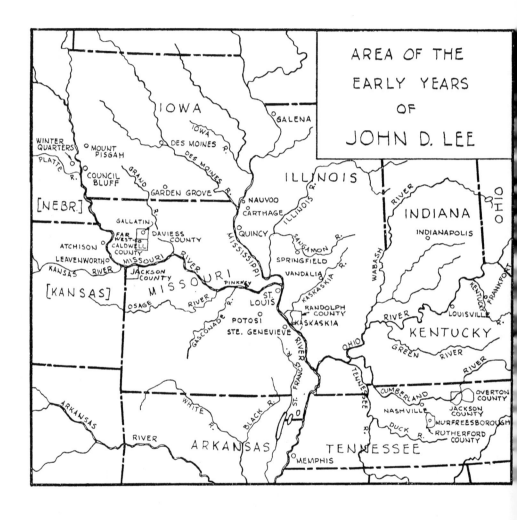

AREA OF THE
EARLY YEARS
OF
JOHN D. LEE

1838
Defender of the Faith

John D. Lee knew little of the history of the church he was about to join. He had heard how the fourteen-year-old Joseph Smith, emotionally spent with religious revivals and confused by conflicting claims of the various sects, had gone to his Bible for guidance. As if by design, he opened the book to the Epistle of James, Chapter 1, verse 4: "If any man lack wisdom, let him ask of God that giveth to all men liberally and upbraideth not, and it shall be given him. . ." The boy did ask God. To him, in answer, appeared God the Father and His son, Jesus Christ, to tell him that, if he proved faithful, he might be instrumental in reestablishing the true church of Christ upon the earth. After his own experience, John D. Lee could easily believe this story.

He learned, too, of an ancient civilization upon this continent, and of its records on the mysterious Golden Plates which ages ago had been hidden in the hill Cumorah in western New York. From these plates, carefully shielded from the eyes of all but a few select men, Joseph Smith had translated *The Book of Mormon*. Of the full truth of this Lee now had no doubt.

The Church of Jesus Christ of Latter-day Saints, even now called the Mormon Church because of the book, was organized at Palmyra, New York, on April 6, 1830. Beginning with only six members, it had grown by leaps and bounds until in just eight years it boasted thousands, with new converts every day. Lee knew little of their troubles first in New York and later in Kirtland, Ohio, and cared even less. He had heard of the violent persecutions which had driven the Mormons from Jackson County, Missouri, but felt that as the ministers had all combined against Elder King, so the powers of Satan would marshal all their forces against the true church of God. West was the direction in which all were moving — west, where there was space and freedom. Perhaps God was behind it all, shaping circumstances to test his people and to bring them to the place He had chosen. For Lee the past held little that was important; the future was full of promise.

The Lees arrived at the outskirts of Far West on June 4, 1838. For miles in every direction they could see the people breaking land, fencing it, building homes. As if by magic, the whole prairie was being transformed. Actually, the first surveys for the city of Far West were

made a year earlier, having begun on April 7, 1837, at which time the
first town lots were sold. So great was the inrush of settlers that in
less than three months ground was broken for the erection of a
temple. By November 10, the officials had voted to enlarge the city to
a two-mile square, and now the whole plain was becoming one great
settlement.

We learn something of this yeasty period from the diary of William
Swartzell, another convert.[1] He had walked from Ohio to Far West,
carrying only a knapsack containing a change of clothes, letters of
introduction, and the small record book in which he jotted down each
day's experiences. He arrived just one week ahead of the Lee-Stewart
group, and secured employment as cook for the surveying camp.
Every day he recorded the work as the survey extended farther and
farther out, marveling at the numbers of people who arrived daily
and the speed with which each newly staked area was occupied. In
the town itself were six Mormon stores, all doing a thriving business.
The press which had printed the first two issues of *The Elder's Journal*
in Kirtland, Ohio, had been moved and would put out the third issue
on the following July 3. Word had come that the remaining saints of
Kirtland would leave there at once, which would swell the population
of Far West by more than five hundred souls in one company.

On June 10, John D. Lee and his wife attended meeting in Far
West, and for the first time saw Joseph Smith and heard him speak.
Mormon literature teems with accounts of the impression the youthful
prophet made upon his followers. George Laub told of the thrill of
"striking glad hands" with this man for whom he instantly felt a
greater affection than for any other person on earth; John Taylor
reported than an electric current ran up his arm when the Prophet
grasped his hand. Brigham Young, older than Joseph and a hard-
headed man of affairs who waited three years before he was converted, was so stirred at his first meeting that he spoke of it as "like a
fire in my bones."

Lee had come prepared to be impressed, but the reality exceeded
his expectations. He thought Joseph Smith carried an air of majesty

---

[1] This pamphlet is very rare. One copy is in the New York Public Library and
another in the Missouri Historical Society. A typescript made by Dale L. Morgan
is in the Utah State Historical Society files.

The fly-leaf of the diary reads: MORMONISM EXPOSED, BEING A JOURNAL OF
RESIDENCE IN MISSOURI from the 28 of May to the 20th of August, 1838, together
with an Appendix, containing the revelation concerning the Golden Bible, with
numerous extracts from the 'Book of Covenants,' &c., &c., by WILLIAM SWARTZELL,
sometime Deacon in the Church of 'Latter-Day-Saints,' commonly called 'Mormons,' PEKIN, O., PUBLISHED BY THE AUTHOR. A. Ingram, Jr., Printer, Pittsburgh.
1840.

that made him seem taller than his six feet as he faced the audience, and more handsome and commanding than an ordinary man. Attracting every eye and holding every heart by the sheer magnetism of his personality, he played upon the congregation as though it were a musical instrument responsive to his slightest touch. When he spoke of the beauties and mysteries of the kingdom, he brought out the melody in deep, strong tones, into which with great skill was interspersed occasional light, sparkling notes of humor.

So great was the press of people around the speaker at the close of the service that John D. did not meet him. His time would come, he told himself. His immediate problem was to select a location, make some purchases, and become established before winter. The season was so far advanced that he had no time to lose.

After walking about the city and riding horseback over the outlying area, he and Levi decided that they would do better where there was more land available. They finally settled twenty miles southeast of Far West, near where the Stewart brothers had already stopped. They named the place Ambrosia, and there on the following Sunday, June 17, 1838, Lee and Aggatha were baptized.

As he stood facing Daniel Cathcart in the clear stream where the water was above their knees, it seemed he was enacting a pageant. After the brief prayer, he was laid for an instant full length upstream, supported by strong hands. As he came up, his hair washed back from his face, his clothes dripping, he felt that there was more than just symbolism in all this. He felt cleansed in spirit, as though all that was dross and cheap in his nature literally had been washed away. He was ready to dedicate his life to the work of God, and to put the welfare of the Kingdom before everything else. This was the most important day of his life; a date to keep as an anniversary.

He set to work with renewed vigor. He had a beautiful location for his home, land with deep, rich soil, a fine stream of water, a clump of trees for firewood, and a small lake stocked with fish. Aggatha said they had everything they had left behind and more — except for two little graves. She too had been stirred at her baptism and now lent her full strength to the work until soon they had a small sod house built and crops growing.

Within a few weeks trouble stirred the air. Missourians, watching the companies arriving daily and seeing the system and industry with which the people set to work, began to threaten and harass outlying farmers. As the Mormons increased in numbers they began to talk of defending themselves. Should a man stand by and watch his home burn, see his cattle stolen, his family driven out to huddle in the underbrush like frightened animals? Men who had experienced such treatment in Jackson County only two years before, men who still bore the scars of whip lashes on their backs were ready for action.

That Fourth of July, 1838, was the occasion for an elaborate celebration. There was an impressive parade which included bands, floats, and cavalry, with a spirited meeting on the public square. Brother Sidney Rigdon, orator of the day, grew eloquent in the recital of past grievances, and concluded that:

> . . . that mob that comes on us to disturb us, it shall be between us and them a war of extermination. . . Remember it then, All men! We will never be the aggressors; we will infringe on the rights of no people, but shall stand for our own until death. . . This day we then proclaim ourselves free, with a purpose and determination that can never be broken. . .

Shortly before this a secret organization had been effected, which became known as the Danite band. When William Swartzell was initiated on July 21, he said there were many ahead of him. Joseph Allen Stout wrote that, ". . . mobs began to rise and commit depredations till we were forced to resort to arms in order to save ourselves and property. The Church organized under captains Tens, Fifties, One Hundreds, and One Thousands. . . They [the Missourians] called our organization the DANITE BAND. I belonged to the 3rd fifty led by Reynolds Cahoon." His brother Hosea was also a member, evidently an officer, for years later he wrote that ". . . we went on again performing as we rode some Danite evolutions of horsemanship as we practiced in the War in Davis County Missouri in the fall of 1838." At another time he noted that "After drilling a while I took them through the old Missouri Danite drill."

John D. Lee early became a member of the band, for though he had no grievances to avenge, he was ready to defend his people. The members swore to stand by each other and their church leaders in any emergency, and had secret signs and passwords by which they might identify other members. These they promised, on pain of death, never to divulge.

Tensions began to mount. The election at Gallatin on August 6, 1838, set the match to the powder keg. All the Mormons from the outlying farms had gathered in to cast their votes. Some of them, like Lee, were relatively new and unacquainted in the area. The town itself consisted of only about ten buildings, three of them saloons; the rest, houses. Near the polls lay a pile of oak sticks the outside of which had been cut off for shingles, leaving the hearts about four feet long and seven pounds in weight; a perfect size for use as clubs.

The first Mormon to approach the polls was "Shoemaker" Samuel Brown, who was accosted by one Dick Welding, a Missourian.

He asked, "Are you a Mormon preacher, sir?"

"Yes, sir, I am."

"Do you believe in healing the sick by laying on of hands?"

"We do."

"You are a damned liar, and Joe Smith is a damned imposter."

With that, Welding struck Brown with his fist, knocking him down. Immediately another Mormon sprang to the assistance of the hapless Brown, which instantly brought a group of Missourians into the fight and resulted in a free-for-all. In the confusion Lee saw John L. Butler give the Danite sign of distress, and grasp a club as he cried out, "Charge, Danites!"

Instantly Lee jumped into the fray along with seven others who had recognized the sign, which both he and Swartzell described as ending by "placing the right hand to the right temple, the thumb behind the ear."

These eight men swung their oaken clubs with such force and purpose that the fight was over quickly. John L. Butler, who had floored a man with every blow, rendering several unconscious, mounted the pile of lumber.

He said, "My ancestors fought in the American Revolution to establish a government where all men have equal rights, and I aim to have mine if I have to fight for them. As to my religion, that is between me and my God, and is nobody's business. But I will vote here today or die in the attempt."

Word of the trouble spread quickly, the story growing bigger with every telling. At Far West, William Swartzell wrote in his journal on August 7: "This day an express arrived from Gallatin in Daviess County that the Missourians had raised a mob against the brethren, and killed two of them and would not permit them to be buried. There was a great fight on the election ground in Gallatin . . . stabbing with knives, throwing of stones, clubs, staves, . . . Brother Butler knocked down and laid open, in a frightful manner, the skulls of several citizens with a bludgeon."

According to Swartzell, the Danites did not wait for retaliation, but began foraging the countryside, driving off cattle and carrying off loot of different kinds, justifying themselves with the thought that they were taking back only a small part of what they had been robbed of in Jackson County. David Patten led one group to Gallatin, scene of the election-day fight, looted the store, and set fire to the building. In other areas they "took honey which they called sweet oil, hogs which they called bear, and cattle which they called buffalo." Other foraging groups were led by Major Seymour Brunson, Alexander McRae, and Captain Jonathan Dunham. Lee admitted that he had participated in some of these, but insisted that none of them did any burning or killing, though they did take cattle, bedding, foodstuff, and guns. Bands of Missourians also scoured the countryside committing similar depredations.

On August 30, Governor Lilburn W. Boggs called out the militia to try to restore peace, but all during September civil war reigned in northern Missouri. By October 11, the saints began moving into Far West from DeWitt and other communities, and on October 15, the Prophet began to organize for war, preparing Far West for a siege by throwing up bulwarks against cavalry attacks and having shops work round the clock to knock out such weapons as they could make from the available steel. This action was considered treason.

False report followed so closely on the heels of exaggerated report that neither side knew exactly what was going on. For example, word went to the governor that an entire company of militia, fifty men, had been killed by the Mormons, when actually the group had suffered no inconvenience but had instead raided a Mormon area and taken three men captive. On the other hand, Joseph Smith was told that the mobbers had captured Nathan Pinkham, William Seely, and Addison Green, and planned to kill them at sunrise.

Mormon reaction was immediate. A rescue party was organized under David W. Patten, Captain Fear Naught, as he was affectionately called; a man born to lead. Six feet-one tall and all muscle, his black eyes flashed with the confidence of one who thinks he is literally fighting God's battles. Secure in this belief, Patten took little precaution, assuming that he would have a special protection.

Many stories were told and retold of the spiritual power of this man. One was to the effect that he was at one time sent with a small company of men to rescue a family on an isolated farm. They found the home burned, the mother in the last stages of pregnancy making her way on foot across the prairie, with several small children around her. From the excitement and fright she had received, it seemed that her child might be born before they could reach shelter, and to further complicate matters, a heavy prairie storm was rolling up. Some large drops were already beginning to fall.[2]

David Patten stopped his party as they came up to the little group. He dismounted and stepping aside into the tall grass, knelt in prayer to ask God to honor his petition. Then returning he stood at full height and lifting his arm toward heaven, commanded the storm to be

---

[2] Lycurgus A. Wilson, *The Life of David W. Patten, the first Apostolic Martyr,* (Deseret News, Salt Lake City, 1900), p. 63.

stayed until the woman could be brought to shelter and properly cared for. Those present said that the rain stopped, the clouds parted, and they proceeded to their destination without complications. Surely a man who could control the elements would be more than a match for any Missouri mobbers.

Such stories repeated had built up a false feeling of security. The company, consisting of some forty-five men, set out from Far West about midnight, expecting to surprise the Missourians in their camp and rescue the three brethren. Captain Patten divided his men into three groups, one under his own command, a second under C. C. Rich, and a third under James Durfee. They routed the mob and rescued the prisoners, but in the exchange of shots one Missourian was killed and six were wounded, while of the Mormons Gideon Carter and Patrick O'Bannion were killed in the first exchange of fire. The mob was put to rout, but one stopped long enough in the shelter of a tree to fire a parting shot at the leader, a large man in a white blanket coat with the pink of the eastern sky behind him to make him stand out as a perfect target.

"How are the mighty fallen!" John D. Lee exclaimed later when he came out with the wagons to help carry back the wounded and bury the dead.

A shot in the head or the heart is an instant and relatively clean death, but a musket wound in the bowels means lingering and suffering. During the fifteen hours it took for David Patten to die, he retained consciousness and suffered excruciating pain.

His death affected his companions profoundly. They thought, as he had, that he was immune to bullets. It broke the morale of the saints, for it gave them a glimpse of what war might actually become. How empty now seemed Sidney Rigdon's threats that they would conduct a war of extermination! That his sword would never again be sheathed until Missouri was conquered now seemed vain, idle boasting.

But the battle of Crooked River was most important in that it gave Governor Boggs, always willing to believe the worst of the Mormons, another excuse to act officially. The distorted report that came to him pictured the Mormons as aggressors in a large-scale civil war. As if to confirm it, on the very same day came sworn statements from two disaffected members of the church, Thomas B. Marsh and Orson Hyde, to the effect that the Danites planned to sack and burn the towns of Richmond and Liberty.

The combined evidence brought forth the "Extermination Orders" and called into action the full military force of the state. "The Mormons must be treated as enemies and must be exterminated or driven from the state, if necessary for the public good," the orders read.

At this time, John D. Lee was at Far West with the Mormon force.
As one of the Host of Israel it was his duty to be there; as a Danite, he
should be in the vanguard, ready to lead in any attack. He and
Aggatha had agreed that she and little Sarah Jane should remain at
the cabin on the farm and take their chances there. At least she had a
cow and hay to feed it, and she had vegetables in the ground and food
stored. If the mob came, the worst she would expect would be that
they would burn the house and take the cow. Certainly they would
not kill an unresisting woman or her child. The poor who had crowded
into Far West were having real difficulty in getting food enough to
keep alive, and the danger of their being killed in battle was much
greater than hers would be on the farm.

Therefore, John D. held down his outpost behind a pile of lumber
facing the road to the town. Beside him were his bullets laid out
ready, his cap box open. Some Missouri troops were drawn up out of
range of the Mormon guns, hoping to get possession of the town by
stratagem. But the morale of the Mormon men was high. When word
came that General Lucas was approaching the town with six thousand
men, Lee's response was "Let him come!" Outnumbered though they
were, he felt that with the help of God they could put any foe to rout.

For two days the armies had faced each other, each loath to begin
action. Then close on the heels of the exterminating order came the
story of a terrible massacre at Haun's Mill, a massacre wherein a band
of armed horsemen, yelling like savages, rode upon the little settlement and began shooting. Some of the people took refuge in an old
blacksmith shop, where they were surrounded and shot down without
mercy.

David Lewis, one of the few to escape, later wrote his account in a
clear firm hand, though with phonetic spelling eloquent of his lack of
formal education.[3] He named every man and described the manner
of every death:

> . . . the first man that fell was Simon Cox, he was standing
> close by my side when he received the fatal blow, he was shot
> threw the kidneys, and all the pain and misery I ever witnessed

---

[3] The original journal of David Lewis is in the hands of Franklin Lewis, Vernal,
Utah. A typescript copy is at the Brigham Young University library.

The journal was begun on January 18, 1854. The writer describes himself as
follows:

"I am now in the thirty ninth year of my age and on the 10 day of next April I
will be 40 years of age. I am six feet one inch high my weight two hundred
pounds I am preportionably built with black hair and blue eyes I am fare skined
and in the full vigor of life and health." The writer was called south with the
Indian missionaries in 1854, and died the next year.

a poor soul in his seemed to excell, it seems as though I could now hear him scream, They came about four o'clock in the afternoon and continued about one hour and a half. . . Sutch groans of the dying, sutch strugeling in blood, I hope that none that reads this account may ever have to witness, unless it is in avenging blood, which must stand against them until it is avenged. . .

He went on to tell how Brother McBride, a very old man, gave up his gun and then was shot with his own weapon. Not content with killing him, Jacob Rodgers grabbed an old scythe blade and hacked his face to pieces. The mob finally entered the blacksmith shop and put a stop to the suffering of all the wounded by closeup shots in the head. When one discovered two little boys hiding together under the bellows, they were dragged out and deliberately shot in spite of the remonstrances of some of the mob. "Little shoots make big trees," David Lewis quoted the executioner as saying. "Nits make lice," another added.

The messenger who brought the news to Far West and gave a firsthand account of the scene where men had turned to fiends, made vivid what could happen to this little fortress, should it be captured by an army fired by the same mob spirit.

The Prophet decided that he must capitulate, lest the carnage be repeated at Far West with far more disastrous results. Supported by the "Exterminating Orders" and with the full force of the state militia, General Lucas had them at his mercy. Messengers were sent to the army headquarters to negotiate and bring back terms of truce. These proved to be severe indeed. The Mormon leaders were to be taken prisoners and tried for treason, the people should all leave the state immediately in a mass migration, every man must surrender his arms and sign over to the state of Missouri all his property except such as would be absolutely necessary to his leaving.

Joseph immediately called his soldiers together and said: "You are good and brave men, but we are faced by ten thousand soldiers with instructions for our extermination. I know that you are willing to die with me or for me. God knows your hearts and he has accepted your offering; I accept it also. But it is best that I and a few others surrender ourselves in order that our wives and children may be spared."

He went on to tell them to bring every piece of plunder to a central place, so that no item could be identified with an individual, lest a man be hanged for the theft of a bridle or saddle. Those who had been at Crooked River might do well to leave at once by the north gate and get away unmolested while enemy attention was centered in the other direction.

"Be of good cheer," he concluded." Pray for me day and night and for those who are with me, that we may speedily be delivered. I bless you all in the name of our Lord Jesus Christ."

Hurrying back to his place on the rampart, Lee watched them leave. Lucas and his army had already started their march toward the city and were within a quarter of a mile from the breastworks when Joseph and his companions came out, a small procession in the afternoon sun. George Robinson, son-in-law of Sidney Rigdon, went a short distance ahead carrying the white flag; behind him a few steps walked Joseph, calm and erect, in Lee's eyes more heroic than he had ever looked before. Just behind him the other three walked abreast, a short line of big men: Sidney Rigdon, twelve years older than Joseph, dignified, experienced; Parley P. Pratt, whose eloquent tongue had swayed audiences and appealed to the most learned; Lyman Wight, the impetuous, fearless man of action who on one occasion had dared to defy even the Prophet himself. Wight early had been dubbed "The Wild Ram of the Mountains," and had loved to dress the part, with a bright scarf around his head, his shirt open, and a wide belt displaying knife and gun. Only a week or so before he had led a raid on Milport. Today he walked bareheaded, simply clad.

As they approached, a cheer arose from the army. General Lucas with a guard of some hundred men immediately surrounded them and declared them his prisoners. There were shouts of triumph, curses and jeers from the soldiers, while behind in Far West fear and consternation reigned.

In the meantime, the men who had participated in the battle of Crooked River had escaped, leaving in small groups. All suffered from cold and exposure, but one group consisting of Samuel Smith, Benjamin L. Clapp, Lorenzo D. Young, Phineas H. Young, Charles C. Rich, Hosea Stout, and others came near perishing in the storm.

The army immediately took possession of the city of Far West, searching the houses, taking whatever they saw that they wanted. At the Prophet's home they drove the family out and literally stripped the place.

By nightfall word came to the town that a court martial had been held and their leaders were to be shot at sunrise. Joseph had enjoined them to pray for his safety, and this they did singly and in groups, some keeping vigil all through the night. The next morning when General Doniphan refused to carry out his orders, the Mormons felt that it was a direct answer to their prayers.

The prisoners had been lined up; the brigade was marched into position. Then the leader, looking at the doomed men, said, "I'll be damned if I will have anything to do with it." To his superior officer he wrote: "It is cold-blooded murder. I will not obey your order. My brigade shall march for Liberty tomorrow morning at eight o'clock; and if you execute these men, I will hold you responsible before an earthly tribunal, so help me God."

This open defiance caused General Lucas to change his plans. The prisoners were brought back into Far West the next morning, Joseph in the prison wagon, the others under heavy guard. The saints were ordered to surrender their arms, each man adding his to the stack in the center of the public square. Each was brought to the official desk which had been set up, where he was to give his name and his previous place of residence. Then he must sign an affidavit relinquishing all right to any property which he held in the state of Missouri and promising that he would leave the state. None were allowed to leave until every man was examined, then in sardonic generosity, General Clark detailed the offenses which had brought this action. ". . . The orders of the governor to me were that you should be exterminated, and not allowed to remain in the state. . . I do not say that you shall go now, but you must not think of staying here another season, or of putting in crops, for the moment you do this, the citizens will be upon you. . ."

John D. Lee passed to the table in his turn, deposited his good Kentucky rifle, two horse pistols, and a sword, and signed all the required papers. He was a prisoner at Far West along with the other Mormons, and would remain so until the examination was completed and each man's arms taken. The Caldwell County record says that "about 630 guns, consisting of hunting rifles, shot guns and a few muskets, some rude swords, homemade, and a few pistols, were given up and hauled off by the State authorities, but it cannot be stated here what disposition was made of them."

Having no property at Far West except his horse, an especially fine gray mare, and his saddle, bags, and other riding gear, Lee spent some time caring for the animal and repairing his equipment. He resolved to appear cheerful and calm and to lose no opportunity to talk to the Missourians. As often as he led his mare to drink, or curried her, one man or another would comment on what a splendid animal she was, and Lee followed any opening for a conversation. Sometimes after a visit the stranger would express surprise that such a man as he should be a Mormon.

One of the officers tried to persuade him that he should renounce the imposter Smith and settle in peace among them. "You are just the kind of a citizen this state needs," he concluded.

"Well, if I am ever convinced that Joseph Smith is an imposter, I shall admit it freely and separate myself from his followers, but until that time, I expect to stand by him and his cause," Lee answered.

At first the officer was enraged and called out, "Blow the brains out of this fool!" When his subordinates drew their guns, he changed his mind. "Hold on," he called. "He is not worth five bullets. Anyway, I like a firm man, even if he is misled."

The surrender had taken place on November 1, 1838, and for more than a week the Mormon soldiers had been barricaded in schoolhouses with no rations issued to them for several days. In the meantime, the Missourians had turned into a mob and pillaged the town, killing animals for sport, rummaging houses, even violating women and girls. Finally, after several days, Lee obtained permission to go out with others under heavy guard and get food from Mormon gardens and fields and to salvage some of the meat from animals that had been killed. The weather was very cold and the snow deep, so that much of it was preserved. By his determinedly good nature and reasonableness Lee had become known among the officers and respected by them.

The treaty stipulated that the soldiers should visit the other settlements, arrest all for whom they had complaints, disarm the men and have them sign the affidavits relinquishing their property and promising to leave the state by the first of April, 1839. General Wilson, with a company was detailed to carry out this program at Adam-ondi-Ahmen, and needing a guide, he inquired of the very officer who had threatened Lee. The officer remembered him as a man of courage and spirit and recommended him for the position.

"Young man, do you live at Adam-ondi-Ahmen?" the officer asked when Lee was brought before him.

"I did live near there," Lee answered, "but I have been told that my house has been burned down. I have a wife and baby there if they have not been killed or died of hunger and exposure. I should like to get back and see how they are."

"Where did you live before you came here?"

"In Illinois. I expect to go back there as soon as we can travel."

"You will soon see your wife and child. I march for Adam-ondi-Ahmen in the morning. Select two companions and accompany me as guide."

Lee chose Levi Stewart and another neighbor, and the next morning left Far West for his home. The ground was covered with snow, so, early in the afternoon, when they came to good shelter in a clump of trees near Waldo Littlefield's farm, the company decided to stop for the night. Lee waited until things were set up and arranged before he approached the officer.

"General, I have come to ask a favor," he said. "I should like to go on to Adam-ondi-Ahmen today. My wife and baby are there without shelter, I'm afraid. Now that the storm has cleared, you can easily follow our tracks in the morning. It's only about eight miles."

For a second the commander hesitated, then, calling an aide, he ordered a pass written which would clear Lee and permit him to leave the state. It read:

> I permit John D. Lee to remove from Davis County to Caldwell County, and to pass out of the state, as he has undergone an examination at Far West and was fully acquitted.
>
> Marrowbone Encampment, Mo., Nov. 15, 1838
>
> R. Wilson Brigadier Gen.
>
> R. F. Cockey, Aid-de-Camp.

Lee rode toward home in haste. The report was true. From across the clearing he could see the charred logs of one corner of the house and the black place where the stack had been. Aggatha and little Sarah Jane were huddled together in the shelter of the unburned corner, over which they had put some boards and a piece of canvas. A small fire burned in front, and a pile of brush and sticks was at one side to keep it through the night. He rode up to the place before she knew he was coming. Her joy at seeing him was so great that she could only weep and cling to him. She had heard of the outrages that had been comitted at Far West and feared him dead.

The next day when General Wilson and his company arrived, they camped not far from Lee's shanty. On his way to report to the general, Lee met Mr. McBrier, a Missourian from whom he had earlier purchased some cattle. He explained that he could not pay for the stock, and that since he was forced to leave the state, he really had no use for them. Would Mr. McBrier take them back? One cow had died, but he would pay for her in anything he had that Mr. McBrier would consider equal to her value. They settled the account, and the Missourian accompanied Lee on to the headquarters. So pleased was McBrier with the arrangement that he introduced Lee to a number of the soldiers and recommended him to the general as an honest Mormon.

This was a very great advantage, for they were now more generous in helping him get a suitable outfit for leaving the state. He was allowed a strong team and a large wagon fitted out with clothing and bedding and necessities for the trip back to Illinois. His one good milk cow he gave to a neighbor whose wife had died and who had a large family of small children. On November 20, they set out from what had been their home.

But winter had now settled down in earnest, with so much snow and such extreme cold that they could not travel. They sought shelter first with a family named Bidwell, and later with one named Morris, as they waited for spring to break. They turned back toward Far West, where most of the body of the saints still remained.

At Far West, Brigham Young and other members of the Twelve were organizing the people so that they could leave in an orderly manner and with a minimum of hardship. On January 29, 1839, a meeting was held at Far West at which a covenant was drawn up to the effect that all men would "stand by and assist each other to the utmost of our abilities, in removing from this state . . . for providing means for the removing of the poor and destitute, who shall be considered worthy from this county, till there shall not be one left who desires to remove from the state. . ." The covenant stipulated that the committee who received property should give an accounting of the use that was made of it, and further protected the signers that they should first use what was necessary for the removal of their own families. Brigham Young was the leading spirit of the organization, getting three hundred and eighty signatures to the covenant. Of the two hundred and fourteen listed in the *Historical Record,* p. 714, one is that of John D. Lee.

Charles Bird was appointed to go down toward the Mississippi River to contract ferriage for the group and to make deposits of corn for the use of the saints as they came along. When the weather permitted, the people began to leave in small companies as fast as they could get ready, traveling overland to Richmond, thence down the Missouri River and up the Mississippi to the neighborhood of Quincy, Illinois.

It was mid-February before John D. and his family made the trip, but in the meantime he had a number of important experiences while he was yet in Missouri. He became acquainted with Father Smith, as everyone called the Prophet's father because he had the same name, visited with him often and listened to his counsel. This greatly strengthened the faith of the new convert. Then he was promoted in the Mormon priesthood; he was ordained a Seventy under the hands of Joseph Young and Levi Hancock, and set apart as one authorized to preach the new gospel. Even more important, he was given a blessing by Patriarch Isaac Morley. These patriarchal blessings could be given only by men especially ordained, and given only to members in good standing. Dated Caldwell County, December 1838, it reads in part:

. . . Thousands shall hear the everlasting Gospel preached from thy lips. Kings and princes shall acknowledge thee to be their father in the new and everlasting covenant. Thou shalt have a numerous posterity, who shall rise up and bless thee. Thou shalt have houses and habitations, flocks, fields, and herds. Thy table shall be strewed with the rich luxuries of the earth, to feed thy numerous family and friends who shall come unto thee. Thou shalt be a counselor in Israel, and many shall come unto thee for instruction. Thou shalt have power over thine enemies. They that oppose thee shall yet come bending unto thee.

Thou shalt sit under thine own vine and fig tree, where none shall molest or make thee afraid. Thou shalt be a blessing to thy family and to the Church of Jesus Christ of Latter-day Saints. Thou shalt understand the hidden things of heaven. The spirit of inspiration shall be a light unto thy path and a guide to thy mind. Thou shalt come forth in the morning of the first resurrection, and no power shall hinder except the shedding of innocent blood or consenting thereto. . .

Lee prized this blessing highly, for it was a very personal document directed to him alone and not intended for reading by anyone else, certainly not for the public. He read and reread it so many times that he committed most of it to memory, and he pondered the meaning of every phrase. He knew that the term "kings and princes" possibly did not refer to earthly potentates, but to the gifted who might be waiting for him to bring them the Gospel so that they could take these high positions in the eternal worlds under God.

The promise of earthly wealth he knew he could fulfill, because he had a gift both for improving whatever he had to make its value increase and for trading to advantage. To one in his present homeless condition, the promise that he should sit under his own vine and fig tree without fear was truly a comfort. The thing that affected him most, however, was that part which said that he should understand the hidden things of heaven and that "the spirit of inspiration shall be a light in thy path and a guide to thy mind," for because of this he became an interpreter of dreams and one who, when uncertain as to his course, asked for guidance and after due meditation followed whatever inspiration or hunch he received.

The promise that he should come forth on the morning of the first resurrection "and no power shall hinder, except the shedding of innocent blood, or consenting thereto," was the one which many years later would cause him the most agony of soul. This sentence appears to have become a part of the temple ordinance in the Nauvoo Temple, for eight years later in February, 1846 George Laub, describing his experience in the temple wrote: "And we was sealed up to Eternal Life to come fourth in the morning of the first Resurection and nothing Can pervent us from coming fourth in the first Resurection only the Sining aganst the holy Ghost which is the sheding of inocent Blood or concenting to the Same."

Although this was pronounced upon all who went through the temple, Lee at the end felt the weight of it so keenly that he was able to face a firing squad, secure in the belief that by giving his own life he would atone for the violation of this one condition which would endanger his status in the hereafter.

But in December, 1838 his first concern was to get his wife and family back to Vandalia where they had relatives and friends. They arrived in that city less than a year after they left. How much had happened in those few short months! Lee was sure of one thing, however. If he had been strong of belief when he set out to join the saints, he now knew of a surety that he belonged to the only true church of God upon the earth. He had fought for the faith; he had suffered for it. The voice of the Prophet had filled him with a burning zeal and his ordination as a Seventy had commissioned him to go forth and preach. What better time than now? While Joseph was in prison, while the Missouri saints were reestablishing themselves, he would go on a mission.

1839-1843
The Missionary

The two young men plodded wearily along the country road. It was early April, and spring was at its best in southern Illinois; however, John D. Lee was more concerned with his blistered feet than with the beauties of the landscape. Levi Stewart was dragging along, too, as though he must consider each step before he made it. They each carried a small bag containing a change of socks and underwear, a *Bible* and a *Book of Mormon*, but had not a penny between them. Like the apostles of old, they went without purse or scrip to spread the new Gospel.

They had planned this mission together, believing that if they left their wives with shelter and food for at least six months, all would be well. Now, after two days on the road, they began to doubt the wisdom of their course. Every house where they had stopped had been a humiliation, either a cold refusal or a torrent of abuse. No one would hear their message, much less give them a meal.

It was dark when they stopped at what seemed to be a public house, though the steps sagged and the porch was warped. The young man at the desk eyed them suspiciously.

Since it was his turn to ask for accommodations, John D. began, "We are ministers of the Gospel, and we are traveling with out money and preaching without price, depending upon the people for food and lodging. May we stay here tonight?"

The young man shifted his quid and spat toward a bucket of sand.

"Well, I don't own the place, and I couldn't give you any grub if I did, on account of how the cook is gone and the pantry locked. Got no bed, neither, but there's them benches you can rest on if you're a mind to."

Since this was better than lying on the ground, they thanked him, took off their shoes, used their rolled-up coats for pillows, and stretched out. John D. Lee could not sleep, weary as he was. The bench was hard, true, but it was not this nor his empty stomach that kept him awake; it was the gnawing distrust in the back of his mind. Had he been foolish to start on this mission? What made him think that he could preach? He knew so little of this new gospel; he had no experience. How could he convert a man to his new faith if he couldn't persuade one to give him a meal?

If he had stayed at home, he could have built a house for Aggatha. He could have earned money with which to set himself up when they joined the body of the church again. In the midst of these despondent musings there flashed into his mind the words, "Whoso putteth his hand to the plow should never turn back," and then, "Rejoice, and be exceeding glad, for so persecuted they the prophets which were before you." Suddenly he was filled with a warm glow, similar to the exhilaration he had felt the night he had finished reading *The Book of Mormon.*

Writing of the incident many years later, he said ". . . the desire to go on burned like a fire in my bones; I was renewed and refreshed from head to foot, and determined to put all my trust in God and go ahead." He called this place "The Fasting Inn" and wondered if his experience here did not coincide with that of the Prophet Joseph when he rebuked the guards in Richmond jail. At any rate, Lee now shook off the shackles of doubt.

Before light the missionaries were on their way, for Lee had predicted that they would get a good breakfast soon. He was right. A man working in his yard sang out a cheerful greeting as they approached, and after a short visit, invited them in. He not only served them an excellent breakfast, but gave them food to carry along so that they would not be hungry before night.

Cheered and refreshed, the past discomforts were forgotten and they reminded each other of the many miraculous experiences of other Mormon missionaries. Samuel Smith, the first to be sent out, had been so young and unsure of himself that he could not sell a single *Book of Mormon.* He finally persuaded the wife of Parson John P. Greene to accept one free, with the result that she not only read it herself, but took it to her brother, Phineas Young, who was instantly converted by it. He passed it on to Brigham Young, whose wife read it and gave it to the wife of Heber C. Kimball. The net result was that four of the most influential families of the church had been converted by the book which Sam Smith could not sell.

Each recalled that Parley P. Pratt had converted himself to the church even before he met the Prophet, and that it was he who had converted John Taylor. Just as remarkable was the fact that Wilford Woodruff was ready for baptism after listening to only one sermon — and that by the bashful, slow-spoken Zera Pulsipher. There seemed no end of examples to show that the field was ripe and ready for the harvest.

Their missionary work began in Jackson County, Tennessee, where Levi's relatives lived. He remained there, and John D. Lee pushed on to work in Rutherford County and the towns near Nashville. The only account of this mission is the one written from memory and published in Lee's *Confessions,* but on the flyleaf of the diary of his next mission he notes: "during a short mission that I took in 1839 I Baptized 27 persons of which I have kept no record." From this and from the story in the *Confessions* it is clear that Lee did much of his missionary work in the same general area.

He remained on his mission only six months, returning to Vandalia on October 1, 1839. During that winter he worked with his brother-in-law, George Hickerson, in a trading operation, buying produce from the farmers and exchanging it for goods in the city. He also preached so effectively to his wife's people that he was able to baptize the whole family, except the father. His own sister, Elizabeth, on the other hand, would have nothing to do with his new religion nor with him.

Early in 1840 they learned of the new city which was being built on the east bank of the Mississippi River, in Illinois. The Prophet had finally escaped from his enemies after months in a dark, damp jail, where for a part of the time he was heavily chained, and was now supervising plans for a new church headquarters to be laid out on a large scale. Lee at once felt that he must join the body of the saints, to be where he could associate with the leaders and hear the Prophet.

Thus traveling again with their Stewart neighbors, Lee and his family set out. They arrived early in April, 1840 at Nauvoo the Beautiful; a fitting name for the young city. The squares were neatly laid out, covering and erasing the former town of Commerce, filling the area where the river made a wide bend and spreading back onto higher land on the plain. The temple site was reserved on a high elevation, and this time, the Prophet Joseph said, it would stand completed and be used to fulfill its purpose.

The newcomers found stores and shops selling goods and some businesses already in operation, among them a steam flour mill, a sawmill, and a tool factory. There was talk of a foundry soon to be established and a ceramics and dish factory to employ the skills of the English converts who were arriving in ever increasing numbers. At the edge of the town was the large community farm, where new arrivals could work for food until they were established in their own trades. The papers boasted that two hundred and fifty homes had been completed the year before and nearly twice as many in 1840.

In general, the health of the people was good that spring. Early settlers told them of the plague of the last summer, when so many were ill that there were hardly enough well to care for them. This, they felt, was due to the year of persecution and privation which they had passed through earlier. There had been many deaths, too many, but there had been also some miraculous healings. Henry G. Sherwood, Benjamin Brown, and Joseph B. Noble were among those who had been restored to health by the power of God on an eventful day, July 22, 1839.

But the case which was most often told was that of Elijah Fordham. At least eight or ten of the leading brethren, among them Brigham Young, Wilford Woodruff, Orson Pratt, John Taylor, and Heber C. Kimball, witnessed the miracle and bore testimony to it. When they arrived at the home of Brother Fordham, he seemed to be breathing his last. His breath came in short gasps, his eyes were rolled back and glassy, his jaws set. Joseph took his right hand and held it firmly, looking into his eyes, as if to draw him back from the shadows. When at last it seemed that there was a glimmer of consciousness, Joseph leaned close and asked, "Do you know me, Brother Fordham?"

"Yes," the answer came in the faintest whisper.

"Do you have faith that you can be healed?"

"Too late, I'm afraid. If you had come earlier —"

"Do you believe in Jesus Christ?"

"I do. Sure, I do."

For a minute Joseph remained silent, still holding the sick man's hand, still searching his face for returning life. Then in a deep, intense voice which shook every listener like an electric current, he said, "Brother Fordham, I command you in the name of Jesus Christ to arise from this bed and be made whole."

Instantly Elijah Fordham started to raise up, and with the Prophet's supporting hand, came to a sitting position. Then kicking the poultices from his feet, he asked in a clear voice for a bowl of bread and milk. After he had eaten, he dressed himself and walked with the group to the home of Brother Noble. Though there he was forced to rest, and even passed into a faint for a short time, he was restored to health still to work among the people. It was thrilling to hear these stories of healing, however, the number of graves gave them all serious concern.

The people were gathering like bees to a swarming limb, crowding in daily overland and by boat. All who had lost their property at Far West were given a free lot in the city, while newcomers, especially those who had money, paid up to five hundred dollars for a lot, depending upon its location.

Lee secured a place on Warsaw Street, where he built a small, comfortable home and fenced and improved his lot. Here on August 26, 1840, his son, John Alma, was born. When the child was only four months old, the father was asked to go back to his mission in Tennessee, since some of his friends there felt that he could add many members to the church.

The diary of this mission is well preserved in a small book and is an excellent commentary on the character and activities of its author. In addition to dates, places, and distances traveled, it contains speeches, scriptural quotations, original verses or acrostics, and some drawings. He moved among the homes of his friends, never lacking for invitations; he debated with local ministers and held meetings. In Overton County he made his headquarters at the home of a wealthy man named Armstrong, whose wife Nancy was converted and baptized. In Rutherford County he stayed at the home of Isham Gilliam, where again he was given a private room for study and meditation, and was encouraged to attend school. On March 22, 1841, he wrote:

> . . . Being prevailed upon by some of my friends in Rutherford who felt interested in my well being offered to pay my tuition if I would go to school as my education was very limited I kindly accepted of their proposal and began my studies on March 22 under Mr. Hugh Montgomery, a celebrated teacher, I first studied arithmetic. . .

For a short time he continued his studies, but one day there was no teacher, and word came that the professor was "very much intoxicated." Accordingly a new tutor was hired, Mr. Johani Rowen, under whom Lee studied spelling, grammar, and arithmetic. Later the student converted the teacher to the Mormon faith.

There was something about this young man, still in his twenties, which appealed to these people. He was not particularly handsome, his ash blond hair was straight and apt to be unruly, and his cheek bones prominent; but his ruddy complexion, his ready smile which revealed a set of fine, sound teeth, his bright blue eyes, and most of all his vitality and enthusiasm, attracted those with whom he came in contact. Women especially responded to him, as the number who later followed him to Nauvoo gives evidence.

He always made himself useful wherever he was. His diary tells of helping Miles Anderson clear a piece of land, replant corn, and harvest his wheat. At the Gilliam home he "stocked" a plow, made bee stands, extracted honey, cut the husband's hair, and mended shoes.

Lee accepted favors gracefully as being contributions to the work of the Lord rather than as gifts to him personally. When Mr. Gilliam offered him a young mare that had been severely wounded by a gun shot, Lee immediately dressed the wound and nursed her back to health. Then he traded her for a horse, which he exchanged again, giving fifteen dollars to boot, for a very fine animal which he could ride proudly. A partial list of gifts includes the following:

. . . Miss Mary Sanders put a new lining in my stockin
Mrs. Gilliam (Caroline) made me a present of a pair of flannel drawers, for which I felt thankful, I very much needed them, for my old ones were considerably worn.
. . . Miss Nancy Haley made me a present of a pair of socks. . .
. . . Mrs. C. Gilliam mended my coat
. . . Sister Patsy Pace gave me a pair of socks. . .

Finally the congregation of his friends, anxious that he make a good appearance, took up a collection for material out of which to make him a suit.

May 1 . . . I received a present of a cloath coat vest and pantaloons The cost of the coat $23.00 as a conterbution was made by Ishum Gilliam D. M. Jarratt & Jacob Wright also a part of the trimming by P. C. Tally the vest pattern by Mr. Jarret & Ramsey of the Christian order the pantaloons by Caroline Gilliams, pants and vest made up by Miss Mary S. Saunders in the most able order. The total amount 31 dollars. In this they have manifested a spirit of benevolence to me a stranger, in a strange land, for which I feel truely greatful to my friends and likewise to my Heavenly Father, for opening there hearts to administer to my wants and necessaties. And as they have clothed me in the name of a deciple of Jesus Christ they have wrought a good work, yea even a work that will stand as bright as the noon day sun, for thus saith the Savior, He that will give one of the least of my servants a cold drink of water in my name, shall nowise lose his reward. . .

His thanks would be his only pay, except for the little acrostic verse written for each personally, the name spelled out in the letters which began each line, like a secret between them to be treasured after he was gone. The women who mended his socks and underwear, embroidered his vest, and tailored his suit, were all the more fond of him as a result, sewing their affections in with every stitch.

His greatest triumph was the baptism of Mrs. Caroline Gilliam. On June 13, 1841, he wrote that she "came in for baptism stating that she felt perfectly willing to cast her lot with ours, a lady of the first rank in our country with an estate between ten and fifteen thousand dollars."

The next morning a group witnessed the baptismal ceremony. Lee, remembering how deeply he had been stirred at his own baptism three years ago, understood the emotion of this young woman as emerging from the water, she wept with joy and pled with her husband to accept the truth also. In spite of her embraces and pleadings, he was unmoved.

Lee now returned home, having been away for six months. He arrived at Nauvoo on July 19, and once more set about the business of improving his home and earning a living. He remained at home eight months this time, during which conditions at Nauvoo reflected peace and prosperity. In the summer, 1841 the apostles who had been in Europe for two years returned to report phenomenal success in their proselyting. The temple and the Nauvoo House were being pushed; many neat cottages were taking the place of the more crude original dwellings. By the spring of 1842 the population of the city was estimated between eight and ten thousand.

The call now was for all who could do so to gather to Zion. With this in mind, the authorities again sent Lee out to his former mission area. This time he was gone only two and a half months, leaving Nauvoo on March 18 and returning May 20, 1842. He was warmly greeted by his friends, who "collected together & wished I should prech to them as they were starving for the word of Life & salvation." On a baptismal day held April 12, he baptized twenty-three persons, among whom were Mary V. (Polly) and Lavina Young, both of whom later would become his wives, along with their parents and brother David. His record contains several poems encouraging his friends to come to Nauvoo.

Throughout the summer Lee was with his family again. He had missed the military parade of the legion held on May 7, at which time Joseph Smith and John C. Bennett had ridden side by side as they reviewed the Mormon army of twenty-six companies, totaling two thousand men. At the conclusion they staged a sham battle for the entertainment of the spectators and the experience of the soldiers. The noise and dust, the clashing of arms, and the general confusion gave it all a very real appearance, and somewhere in the melée the Prophet's life was endangered. The near accident fanned into flame the smoldering differences. Bennett was accused of conspiring to bring about the death of Joseph Smith and was excommunicated from the church. Within a fortnight he resigned his position as mayor of Nauvoo, and Joseph Smith was appointed to fill the vacancy.

Though Lee missed the parade, he was back in time to help escort

Bennett to the meeting where judgment was passed on him on June 23. Lee had been restored to his position in the guard and was a private watchman at the home of the Prophet. During much of this summer, the Prophet remained in hiding, coming out in August to make one public speech in which he appealed for young men to go out on short missions in adjoining states to help counteract the stories that were being circulated by Bennett. At the close of the service, three hundred and eighty volunteers pressed forward and asked for the privilege.

This time Lee visited the place of his birth, Kaskaskia. He set out on September 21 and traveled with Brother Twiss. On the way out and back he spent time at the home of A. P. Free, whose family he converted, and whose daughter Louisa later would become his wife. He visited his Aunt Charlotte Conner, where he was royally received. He made the place a headquarters, spending several nights there, accepting small gifts, and leaving with a load of dried fruit which he helped his cousin, Edgar Conner, to sell in St. Louis. He baptized only six persons on this trip of six weeks.

Through November and December Lee remained with his family, but by mid-January, 1843 he was off again, back to the branch of the church he had left in Tennessee. He traveled with Brother Henry B. Jacobs, and as usual recorded in his diary the travels and doings of each day.

He detoured for another brief visit to the home of his Aunt Charlotte, where he made an ox yoke for Edgar, repaired some chairs, and helped out about the place, in return for which "Old Aunt Charlotte made & presented to me a shirt which I much needed" besides washing and repairing the clothes which he already had. He could not impress her with his gospel message, so left them all with good feeling, never to see them again. He recorded that "from Aunt Conner I obtained the geneology of my fore parrents," but he did not include it in the diary and to date the family have not found it.

Back in the vicinity of Murfreesborough at the scene of his other missions, he filled the record with the names of old friends and converts. Here again he had remarkable success, recording the names of twenty-eight who were baptized, among them Miss Caroline Williams, who also later would become his wife, Captain John H. Redd and family, Wilson D. Pace, Harvey A. Pace, William Hickman and Mary Ann Hickman. On June 5, 1843 he baptized John Holt and Mary his wife, "Sister Holt that but a short time before was conveyed in a carriage to the water, her health being so much impaired as to prevent her from walking a few rods, was imediately relieved of her illness."

Another seeming miracle was recorded on July 26 "when we came to brother Pace's we found sister Pace lying low of a fever which by

the prayer of faith was restored to perfect soundness immediately."
His influence as a preacher was great here because he had built up a
large and loyal following, and all the members and friends were eager
to entertain him and to support him in his meetings. Such instances as
the following were told abroad as evidence that he truly had the gift
of healing:

> June 13, 1843 . . . Rode to Br J. Thompson found him
> verry ill, of a fit of the rheumatism deeply seatd in his Back
> sholder & head in so much that it reduced him to a constant
> misery & distress boath day & night — seeing or perceiving that
> he had faith to be healed, I administered to him according to the
> order of the gospel — in the name of Jesus. And his health was
> instantly restored & he springing up began to praise God with
> joyful acclimations.

The *Times and Seasons* for September 11, 1843, published a long
letter from John D. Lee, saying that "after an absence of several
months, I have returned to our beloved city," and summarizing his
activities while he was away. He felt that now he had really filled a
mission: five times he had been out and back, and the total months
was more than the two-year requirement; more than a thousand
people had heard his message and more than a hundred of these had
accepted it and become members of the church. With this obligation
filled, he was now ready to stay at home and help to build up the
kingdom in Nauvoo.

1843-1844
The Gathering Storm

Life in Nauvoo was exhilarating. Everywhere was evidence of such vigor, robust vitality, present accomplishment and future promise that the very air was electric. Converts continued to arrive in companies, the number from Europe increasing every season. There was work enough for all, and everyone was at work. But there was play, too. Band and choral concerts, dances and sociables, Saturday afternoon baseball and athletic contests provided public entertainment; while regular quorum meetings — often a compound of exhortation, faith-promoting stories, good cake and wine, dancing, singing, laughter — cemented the fellowship of special groups.

Lee enjoyed all this immensely. He was at his best in a crowd, whether at work or play, for he always lent his full support to every activity. One of his regrets at leaving for a mission was the thought of the good times he would miss and the history-making activities of which he would not be a part.

One of the events which stirred Lee most was the kidnapping of the Prophet in June, 1843 by officers from Missouri. Here in America, in the free state of Illinois, a man was taken prisoner by officers without a writ being served or a paper shown. But Joseph outwitted them by going to an upper window in the house where he was being held and calling out the window to passers-by his need for a lawyer. Word reached Mr. Cyrus Walker, a criminal lawyer who was in town campaigning for a seat in Congress. He quickly took the part of the Prophet, had writs served on the officers who had acted illegally, and set out with the company toward Quincy to present the case before Stephen A. Douglas.

Excitement was intense in Nauvoo when the word came of the kidnapping. All forces were quickly mustered and set into action. The cavalry of one hundred and seventy-five men set out with such haste that they rode some of their horses to death. Charles C. Rich with a picked group scoured the country to the north while the *Maid of Iowa* with a crew of eighty men patrolled the river.

When Judge Walker and his group met the Mormon horsemen, they decided to go to Nauvoo rather than to Quincy. Messengers ran ahead with the glad tidings; the band led the populace out to meet them and to escort their Prophet to his home in a cavalcade of rejoicing, for their leader whom they feared to be dead was among them safe and in high spirits. This event was one in which Lee gladly would have shared.

By this time there were currents running deep in the basic philosophies of the church which would change the lives and fortunes of many of its members. One grew out of the belief that the second advent of Christ upon the earth was near at hand, a great and dreadful day when the earth would be cleansed and His Kingdom be established. The idea grew of an actual physical kingdom with a center around a temple. By this time the Prophet was considering a move west again to the Rocky Mountains, a peaceful, orderly move to a place of the Mormon's own selection.

To implement this there was organized a secret Council of Fifty, a group of men of practical skills in all trades, loyal men of good judgment and frontier experience who could help to build the new Zion. The revelation which commanded that the organization be brought into being was received on April 7, 1842, and at once such men as George Miller, Benjamin F. Johnson, Charles Shumway, Alpheus Cutler, Theodore Turley, Joseph L. Heywood, Edward Hunter, and others were called to the council. It was not until almost two years later that the organization was completed, when on March 11, 1844, they "held another council at Nauvoo about the saints moving to the mountains." Much will be said later of the importance of this group.

The doctrine which touched many more lives closely was that of celestial marriage, or a plurality of wives. Joseph Smith had talked of this several years earlier to a few close friends, but not until 1842 did he present it to these chosen few as a commandment, a direct order from God, reinforced by an angel with a flaming sword. That year, on April 5, the Prophet took his first admitted plural wife, Louisa Beaman, with her brother-in-law, Joseph B. Noble officiating in the ceremony. In less than a year he had added four others to his household.

This was a stoutly guarded secret, being divulged to only a few at a time. At a private meeting on May 5, 1842, Joseph explained the principle to Brigham Young and Heber C. Kimball, who had just returned from missions to England. Within six weeks, after much hesitation, both had taken plural wives. The word spread slowly at first, with each man initiated required to take at least one extra wife to fill the law. Each must keep his secret closely locked in his own heart. Some idea of the way the doctrine was passed around is shown by the following, gathered from personal diaries: On April 1, 1843, Joseph Smith explained the principle to Benjamin F. Johnson; on April 11, 1843, Erastus Snow arrived in Nauvoo from his mission in England and was personally taught the law of plural and celestial marriage by the Prophet himself; Lorenzo Snow and John Benbow with his wife Jane all learned of it in April, 1843. William Clayton, one of Joseph's secretaries, who had been taught the law more than a year earlier, married Margaret Moon as his second wife on April 27, 1843. On the following July 12, the revelation was written for the first time, and Hyrum Smith, hoping to convert Emma, the Prophet's wife, read it to her. She promptly destroyed the paper, but not before a copy had been made.

The seeds of real trouble were sown when the document was read to the High Council on August 12, 1843, for among the group were two who refused to accept it, and who looked upon the whole program with such increasing distaste that they withdrew from the church and revealed the secrets.

When John D. Lee arrived in Nauvoo just at this time, mid-August, 1843, he found the city full of new homes and public buildings. The Masonic Temple was almost ready for dedication, the arsenal was completed and in use, the walls of the temple were up to the second story. Lee was at once restored to his place in the guard, under his old friend, Albert P. Rockwood. From this group he learned of the Council of Fifty, with its inner circle who were known as "The Living Constitution," the executors of the law.

When on December 29, 1843, forty men were chosen as special city police, Lee was the seventh to be selected. His duty included guarding the home of the Prophet, which he regarded as a great privilege, for the more he saw of this man, the more he honored and revered him. Of all who had lived upon the earth, Jesus Christ alone excepted, this modern prophet was greatest in the eyes of John D. Lee.

For a daytime assignment, Lee was asked to assist Joseph Young in building a hall for the Seventies, a two-story building with a large upper room to be used by the Council of Fifty for their secret meetings. His summer's task was to secure the needed materials; to make brick for the walls and get lumber from the excess that was arriving from the Wisconsin pineries for the temple.

Now the shadow of impending trouble began to fall upon the church leaders. There were rumblings of discontent within the church and threats from their neighbors without. Accusations of immorality among the leaders were whispered among the saints; the number of unmarried mothers caused gossip unlimited, questions asked which could not be answered. That this new law of home life could be properly sanctified, the work on the temple was pushed above everything else, yet through it all the leaders all stoutly denied that there were any irregularities.

The citizens of the surrounding area resented the fact that, since the Mormons voted as a unit, they could determine the outcome of any election. They watched the Nauvoo legion, now increased to four thousand men, drill and parade with deep misgiving. Here was an army to challenge the authority of the state, a formidable tool in the hands of a power-hungry zealot. Were they wise to let such a threat grow up in their midst?

To quiet accusations against himself on the political front and to distract attention from the matter of plurality of wives, Joseph Smith, on January 29, 1844, declared himself to be a candidate for the presidency of the United States. Though he knew that he would not be elected, he thought such an announcement would clarify his position with both political parties because it would mean that his own followers would vote for him. It would also be good publicity for his church. He promptly called one hundred additional missionaries to go out to campaign and preach his gospel.

Fortunately, Lee's diary for this mission is extant. One needs only to compare it with the earlier ones to see the maturing of a callow youth to a man confident almost to the point of arrogance. No longer is he the humble boy, grateful for the smallest favor and eager to help with family chores, who would act as barber, shoemaker, or farm hand to pay for board and lodging. Now he is the emissary of the Prophet of God, come to warn the people and bid them prepare for great events near at hand. The very handwriting has changed from the small, labored letters to the free Spencerian script of a hand accustomed to the pen. Though there are a few geometric designs, as in the earlier records, there are no acrostics. Perhaps he felt that the long, elaborate one published in the *Times and Seasons* for March 1, 1844, made all others seem insignificant. Spelled out, the title was JOSEPH THE GREAT PROPHET OF THE WESTERN EMPIRE OF STATES, with each letter the beginning of a line. It was not really an eulogy of the Prophet, but an invitation to all to "Enter our sanctum Nauvoo's holy ground," along with a vivid description of the judgments to come upon the earth in the last days.

In other ways this diary follows closely the pattern of the earlier ones, the daily entries giving account of the distances traveled, the visits made, the dialogues of ministers, and the accommodations secured. But here the similarity ends, for now the author consciously tries fine writing.

The first page notes in large letters: "John D. Lee Journal bought in St. Louis May 29th, 1844 price 25¢ No. 4. From this last we assume that he had filled three journals before this one. The book begins without further preamble:

At just 9 in the morning I took leave of our beautiful city on board the steamer Osprey which soon conveyed us from the sights of Friends homes and connections leaving us only to reflect on scenes of past enjoyment while in the bosom and society of a people so near and dear to us. . .

This time he was leaving Aggatha with her three children and another to be born in his absence, and also his activities in the community which were both enjoyable and remunerative. But, as always, his first loyalty was to his church.

The importance of our mission came rushing into my mind banishing grief and anguish by restoring peace and comfort as a friendly mentor — the author of relief. I lifted up my voice in supplication to the author of all good demanding protection at his hands in behalf of myself and family, while engaged in the work of the ministry. . .

Instead of trudging along on foot as he had done earlier, he traveled on a luxurious steamboat, "up the Ohio River at the lively rate of ten miles an hour."

At the mouth of the Kentucky River they separated from the main body of elders whose assignments were farther east, while four, including Lee, were to labor in Kentucky. Soon they separated again, Brothers Owens and Frost going overland to Frankfort while Akes and Lee traveled on by water. At their first stop, they met friends in the family of R. C. Steele, who not only gave them food and shelter, but secured a free passage for them on their way. Lee wrote in appreciation:

The generosity Friendship and philanthropy exercised in our behalf by these kind and Benevolent Friends shall ever be fresh in my memory . . . may the light of Heaven Brighten their Prospects and speed them on their way to the Bright Mansions of day. . .

On his way he called on Colonel Haskett and asked permission to deliver a lecture in his house. When he learned that Lee was a Mormon, the Colonel refused, whereat Lee set about to show him his error. In conclusion he said:

Furthermore I, one of the servants of God bring salvation to your door the privileges of which is afforded to you without money or price on the terms of the Gospel if you receive it you will be blest with eternal life — reject it and you will seal your own damnation. Now I am clear of your sins they cannot be required at my hands in the Great Day of accounts Now I leave you & submit your case to God Stop stop said the old professor, dont be in haste — stay all over night with me you are quite welcome so to do I answered no, if you wish to hear a Mormon you must now put yourself to the going where I preach. Between sunset and dark Preached at Mr Lewis's who met me with the same usual kindness. . .

Soon they were in such demand that they sent word for the two men who had left them earlier to come and help them meet their appointments. Instead of traveling two together, they went out singly to their preaching assignments and gathered at intervals to exchange experiences and plan their work.

Nowhere was there any mention of politics. These men were interested only in winning people to their belief, and Lee gives some of his discussions and sermons in great detail. Nothing pleased him more than to have a person declare publicly his conversion. On Saturday, June 22, he recorded one such instance, when after inviting any in the audience who wished to do so to speak:

He proceeded as follows — my religious views are not changed as in all probability may hereafter be conjectured of some at least although I have been connected with the Baptist and also with the reformers, yet I have never bound myself down to any creed further than the Bible authorizes. . . Under this consideration I attach myself to this people believing it to be my duty so to do for I most assuredly have heard the gospel by these men & with them am willing to cast my lot & share their persecution that I may be worthy to partake of the Glory of God at his coming. . .

The journal continues with the detail of their proselyting, their failures as well as successes. At times Lee puts down the words he would like to say, calling some of the preachers "long-faced, sanctimonious, hypocritical Pharisees" who belch out their own confusion. At another time a large company gathered "to hear me elucidate upon the principles of life and salvation." Such expressions did not appear in his earlier writings, for then he was less sure of himself.

Joseph Smith and his brother Hyrum were killed by a mob at Carthage jail on June 27, 1844, but word of it did not reach the missionaries until July 5. Lee could not believe that the report was true. Surely God would not allow His Prophet to be killed by an assassin's bullet! After all the times he had been imprisoned and released, after all his miraculous escapes, this could not have happened. The Elders gathered together to talk of the terrible report and decide what they should do. They withdrew to a secluded place and joined in prayer, asking for God's inspiration and guidance and for an assurance on the matter. Lee led in the prayer, and when they arose from their knees announced that as for himself, he thought it was a false report. The others could return to Nauvoo if they wished, but he would remain until the story was verified. It was such a fruitful field that he felt constrained to stay.

The next day he could hardly go on with his work, so occupied was he with thoughts of the Prophet, "the man who was more dear to us than all the riches and honors that could be conferred upon us by a thousand such worlds as the one we now inhabit." He remembered Joseph as he had played and wrestled with the boys, as he had walked away from Far West, so heroic and calm, into the hands of his enemies, as mounted on a white horse and dressed in his uniform he had commanded the legion. But the most poignant memories were of the times when, before a large congregation of faithful saints, his face became illuminated as with a white light. Never as long as he lived could John D. Lee speak of Joseph Smith without a deep emotional ring.

His mind continued to worry with the problem until he had an answer. Writing in his diary a few days later, he told how he had remained in solitude for several hours, during which time it was made known to him that the story was true. He said:

A personage whose face shone as lightning stood before me and bid my fears depart. Your mission, continued he, and labors are accepted — as were the 12 and 70 that were sent out by the Son of God. They supposed that their labors were lost when their leader was taken and crucified instead of being crowned King (temporal) of that nation as they fondly expected — So it is with you — instead of electing your leader the chief magistrate of this nation they have martyred him in prison — which has hastened his exaltation to the executive chair over this generation — so now return home in peace and there wait your endowment from on high as did the disciples at Jerusalem, for this circumstance is parallel to that. . .

Somewhat resigned, Lee continued his missionary labors for almost a month, during which time he baptized about a dozen new members. On August 4, he wrote,

This evening I received a letter from Nauvoo which came through Mr. Marshall In it or from it I obtained the fatal news of the death of our beloved Bros. Joseph & Hyrum and of Br Taylor's —

editor — being wounded having 4 bullets shot through him the
feeling of grief and anguish opperated so powerful upon my
natural affections as to destroy the strength of mind and rendered
it almost impossible for me to fill my appointments — some of
which I disappointed. . .

He did remain long enough to organize the group and to perform
several baptisms, though some he postponed until he should come
again. "I will here remark that Parson Steele a licensed minister in
the Baptist church came privately like Nicodemus of old and demanded admission into the church of God, confessing his religion and
system to be false, but owing to the distance to the water, and short-
ness of time to attend to the ordinance, I was under the necessity of
omitting his case as well as many others until my return, as I intend
to start on the morrow." His friends in that vicinity raised $5.10 among
them and he sold a *Book of Mormon* for $2.50, so he had enough for
passage on a small boat.

His account of his trip home gives a good picture of flood conditions on the Mississippi River.

Sunday 18th [August 1844] we landed at St. Louis nothing of
moment occurred on my trip from Louisville to this place with
the exception of destruction by high water which was truly distressing. For in fact the whole Mississippi Valley from 30 miles
above the Missouri River down to the mouth of the great Mississippi was entirely inundated in water — from 3 to 20 feet —
sweeping before its wild deluge stock, grain, fences and buildings,
leaving nothing behind but desolation. . .

Tues 20 I reached home safe. Found all my effects in good
order — for which I close by offering a tribute of Praise to Him
that has guided me safely home in peace.

Tues 20 distance of this month by water 1000 miles, by land
over 100 miles.

August 20th 1844 End of Mission.

This indeed was the end of his career as a missionary, for never
again did he go out to proselyte formally, though he never lost an
opportunity to talk in private or to preach in public. His return to
the city, with the Prophet dead and buried, was a sad one, in spite of
his eagerness to be home with his family again.

1844-1846
Driven Again

For weeks after the burial of their Prophet, the saints in Nauvoo were so numb with grief that they could hardly carry on church activities. They met each other with empty, sorrowful faces, wondering what further horrors might be in store for them. Until the members of the Council of Twelve should return from their scattered missions there could be no delegation of authority, and without leadership there could be no purposeful activity.

The meeting in which Sidney Rigdon and Brigham Young contended for the right to direct was held on August 8, in the regular place at the grove. Nearly eight thousand faithful saints gathered, jamming the place to capacity, crowding on the seats, sitting on the grass, standing around the back and sides. During the morning session, Sidney Rigdon used all his powers of oratory to show that because he had been first counsellor to Joseph and had shared in making the plans, he was the logical person to assume the duties of president. He claimed also to have had a revelation to show what a mighty work the church would accomplish under his direction.

What happened in the afternoon session when Brigham Young rose to speak has become legend. He had not said two sentences before the audience was alert, electrified. Among the multitude were those who declared that he spoke with the voice of Joseph; some people sitting on the grass leaped up to see if it were not in reality the youthful Prophet returned. Others thought his bearing was that of the departed leader, while still others testified that his face was illuminated with the same supernatural radiance that on rare occasions had lighted the Prophet's countenance. All were agreed that "the mantle of Joseph fell upon Brigham," and voiced their approval of him in an overwhelming vote of confidence.

John D. Lee did not arrive in Nauvoo until ten days after this meeting, but he accepted the decision with all his heart. He felt a close personal allegiance, for while he had maintained a half-worshipful distance from Joseph Smith, he had worked hand-in-glove with Brigham Young. That the feeling was mutual is shown by the fact that Lee was at once put into important positions.

His first assignment was to complete the Seventies' Hall which he had started the summer before. Since his chief article for trade was unskilled labor, he set up a brick mill, knowing that he could sell or exchange his surplus. The lumber he could get from that left from the temple. The chief source of cash was from the Seventies themselves. When the reorganization was effected on October 8, 1844, and he was made their general secretary, there were but twelve quorums of seventy men each. Within a year the number had increased to thirty-two quorums. From every member Lee must collect five dollars, for which he must issue a receipt and certificate of membership.

He was too busy to keep a daily account during that fall and winter, but from other sources we learn something of his activities. Hosea Stout, captain of the guard, several times recorded standing guard with Brother Lee. On December 24, 1844, Stout named Lee as the third of seven members in the "Seventies' Library and Institute Association." A later entry shows that the guard had been reorganized and that Lee was among those who were dropped. Of this Stout wrote:

Feb. 8, 1845   In the morning I went to the City Council to have some business transacted for the police, as it was the time that the old Council went out and the Council elected last Monday took their seat. . . Daniel Carn flour inspector for the city, with the privilege of having agents. Jesse P. Harmon also appointed Pound Master; John D. Lee Water Master. I was much pleased with the good feeling manifested toward the old police by the Council, who seemed willing to extend the hand of patronage to us after we had spent the winter thus far without any remuneration and kept up the guard to the satisfaction of the Twelve and other Authorities and now they in return were willing to put some business into our hands to afford a small compensation for our support.

During all this time, the principle of celestial marriage continued to be practiced by more and more of the leading brethren. It was also being discussed by the sisters. Sarah Sturdevant Leavitt wrote that, "It was whispered in my ear by a friend that the authorities were getting more wives than one," and being of stiff Puritan training, she was deeply troubled. As was usual, she turned in fasting and prayer to God until she received an answer. She thought she had a view of the celestial kingdom, and that was the order there. "and Oh how Butiful I was filed with Love and Joy that was unspeakable." But she was given to understand also that "it would dam thousands it was to sacrid for fools to handle for they would use it to gratify their Lustful desires." Writing as she was, many years later, she admitted that "I have seen so much wrong Connected with this Ordinance that had

I not had it revealed to me from Him that cannot Lie I should sometimes Doubted the truth of it."

Sarah was not called upon to live this law because her husband died
the next year, but many another woman, after having a similar manifestation, was put to a lifelong test. The conversion of Vilate Kimball
was a close parallel to that of Sarah Leavitt; Eliza R. Snow had a
similar period of fasting and prayer before she saw the light. Bathsheba W. Smith took a few months to become converted, but when
she did accept the principle she wrote that, "firmly believing that I
should participate with him in all his blessings, glory and honor;
within the last year, like Sarah of old, I had given to my husband five
wives, good, virtuous, honorable young women."

A recently acquired diary of John D. Lee tells of his activities
during the late fall and winter of 1844 and on until January 17, 1845,
so that we may know accurately of his doings. By December 20, 1844,
he had finished the Seventies Hall, the dedication of which lasted
during the Christmas holidays, with two quorums at a time occupying
it for an evening of meeting and celebration. Next, he was assigned
to build a home for Brother Joseph Young, the president of the quorum,
and decided to erect one for himself also. "I would here observe that
by the request of Pres. B. Young I exchanged my possessions on
Kimble and Warsaw street for the place owned by S. B. Frost. . ."
This, he explained was to place him nearer his work with the Seventies
Hall, and also to be near the home of Brigham Young. As to his own
building, he said:

> In the meanwhile I had an opportunity of teaching of the
> broad sword exercise as taught by Mr. Horace Stanley — the
> benefits of which I soon availed myself of — and soon commenced
> teaching the science myself in the city — by which I was enable
> to help myself to about $5000 in tithing labor &c for which I was
> enable together with avails of my labor otherwise to build quite a
> house about 50 feet in length — breadth 23 feet 2½ storys above
> ground —

Peace and prosperity reigned in Nauvoo during the closing months
of 1844 and through the spring and summer of 1845. Now with a
large home and a standing in the church, Lee himself became one of
the elect who might practice celestial marriage. Of it he wrote:

> About this time my family began to increase by the Law of
> Adoption. Feb 5, 1844[1845] Nancy Bean was adopted into my
> family April 19, 1845 Louisa Free was also admitted — taking
> upon her my name. On the same day Caroline Williams was

registered on my list — and on the 3rd day of May 1845 Abigail
Woolsey, and Rachel her daughter was likewise acknowledged
Frid 3d May at 7 p.m.

Lest there might be a misunderstanding, he wrote them all over
again immediately and on the same page:

Nancy Bean was adopted Thursday 10 p m Feb. 5th Louisa &
Caroline adopted Saturday the 19th April 1845 Abigail & Rachel
Friday 3rd day of May 1845

Because he gave the year 1844 first as the date for Nancy Bean and
did not give the year at all on the second listing, there has been some
question as to whether or not she had been married to him a full year
before any of the others. He clears this up in the *Confessions* when he
writes (p. 166)

My second wife, Nancy Bean, was the daughter of a wealthy
farmer who lived near Quincy, Illinois. She saw me on a mission
and heard me preach at her father's house. She came to Nauvoo
and stayed at my house three months, and grew in favor and was
sealed to me in the winter of 1845. My third and fourth wives
were sealed to me soon afterward in my own house. . . Amasa
Lyman officiated at the ceremony At the same time Sarah C.
Williams, the girl that I had baptized in Tennessee, when but a
child . . . stood up and claimed a place in my family. . .
In the Spring of 1845 Rachel Andora was sealed to me. . . She
was a sister to my first wife. Her mother, Agibail Sheffer, was
sealed to me for an eternal state. . .

From the diary of Hosea Stout we learn that Lee was indoctrinating
others into the new principle, for Stout mentions discussions on
"Eternal Exaltation" and other spiritual matters. On Saturday, May
19, he wrote that he was "sent for by Brother Lee who wanted to see
me," evidently as a witness to Lee's double marriage. On the very next
day Stout recorded that "Myself and wife and Lucretia Fisher, went
to Brother John D. Lee's to a social meeting. . . President Amasa
Lyman, Brother Lee and wife, and others were present." Though he
makes no mention of the ceremony, his family Bible gives this as the
date of his marriage to Lucretia Fisher. On June 30, when he took his
second plural wife, the nineteen-year-old Miranda Bennett, he told of
going to the home of Charles Shumway, where quite a crowd had
gathered and where, "We had a short address from Br Lyman and
after drinking what wine we wanted we dismissed all being very

John D. Lee's Home in Nauvoo

Courtesy of the Latter-day Saints Church Historian's Office, and Mrs. Manetta Henrie of Provo, Utah.

much edified by the remarks of Bro. Lyman." That the ceremony was not recorded is another evidence of how secret it was.

For the ordinary members of the church not initiated into these rites, this was a happy time. Though they missed their Prophet, they knew that his passing had eased tensions generally, so that building went on and social life was gay. Stores carried a plentiful supply of goods, which they traded for wheat, corn, or other staple products. From the outlying settlements people peddled their berries, fruit, and vegetables from door to door; skilled workmen were much in demand and common laborers could always find employment on public projects.

True, the Prophet had predicted that the church would yet move west and be established in the Rocky Mountains, but that seemed in the hazy future. As the walls of the temple reached their full height, the spirits of the people rose with it. The Junior Legion drilled and trained and paraded; baseball fans had their Saturday afternoon entertainment. Hosea Stout wrote of attending "a grand concert" in the Music Hall, where the Twelve and other authorities "were provided with as much beer wine, cakes &c as we could eat and drink."

No new citizen could have been more enthusiastic than was young Irene Hascall Pomeroy, a bride of less than a year. Writing on June 2, 1845, to her mother in New Salem, Massachusetts, she could hardly find language eloquent enough:

> . . . I cannot wait any longer before I tell you what a beautiful place Nauvoo is. I was very much surprised to see such a pretty city. . . It is the prettiest place I ever saw for a large place; as far as we can see either way are buildings not in blocks like other cities but all a short distance from each other. The ground between them is all cultivated it looks like a perfect garden. . .
>
> I have been to view the Temple. It is a splendid building. The top stone was laid with Praises and Hosannas the morning before I arrived, . . . The roof is partly on. It never went so fast before. . . They are now encouraged and think they will be able to have meetings and commence endowment before snow falls. More than three hundred are at work on it and the rest help by paying their tything &c. . . All is peace and harmony. . . We hear the laborers sing and shout as they raise the timbers.

In every letter she repeated her praise of the beauty everywhere, even interrupting herself in the middle of one to run out and measure a corn stalk. "It measures eleven feet and a half. I presume I could find one twelve feet," she wrote triumphantly on her return. "Sister

Pond just brought in an ear and laid it beside my letter; it is as long
as this sheet and large enough to roast or broil."

She was so eager to have her mother come and bring her younger
brother Thales. The fact that her father refused to leave his home and
his aged mother should not keep them back. Their eternal salvation
was at stake. "Let Father stay if he must, but you two come quickly
to Nauvoo. Have no worry about how you will live when you arrive;
just get here. And instead of cluttering your journey with a lot of
things, bring what money you can" — this was the theme of every
letter.

Food was cheap in Nauvoo, she insisted, and gave prices to prove it:

Flour is 3.75 a barrell, butter 8 to 10 (cents) per lb., eggs 4 to
5 cents a dozen, sugar 10, molasses 40 cents per gallon, pork 5
cents per lb, milk 2 or 3 cts per qt. corn 27½, potatoes 25 and dry
goods as cheap as in New Salem.

After she had been there a month she reported that they had not
yet spent a dollar in cash for food. Francis had worked for a bushel
of wheat or four of corn a day, which they had exchanged at the store
for staple items, while from the abundance of their neighbors' gardens
they had fresh peas, corn, squash, beans, and cucumbers. Her husband
had picked a bucket of luscious blackberries, and had secured a cow
and six hens to help with the family economy.

She promised the eleven-year-old Thales that he could become a
member of the Junior Legion, an organization of some two hundred
and fifty boys who trained every week and marched in the parade on
July 4. He might even have "a real cap (not an old hat with a feather
in it) and some white pants trimmed with red."

But toward fall her joy became tinged with worry as reports came
in of trouble in the outlying settlements. One of the first acts of
violence was against the village over which Isaac Morley presided.
Here every house was burned. Now Irene wrote:

I have delayed sending it of late on account of the persecution
which has been raging against the Mormons in the neighboring
villages, . . . I believe in most instances their lives have
been spared but they have burned their houses, their barns filled
with grain and drove those out that were sick and not able to get
out without help exposed to the hot sun. Such cruelty! The mob
said they were going to drive every Mormon from the state. They
could not raise force enough to attack the city so they took the
adjoining towns. One hundred and twenty teams were sent from
here to Lima to rescue the people and bring them and their
goods and grain to Nauvoo. . .

The next week she added that school had closed because three families had moved into the schoolhouse. "All is peace at present; the people of the adjoining towns wish the Mormons to sign a treaty that they will leave in the spring if they will let them live here in peace this winter."

Among the newcomers who were ready to resist the mobber with force was John Steele. An Irish shoemaker, he had joined the church just three months before in Glasgow, Scotland, and with his wife and baby daughter had arrived in Nauvoo on July 8, 1844. He wrote with warmth of "the many fine buildings, costly mansions, fine farms cultivated around the city, plenty of woodland close by and a beautiful situation, several stores, and upon a high commanding bluff our magnificent and beautiful Temple!" As he put in his days of tithing labor on the roof, he delighted to view the scene, the prairie land beyond and the river opposite, where a busy commerce was carried on.

He and his wife found work at their trade, she stitching the uppers of the shoes and he putting on the soles and heels. Here was rewarding labor and wholesome, friendly association, a Zion indeed. When word came of the burning of Morley settlement, John Steele was ready to fight, and was glad to be detailed to "get the old sow and little pigs," the cannon and shot, to defend the temple. These were neatly covered with straw in an old wagon box.

Next he was ordered to go in defense of the carding machines at Macedonia. Five wagons, each carrying ten armed men, set out in the late afternoon, and made their headquarters in the village in front of Uncle Billy Perkins' home. John Steele was first to volunteer to stand guard over the buildings, and when the captain ordered him to load his gun, he remarked that "I never tasted anything so sweet in my life as did that powder." So eager was he for action that he ran out to stop a wagon, catching the horses by the bridle bits and calling out to stop, only to find that the men were friends, Ute Perkins and Long Andy.

Lee wrote that things had gone well until September 20, 1845, when "men belong(ing) to their father the Devil filled with his spirit commenced depredations on the Saints by burning their dwellings robbing and plundering their property driving them from their peaceable homes and possessions. . ." The saints were advised to offer no resistance, that the public might know that they were not at fault. Finally the county sheriff, J. B. Backenstos, "a noble hearted patriot," came to their assistance with troops, and there was again a state of civil war.

After more than a hundred Mormon homes had been burned, a meeting was arranged between the leaders of the church and General James A. Hardin, Senator Stephen A. Douglas, W. B. Warren, and

J. A. McDougal, commissioners from a convention held in Carthage. They agreed that all violence should cease on both sides, and that the Mormons should be allowed to remain unmolested until "the grass grows and water runs in the spring, when they shall all dispose of their property and leave the state."

With only five months in which to make preparations to move more than twenty thousand people, the smithies and carpenters and wheel-wrights must work around the clock to make wagons. The combined wisdom and energy of Brigham Young and the Twelve, the Council of Fifty and the City Council, and of every member of the church was needed, for many immigrants had exhausted their resources to reach Nauvoo from Europe and had nothing on which to go farther. Yet Brigham Young declared repeatedly that no one should be left behind who wished to go; the whole undertaking would be a cooperative one.

In the midst of all their trouble the saints continued to work on the temple, determined that it should be completed and used for their sacred ceremonies. John D. Lee recorded that "Nov 28th 1845 I was called upon to assist fitting up the rooms for the endowment in the House of the Lord — 10 days & I might as well say nights I was engaged in preparing the rooms refered to & on Thursday at 5 p.m. Dec 10 1845 myself and wife received our(s). . ."

From this date on until the book is filled on January 25, 1846, Lee spent most of his time in the temple, helping with the general arrangements, officiating in the ceremony, keeping records. There were times when he didn't have time to go home to sleep, but spent the night on one of the "sophias" in a side room, where wrapped in a comforter, he rested well. He noted carefully each day's activities until January 13, when he wrote that:

> I will here observe — Pres Brigham Young called & set me apart for the purpose of keeping the records of sealings . . . which were sacred and precious — & will of course be handed to future generations — quite a number of cases having allready occured without ever having been recorded & what was recorded was not in a correct form consiquently had to be rectified — which of course produced much labor which has been our occupation through the week. Finding the task more arduous than what we expected — Br Franklin D. Richards was appointed to assist in getting the records properly arranged & up with the opperations of . . . each day

He was first eager to have the wives who had been previously married to him at his home go through the temple ordinance. On December 19, 1845, he recorded that "I called in at Br J Beans &

notified Nancy his daughter to cleanse her body by washing in clear water & purify her heart by humbling her self in fasting and Prayer & come up to the Temple. . . She manifested some dissatisfaction and said that she chose to wait a little longer until her mind should be reconciled."

Four days later Nancy did come to the temple, accompanied by Rachel. Perhaps the fact that she was eight months pregnant would account in part for her reluctance. Later all of those who had been married before this time — Louisa Free, Caroline Williams, Abigail Sheffer, and Rachel Woolsey — came in together for the official sealing ceremony.

At this time another ceremony was instituted, which though it was of short duration and never widely practiced, was significant and important while it lasted. This was the adoption of young men and their wives to one of the leaders. The idea behind it was that in establishing the Kingdom of God upon the earth there should be also a celestial relationship. If the Prophet Joseph were to become a God over a minor planet, he must not only have a large posterity but able assistants of practical skills. Brigham Young had been "sealed" to Joseph under this law; now he in turn had some thirty-eight young men sealed to him.

Of this number, John D. Lee was second. He seemed to regret that he was not the first adopted son, as his position as secretary and recorder might have warranted, but deferred to Joseph's personal guard, Albert P. Rockwood, because of his seniority. All of the men thus joined in the covenant seemed brothers in one sense, and for some of them Lee developed a genuine affection. Among others, jealousies grew up as they competed for favor.

In the same way, Lee had eighteen or nineteen young men with their wives adopted to him, most of them those he had brought into the church. He often spoke of them as George Laub Lee, W. B. Owens Lee, Miles Anderson Lee, James Pace Lee, Allen Weeks Lee, William Swap Lee. Once he referred to "Thomas Woolsey, my first adopted son," and again to "Wm. J. Phelps, an apostate from my family."

For details of the adoption ceremony we are indebted to George Laub, who kept a daily diary during this period. Laub was an unmarried man of twenty, a member of three years' standing, a skilled carpenter and joiner by trade. He had grown up an orphan, so had no opportunity to attend school. His hands, expert with saw and hammer and adz, were awkward with a pen; his spelling was phonetic, but his writing clear and forceful.

Though he had been through the temple on December 19, he was not adopted to Lee until the day he was married to Mary Jane McGinnis. This was February 5, and Amasa Lyman officiated.

. . . I and my wife Mary Jane with many others was adopted
into John D. Lee's family, this I took upon myself the name of
Lee in this manner, George Laub Lee and my wife's name Mary
Jane Laub Lee in such a way that it cannot be seaparated by
covenanting before God, Angels and the Present witnesses we
covanant together for him to be as a father to those who are
sealed to him and to do unto them as he would unto his own
children and to councell them in rituousness and to teach them
all the Principles of Salvation and to share unto them of all the
blessings to comfort these and all that are calculated to make
them happy Both in time and in Eternity. Now we did also
covanant on our side to do all the good for his upbuilding and
happyness both in time & Eternity this was done in the hous of
the Lord across the alter as was prepared for this Purpose of
ordinances.

The young man was so impressed that he wrote the account in full
a second time in almost the same words, concluding, "Father Lee
being filed with the Spirit Embraced us in his arms and bless us in
the name of the Lord . . . that we should become mighty upon
the Earth and our names to be honorable in all generations."

The leaders met often to discuss plans for leaving and to decide
upon their destination. On December 3 they heard Parley P. Pratt
read from Fremont's Journal; on the nineteenth they spent two hours
"reading and listening to a California pamphlet;" on the thirty-first
they examined maps of the western country. Their real problem was
a more practical one, for when they checked on January 13, they had
only seventy wagons ready to move across the river.

Lee's diary of this time deals with private matters. For example on
January 12, he gave something of a picture of his home and its
activities:

. . . I drove to Br A P Free's & took my wife Sister Louisa
Lee home . . . when I reached home again I found several
of the High [council?] were collected at my house & had in the
South part of the 2nd story about 30 in No Bro Jefferson Hunt &
daughter Br Bean & family in connection with many other good
friends who helped pass off the even — We had a variety of
music — we enjoyed ourselves well . . . after our merriment
ceased we bowed in prayer. . .

Hosea Stout's diary, on the other hand, is in sharp contrast. He was in
charge of the police and watching for spies, eavesdroppers, and

enemies of the church. and preparing for the western move. On Friday, February 5, he wrote:

> The people was busy at my house preparing to start Hunter & I then went to the river at Kimball's landing to see how Capt Jones came on preparing the boats for crossing the river All was well and the boats was in a forward state for use . . . we made arrangements with Captain Jones to take about twenty of the guard and cross the river to Montrose and bring back to boats. . .

By early February the Missourians became restless. Again there were outbreaks of violence which convinced the leaders that some of them must move. The fact that the weather was still mild made them hasten their preparation.

They had now a fleet of flatboats, old lighters, rafts, and skiffs. Charles Shumway had gone across ahead on February 4, with his company — a group of fifteen wagons. Their business was to select a campsite suitable with regard to wood and water and to clear it and assemble fuel for those who would soon follow.

Again we must look to George Laub for details of the exodus of John D. Lee and his family. Writing under date of February 12, 1846, he says:

> . . . Myself and John D. Lee, Nancy Lee and Polly Lee took up our line of march for the west for pertection from our Enemys who were seeking the lives of the Twelve. . . Now this evening we got on a flat boat and crossed the Mississippi River into the State of Iowa . . . there many of the Brethren struck up their tents. . .
>
> Now I took across from the State of Illinois one waggon, Two Horses one cow and Provision soficant to sustain them for about Two months or more . . . then I returned again to my place of abode to commence making wagens for Lee's family . . . as I was appointed to doo so. . .

Though this entry tells us a great deal, there is much that it does not say. It fails to mention the fact that Nancy Bean Lee had with her a tiny daughter not yet a month old, born on January 15, when Lee was too busy at the temple to know or record the fact in the last real entry in the book. Polly Ann Workman was a younger wife, one of the last taken before they left Nauvoo. It appears that these two girls were congenial and wanted to be together. Nancy was the first to bear a child under the new covenant, and it was thought she should be out of the city in case of any investigation.

They found Hosea Stout with his three wives set up in a large tent, with a good fire going. The newcomers were glad to take shelter there, for the weather had turned very cold. The Stout group told a tale of horror about the river crossing. The water had been extremely rough. They had seen a skiff loaded with wood and operated by a man and two boys go down, and had heard the screams for help as the water covered them. Fortunately, they were rescued. Worse still was the wreck of a large ferry boat loaded with two wagons, two yoke of oxen, and about twenty people. Pandemonium broke out on their craft when a mischievous boy spit some amber into the eye of an ox. The animal, crazed with pain, jumped overboard, and his mate in threshing about kicked off some planks in the bottom of the boat, so that the boat went down and "in a few minutes we saw them scattered on the surface of the water like so many wild fowls . . . some were on feather beds, sticks of wood, lumber or any thing they could get hold of and were tossed & Sported on the water at the mercy of the cold and unrelenting waves. . ." All the people were finally rescued, though one yoke of oxen which was fastened to a wagon drowned.

Through all this, Hosea's wife and little son were both very ill, the child with a high fever. Lee and his group thanked God that their own crossing of the stream had been without incident and all had landed in good health.

Nancy and Polly Lee found many girls here in the same condition as they were. In the company which had landed on February 9 were Bathsheba W. Smith and the five virtuous young women she had given her husband as wives the year before. Within the month one of them would die in childbirth and her child with her. Also with the group was Zina D. Huntington, previously the wife of Joseph Smith and now of Brigham Young. In the last weeks of her pregnancy she had come ahead in the care of her elder brother Dimick. She gave birth to her son in the wagonbox, attended only by Mother Lyman. With the luxury of a cup of coffee and a biscuit to sustain her, she came through her ordeal. "I did not mind the hardship, for my life had been preserved, and my babe seemed so beautiful," she wrote.

Everywhere were young women with babes in their arms or under their aprons. Eliza R. Snow reported that, "I was informed that on the first night of the encampment nine children were born into the world."

There were many problems connected with the life of these exiles in their temporary camp. First was the cold. A tent firmly set, banked with sod around the edges provided shelter against the wet and cut the wind somewhat, but did not keep out subzero cold. Community bonfires glowed in the center of each group of tents or wagons, near which people gathered and turned constantly that one side might not freeze while the other sizzled. Inside the tents, babies were changed and dressed beside the glow of red coals carried in on shovels and placed in a scooped out hollow.

There was also a great concern for the poor cattle which were exposed to this bitter weather without food. How could the company move on to the mountains if their oxen and horses were frozen? The calendar said it was past mid-February; spring must come sometime. Surely God would not subject these, His special children, to too much suffering.

Brigham Young and his families arrived in camp on February 15. As soon as they had their tents and wagons placed, he called all the men together for a council. One wagon was rolled into the center of the enclosure to be used as a stand which he mounted, while his audience stood facing him near the fire. He reminded them that if all were to reach the mountains, they must have order in the camp. They must be organized into workable units, but there must be first a census taken in which the name, age, and birthplace of every person should be recorded. Second, they must build a large, central crib to hold the grain for the animals, and Brother George W. Harris would be in charge of it to parcel out to each man according to the number of animals he had to feed. They had already been able to purchase several tons of timothy hay for forage.

Benjamin F. Johnson was appointed to take charge of all lost articles. The signals for meeting would be the raising of a white flag when all the people in the camp should come; a blue flag would summon the captains. Of the first such meeting Lee wrote:

Feb. 18 . . . the male members of the camp were called together near the bridge on the east side of the creek. Presant of the Twelve Pres. B. Young, H. C. Kimball, P. P. Pratt, G. A. Smith, O. Pratt, Willard Richards and Amasa Lyman. At 10 Pres. Brigham Young took the Stand (J. D. Lee clerk) and called on the Capts of 100 50's and 10's to collect from their several companies money to purchase Factory Drilling and bed ticking to make wagon covers and Tent ends and put it in the hands of John D. Lee — we will send it to St. Francesville Mo and obtain the cloth — it can there be had low so I understand.

The next day, with $50.95 and two companions to accompany him, Lee set out on his errand. The river was almost blocked with ice, too dangerous to cross large boats and not solid enough to hold a wagon.

The men steered their small boat through, and returned three days later with the cloth.

Soon afterward, Lee received word that two of his brothers-in-law, James and Reuben Woolsey, were in custody at Nauvoo charged with theft, so "I laid my wishes before my Father, the Pres of this church who sanctioned my intentions & bid me go & prosper in the name of the Lord and that he would render me all the assistance that he could in seeing to my family that was here as I had 4 of them along."

This time Lee was hauled to the river bank in a buggy, crossed the stream on ice, and at once set about to settle his affairs and bring out Aggatha and the children and as many of those who had joined his family as he could. He secured the release of the Woolsey brothers; he turned his fine home and all his property into the hands of the church trustees, Babbitt, Heywood and Fullmer, for eight hundred dollars to be paid in teams and store goods. Since the trustees could not guarantee teams before April 6, he traded his credit with neighbors who would not be ready to leave before that time. Thus he was able to secure four full outfits with two span of oxen and two of mules, besides his fine riding horse which he had kept out of any trade.

Aggatha must leave the comfortable home with the furniture and nice things she had collected, and had enjoyed for a short time only. She must content herself with parched corn meal sewed into heavy sacks, dried beans, wheat, salt pork, and other staple foods, all packed to conserve every inch of space. She could not resist putting in the clock and some flower seed tied into small bags. Not only must the medicine box be taken, but it must be readily accessible, as well.

Again we depend upon George Laub for the details:

. . . Now after John D. Lee had crosed the first time the camp stoped several days in the Iowa teritory in concequence of the cold wether and the snow storm. Then he returned and took the residew of his family, this was on the 4 day of March when I crossed with him. . . So now I took my leaf of them after wishing them Peas and prosperity on their jurney. I gave Father Lee the parting hand and we Embraced Each other in our arms for sorrow was in my heart to part with so good a friend.

Now there was in Number in this last part of his family J. D. Lee, Agathan & Rachel, Martha, Loiza, Horas Bowen and wife, James Wolsys wife & Mother Wolsey & Hyrum & Brother Workmans Son &

The abrupt closing might indicate that Laub had other names to add — perhaps those of Aggatha's four children. One thing the entry does show is young Laub's complete devotion to his adopted father. He returned to Nauvoo to manage Lee's affairs and follow three months later. He emphasized the fact that he had crossed the river "twist" (two times) in one day, which was something of a feat in itself.

The ice had finally broken up in the river, so they ferried the wagons on flatboats. On the opposite shore they found the roads thawed and the mud so deep that it took them four days to cover the nineteen miles to camp.

1846

Across Iowa

As soon as the little wagon train arrived at the main camp, Lee set about to bring his record up to date by filling in what had happened during his absence. This daily account, as yet unpublished, gives so much of the doings of the secret Council of Fifty, that it seems appropriate to pause here for a brief discussion of that organization.

As was suggested earlier, a basic teaching of the early Mormon Church was that the second coming of Christ was imminent, and the saints should prepare for it by building temples in which to purify themselves. They must also establish the kingdom of God, an actual, physical kingdom of homes and industries, of culture and beauty and righteousness. To implement this, the Council of Fifty was organized of practical men of the earth, skilled, educated, superior men who were not to direct the spiritual affairs, but were to help to make, interpret, and execute the laws and plan for the general welfare.

Before his death, Joseph Smith talked of a move to the west, where the kingdom would be planted in the tops of the mountains. On March 11, 1844, both the Prophet and Brigham Young wrote of the organization of the Council of Fifty, though it would seem that the actual revelation authorizing it had been given on April 7, 1842. Every man was selected for two qualifications: his skills or abilities and his complete loyalty to the church. Every man sensed the honor and responsibility of his position; each felt that he had been especially called by the highest authority of God upon the earth.

Martyred for the cause, Joseph Smith had even more influence now than before and the men selected by him felt that their call and responsibility was equal to that of Brigham Young. So great was their zeal that they gladly subordinated their personal ambitions and the welfare of their families to the business of leading the modern Israel through this exodus to their own Promised Land. Brigham Young knew that his power lay chiefly in cooperating with these fifty men, listening to their counsel and abiding by group decisions.

During the days in Nauvoo before the death of the Prophet, the Council decided upon economic questions, established businesses, secured materials for building the temple and public buildings, stood guard over the leaders, dealt with spies and apostates, pledged themselves to help the poor, prepared for the exodus, and decided who should carry out the various duties attending it. A list of the names of the Council includes the leaders in every enterprise, yet the meetings were so secret that few of the people knew of the organization.

Lee's record, more than any other yet found, brings out the importance of the Council of Fifty, which he designates as the YTFIF, or the word "fifty" spelled backwards. Naming a few of the members one sees clearly their importance. Almon Babbitt, Joseph S. Heywood, and John S. Fullmer were to remain in Nauvoo, sell the property of the church, help the saints get their outfits ready, and keep careful records of all, even the enemies of the church. Lyman Wight was in Texas, whither the Prophet had sent him to learn the possibilities of a final settlement there; James Emmett started after the Prophet was dead to carry out an earlier assignment to explore in the northwest for a possible place for a home for the Church. George Miller, always in the vanguard, always building bridges, fencing, clearing, and planting fields, resented the dictation of Brigham Young, declaring that his own orders had come from the Prophet. Charles Shumway took the great responsibility of crossing the Mississippi first, selecting the first camp sites, and preparing for the larger emigration.

Though these exiles were only a small part of the church, they included many of the leaders. In keeping the minutes and writing up the various assignments, Lee shows clearly the problems with which they were confronted. The most pressing need was food, so trading groups were sent out, and the band gave concerts in nearby towns, at one place reporting a clear gain of "$25 and 70 cts." Captain John Scott and his artillerymen left their heavy guns stuck fast in the mud while they took a contract from farmers to make two thousand rails in exchange for flour and pork. Still another group contracted to shuck corn for every seventh bushel and the shucks and fodder, these last items to provide chewing material for starving cattle.

The chief obstacle lay beyond their control: the weather. After the snow stopped and the cold moderated, the rain began, daily constant rain that seemed as if it would dissolve and leach out all the religion in the entire camp. Fires could not be kept going, bedding and clothes could not be dried, nor could wagons be moved. There was neither time nor a place for a general meeting, so instead of getting warmth of spirit from one another, each was forced to fan the flame of faith under his own wagon cover.

The council met almost daily. Should they sell the temple at Nauvoo? Should they select a hundred men, fit them out, and send them to the mountains this season? If so, who would they be? What of the families that would have to be left behind?

Clearly no one could move now. All were too heavily loaded for one thing, none had food enough, and the roads were still impassable. To correct the first condition, on the first clear day, March 14, they made a cache of "certain valuables." Hosea Stout was more specific, writing on March 9 that "it was also decided to light up the loads of the Artillery by burying up the ball & shot in the ground and getting them some other time." Two days later he was out in the rain and reported "we came across H. G. Sherwood surveying & taking the points of the compass from certain objects where the cannon balls had been buried.   . ." It would seem important to have an exact location of the spot in order that the ammunition might be found when needed. The directions read:

> Certain deposits near ——— (viz) beginning at an augur hole in the west side of a white oak tree near the roots running thence w with the needle pointing 80 degrees N L 130 links to a black oak tree thence 39 links to another black oak tree thence 23 links to a mound with a pit on the south side of said mound making in all 192 links in a direct line from said white oak tree — thence from said mound south with the needle pointing 10 degrees E.L. & 135 links to a stone about 15 inches long & about 7 to 9 inches square at the upper end tapering to about 5 inches at the other end — set in the ground on the east side near the root of a forked black oak Tree forked near the ground.
>
> Witness: Joel Terry
> John Scott   Warren Snow
> John Farnham   Henry G. Shearwood
> George G. Johnson   Surveyors

Soon this area was to become a burial ground, for the next day two deaths occurred: Sidney Tanner's fifteen-months-old child died from brain fever and worms, and Edwin Little died from consumption and overwork. Both graves were located with relation to the augur hole in the white oak tree.

With the coming of mild weather, some of the guard were permitted to return to Nauvoo, but were required to leave their wagons with the council, an order which caused much protest. Such were the conditions, however, that though the people inched ahead as best they could all during March, they covered less than a hundred miles in thirty days.

From April 10 to 18 Lee went on a trading expedition, taking seventeen wagons and some horses for trade. At Miller's station he met Patrick Dorsey, who was suffering with extremely sore eyes. Lee reminded him that God could heal any of his children who had faith. He placed his hands on the sick man's head and asked God to restore him to health. The result seemed miraculous. Dorsey was so over-joyed and grateful that he was ready to do business in a generous way, and more than glad to exchange provisions for Lee's property in Nauvoo. Of this, Lee wrote:

> I reflected a little and gave him a list of city property at Nauvoo that I would turn out to him at one-fourth its value, for such property as he wanted to turn out to me. He said he had twelve yoke of oxen and some twenty five cows and other stock; four bee stands, three wagons, powder, lead, blankets, thirty rifles, guns, knives, tobacco, calicoes, spades, hoes, plows, harrows; also twelve feather beds and all of his improvements. . . All the above property he turned over to me and I gave him deeds to property in Nauvoo. . .

So once again Lee had justified the confidence of Brigham Young, who sent him repeatedly to act as purchasing agent for the group.

On April 18, they held an important council meeting at which were present five of the Twelve Apostles; Brigham Young, Heber C. Kimball, John Taylor, Parley P. Pratt, and Willard Richards, and Newell K. Whitney, George Miller, Wm. Clayton, John Smith, Samuel Bent, J. M. Grant, George D. Grant (Young), Charles Shumway, Theodore Turley, Philip B. Lewis, Erastus Snow, John D. Lee, and Peter Haws of the YTFIF. The next day Benjamin F. Johnson, Father John Smith, Albert P. Rockwood (Young) and Daniel and Orson Spencer had arrived to bring the total to eighteen members.

The members of the council and the captains of the various groups were asked again to make a complete inventory of all the outfits in their care, of the foodstuff on hand, and to offer suggestions for future policy. On Sunday, April 19, a general public meeting was called, the first real service in more than two months. Lee's minutes of this gathering are careful and complete, preserving the flavor and idiom of each speaker.

The question for discussion was the ever recurring one, "Who shall go on to the mountains?" None was really equipped to go, but all were eager to be on the way. Brigham Young began by warning them that they would have short rations, that they would experience much sickness, but he concluded with the promise that "If this people will harken to counsel they will have good health from this time forth & before we get to the top of the Mountains that women that cannot walk 1 mile now can then walk 20 miles a day. . . There is Dr. Richards the Historian that has to be poulticed all over will then skip like a boy with his gun on his shoulder running after deer elk & Buffalo. . ."

Elder Kimball testified that "I have been with my brethren in England when we subsisted 3 days on a penny loaf of bread which was not larger than my fist & we were abundantly satisfied. . ." Elder George A. Smith confessed that he wished they had more, but promised not to murmur. "I find that Smoke Rain Snow wind or hale is good for my health for I am feeling it improving and there is Amasa Lyman that has been almost helpless in times past walking now with his gun on his shoulder and if Dr. Amasa & I get young and sprightly as boys — well, then we will acknowledge him a prophet. . ."

George Miller remarked that "I don't mean to brag but I can outrun any horse in the camp."

It remained for Lorenzo Young to prick the bubble. He reminded them that some, when they left Nauvoo, thought they could accomplish the whole journey on two or three bushels of parched meal. "Have they been able to sustain themselves thus far — no, they have not only eaten all the food in the camp and have complained of hunger already. Therefore brethren — don't let the bump of Ideality get so high & be carried away in anticipation to that extent that you will venture to take a journey of 12 months upon the scanty allowance of 4 ounces per day, as Bro. Miller would feign make you believe. . ."

As a result of this meeting it was decided that all should organize and pitch in right there to plant crops. Men wishing to return to Nauvoo were ordered to "Let your families be! What can you do at Nauvoo now? Nothing but eat. . . They will manage better without you than with you. Go and do what I command you — that you open a farm and raise something to feed them when they arrive."

More rain delayed the program for another week, but on the next Sunday it was clear, and again the saints gathered for meeting. Now Brother Brigham spoke out sharply against waste, against pieces of bread lying around and dishes of flour and meal half used, of taking more meat out of the brine than could be cooked at once. He then gave the general plan; they would clear and fence and plant here, leaving some to care for the crops, then move ahead about forty miles and clear and start another place, and on again.

Found that there were 359 men available independent of those Traders, herdsmen & others & were disposed of in this manner 100 men to making rails — 10 to building fence & 8 to building houses 12 men to digging wells 10 to build a bridge the remaining of the available men were not disposed off but were left to clear plough plant etc. . . moved & carried that Jas Allred oversee the fence making department & that Father John Smith boss the house building department & C C Rich Jas Pace Lee

L D Wilson & S Markham boss or oversee rail making — Daniel
Spencer to Superintend the Farming department Jacob Peart to
Superintend the well digging department A P Rockwood the
bridge making department that Pres boss him and all the whole
camp also that Pres Young Kimble & P P Pratt & C C Rich corner-
men on the buildings.

The result was that the camp was called out at six the next morning
and soon the sound of axes and mauls was echoing over the countryside, according to the recorder, "keeping perfect time."

In the meantime, the saints at Nauvoo had enjoyed comparative
peace. During the first cold months and the long weeks of rain they
had shelter and warmth. While all were working toward getting ready
to leave, they continued with their church meetings and public activities. The carpenters labored at the temple by day and attended
services in some of the rooms at night. One of them, young Samuel
Richards, kept a diary account in some detail of these. On Sunday,
March 15, he wrote:

> . . . In the evening was with the Quorum in the temple until
> after 12 oclock at night. The Sacrament was administered, and
> great blessings were enjoyed. Tongues, Prophecying, and the
> angels attended us. Their glory filled the house in so much that
> many witnessed it throughout the city and testified thereof, that it
> was the brightness of fire.

On the following Wednesday he reported that the temple was "filled
with an exceeding bright light, the gift of Tongues & Prophecy was
much enjoyed." The next Sunday there was an even greater outpour-
ing, until one of the number suggested that they unitedly pray "for
the Prophet Joseph to come into our Midst and converse with us."
Older and wiser members protested, saying that such a course would
not be fitting, so each was content to receive his own personal
inspiration.

When April followed March and few Mormons were leaving, their
enemies began to be restless. The promise that they would all move
as soon as "the grass grows, and the water runs" was not being kept.
Though some were working toward getting their outfits, others were
still putting in their time on the temple. On April 23, Samuel Richards
told how the carpenters swept up their shavings "after which it was
voted that Bro. Angel go and inform the Trustees that the hands were
ready to drink the Barrell of Wine which had been reserved for them."
The painters continued their work until the evening of April 29, when
a group of the workers and their wives met in the attic and "had a

feast of cakes, pies, wine, &c, where we enjoyed ourselves with prayer, preaching, administering for healing, blessing children, and music and Dancing until near Midnight. The other hands completed the painting in the lower room."

Plans were made for a three-day dedication of the temple, on May 1, 2, and 3. On the evening of Thursday, April 30, the priesthood in charge met for the real service, a small, earnest group of thirty men dressed in their priestly robes. The next morning the building was again dedicated in the presence of strangers and all who would pay one dollar for admittance, the money to be used to help pay the laborers. On Saturday a second ceremony was performed, and on Sunday a third, open free for all the saints. Here Orson Hyde proposed that they sell the building, and a vote was taken with but one dissenting voice.

Samuel Richards had been called to go on a mission to England, but he proceeded to get an outfit and provisions to take his bride of a few months to join the saints who were on the way west.

During May the largest organized and best outfitted groups left Nauvoo. Amos Fielding, approaching the city on June 1, said that in three days of travel he counted nine hundred and two Mormon wagons headed west. Among this number was Francis Pomeroy, his wife and baby, her mother and brother. Irene's fervent letters from Nauvoo finally had persuaded Ursula Hascell (later spelled Haskell) with her son, Thales, to join the body of the saints, leaving her husband at home. Now it was the mother who wrote back to neighbors in New Salem, Massachusetts, a report of their doings.

Nowhere does this lady suggest that they are saddened by the move, nor does she hint that it is a hardship. On the contrary, it is wonderful; an adventure toward the new Zion and an assurance of eternity hereafter. The food is good, she insists, "hot biscuits with honey and butter and a cup of good coffee are not too mean a meal." She mentions fresh meat, game, and fresh berries. She said she had never slept better in all her life. Of the wagon and outfit she wrote:

. . . The wagon is long enough for both our beds made on the flour barrels, chests and other things. (Thales and I sleep in the back and F and Irene in the forward end While we are traveling if we are too late to pitch our tent) It is painted red. It has eight bows eighteen inches apart; a hen coup on the end with four hens. We had two webs of thick drilling. We put on one cover of that, then three breadths of stout sheeting over that and then painted it. The heaviest storms do not beat through, only a few drops now and then. Our tent is made of drilling sixteen breadths in the shape of an umbrella, a cord three feet long on the end of every seam and a pin on that to drive into the ground, then a breadth of sheeting put on the edge to let down in cool weather and fasten with loops and pins in the ground. . .

This, perhaps, represents the outfits of the better-to-do of the people. Now in warm weather, with grass for feed along the way, they could travel in less than two weeks the distance the others had taken almost four months to cover, with little discomfort to either themselves or their animals.

While this was true of a good part of the Mormon emigrants, there were still those behind who had no means of moving. The first real persecutions began in July when eight farmers who were harvesting their grain near Nauvoo were cruelly whipped, two of them nearly to death. That hurried such families as could go to leave, but those who had no means of transportation were subject to threats and abuse, until by September things had reached a stage where there were gun battles in which blood was spilled on both sides and the last Mormons were driven to the river on foot. There they were met by friends who took them across and on to join the group, in accordance with the promise made so repeatedly that none should be left behind who wanted to go.

Meanwhile the pioneers were building temporary farms and shelters and moving ahead, leaving them for others who were following; Garden Grove, Cutler's Park and Mount Pisgah.

Lee had been forced to leave a part of his "family;" that is, seven of his adopted sons with their wives and children, behind at Mount Pisgah. He shared his foodstuff with them, gave them three good milk cows, some seed potatoes, and his blessing. He did not name those who went on with him, but said that there were "twenty souls, 24 head of cattle & 4 mules & 1 horse rather a mare 4 waggons besides 2 horses & a waggon belonging to Benj. McGinnis." (This man was the father-in-law of George Laub).

When June came, Brigham Young and the council could see very well that they could not push on to the mountains that season. They would get to the Council Bluffs, perhaps cross the river, and set up a winter quarters until those who were to make the trip could be better prepared and those who remained behind could be left with shelter and food.

The two hundred wagons which constituted the central company moved ahead in order, and Lee was so impressed that he wrote, "When we had crossed the river and ascended the hill a more grand & sublime scene was seldom witnessed the high Rolling green elevated Prairies were lined with waggons & almost covered with heards for miles." Out on the prairie, at what Lee called "The Pleasant Prairie

Encampment" they halted for a complete reorganization of the camp, in which Lee lists the order of the wagons and gives the names of every teamster and of the captains over each group.

At every stop the YTFIF met and counseled, determining the tasks of the various ones, deciding who should move ahead and who should stay behind to manage the farms and settlements.

They pushed ahead to the Bluffs where a part of the Emmett Company awaited them, crossed over Mosquito Creek on the bridge built by George Miller, and halted while the women gathered ten bushels of wild strawberries. Had it not been for the mosquitos they would have made a permanent camp here.

Brigham Young counseled them to have no doings whatsoever with the Indians or the traders. Individuals who tried to trade would most certainly be taken advantage of; one agent representing the group could drive a better bargain. He also told them not to talk to strangers nor speak of their plans. Each herdsman should collect and hold all creatures that had a tail and horns, whether the animal belonged to his immediate group or not. The business at hand was to get across the river and out of Indian territory, to which end they would build solid boats to carry the whole migration over, as they came along.

Nearly a month earlier, President Young had suggested that Lee take a trading train of wagons to the settlement, but the weather and other pressures had prevented it. Now that they were at a camp that would be permanent for a while, at least until strong boats could be finished, it seemed a good time to carry out the plan. On June 15 he was told to unload his wagons and prepare for the journey. At the same time word was sent out among the people asking that anyone who had anything he wished to trade should bring it in. Lee kept a careful account of the cash entrusted to him and an inventory of the property put into his hands, with a value set upon each item. His diary says that he left on Sunday, June 14, with seven teams for Brigham Young, two for Willard Richards, and several more from the first company besides his own, loaded with "traps such as feather beds, fine counterpanes, quilts, and such goods to trade for supplies, beef cattle, oxen, and cows."

At this point he left twenty-two pages of his record blank, evidently intending to write in the details of general camp history later. His own personal account book, and the record of his trip and its transactions, would be kept in a small pocket book and not placed in the church record except in summary. Whether Lee was away for six full weeks, or whether he was too busy with other things to make the careful record, we cannot know; we know only that on July 31 he picked up the story of doings at Headquarters of the Camp of Israel.

Many things had happened during his absence. More than five

hundred wagons had crowded to the Bluffs and many had been crossed over the river near what would become Winter Quarters. The evacuation of Nauvoo was at its peak; the road all across Iowa was alive with wagons as thick as a string of migrating ants.

Most important was the arrival on July 13 of Captain Allen asking for five hundred men to march with the army to Mexico. So bitter were most of the Mormons about the treatment they had received and the lack of protection at the martyrdom of their prophet that none wanted to enlist. Brigham Young had to use all his persuasive powers, visiting all the camps and back stations, encouraging, urging, almost commanding men to join. They were going west anyway; if they could go across with their food and clothing provided by the government, they might well contribute a part of the cash pay — seven dollars per month, with six months in advance — toward the expense of the general migration. That would greatly simplify things for the Mormon leaders. President Young had pulled all the strings he could through Jesse C. Little to get this call, but now he was to have some difficulty to raise the quota. He appealed to those within the age limits of eighteen through forty-five, he urged and encouraged and admonished. He promised that they would not be called upon to shed blood, and that if they lived their religion they would be protected.

Four groups of one hundred each were finally raised, and after they had marched away, the fifth was made up. But many concessions had been made. Seven boys too young to be enlisted as regular soldiers were taken along as assistants. Thirty-three young men took their wives; twenty others took their wives and children, the families ranging for the most part from one child to five. The outstanding exception was made in the case of Captain Jefferson Hunt who took two wives and a total of eleven children. In the group were six women, each of whom carried her own secret knowledge that before six months had passed she would give birth to a child. But children had been born on the road before, and each preferred to take the chance in company with her husband. Only one, the wife of Captain Jesse D. Hunter of Company B, died and left a living child; at least two others lost their babies at birth or soon after.

Lee himself did not go. However, he used his influence to send three of his adopted sons. First Lieutenant James Pace, Second Lieutenant Andrew Lytle, and Third Lieutenant Samuel Gully, with two of the teenage boys, Byron and William D. Pace, were among those who went along.

The help of these able-bodied young men was sorely needed by the camp, but the money they sent back by Parley P. Pratt helped greatly in fitting up the needy saints.

Lee says nothing of all this, nor of the details of the mustering in. This information was evidently intended for the twenty-two blank pages. His first entry after his return, July 31, makes clear that there was sickness in camp, for on that day Presidents Young and Kimball "laid hands on" the head of his oldest daughter, nine-year-old Sarah Jane, and prayed for her recovery. Later in the evening President Young administered to his youngest son, John Brigham, and Dr. Sprague also visited him without success. This child was the son of Louisa Free, whom Lee had married on April 19, 1844. While the actual date of the boy's birth has not been found, it appeared he was then more than a year old.

Since he was keeping a church record, Lee rarely mentions his family affairs. Only once on Saturday, May 2, 1846, he had written:

. . . this morning I lay rather late, having neither bread nor meat in my tents, still having 28 persons to feed. I knew not where to go — however, I got up & walked east — & soon met a man that proffered to lend me both flour and bacon. . .

On the first of August, he wrote of official business and of the decisions to remain there for the winter and to write to George Miller and others ahead so that they will not try to send anyone over the mountains before the next year. Then after taking the description of a villain who had passed off counterfeit money, he remarks that some of his family are gaining from their affliction, but his young son is no better. Dr. Sprague visited the sick of his family and pronounced some of them dangerously ill. But the following day Lee notes that he "found some of my family improving."

The next three days were employed in selecting winter quarters; with daily meetings of the Council of Fifty and those of the Twelve who were present; and with the business of all hands working to cut the wild hay for winter feed and twelve members of the YTFIF to lay out the settlement.

Early in August, Thomas L. Kane visited the headquarters of the saints. He had become acquainted with Brigham Young and the other leaders the preceding June while they were raising the quota of men for the Mormon Battalion, and he had been nursed through a serious illness at that time. He had visited the deserted city of Nauvoo and later spoke and wrote effectively about the desecration of the temple and the great losses which the people had sustained. Many years later he was to intercede for them again and to act as a peacemaker between them and the representatives of the government. So friendly did he become and so solicitous for their welfare that many people believed

him a baptized member of the church, his membership kept a secret
lest it should lessen his influence in the East.

As soon as he arrived, Brigham Young called a private council in
which he "said to Col. Kane with reference to our settlements in the
California's we do not intend going & settling the majority of our
people on the course or near the Bay of San Francisco — but intend
settling the greater part of our people in the Great Basin between
the mountains near the Bear River valley. . ." Governor Kane reported that their greatest enemy, the ex-Governor of Missouri, expected
to be appointed the executive officer in California. He also suggested
the type of letter which Brigham Young might write to the President
of the United States to court good will.

A few days later, when Col. Kane was taken ill again, Lee mentioned the public prayers in his behalf, reported that they had shaved
his head and given him repeated baths to reduce his fever, and sent
posthaste to Fort Leavenworth for medicine for him. All this, along
with the ordinance of administration, finally combined to restore him.
Mormon legend says that that when Brigham Young promised him that
he should live to old age, be married and father children, Kane did
not believe it because he had been so frail and sickly.

Through all these months we should know little of Lee's family life
except for George Laub's account and Lee's later *Confessions*. There
is some evidence that Aggatha was not happy about the plural wives,
for on August 8, 1846, he did write: "by council I removed a part of
my family (namely Nancy) to my son Wm. P. Lee (William Pace) &
placed them in the 2nd 10 in Co. No 1 Louisa with a wagon I removed
to the same 10. . ." These two girls are the only ones who had
borne him children under the new order, Nancy a daughter, then
called Eliza and later named Cornelia, and Louisa a son, John
Brigham.

Perhaps Aggatha's condition would aggravate her jealousy, for just
a week later, August 15, Lee wrote that "About 5 o'clock A.M. Aggatha
Ann Lee wife of John D. Lee brought forth a large likely son & called
his name Heber John after 2 of the apostles. . ." Many years later,
on August 20, 1866, Lee was to explain the actions of a rebellious son
of Aggatha thus: "these children were begotten in the days of trial
when plurality was first introduced; consequently the spirit of aleana-
tion & disaffection were entailed upon the children, hence our last
children are hoped to be the best."

Lee's account is illuminated throughout with observations on many
subjects. Always he was concerned for the cattle, telling of animals
that are exhausted, oxen that fell in the yoke, horses bitten by rattle-
snakes. Cures were sometimes effected by dosages of oats heavily

seasoned with tobacco and salt. In extreme cases, they invoked the help of God, as on March 11, when:

At Indian creek one of his horses sickened with bloating colick Elder Hall & Luallen layed hands on him & he recovered immediately & went on about 2 miles when he was again attacked much more violently than before they tried to give him medicine but could not succeed the horse layed on his side with his foot over his ear. Reuben Strong said he believed there was life in him yet, and proposed to lay hands on him but some doubted whether it was right to lay hands on a horse or not. Elder Hall replied the prophet Joel has said that in the last days the Lord would pour of his spirit upon all flesh & this satisfied the Brethren & Elder Wm Hall, R. R. Strong, L. Manette, Jos Chaplain, Marin Potter, & one more laid hands on the horse and commanded the unclean and foul Spirit of whatever name or Nature to depart and go to Voree and trouble the Saints no more when the horse rolled twice over in great distress vomited & purged next morning was harnessed to a load of about 12 hundred & performed his part as usual.   .   .

Lee did not pretend at any time that all was peace and harmony among the saints. He told how one James W. Hemmick challenged Wilbur J. Earl to fight a duel, whereupon Brigham Young by order of the council commanded that he be discharged from the camp forthwith and not be numbered with the saints. Three days later the two met before the council to air their grievances, but almost before they had started, the verdict was given — there was no cause for hard feelings on either side and "that the subject be *forever* dropped."

Another incident happened on May 6, when "between 10 & 11 this evening a waggon containing Erastus H. Derby & Emiline Haws was suddenly upset & is believed by some boys in the camp." The next morning, "Emiline Haws believing & pretending that Benjamin Denton was concerned in upsetting the waggon the previous evening threatened revenge & while at breakfast about 8 o'clock threw a cup of boiling coffee in his face which penetrated his eyes. Doct. Sprague was immediately called to his assistance & concluded it was doubtful whether he would ever see again."

Some members of the YTFIF investigated the matter, talked to the girl's father, read some of her letters, and in general considered her conduct. Since no further mention was made of the affair, it would seem that the young man was not permanently injured and the girl was not punished.

Though Lee felt called upon to record some unpleasant incidents, he did not always pass judgment, as in the following case:

June 8 . . . All went well today with the exception of a little confab between Bro. J. Pack & Howard Egan, the former wishing to take his place in front of the latter in traveling the road contrary to his wishes smote his team with a stick 3 times when Bro. H. E. with a blow of his fist brought him to the earth and then kicked him for falling. This however can alone be attributed to the weakness & depravity of mortal man for they are both good men. . .

In August, all else was subordinated to the business of preparing for the winter ahead. They stopped first near a grove and effected an organization with Alpheus Cutler in charge and eleven others of the Council of Fifty to assist him in building a community. This place, called Cutler's Park, really became a suburb of the Winter Quarters which was located three miles farther on. But through all these uncertain days there were many meetings of the council and much exhortation to the camp. The people were told not to discuss their business or destination, nor to preach. Furthermore, "with reference to sealings, there will be no such thing done until we build another temple . . . let no man hint such a thing from this time fourth. . ."

The business of plurality of wives was no longer as carefully guarded as it had been in Nauvoo, although there was little public reference to it. Yet in his speech on June 7, Brigham Young lay forth the duties of the sisters in plain language:

. . . I would tell the Sisters their duty but should I — Don't let some man go and cut a gad & whip his wife before night . . . that is, speaking in general terms — it is the duty of all my wives & all other women to mind their own business — keep themselves — houses or tents clean & not to dictate my business or the Priesthood or want to know where I am going or where I have been slept last night . . . it is their duty to bear all the children they can lawfully & raise them up in the name of the Lord watching over them & seeing that they are kept from playing with ungodly children from falling in rivers or exposing themselves to sickness & dangers & teaching them to reverence the Priesthood & when she has raised up to deliver them up to their fathers. . .

Orson Pratt was not so pointed but did make it plain that "we are under the Celestial Law & governed by the same God Spirit & Priesthood as the ancients were," and had the same kind of patriarchal family life as did Abraham of old.

Lee always reported the words of Brigham Young with great fidelity, preserving even the vulgarisms and the extreme statements. Speaking to the wives of battalion men he said, "I saw women slinging snot saying we will never see the 1st cent of what our husbands sent us. . ." and then proceeded to explain that they had used the money to buy staple necessities at wholesale prices and that all would benefit. . . "then stop your whining about losing your money & saing that the 12 will keep it etc. for I will not bear it — my brethren shall not be slandered by such poor miserable whining cursed apostates — if they do not stop — we will stop their wind — Now run & tell that we kill folks. . ."

Still another item of interest lies in the fact that in all their frequent enumerations, they never give the number of women or young children. On August 12 they made a careful census of the first company, which was that of Brigham Young and listed "325 men & boys over 10 years old, 359 wagons, 146 horses, 1264 oxen, 848 cows, 49 mules, 416 sheep," but no word of women and children!

Perhaps this is not so strange after all, when we consider that Brigham Young brought seventeen wives out of Nauvoo, John D. Lee had ten, George A. Smith six, and Heber C. Kimball listed thirty-two.

Throughout August the leaders were concerned with preparing a central headquarters for winter, providing shelter and food for the hundreds who were daily crowding in, preserving the wild grass hay for winter feed for the stock, and protecting as best they could the general health of the community.

On August 28, about dark, President Young visited John D. Lee in his tent. "I have a very dangerous but responsible mission for you to perform," he said. "I want you to follow up the Mormon Battalion and be at Santa Fe when they receive their payment. Can you go?"

"I am willing to do whatever I can to further the cause," Lee answered without hesitation. "But you know my condition. My wife is not well, her babe is not two weeks old. My families are not provided for. My most reliable adopted sons are with the Battalion and George Laub has not yet arrived."

"Go, and God will protect you," Brother Brigham said, laying a firm hand on his shoulder. "I shall see that your families do not want. It is most important that we have what money we can get if we are to have food to survive this winter. Even then I have a heavy heart when I think of what is ahead."

Thus Lee accepted one of the most important assignments of his career.

1846
To Santa Fe

Aggatha might well have protested this trip. Her baby was not yet two months old, they were living in a tent and wagon box, and winter would soon be upon them. But her faith was such that she too was willing to place the interest of the kingdom above her private needs, with the assurance that in so doing all would be well. Five times she had sent him out on preaching missions. During the seven months since he had first set his face west across the river, he had been sent on at least four different trading or purchasing expeditions. This would be longer and more dangerous, but she had some pride in the fact that of all the men available, Brother Brigham should choose her husband as best qualified to fill the assignment.

Since the success of the trip, his very life even, might depend upon the secrecy of his going and coming, Lee's wives were instructed not to know anything at all about it. In his absence each must manage as well as she could with what she had or could get; she must look to her parents in any emergency and turn to Brigham Young for extra food or medicine.

Lee had for his companion Howard Egan, a frontiersman who was a stranger to fear. They were fitted up with a light wagon, well covered, and drawn by a span of mules. Traveling with him also was one of his favorite adopted sons, James Pace, who had brought mail from the battalion and was returning with mail for them. Important also was their little dog, Trip.

Lee kept a careful diary of this journey, noting the distances traveled each day, camping places, nature of the terrain, and the people they met or passed. Many years later he wrote from memory of the trip, preserving the story with remarkable fidelity. Nearly every day he took time to record the unusual, the approach of a large black bear in the night, the prairie dog mounds in one of which he found an owl and a rattlesnake keeping the owner company. Most of all he was excited with the buffalo herds he saw on the plain. He "would like to have taken chase could we have carried the meat & skins, but to leave them to waste would be wrong." On September 14 he wrote:

. . . When light came we found ourselves surrounded by 1000's of buffalo feeding on the plains within 300 yards of us

perfectly quiet. I took 15 shooter & walked within 60 or 70 yards
of them, stood and looked at them some time, and it was as much
as I could do to refrain from shooting. . .

He described various reptiles, but was most astonished at the first
tarantula he had ever seen:

> . . . They resemble our common black spider — though much
> larger — some of them are as large round as a tea saucer have a
> white spot in the forehead & on the back legs wooly & are said
> to be poisonous. . .

In the same detail with which he described the country and the
animals, Lee told of his experiences. He did not spare himself in any
way, repeating verbatim criticism of himself by Jefferson Hunt and
others, and telling frankly every happening.

Lee and his companions caught up with the battalion on September
17. He had hoped that the commanding officers would call a halt and
let the men rest while he delivered the mail he carried. Perhaps he
might also read the message that he brought from Brigham Young.
But no attention was paid to him, so he traveled along behind the
group.

The letters which had reached Brigham Young had been full of
complaints against the army surgeon, Dr. George B. Sanderson, called
by the Mormon men "Doctor Death." Without exception, they protested that he prescribed calomel powder for whatever ailed them.
At first he gave it to the men in papers, with instructions as to how it
was to be taken, but when he learned that many were throwing the
medicine away, he administered it himself from an old iron spoon.

Daniel Tyler told how "the sick man was compelled either to take
the medicine quietly, have it forced down him, or be left to perish on
the plains; of course, on reflection, he chose the former."

Lee and Egan overtook the company on the day that Alva Phelps
was buried. Tyler wrote of how Phelps had begged not to have to take
the medicine, whereupon with horrid oaths, the doctor had forced it
down him with the old rusty spoon. "A few hours later he died, and
the general feeling was that the doctor had killed him. Many boldly
expressed the opinion that it was premeditated murder."

Since he felt that he represented the authority of Brigham Young,
as soon as Lee was introduced to Lieutenant Smith, he too began to
protest the treatment of the men. He began with the case of Alva
Phelps because it was already on the lips of the men. He reminded the
commanding officer that, "not withstanding his entreaties the Dr.

poured an even spoonfull of calimal down him & about twice that amount of spirits of turpentine, which ended his career."

Lieutenant Smith replied that he was not responsible for all the doctor did, but that he himself did not designedly oppress any man. Lee quoted his rejoinder as:

". . . said I if you are the man that made one of the soldiers get down off his horse & damn him threatening to tie him to the waggon there drag him like an ox (when he was scarcely able to stand alone burning with fever) unless he would report himself to the Dr. (death) & take whatever he should prescribe & when the sick man begged the liberty of being nourished with food and might hereby [be nursed by] one of his brethren who was very skillful in baffling deseases, your reply Sir was what if you ever knew of our Drs. administering medicine to any man in this Bat. that you would cut his throat the Sergeon was the man to prescribe, & administer medicine when you were knowing that the same time that he gave double portions of calomel through spite saying that he did not care a dam whether it killed or cured and the more killed the better that the dam rascals out to be sent to hell as fast as possible. . .

At the close of the discussion Lee said that "I expected that he would have challenged me for a Duell but instead of that he never resented the first word." Perhaps it was because at that juncture they came upon a slough in the desert. The day was warm and the road dusty, and it had been fifty miles since they had seen water. Although it was:

". . . ½ buffalo urine at least notwithstanding the Brethren would rush into the midst of it & suck & strain the water through their teeth to keep back the live (as well as the dead) insects & mud from being swallowed wholesale & after quenching their thirst filled their canteens out of the tracks of the oxen & mules. Others not having strength to reach the swamp were prostrate by the way — some of their friends would carry drink to them & as much as they could they would be put into waggons privately risking the consequences notwithstanding the threats of the commanders — I had 3 to 4 sick which was in reality more than our little carriage was able to bear up with safety. . .

Finally Lee called a meeting of the officers at his camp, but no one came. Later they sent for him to a meeting of their own in the tent of

Captain Jefferson Hunt, for as the captain said "it was customary for the man that appointed the ball to open it." Each man had a right to express himself, but Capt. Jesse D. Hunter seemed to summarize for them all:

> . . . Bro Lee has not as much right to be hurt as we have. He came here & assumed the right to dictate to this Bat. & even went so far as to light on our commander & seargon (Dr) whom we have appointed & abuse them which we considered to be an insult & that he was out of his place & if he bore that express to Gen Kearney he must wait till we give him liberty of having this honor. If we have got ourselves in a bad scrape, we are the boys that can get out of it ourselves & when we want help we will call on him. . .

Captain Hunt accused the visitors repeatedly of stirring up the battalion to revolt and threatened to have Lee arrested if he did not keep his place. Lee, on the other hand, felt that the men were being badly treated and that if they would follow the advice of Brigham Young, they might have one of their own number to take the place of Captain Allen, who had died at Fort Leavenworth on August 23, 1846. With a Mormon in command, they might be allowed to administer to their sick according to their own pattern.

Through all the long discussion, Egan said nothing, nor did he speak until he was invited to. Then he explained simply that the reason he was silent was

> . . . he saw that they did not want any council, so he thought in as much as they had burned their backsides they might sit on the blister. . .

All was finally settled and good feelings restored all around; Captain Jefferson Hunt offered free board to the visitors while they were with the group and Lee advised him to

> . . . elude or thwart all plans, snares, or schemes that may be laid for the injury of this people
>
> 1st When anything of this kind is proposed, I would as a matter of policy beg the liberty of a few hours to reflect before giving an answer. Then calling all the officers of the same grade, with the wise old men that hold the Priesthood . . . convene together with humble spirits in prayer before the Lord that his wisdom might be in your midst to direct you in your deliberations. . .

Just before they reached Santa Fe an express from Fort Kearney instructed the Mormon Battalion that Lieutenant Smith was their head and that Captain Cooke was put in charge of the whole battalion. This made Lee feel that he had failed in his mission, that perhaps his very zeal for his fellows had worked against his purpose. At any rate he named the encampment for the night, "Valley of Repentance."

His descriptions of Santa Fe, its general location and surroundings and of some of the ancient ruins of the area are exact and vivid. As to the city itself "a stranger at the first glance would conclude that there was not a room in the whole city that was fit for a white man to live in but to the contrary some of their rooms are well furnished inside — floors excepted —" He visited the stores and purchased three Mexican blankets and some other articles, and took time to describe in detail the load of wood carried by four small jennies (female burros) who were fastened together with cross pieces and the wood loaded directly on their backs, driven without bridles or lines. "Around the walks in all public places are found Pine nuts, apples, peaches, pears, large grapes, bread, onions, boiled corn, mellons &c sold by women & girls. . ."

He was disturbed that several of the men of the battalion "got on a spree" and some had to be in the calaboose, and that others had attended a ball sponsored by the Spaniards and the Missouri volunteers, with tickets at two dollars each — money that might otherwise have gone to help the destitute saints. "The commanders said they took this course to gain friends, but I am certain that the Bat. lost 10 lbs. of influence to where they gained one ounce of credit or pleasure."

When Lee heard that about twenty-five of the battalion men had been placed on the sick list and were to be discharged from the service forthwith, his indignation knew no bounds. He at once told Adjutant George P. Dykes "that I would consider it more honorable to command those men (sick) to be shot & thereby to put an end to their suffering — than to leave them here to rot among prostitutes — without a friend to assist them . . . and that the man who raised his voice or assented to this move would have to atone for the sufferings and lives of those men." He immediately went to the Captain and other officers to protest the action.

But perhaps John Steele did as much to secure a reversal of orders as did Lee. His young wife and little daughter had come along with him, walking as he did. Now to have them assigned to go back with the group of sick men angered him until he did something about it. There were about twenty women along, each of whom had an able-bodied husband. John Steele tried in vain to get the group to support him, but none dared until John Hess said that if he were fortified with a good stout drink he would go along to face Colonel Cooke. Steele wrote:

> We went and found him in a long low cellar with about 30 officers. I asked which of the gentlemen there is Col. Cooke. Then there arose a man from the other side of the table, measuring about 6 ft four inches. I told him I understood he had issued orders for all the sick men and all the women to go back to Bent's Fort. He said yes that was so. I told him I had my wife there and would like the privilege of either having my wife go on to California with me or going back to Bent's Fort with her. He spoke very saucy and said he would like to have his wife along with him (but he never had a wife). I told him very likely his wife was in Washington or some other good seaport town among her friends, while mine was in Santa Fe among her enemies, and to have her left there with only a squad of sick men, I would not stand it, and the more I talked the more angry I got until at last I could have thrashed the ground with him. . .

At any rate, between them they had the order changed so that the husbands who wished to do so accompanied their wives. Lee asked for two men to go back with him, but could get none released except by having their names put on the sick list and reducing them in rank.

Lee always spoke of Lieutenant Smith in terms of scorn such as "that little wolfish Lieut." Now he said that Roswell Stevens was placed on the sick list, "which through him out from under the command of the Devil," and enabled him to return.

There was great excitement in headquarters when it was discovered that two expensive gold watches had been stolen, one from the pilot and one from "the old Dr." meaning their Doctor Death. Lee seemed to have no idea of who had taken the watches, but writing many years later in his *Confessions,* he intimated that his own men were the guilty ones, but that at the time he knew nothing of it. Considering the hatred they all had for the doctor, it is not likely any of them would have considered it too sinful to steal from him.

The return trip was made in great haste, for with some twelve hundred dollars in their possession, they would need to hurry. They had trouble in Santa Fe getting mules for the journey, so again one of his men lifted one or "consecrated" it for the use of the church, took it out a day's travel ahead and secreted it in the brush. Now they traveled in haste for fear of pursuit, making forced drives until at three different places they had to leave a worn out animal, "for the use of Cousin Lemuel," as Lee facetiously called the Indians.

Yet quite unexpectedly, even miraculously, they secured fresh animals, the stories of which have become legends in the Lee family. At the time he wrote:

Nov. 3rd 46 . . . at the distance of 15 ms more fed again, here we found a good young mule with the harness & rigging on which had doubtless run off in time of Mann's engagement — she came in good time we hitched her in the waggon & traveled 10 ms

Just two days later they had an even greater streak of luck:

Fri Nov 5th '46 . . . Started at 7 drove 8 ms where we discovered 5 mules with ropes on that had been taken by the Indians from Capt Bulliard & co 2 days before. This certainly was the ram caught in the thicket as 3 of our mules were about past traveling the 5 just made a change all around which when we had done we thanked the Lord for this peculiar manifestation of his good will & went on our way rejoicing

His later account tells how they saw the horses feeding among a herd of buffalo and coaxed them with grain in a nose bag or on a canvas such as those from which they had been accustomed to eating.

Although they saw some evidence of Indian depredations and heard of other companies that had been attacked, they traveled in safety. At one time they did meet some Indians, but talked to them in a friendly manner and passed on unmolested.

Their one loss was the gallant little dog that had warned them of every approaching night animal. One night he took it upon himself to chase a wolf from the camp and got too far away. Lee wrote that they had named the valley "Trip's Defeat" because here he had been "overpowered by 6 large wolves."

His account ends with his arrival at the last stream:

Friday Nov 19th 1846 Morning clear heavy frost ground hard frozen eat breakfast at light paid 13¢ each crossed the Nishan at Moreleans Ferry paid 40¢ here I met with Sister Nancy Daly an old acquaintance who wept with joy I presented her a handsome stran of Mexican beads as a token of friendship

The Sister Nancy Daly was one of Lee's converts on his second mission to Tennessee. Her name appears on the list of friends who made him gifts as he left the mission.

1846-1847
Winter Quarters

When John D. Lee walked abroad in Winter Quarters that morning in late November, he was amazed at the transformation. The camp of wagons he had left had become a city laid off in forty-one long, narrow blocks, some of which contained twenty homes. There were 528 log houses, 83 sod houses, and many dugouts against the hill, but there were still many families in wagons and tents; his own among them. He noted houses of many types, from Dr. Willard Richard's "with 8 sides and covered with dirt & forms an oval and is called by the names of the Octagon, potato pit, apple heap, coal pit, round house, the Doctor's den," to Hosea Stout's own, which was twelve feet square on the outside and still without window or door.

According to the census, there were in the camp 3,483 souls, of whom 384 were ill, and 75 others widows or wives of missionaries or battalion men, who would be dependent. Even the most optimistic could see a hard winter ahead, but few dreamed how hard.

As for Lee, he made his report to Brigham Young, handed over the twelve hundred dollars, met with the council and gave a general account of his trip, and received their approving vote. Then he set about on a building program. By December 1, he had one cabin finished, covered with sod, and daubed inside and out with mud; in two weeks he wrote that the second was done, including the chimney and hearth stone. By the end of the month two additional ones were completed, so that his wives and children could have warmth and shelter.

Mrs. Hascell, who had written with such enthusiasm about their traveling conditions, now told the folks back in New Salem about the setup in Winter Quarters. She and her daughter and family had a cabin of split logs, covered with lumber and shake shingles, with a brick fireplace and hearth, a solid door, and a window of four 10 x 12 panes of glass for which they had paid eight cents each. The built-in beds were made private by curtains; the furniture consisted of two chairs, the flour barrels, boxes of supplies and Irene's chest. Earlier she had listed the plenty of food they had: flour, hams, sausages, dried fish, lard, sugar, coffee, rice, and raisins. Now they had gathered black walnuts that grew in abundance and wild plums, which made such excellent preserves and pies, and which dried would supplement their diet all winter.

In addition, they lived across the street from the store which, Irene later wrote her cousin, was stocked "with every necessary English and West India goods, coffee, sugar, molasses, saleratus, etc." As herdsman for the company cattle, Francis could draw up to two dollars a day from the store.

In the same way, George Laub, who had left Nauvoo in June and arrived here in early October, built himself a good log house, laid up enough feed for his cattle, and had steady employment on the Council House which would give him goods from the store. His skill with carpenter's tools was a real asset.

As soon as his homes were completed, Lee was sent to Missouri on another trading mission. The bishops of the twenty-two wards had each made a survey of his ward and found that the food supply was almost exhausted, which meant that staple items must be bought in bulk. Eighteen-year-old John Pulsipher had already brought in one load of corn, and was to spend the entire winter going out and back, so great was the need and so few the able-bodied to help fill it. While Lee himself supervised this train of wagons, his outfits went later in the hands of his adopted sons.

On the day before he left, Lee was married to Emoline Woolsey, younger sister of Aggatha and Rachel. Brigham Young said publicly that there would be no more sealings while they were in the wilderness, but for Lee he made an exception. After noting at ten p.m. that Emoline had come to spend the night at the camp, Lee wrote with characteristic frankness:

> Dec. 21 [1846] About 6 eve Pres Young by permission, not according to law, as the sealing ordinances were stopped when the Endowment stopped in the Temple . . . solemnized the right to matrimony between Emoline and myself. Charged the family to lock these things up in our breast and there let them remain. After attending to the ordinance I presented him with a box of sardines.

Lee was delayed in leaving because two of his young adopted sons, Thomas Johnson and Truman Gillett, who had been sent to bring in the mules, had been forced to spend the night in a tree just out of reach of a pack of hungry wolves that circled about, howled, and jumped at their feet, only a few inches out of reach.

Lee's outfit consisted of two four-mule teams and two large wagons. He was gone three weeks during bitter weather, where a delay or camp out meant real hardship. On his way out he purchased one load which included salt, dried fruit, whiskey, molasses, honey, tallow and fish, and sent it back by a gentile who was on his way to St. Joseph via Winter Quarters. In addition to the corn which Lee purchased, he got four bushels of white beans at forty cents a bushel and six large dressed pigs which totaled about twelve hundred pounds.

For the most part, the trip was uneventful except for time (with the thermometer at 13 below zero) when he broke an axle on his wagon and the boy driving the other outfit ran off a bridge, tipping the load out into the snow. They were delayed a full day repairing the one wagon and reloading the other. In general, however, he had a genius for getting to shelter among friends.

Young John Pulsipher in his diary tells of having camped on the prairie all night, and being beset by wolves. "The way I made the firebrands fly in defense of myself & cattle was not very slow," he wrote. On January 14, he set out on his third trip for corn, and immediately upon his return, he started again. In his part of Winter Quarters there were so many poor and dependent that someone must bring in supplies for them. In just one hour his father counted seventeen people who came to plead for food or medicine.

On January 31, Lee sent his teams again into Missouri, this time under the direction of three of his adopted sons; George Laub, Thomas Johnson, and William Woolsey. George Laub recorded their doings carefully, each day's journey, each transaction, prices and amounts. They contracted to pull corn for David Henderson for the sixth row; then they moved on to Samuel Winterbottom's farm where a number from Winter Quarters were employed, among them others of Lee's adopted sons. Here Laub earned fifteen bushels himself; nearly as much as Truman Gillett would get for teaching school.

As they prepared to return to Winter Quarters, Tom Johnson insisted upon a division of the corn, "swore that he was not agoing to be a negrow for John D. Lee any longer . . . for said he would sooner goe to hell and take another probation than to do it any longer. I told him we had come for corn for Father Lee and I want he should have mine as I went for him." William Swapp, who was also along, decided to stay and work another month longer, as this seemed the most profitable employment he would find during the winter.

But Pulsipher and Lee and all his young men were only a few of those who went for provisions or in search of work. On the other hand, many people found the winter interesting and exciting. Throughout the fall men worked on the Council House, and after the walls were up and the roof on, it was decided to put a good floor in so that the people might enjoy themselves in the dance, or "praise the Lord in the dance," as they had done in the temple at Nauvoo. This entertain-

ment began before Christmas and extended through the holidays, with
different groups assigned for different nights, that all might enjoy the
new building. George Laub wrote on January 28:

> "I and my wife Mary Jane attended and it was a joy and comfert
> to our souls. The dance was opened by prayer by H. C. Kimble by
> each calling on their pardner and kneeling on the flor in our devo-
> tion to our heavenly Father to bless the musick & the people."

Perhaps the best description of their activities is one from the pen
of Mary Parker Richards, who was waiting for Samuel to return from
his mission:

> Tues 26th January 1847 The weather comfortable Early in the
> morn. Sister Chester Snyder sent for Jane and myself to come to
> her house for a quilting. We went stayed a little while there
> Henry came and informed me that Bro Godard had come to invite
> me to a party at the Counsel house. Sister Snyder excused me and
> I went up to our tent — found Bro G. waiting for me, so I got
> ready as quick as possible and accompanied him called at Bro
> Hendrix and got his wife and about 4 o'clock entered the Council
> Hous. Bro G. took me onto the floor the first dance — here for the
> first time I joined with those who praised God in the dance When
> this figure was formed it being the first, and Bro. Rockwood being
> at the head, according to order we all kneeled down and he
> offered up a prayer. We then arose & danced the figure, and so
> praised God in the dance. I danced with Bros Dewsette, W.
> Cahoon & Grant, and others, and once with Bro Brigham, the
> moneymusk. had a very pleasant party and some good refresh-
> ments About 11 o'clock every man took his partner or partners &
> marched 3 times round the room. We were then dismissed with
> the blessings of God. Bro. G. accompanied me to sister Janes
> where I spent the night.

Two nights later she went with Elsy Snyder to the singing school,
gathering up other girls en route. There was a large crowd present,
more than there had ever been since they left Nauvoo, and they sang
an hour and a half after which they danced until eleven-thirty. . .
Lee might not have been present at all the dances, but he records
that "The band was refreshed during the 4 days recreation at the
expense of J. D. Lee and A. P. Rockwood. Room crowded."
So the winter wore on. Men who had finished the Council House
were next set to work on a gristmill and millrace, for people could
hardly get the proper nourishment from either the corn or wheat

unless it could be ground. True, many soaked the wheat and cooked the whole kernels; many learned to make edible hominy from the corn. But mostly they lined up at Brother John Van Cott's for a turn at his hand mill because he did not charge a toll for its use. Others had hand mills, too; few were as generous as was Brother Van Cott.

Through December the work on the mill went on. Then Brother Brigham approached Brother John Neff, who had owned and operated a mill near Nauvoo, for financial aid. At first Brother Neff refused, saying that he was not going to contribute anything to support the "whores of the Twelve." In a very short time after this Brother Neff's twenty-year-old son became suddenly very ill and died before they had a chance to use any of the well-known remedies. President Young preached the funeral sermon; Brother Neff was convinced that this was the chastening hand of God and freely gave of his money and skill to get the mill going. Mrs. Ursula Hascell wrote proudly in early April that "the Mormons have built one of the best grist mills that ever was run in the states. . . It ground twelve bushels an hour when it first started but they took it down to six bushels when they made a business of it."

In order to keep as many as possible employed at constructive work, the leaders encouraged handicraft of all kinds. Sylvester Earl was appointed to teach basket making, an art in which several of John D. Lee's wives became expert, to their great advantage later. There were willow baskets of various sizes designed for different uses — large, coarse, oval-shaped baskets with two handles for carrying wet clothing, square baskets with lids for food containers, small decorative baskets for household notions, standard half-bushel measures. The idea was that by spring they should have marketable items which might be sold or traded for supplies. The women had also quilting and sewing bees, and classes where children's clothing was made from the backs of men's pants or the less worn shirttails. Such projects helped to keep up the morale of the camp, along with the singing schools, dances and sociables.

Lee himself was often troubled because, at the order of Brigham Young, he had purchased goods at wholesale for the store, and now some of the wives of the battalion men were asking for an accounting and complaining that they had not received the value of the cash their husbands had sent. Repeatedly and with emphasis, their leader explained that this was as it had to be, but the whole arrangement set up a chain reaction which caused Lee to suffer loss of prestige, in spite of the fact that he joined in all activities, gave without stint of his time and energy, and even reported that the band was refreshed every night during the holiday celebration free from the stores of Rockwood & Lee.

In the meantime others besides Brother Neff were shocked at the practice of polygamy. On February 16, Brigham Young called a family meeting where he explained the principle at some length, justifying the practice on the theory that men who held the priesthood should be allowed to raise up a righteous seed in order to "hasten the consummation of His purposes in this dispensation."

Here also the law of adoption was discussed, and the fact that it was all done with Joseph the Prophet as the head seemed to iron out most of the jealousy. Father Morley said that "Joseph the martyred Prophet had gone to prepare the way for us, and can do more for us than he could do provided he was here." Brigham Young asked that they no longer call him "Father Brigham" but "Brother Brigham," for he was only one of them, all working for the exaltation of Joseph and expecting as his reward a position subordinate to him.

Again Brother Brigham made Lee an exception to the publicly announced policy of no sealings until they should reach Zion, for on February 27 he gave Lee three additional wives. Here again it was the women who took the initiative in asking to be sealed, for each desired a place in the kingdom to come and security in the present. The first of these three, sealed in one common ceremony, was Nancy Gibbons Armstrong who had been converted by Lee on his second mission. She had left her husband and the comfortable home where she had servants at her command to join the saints, bringing with her a large sum of money and such goods and jewels as she could. She made the proposal herself, first to Lee and then to his wives, declaring her love for him, her belief in the principle, and her willingness to share with them any adversity.

The other two girls were sisters, Mary Vance (Polly) and Lavina Young. Lee had converted their whole family while he was on his first mission; in fact, they were the two girls he saw in the dream and their father the ferryman who prepared the way for his first meeting in his new field of labor. Their father, mother, and brother David had already been adopted into Lee's family. During his mission these two girls had helped to make Lee a new suit; now they presented him with a new coat and a pair of pants of their own handiwork as a wedding gift, while Nancy Gibbons added material for a new collar and cuffs.

Thanks to Lee's careful record, we have the full information on these three women; their date and place of birth and the names of their parents.

Toward spring, Lee's family troubles multiplied. There was sickness among them. He himself became so ill that he was revived only after "Father B.Y. brought and laid on my brest a cane built from one of the branches of the Tree of Life that stood in the garden of the Temple." He was temporarily restored, but soon fell ill again.

Through these months Louisa Free seemed to be his favorite wife. He visited her and her little son, John B., often at her father's house; he took her and Aggatha with him to a dance in the Council House. When he was ill, she sponged and anointed his body, and at one time "lay and embraced me in her arms for two hours." When she was taken down herself, he called to see her every day and finally wrote that he had removed her to his house where he could look after her.

Polly Ann Workman, on the other hand, had fallen into disfavor. She was independent and headstrong, and six months earlier had gone back to Mt. Pizgah against his orders. When she returned she was often "verry turbulent and unruly and arbitrary, using unbecoming words in the family." He finally told her that she would do better to leave his family if she would not reform, but she continued to "make a perfect hell" for him. Finally he suggested that she return and keep house for her brother, and provided transportation for her with some of his own teams back to Mt. Pizgah. From this time on, she does not appear again in his record, though years later in his *Confessions,* he wrote that he had often regretted his action in sending her away. [She went to Des Moines, Iowa, where she married John Bennett. She did not come west.]

Nancy Bean also had her problems during this time of sickness and general adversity. Though she had come back to his home promptly upon his return from Santa Fe, she had returned to her parents while he was gone on his winter trading expedition. On March 10 she wrote him a kind, conciliatory letter, asking for "a word from me to know what my feelings are, what she might depend upon." Lee himself was a kindly person who might have met her half way, but he read the letter to his Father in the Covenant and was advised to give her the strict conditions under which he would accept her back.

A week later her father came to Lee with word that she and the little Eliza were both ill with swelling in the throat. Lee was sharp with him: Nancy had left without his permission or sanction; before he would assume any responsibility for her, she must return and place herself under his care. Ten days later she wrote again, this time asking him to come for her, as she desired to return, but again he was advised not to be in a hurry. The next day, March 28, she arrived home by some other means, and Lee accepted her into his family.

All this was a part of the pattern adopted. A woman should know her place and keep it, her first and chief business being to respect the priesthood which her husband held and to love him so completely that she did not question him, but would make his will her law. She was to bear and rear children and train them in righteousness, teaching them also the proper honor and respect due their father. A man was to hold himself above the whims of any woman, and while he should treat his wives with kindness and tenderness, he should not allow them to sway his decisions or deflect him from his duty. Brother Brigham always spoke with consummate scorn of any man who should bend to the will of a wife.

The winter was long and severe. In late January the river froze from bank to bank, and on March 2 Lee reported that his teams were still dragging wood across on the ice. In early March came a thaw that brought floods large enough to wash out the millrace; then on March 9 came a shift of the wind and a fall in the temperature that resulted in an ice jam which formed a solid bridge across the river. People reminded each other of the more miraculous one which had spanned the Mississippi nearly a year before, a highway over which modern Israel, or about a hundred wagons of them, could escape from their enemies. Lee counted this one here another special providence by which he at once was able to set three mule teams to drawing wood over the river on the ice that his four homes might be warm.

Before January was out, blackleg had appeared in camp. By mid February Lee reported several of his family ill, but of them all he seemed most concerned for Louisa Free. He described her condition as "a rheumatic affection, canker, or I was going to say gout," the cause of which both Brother Brigham and Doctor Richards said was the result of the impure air which they had inhaled into their bodies, the dregs of agues and colds which settled into their feet and legs. Over exertion and fatigue were contributing factors, of course, but no one as yet had as yet suggested that the real cause was a diet deficiency. The regular remedy, a mixture of sulphur, whiskey, and bloodroot was administered to cleanse Louisa's blood.

In April, Mrs. Hascell included in her otherwise cheerful letter the sad news that every one of Brother Pond's children except Loenza had died, dropped off one after another, while Sister Pond would probably never recover the use of her feet. Dear Sister Pond, who in Nauvoo had been so generous with Irene, who had carried green corn, peas, squash, and cucumbers to all the neighbors, now sat with her legs black and swollen, her toes like dried blue plums. Brother Pond's health was very poor also, while little Elizabeth was a mere skeleton.

John Pulsipher, despite his efforts to secure enough food, still had to witness death from starvation. Of it he wrote:

When the warm weather came the sick began to recover, they could get some vegetables which consisted of pig weed greens & some wild roots like potatoes ½ inch in diameter — very good. Yet many were cripples — their legs were black and dried up & seemed dead & the flesh would rot and drop off from some to the bones.

What the number was that died I can't tell, but it far exceeded anything that I ever witnessed before. . .

In the early spring before they could start working the ground, Father Zerah Pulsipher made a large seine, four yards wide and forty long, and with a skiff went up the river and caught fish which he sent home by the loads. This also proved to be excellent medicine for the sufferers.

But it was not only the people that suffered this winter. There was also "the greatest destruction of cattle that I ever saw. Father lost 1/3 of his and all his sheep but one. . . We had plenty of hay — they would lay and die with the head to the stack & the belly full" young Pulsipher wrote, after telling how he and his little brother Charles had saved their pennies to buy a ewe, and how their flock had increased to five. Now they all died with the rest.

Even in the homes of some of the leaders the diet had been too exclusively corn and bacon, so that the scurvy set in among them also. Apostle George A. Smith had insisted that if they could get a few potatoes to go with what they had, the health would improve, yet one of his wives and four children died before any food supplement came. On March 16, one of John D. Lee's teams, driven by Brother Bird, arrived in camp with a load of potatoes to be used for seed. The next day they were distributed to those who could pay fifty-six cents a bushel for them.

Brother George A. purchased some, cut out the eyes to be stored for planting and handed chunks of the remaining part to his wives and children with instructions to eat them raw. Immediately they felt better! They felt so much better that Brother Smith started preaching raw potato additions to the diet everywhere. Don't even peel them, he said, though with the scarcity, the eyes cut out for seed would leave little enough of peelings. Brother Smith preached and planted and cultivated potatoes until he became known as "the Potato Saint," he was so determined that never again would his people lack for potatoes.

Better still, the herdsmen found some clumps of horseradish growing in sheltered corners of old Fort Calhoun and brought it into camp. Again it effected an almost miraculous cure for the scurvy. Now everyone who was able to get out of doors at all hunted for green herbs, the slender reeds which marked the place of wild onion, the sweet, succulent tubers of the artichoke, and within a few weeks the general health of the camp was greatly improved. But by now more than six hundred people had been buried in the grave yard on the hill — six hundred men, women and children who with a little less exposure to the elements, a little more food, or more variety in their diet might have been in good health. Six hundred people could have founded a city of their own in Zion could they have survived this one winter.

For those who remained the attitude was best expressed by William Clayton a few months later:

> "And should we die before our journey's through
> Happy day! All is well!
> We then are free from toil and sorrow too
> With the just we shall dwell."

So the bereaved were comforted, and the survivors soon looked eagerly toward the Zion in the tops of the mountains. No one in John D. Lee's family died during that terrible winter; even Louisa was completely restored to health. As he took his careful minutes of the meetings, Lee hoped that he might have the honor to be chosen among that first select group.

1847

Summer Quarters

In spite of sickness and death, and the inclemency of the weather, the first thought was the move to the mountains. A company should be on the road early enough to arrive in time to plant and harvest a crop. It would be impossible to take any families; only a part of the Council of Twelve and the Council of Fifty should go, accompanied by a few vigorous young men skilled in frontier life. Among them must be at least four blacksmiths and four carpenters to keep the outfits in repair, and expert teamsters, farmers, and hunters.

Their wagons should carry only necessities — provisions, seeds, tools — and only three men to each wagon, so that they might sleep in the wagon-box and do away with the complication of tents. Every animal must be freshly shod, with extra shoes and nails along for replacements.

Their past travel experience had taught them that one of their greatest problems would be the fording of streams. How could they provide in advance for this contingency? After much discussion, they decided to build two rawhide boats to carry along, and assignments were made for the necessary hides and timbers. This experiment was to prove valuable to them later.

Though he was especially eager to be one selected to go, Lee had an intimation that he would not be chosen when Brigham Young asked him to furnish one wagon and two adopted sons as teamsters, suggesting Rufus C. Allen and Thomas Woolsey. A few days later he called Lee in for a private discussion with George D. Grant, in an effort to iron out differences that had risen between them. He had decided not to take either of them, he said, but to leave them in charge of his family affairs.

"Brother Grant is not acquainted with doing business and keeping books, but he understands rigging wagons. Brother Lee is better qualified to take care of business," he said.

All their plans were again thwarted by the weather. After a regular spring thaw, it turned cold again on March 9, so cold that all hope for an early start was abandoned. On March 23 Brigham Young called together thirty-eight of his adopted sons to counsel together as a group. After explaining the general program he said, "Come, brethren, who will be set apart to stay and farm? Here is Brother John D. Lee, George D. Grant, and David Lewis that I will select to farm — Brother J. Bushbie, also. Who will be president?"

"Let our leader appoint the man to preside over us and select the location of the farm and leave his blessing upon it, and we will do as he shall advise," Lee volunteered.

"Let Isaac Morley preside," said Brother Brigham. "He is good-natured and will keep his men good-natured around him." Next he called for the pioneers, and when fifteen men stood, he assigned them to stay and farm also.

"As for a location for a farm, I know of no place equal to a piece of ground lying a short distance above the old fort and about sixteen miles from this point. There is about 600 acres that has been cultivated and is as mellow as an ash heap. We can enclose with very little labor some 2000 acres including the broke land, where you can by industry raise almost any amount of grain. But this is my council — that you build your houses and lots so as to be perfectly safe from the Indians, and that you boil your water before using it, and make beer as a drink. There are roots and barks in abundance in this country that is wholesome and if you will do as I have advised, you will have good health."

With Lee, an assignment was to be promptly carried out. On Monday following the Thursday night meeting, he was on his way with ten loaded wagons. The animals were poor, the season literally between hay and grass, so he was forced to take two days to travel the sixteen miles, and to cut down elm trees that the horses might browse on the tender twigs.

Having arrived on the ground, he must first explore to determine the best location for the homes. At daybreak he was out on horseback with young Tom Johnson, formerly so rebellious, but now in full comradeship. They pulled all the wagons to the site and dedicated the land to the Lord, praying his blessing on the project. The next day he measured off the vegetable gardens for each family, and then called together all who were there to see if they would prefer to operate individual fields or to work together as a family. Five voted to work independently; ten to work as a unit. Thus from the first it was evident that there were factions in the camp, and trouble probably would lie ahead.

On April 8, Brigham Young visited the farm, which was now to be known as "Summer Quarters," or "Brigham's Farm." He brought out Isaac Morley, George D. Grant, Charles Kennedy, John Young and his son Joseph Young to help, but their attitude only seemed to complicate matters. Now, too, Aggatha became upset over family affairs. Either she had not known that her husband had taken his last wives, Polly and Lavina Young, or she was ill with the thought he was courting or paying too much attention to another. She railed out at him and scolded and abused the whole group, until he in turn rebuked her and predicted that she would yet feel the chastening hand of the Lord.

Within a few minutes she became violently ill and continued to suffer great pain until he laid his hands on her head and blessed her, at which she was relieved and fell asleep. It was a humbling and frightening experience for them all.

Things were hard for them all at first, this move to a new place, away from the little they had built up at Winter Quarters. It was easy for tempers to become acid and tongues sharp. Hungry cattle mired in the uncertain flood-bottoms until part of the group was constantly occupied digging them out; famished horses chewed at the budding ends of willows and felled trees, and then gave out under their heavy loads.

Most eloquent of the general temper of the camp is the diary of George Laub, who at first spoke of Lee with genuine affection and tenderness and defended him staunchly against the complaints of others, and wrote his name always as "Father Lee." Then on one unfortunate day he was assigned to bring a load the eighteen miles from Winter Quarters, and the team was so weak that it could not make it. Laub walked in to the farm, and in Lee's absence, borrowed another span of mules to help with the load. Evidently Lee's temper flared for ". . . when he came home and found that I had done as I had he was very angry and used harsh language. This gave me great feelings and we had a hot contention," Laub wrote.

Although they later made peace and continued to work together for a short time, Laub asked to go into Missouri where he could find employment at his trade. He was a skilled carpenter and could command much better wages there than he could at farming; besides he had sprained his ankle badly and walking behind a plow aggravated the swollen joint. So on May 8 he sent his wife with their household goods back to Winter Quarters where she could live in her comfortable cabin until he could establish himself in a job and send for her.

Even before he had reached this decision he wrote in a large hand crosswise over the written page of his diary "BUT IT SEAMS THIS COUNCIL OF LEES SEEKS ITS OWN INTEREST AND NONE ELSE. HE THAT READS LET HIM UNDERSTAND." And he very carefully went back over several earlier pages and blotted out the word "Father" every time it appeared before Lee's name. This grew out of the fact that Laub had wanted to be one of the pioneers, and he thought Lee interfered to prevent it.

But there were others who retained their confidence in Lee. On May 13, Allen Weeks, George W. Hickerson, James Woolsey, and Levi North and their families arrived in camp from Mt. Pizgah, ready to unite and cast their lots with that of their adopted father. James Woolsey was a brother to Aggatha Ann, and George Hickerson was married to her sister Sarah, so they were united by blood. Allen Weeks with his two wives, the Bennett sisters, had been sealed to Lee in the Nauvoo Temple, as had been Levi North. All were his converts; all had young families. Four days after they arrived, George Laub moved out and did not see Lee again for several years.

But Lee had been ordered to farm, and farm he did, from the day they arrived. Everyone worked hard, men, women, children and animals. Some of the beans that they planted earlier were nipped by the frost on May 3, but the potatoes and other garden stuff were thriving. Mid-May found them with six teams going and a program of planting which consisted of fields of corn, squash, and beans. Women dropped the seed, while men built fences, cleared land, or hauled logs for homes. No one was idle, Lee, least of all.

By the time he reported that a hundred acres were planted, the weeds also had a good start. "All hands out today contending with the weeds," he wrote. A few days later he took four plows and fourteen men to clear out Brother Martin's cornfield, where the weeds were waist high.

It was as if he were driven by an unseen force, as if he felt that his part in this great operation of building the Kingdom was vital, so vital that it must not fail. Already they had been delayed a year in getting to the mountains. Unless they here could raise enough foodstuffs there would be another delay. He was responsible to Brother Brigham and through him directly to God for the success of this project. On the other hand, it could not succeed unless he could persuade every person there to carry his full load.

Perhaps nowhere in his career does Lee emerge more clearly than through this summer of 1847 when he matched his strength to the magnitude of his task, impatient with all who would retard the work. He felt that he was literally the instrument in the hands of God in carrying out His design for the establishment of His kingdom. As he accepted the orders of Brigham Young without question, so he expected those under him to render immediate obedience. This often meant friction and contention, and Lee was never willing to admit that he was in the wrong.

On June 6 Levi Stewart arrived from Tennessee, bringing with him Caroline Gilliam and Drusilla Holt. He had been sent in February with the order that he should persuade Mrs. Gilliam to join the saints. Though she had pretended that she was coming only to visit Nancy Armstrong and other of her friends here, she had brought money and jewels as if to remain. While the other women were helping in the garden, she tailored a pair of trousers for John D. Lee. She had supervised the making of a full suit for him six years ago while he was staying at her home, and she took great pride in her skill.

When her husband arrived two weeks later, she did not protest going home with him. He had come out with Mr. Redd, a convert, to look the country over and travel back with his wife. Both men returned, Redd to follow later after the saints were established in the mountains and Gilliam never to join the church.

All through the spring and summer there had been stirrings at Winter Quarters and the settlements across Iowa. With the return of Parley P. Pratt, John Taylor, and Charles C. Rich from their mission, all those who could make the trip west with supplies for a year urged the leaders to go. So six companies were organized in the established pattern with captains of fifty and ten. Among them went the Hascall-Pomeroy wagon, John Neff and others, even some who had been detailed to remain on Brother Brigham's farm with Lee. In addition, another group with George Miller set out to join Lyman Wight in Texas, telling each other that this is where Joseph would have gone had he lived.

This shift of population meant that there were vacant homes in Winter Quarters into which families out on the prairies could move, and land cleared and prepared. This meant that they could face the next winter with the assurance of some comfort and plenty.

At Summer Quarters the friction increased, one complaint leading to another. The initial dissatisfaction over the division of the land had spread into every part of the operation. Through every difficulty Lee's most loyal friend was Samuel Gully; his bitterest enemy, Charles Kennedy. Gully was his adopted son; Kennedy was an adopted son of Brigham Young. Since he had taken charge of the commissary for the Young family, he felt himself equal to, if not superior to Lee.

In mid-July Lee was cited before the High Council at Winter Quarters by John Berry over the loss of a horse. After a long hearing in which several people testified against him, Lee pled his own case and won the decision. Now he would make concessions to Berry, who was after all his father-in-law, and they settled things amicably.

To compound their woes, a violent disease broke out among them. On July 18, Lee wrote that he was called in great haste to administer to Samuel Gully, who was cramped almost to death. Lee's friends all believed that he had the gift of healing, and he himself felt that God was good to answer his prayers. Now during his prayer, the patient relaxed and became easy, though too weak to say a word. He soon recovered fully.

But there were some who could not be saved. First to go was twenty-one-year-old David Isom Young, brother to Lee's wives Polly and Lavina, who died on July 19, 1847. Already weak with consumption, he had no resistance to this new disease.

Now they must have a cemetery. Accompanied by A. P. Free and Levi Stewart, Lee rode to the top of an eminence north of the fort to select a suitable site. From the top of the hill they could see the broad river to the north, the wooded bottom lands where the lush wild berries were now ripening, the cluster of small houses with the gardens around them, and the expanse of the cornfields thrifty and green.

"We should call this place *Fair View*," Lee said, and so it was named. They selected a grassy spot, set up stakes to mark its boundaries and started to dig the grave in the northwest corner. David Young was dressed in his burial robes, placed in a homemade coffin painted green, and buried at sunset that evening.

No record has yet been found of seventeen others who rest at Fair View, but from scattered sources we learn that among them were David Young's father and mother, Lee's wife, Nancy Armstrong, Aggatha's baby, Heber John, and three of the children of Miles Anderson.

Lee himself was finally stricken and for a time was near death, but eventually made a slow recovery. About this time Hosea Stout visited "Brigham's Farm" and reported under date of August 25:

. . . I found a majority of the place sick & in a most suffering condition. Some whole families not able to help each other and worse than all they were quarreling and contending with each other in a most disgraceful manner. . .

They had fine and extensive crops of corn beans cabbage melons &c and had they been at peace with each other, would have been in a fair way to do well. . .

Real trouble began when one of Lee's oxen was caught trespassing on the corn and was tied up by the officer in charge. When Lee came from the farm to get the animal, he was told that he must pay a fine of twenty dollars, either in cash or in butter. He protested that he had neither of these, but would pay in corn or in such other goods as he had. In the meantime, he needed the ox and proceeded to untie and take it. Charles Kennedy interfered and hot words were exchanged which finally led to blows.

Lee's diary for this period is not extant, but Hosea Stout wrote under date of September 22 that "Today reports from Brigham's Farm says that Lee & Keneda had a fight about their stray pen operations up there & Lee came off victorious for he badly worsted Keneda & did not get hurt himself."

Hosea could write with understanding about the troubles of the stray pen, for he himself was in charge of the one at Winter Quarters and knew plenty of trouble with it. Just a couple of weeks earlier he had caught Henry Phelps trying to get his horse out without paying the fine and "I gave him a severe caining & broke a good fancy hickry cane given me by Br Stewart all to pieces. He ran through the lot and cried so loud that he excited the whole neighborhood. . . Henry was a young man about grown & needed all he got for his imprudence for he was a rebellious person. . ." Later he had "quite a knock down" with Charles W. Patten, for which he too was cited before the high council.

Stout was wrong however to say that Lee did not get hurt, for he was humiliated that he had cheapened himself enough to get into a fight. He lost public favor also, for he had beaten Kennedy up badly. So many little irritations had grown to culminate in this — Kennedy's constant criticism, his swaggering attitude, insinuating remarks, but most of all his coaxing away Lee's young wife Emoline and taking her with him to Winter Quarters. Much more than the untieing of an ox was involved in this fight.

Lee was called before the Council on October 3. The hearing lasted for two days, and in the end the decision was against him. He was ordered to apologize, not only to Kennedy, but to the whole group and to assume full blame for the trouble. To refuse would mean to be cut off the church, and that would be more than he could bear. At last he consented to repeat the words of the council, but they sensed that he did not feel properly repentant and insisted that he make a full and free confession of his own. When Lee would not, and word came that Brigham Young was soon to arrive from the west, the matter was left for him to decide.

Many people went out to meet the returning president, but Lee went back to the farm. He preferred to present his case quietly and privately. After a reasonable time, he sent Samuel Gully with a letter to Brigham Young, asking for an audience. It was ignored. Then his wife Louisa worked through her sister Emmeline, who was married to Brigham Young, and between them they arranged a turkey dinner at which the two men met. Though nothing was said about the trouble or the court case, the President could not help seeing that here was a man who had accepted and filled an assignment, that his fields had yielded beyond belief so that he had corn enough to supply all the family and more. It was not hard to be lenient with so faithful a servant.

Again we are indebted to Hosea Stout for information on the final decision. On December 9, he wrote:

. . . There was a council today at which W. W. Phelps was formally cut off the church & John D. Lee's case up. Most of his

wives & adopted sons were dissatisfied with him & I believe it
was so managed to let all go free who chose when 2 wives and
almost all of his adopted children stepped out. . .

The wives were Abigail Woolsey and Martha Berry, both of whom
returned within a week. The names of the adopted children who left
are not given, but the fact that all were set free was a death blow to
the whole system of adoption. It meant that there was no tie more
binding than personal desire, and weakened the ties in the family of
Brigham Young as well as John D. Lee.

It was as well, for most of the other leaders had not entered into
the plan, and they felt that it gave an undue economic advantage to
those who had adopted sons. Polygamy they could accept, because
each who was worthy could secure additional wives as he was able or
as the women approached him and asked for admission into his family.
But adoption, ideally carried out, would give the "father" a decided
financial advantage.

In his family meeting almost a year earlier, Brigham had indicated
that the system was causing jealousy and competition, and "some
would even try to pass right by me and go to Jos. thinking that to get
between mine and the 12." He named Brothers Hyde, Pratt, and
Taylor as some whose feelings had been hurt by this plan. He also
suggested that he had heard some say that "I am not dependent on
any man," with the implication that each could care for his own needs
better by himself than he could through a large, unwieldy family.
Through the remarks of Orson Pratt and others it was clear that "the
major part has rejected this privilege. . ." Wilford Woodruff confessed that he knew little of this practice for "I have never had the
privilege of having anyone adopted into my family." He had been
absent on missions all the time that this was being discussed in
Nauvoo. Orson Pratt was in the same position. George A. Smith confessed that he had "lectioneered" with all his might to get men to join
his family. Throughout the two-day meeting, the law of adoption was
discussed among the leaders, and in spite of all the explanations and
exhortations, there was some jealousy and disapproval of the plan.

The fact that a subordinate like John D. Lee should have a large
adopted family while some of the apostles had none at all would not
help Lee's position among them, and this action to set free all who
wished their freedom would meet with general public approval. It
should have simplified matters for Lee himself, for there could be no
advantage in having rebellious, recalcitrant sons. Though all maintained economic independence after this court order, many remained
friendly with Lee all their lives. A formal decision was reached that
in reality and for any practical purpose adoption was not binding to

the people who had entered into it, thus causing the decline of the practice.

The winter of 1847 was much better than the previous one had been. The people had raised good crops and had provided more of a variety of foods. More than two thousand had moved on to the valley, and as a result, many others now had good houses. At Winter Quarters there was a hum of activity, the store doing a good business, the mill running, the basket factory still in operation, schools in session, even a dancing class held daily.

Now that Lee had one decision against him, another complaint was launched. This was by the wife of Andrew Lytle, with a charge of misappropriated funds, while Lee countercharged that he had issued to her much more than the value of the money he had received the fall before from her husband. The hearing was held in March 11, and Brigham Young was in attendance.

"Have you kept a record of all the items you gave to Sister Lytle?" he asked.

"Yes."

The Bishop then caused the clerk to read the bill, several of the items of which Sister Lytle denied receiving.

"I know Brother Lee's method of doing business," his chief said. "He is very careful and particular in keeping his books and accounts and if he has the items listed under date and amount, I am willing to accept his record, but if I were in Brother Lee's place, I would forgive the debt rather than have feelings between brethren."

In an instant Lee was on his feet.

"I should like to ask the court the liberty of withdrawing the charge," he said. "I should not have pressed it in the first place if Brother Andrew had come to me like a man and asked to talk over our accounts, or if he had expressed his appreciation for what I had done for his wife. I would have just said, 'That is all right, Andrew. Sometime maybe I might be in a tight place and then you can lend me a hand.' But no. He and his wife came into my home and started berating me and insulting my wife. Still I will overlook his hard speeches and withdraw the suit and say no more about the debt."

With that he stepped to the fireplace and made a motion as though to tear the bill in half and throw it into the flame.

"Don't do it," Brigham cried out. "Keep it, Brother John, and file it away with your other accounts to complete all your transactions in this matter. You may find it useful in some future day."

"There has been no man in this church that has done as much for the soldiers' wives and the poor widows as Brother Lee has but myself," he continued. "In fact, he has run and exposed himself enough to wear himself out."

Then he started with Andrew Lytle's wife and proceeded to tell the young husband that "She is a stranger to me, yet I know that she possesses a nasty little whining Peevish Devlish spirit," and continued to berate them all. Finally in a high passion he declared, "Great God! Could a woman trample me in this manner! No! All their council and wisdom don't weigh as much with me as the weight of a flytird. Excuse me for my vulgarity. It is not common for me to use such language, but I know of no language mean enough to suit the case before us."

At the close of the meeting many who had before treated Lee coldly now came to shake hands with him. And to make public his friendship, Brigham Young accompanied Lee home and stayed overnight.

After their supper of bread and milk, they visited long before the fire. Finally after studying the blue flames that flickered along the backlog, Brigham Young said, "I think I should tell you this, John. It may be a comfort to you. A few days after your last trial we were in council one night — Wilford, Heber and I, and your name came up. We discussed the trouble with Charlie Kennedy and the other boys at the farm and all of a sudden — you know how he is — Heber spoke up and said, 'Brother Brigham, I want to prophesy.'

" 'Son of Man, Prophesy!' I said.

"Well, he started out in a solemn voice, 'In the name of Israel's God, this man Lee who now is so much spoken evil of, will yet destroy and trample under his feet, and walk over their graves, those that would destroy him. And most of his family will return to him.' "

For a while Lee could not speak. This was almost too much! Finally in a choked voice he said, "Thank you, Brother Brigham."

Again he was buoyed up, ready for the tasks ahead. He had done the best he could to further the cause, and his efforts had been recognized and accepted. From here on, he would move again with confidence. As for the prophesy, it was such a constant source of comfort to him that twenty-five years later and half a continent away he was to repeat it in his journal almost verbatim.

When George Laub returned from Missouri and, learning those who wished to be released from their obligations as adopted sons might do so, came and asked to withdraw, Lee did not protest, but freely set him at liberty.

"I spoke to President Young about it and Br Bullock promised to put it on Record and my request," Laub wrote.

That these two, between whom there had been such a strong emotional and spiritual tie, should sever the relationship in good feeling meant that later they could be better friends than they could ever have been in the father-son relationship.

And now that Lee was back in favor with his own father, vindicated among his peers and upheld before his subordinates, he could go on with his preparations for the journey west. He could wish for better harmony within his own family, though. He had found that really to live the celestial law a man must be wise indeed; kindly, loving, and tender, but at the same time firm with his wives. More than that, the wives themselves must be tolerant and understanding with each other.

Since the day when Aggatha lost her temper so completely, tensions had been mounting, especially with Nancy Bean. He mentioned her often throughout the spring and early summer as helping to plant and weed in the garden, as going berrying with the group, or visiting at Winter Quarters, or getting turnip seed, as though she were cooperating to the fullest in all activities. She even helped to haul the brick from the old fort.

Yet on July 19 her father "profered to take Nancy and child, board them and take them on next spring for what help and Co. she would be to her mother." Legend in the Bean family says that at one time when Lee ordered Nancy to perform some task, she refused in a sharp and saucy manner and he slapped her or struck her with a switch as though she had been a disobedient child. At any rate, she seemed glad to leave him. The next March he records that she came back and asked for a cow to milk and he refused her saying that when "any of his women left him that he would milk his own cows, but that he had a writing of releasement for her at Dr. W. Richards' office."

Circumstances had made it difficult for him to maintain a good home situation, for he had been called so many times on trading or purchasing missions, not to mention the long trip to Santa Fe, that it is no wonder some of his wives became estranged.

Louisa Free also had gone to live with her parents, though Lee often called to visit with her and seemed to feel no bitterness toward her. She herself had always been cordial and affectionate, but her mother had said harsh and critical things about him during his troubles in court.

Now he would start for the mountains with five loyal wives: Aggatha, Rachel, Martha Berry, and Polly and Lavina Young. Abigail would go along, too, of course, as the mother of the two first wives rather than as a wife herself. Only Aggatha had children: Sarah Jane, Alma, Adoline and Joseph.

1848
Across the Plains

For a year now they had bent every effort toward preparing for the journey to the mountains. In addition to farming, they had kept some men at building wagons, gathering ironwood for the axles, oak or ash for the spokes, and pine to saw and season for the wagonboxes. Each part must have its special wood cut, seasoned, and dried before actual building began. No wagon was stronger than its weakest hook, and one broken felloe could stop an outfit, so they worked with great care. The finished wagon, painted, its wheels tired and soaked in oil, its bolts and burrs all in place, was sturdy, though always heavy — almost a load in itself.

The corn that year yielded beyond their fondest hopes. In spite of inroading cows, vermin, and crows, they raised a total of three thousand bushel. The general distribution probably began in the winter, but through the month of March Lee's record shows that eighteen loads, probably still in the husk, and seven hundred and eighty bushels of "bread corn," shelled, cleaned, and measured into sacks or barrels, went out by team from Summer Quarters.

On April 25, a few days before they planned to leave the farm, a band of Indians arrived, threatening and demanding that they get out. While Levi Stewart rode post haste to Winter Quarters to report, Lee tried to pacify the natives by giving them meat and vegetables and letting them take some kettles in which to cook the stew. They might sleep in the two empty cabins, he told them, but they should not be up and moving about during the night lest one of the guards shoot them by mistake.

Early next morning the band started off, carrying with them the kettles, as though they considered them a gift or payment for the use of their land. Only by a heated protest did Lee get the dishes back, and the Indians left grumbling and angry.

About this time Levi returned with orders to load everything and come to Winter Quarters immediately. Brother Brigham was sending teams to help with the move. Lee himself was putting tires on a wagon which he could not take unfinished and could not afford to leave, but all other hands began to load. Three men on horseback were detailed to round up all the loose stock and get them on the road.

"The camp was in an uproar, or rather a bluster to gather in so short a notice," Lee wrote, but it did not occur to him that they might take a day in which to organize. It had started to rain, but they went right on loading in the midst of the downpour, carrying out corn, furniture, bedding. As each wagon was filled, it pulled out and started back, until by four o'clock in the afternoon twenty-two wagons were on their way.

If any complained at this disorganized, hasty departure or suggested that they wait the rain out and sleep there under shelter, it did not find its way into the record. Might they not have been more safe in the houses under a guard than out on the open prairie? Theirs not to reason why; theirs to obey counsel.

They had no regrets at leaving this place, yet each must have thought of some they were leaving behind at Fair View on the hill, now neatly enclosed in a willow fence. Aggatha would drop a tear for her little Heber John who rested there, while Lee would remember also Nancy Armstrong and all she had sacrificed to join the church and follow him. No one had been more loyal than she, or more willing to help with any task.

There was no time now for introspection or regret, for present needs were too demanding. After only six miles travel, they had to stop to let the horses rest. They waited out the night, wet and hungry. By daylight the sky had cleared and they reached Winter Quarters by noon, in bright sunshine, the boys with the cattle never having gone to bed at all.

Brother Brigham met them, saw their plight, listened to their story, and treated it all lightly. "Said that he felt for them, but the night was short & would pass off like a dream," Lee wrote.

The whole incident is typical of Lee's unquestioning obedience to his leader, even though the situation or his own judgment might suggest other action. Others might complain, but he offered no criticism.

Through the next week Lee was bedeviled with the idea that perhaps he could not get to the mountains this year after all. There was so much to take and he had so little help. Tom Johnson had walked off, George Laub was released April 4, Allen Weeks and Levi North left on April 20. His brothers-in-law, George Hickerson and James Woolsey, had all they could do with their own large families.

One day when Lee was discouraged, he met Brigham Young, who was also short on wagons. Impulsively Lee offered six of his own seven outfits.

"No, John," Brigham said kindly. "Fix up the wagons and get ready to start with the company. I want you to go into the Valley with me." Then he handed Lee fifty dollars in gold and added, "Keep your face to the setting sun." This unexpected gesture of love took Lee so by surprise that he could hardly express his thanks. It did remove all doubt from his mind as to his immediate course of action, however.

Lee's next problem was to help those of his loyal adopted sons who must remain behind. After helping James Pace find a suitable location, he wrote that "I fitted him with a wagon and team, furnished him 4 bushels of seed potatoes, 30 bushels Bred corn, one of seed, four chickens, seven yearling calves, a first rate diamond plow, handsaw, augur, drawing knife, Hamer & Square."

Adolphia Young also remained to help farm, saying that "he never wished to clog the wheel, that he would rather stop here ten years than to hinder the cause 1 minet." Though his disappointment was keen, his loyalty overruled it.

On May 10, while Lee was making his final inventories and packing, the steamship *Mandren* came up the river loaded with goods of all kinds, including three hundred barrels of flour. Again Brigham Young gave him forty dollars in cash with which to buy such necessities as medicines, groceries, powder, and lead. This time Lee, not wishing to be outdone, repaid the favor by giving in return a yoke of oxen.

The order came for all who planned to go in the first company to pull out a few miles onto the prairie, where they might be properly organized. On Friday, May 26, 1848, President Young with his long train pulled out of Winter Quarters, followed by Lee and his seven wagons. After two days of travel they came to the point of rendezvous on the Elkhorn, where by June 1 there had gathered six hundred and twenty-three wagons, the combined company. Here Lee worked at building the wharf and ferry.

At this point they had the first accident of the journey. Little Charley Beer, stepson of John Neff, a lively little boy and a general favorite, fell into the river. Though the alarm was given, he had gone out of sight before help came. Men on the raft followed down the stream, boys ran along the bank, horsemen rode a mile or so further down in case the body should elude the other searchers. When finally he was found, the child was past all earthly help.

John Alger and others prepared a coffin from a large log, from which they cut a length, removed a section with great care so that it would fit back into place securely, and scooped out the center, smoothing it outside and in. They wrapped the body in a piece of white cloth, placed it inside, fastened the lid into place with nails and leather straps, and buried it near the liberty pole on May 27, 1848.

The ferrying of the Elkhorn was difficult and slow. The stream was some eight feet deep and as many rods wide, so they could swim the cattle but must ferry the wagons. Each was wheeled from the wharf onto the log raft, pushed into the stream, and guided across by means of poles and oars downstream to where it was unloaded onto a second wharf. By means of a heavy windlass they would swing and pull the raft back to the starting place. In this way, with a diligent crew of workers, they could cross a hundred wagons a day.

On May 31 the first ninety-nine wagons, with Lorenzo Snow in charge, was organized, and on June 2 it started from the west bank of the Elkhorn. The second group, containing only fifty-one wagons under Zera Pulsipher, followed the next day, and the third with fifty-seven wagons under William G. Perkins the same day. It was here that John D. Lee traveled.

Lee had been chosen by Brigham Young to be captain of the second fifty of the Perkins unit, but since the people were allowed to choose their captain, no one wanted to go with him. Word of his difficulties at Summer Quarters, of his fight, and the court sessions at Winter Quarters provided material for discussion and gossip. Of this Lee wrote that "Through the day some feeling arose through jealousy on account of J. D. Lee's appointment, & fire brands were thrown through the camp by envious Persons in So much that Some left the co."

Hosea Stout, now night guard for Brigham Young, wrote that "Capt Lee had hard work to raise his 50. The people do not like to go with him." Stout himself had just passed through a period of unpopularity, so he could appreciate Lee's position.

Lee made a speech in which he said that he had only the best of feeling toward the brethren, and if he had injured anyone in any way, he would be glad to make restitution. Isaac Morley also spoke in his behalf, assuring the people that he was capable and worthy of the position. Even Brigham Young and Ezra T. Benson reasoned with the brethren, but it was of no use.

The companies started out in order, with each wagon in its place. Twenty-one-year-old John Pulsipher drove the first outfit in his company; Isaac Morley with the "record wagon" was always first in his.

On June 4, Lee wrote that he was up "bytimes engaged in making out returns of the whole co. to Head Quarters," which he sent in by Bro G. Alley. "About 3 p.m. Bro. Alley, the Messenger returned & reported favorable. Said that the Pres & Council was highly gratified with the report. Said it was worthy of Praise." Twelve days later Brigham Young asked about the census, and Lee answered that it had been promptly attended to.

It would seem that the messenger did not deliver it into the proper hands, for no record of this group is found in the L.D.S. archives, and the booklet, *They Came in '48*, compiled by the Daughters of Utah Pioneers contains none of the names of this company, neither wives, children, nor teamsters.

Captain Perkins was an older man, quiet and mild spoken, selected because Brother Brigham felt that he could maintain harmony. Even so, there was some bickering, especially with regard to the positions in the train. Finally, in a general meeting, they agreed to number the wagons and move in order, but there were still those who would have to wait and fall in behind the outfits of others who dallied. Lee's own wagons were so heavily loaded that within a couple of weeks his teams began to be fagged, and in one day on bad road three single-trees were broken.

The first accident in the Perkins train occurred on June 12, when one of Wilson G. Perkins' little girls fell out of the front of the wagon, and both wheels ran over her body. She was picked up for dead and carried to the roadside, where Captain Perkins and Elder Miller prayed over her, and "the Prayer of Faith through the Power of the Priesthood Saved the child, for she rested almost free from Pain from that time on, although the waggon was heavily loaded."

Nowhere was the need to cooperate more evident than in fording streams. At the Loup Fork, for example, all wagons waited until horsemen had ridden across and staked out a crossing, cutting down the bank at the approach and also at the egress. One extra team, sometimes two, would be hitched to the wagon, and with a whoop from the driver and a crack of the long whip, they would plunge in and go diagonally down the stream to come out far below, the distance depending upon the swiftness of the current. With the first to cross, horsemen would ride alongside to guide the lead team to the place where the bank had been cut down so that they could get out without too much difficulty. Once a wagon was across, it would be pulled to one side and left, the teams taken back to help with later ones. As soon as the path was found to be safe, the wagons would cross in a steady line, but none started traveling farther until all were across.

At the Loup Fork, Daniel Miller, captain over ten good outfits, and always independent, decided that he would make his own crossing. There seemed no sense in waiting for all this crowd. He selected a place where the stream was wider and the approach easier, but he hurried his wagons into it without making a careful examination, with the result that he became entangled in quicksand and had real trouble to get some of his wagons out. This time his more haste really meant less speed. As a result, he was cited before the superior officers for insubordination, and for failing to obey counsel. He admitted his error and promised not to repeat it, but they all felt that it was only a verbal admission and that in a similar situation he would likely do the same again.

The arrival of mail was always exciting, though the exchange was only between the captains of the companies. Two horsemen rode the length of the trains from one end to the other, carrying news and instructions and questions. This day they brought the report of a battle which Howard Egan and Thomas Ricks had had with a band of Indians, in which both white men were wounded and several Indians killed. Lee thought of Howard Egan with some affection, careless as he was with his language at times and apt to drink too much if he were in a drinking crowd. But he was absolutely without fear. Not for an instant would he stand to see Indians take off his cattle, no matter how large the band was. Tom Ricks was of much the same temperament.

In this encounter Egan was shot in the right arm just above the wrist, and Ricks in what looked like a fatal spot in the back. Companions came to their rescue and making a stretcher of a buffalo hide, carried Tom back to camp. Although upon his arrival he seemed to be dying, he was restored through prayer and administration. Egan's wrist, which seemed so badly shattered that it looked as though he could never use his hand again, now was healing normally.

It was the same pattern with all, animals or humans. If a horse was bitten by a rattlesnake, they were told to mix spirits of turpentine with tobacco, wash the wound, and pray for the recovery of the animal. When one was poisoned by drinking alkali water, they were to drench it with a half pound of gunpowder mixed with a quarter pound of salt dissolved in sweet milk, the mixture boiled well. This was to be followed by a dose of a pound and a half of salt pork cut into strips. In every case they did what they could and depended upon God for the rest.

Although Lee could never stand to see an animal mistreated, his own were worked to the limit each day. He remonstrated with a brother who was beating a cow; he discharged a teamster for abusing the team. Yet there were times when through necessity an animal was forced to travel until it dropped.

On Saturday, June 17, the group had waited to help the Heber C. Kimball company across the stream and decided to camp there the next day that they might hold a Sunday service all together. In the evening, Lee rode horseback to visit with Brigham Young and Heber C. Kimball. Several others joined them and went in a group around the camps to call the saints to a general meeting the next day. From this point on, in all likelihood they all would not be so close together again.

In the early twilight, Lee made a brief entry in his diary. As he wrote the date, it dawned upon him that just ten years ago on this day he was baptized into the church. It was an overwhelming thought! Putting his book in the tin box at the front of his wagon, he walked away from the camp where he could be by himself. On a little knoll he lay on his back, his hands under his head, while the light died in the west and the stars came out clear and close and friendly. Above him bats and night birds circled; he could hear the frog chorus in the marshy coves along the stream. Campfires spotted the plains, glowing brighter in the falling darkness. The sound of the fiddle and flute and throbbing drum told that a dance was in progress.

Somehow it was not the time for him to dance; he had his own private communion to keep. He pictured the quiet stream between its willow banks; his skin pulled into gooseflesh as he remembered being immersed and then coming up out of the water and the feeling of exaltation which had filled him. How far away it all seemed! How much had transpired in the meantime! Now here he was, scarcely three weeks out on the road, his teams already failing, his wagons so overloaded that each day was a burden and each night a weariness. According to the travel books, the worst of the journey lay ahead. He had never regretted his baptism, from that day to this, and he knew that somehow he would arrive in Zion.

Joseph, the Prophet, had always admonished them to be firm in the faith and to defend the truth; not to defend him as a person, but to defend the cause which he represented. John D. had done that; his whole effort was to help to build up the kingdom of God upon the earth, to help to prepare for His coming. And this journey was a part of the plan. He was proud to be in it, glad to be associated with men like Brigham Young and the others. Though he might overshoot the mark or err in judgment, they knew he could be depended upon.

The music had stopped and people were making their way to the various wagons, calling out goodnights, pairing off, or going in groups. Strengthened in his faith, Lee set out for Aggatha's wagon.

Lee's record gives some vivid accounts of near tragedy on the road. On June 21 he found a boy who had wandered from his own company and hurt his foot so badly that he could not travel. Lee picked him up, bound up his injured foot, and carried him to his father, Brother Biflington, an Englishman from Staffordshire. The child had been missing overnight.

Two days later, at about ten o'clock at night, Brother Jacob L. Workman, captain of ten in Lorenzo Snow's company, came back in search of his son, who, he was told, was very ill and had lain down by the wayside. Lee unhitched a team and gave him a horse to ride in the search.

. . . "Captain Workman went & found his child lying in the open Prairie, returned to Captain J. D. Lee's waggon, wept with Joy & gratitude because his child was yet alive."

On June 25, Lee became severely ill and for three days was not able to travel. Now he found that he had friends. President Young offered him an axle to mend one that was broken, and Brother Webb put it in. Brother Wilson G. Perkins called the group together. He told how, when Lee was appointed to be a captain at the Elkhorn, "Some persons said that he was oppressive and overbearing, & if we did not just as he wanted them that he would Just take up a stick, Knock them down." Now after having traveled with him, "I must confess that he has been as patient, easy and as Mild a Man as I ever saw & no man could fill the office and give more security than what he has done." He then volunteered to take three hundred pounds of Lee's load and haul it all the way into the valley.

His illness had another good effect; his company released him from guard duty and appointed him historian for the group. Captain Daniel Miller assumed the responsibility for the guard.

When on the third day he continued with a high fever, Captain Perkins' wife came to treat him. With the help of her husband, she bled him, gave him an emetic, and put a plaster on his head and temples, which last remedy Lee thought brought about a cure. For some days he was too weak to do much, but was able to travel.

Soon they were in buffalo country. Now all the camp was well supplied with meat, even some extra to "jerk." They contrived this by cutting the meat in long strips, dipping it for a minute or two into a boiling solution of brine, and then hanging it over a heavy cord or light rope which would be suspended between two posts. Underneath they would keep a smudge fire for the night. When they were ready to travel the next day the strings of meat would be looped under the wagon bows to be sun-dried.

Lee had one hunting experience that he was never to forget. He was out with young Byron Pace, and they had already shot a buffalo cow and were dressing it, when Lee saw a large bull not far off. Leaving the boy to go on with cleaning the dead animal, he stalked the bull until he got a good aim and fired what he felt sure was a fatal shot. To his amazement, the bull charged at him with such force that he was nearly knocked down and trampled. For a few rods they ran, the animal's breath hot behind him, the short horns almost scratching his pants. Then stepping aside quickly, Lee brought his gun down with all the force he had across the animal's nose. Though the action stopped the beast, it flipped the gun out of his hand into the grass. Breathless, Lee ran a little farther before he paused to watch the old buffalo, his front legs far apart, sniffing at the gun. Too shaken to carry the argument further, Lee went back to camp. The next morning when he returned with a wagon, he found the buffalo bull lying dead beside his gun. Now there was more meat to dry.

Since the Loup Crossing the companies had never been together again, but were scattered along the plain for twenty-five miles. Now President Young sent word for them all to wait at the Chimney Rock that they might again have a general meeting. Here they decided to break into smaller units of ten-to-twenty wagons that the cattle might have a better chance at feed. Here, too, Lee called upon Louisa Free and visited with his little son. Louisa, with the help of a twelve-year-old brother, was managing one of her father's wagons. The conventional story says that she had with her two young brothers, but, of course, one was her son, now going under the name Andrew B. Free.

As they pulled away from Chimney Rock, there was a great rush among the companies to get ahead, for those in the lead had the best chance for feed and fuel. With the loosening of restrictions, Daniel Miller determined to go on as fast as his teams could travel. From the first he had chafed at being held back by the overloaded wagons and the weak cattle of others. Though Captain Perkins urged moderation, and Lee pleaded with him, he insisted that it was too early to camp, his teams were strong and he would travel a few hours longer to a better campsite. Their companions watched with regret as the ten men and twenty-two wagons left. Among the men leaving was B. F. Pendleton, the only blacksmith.

Under date of July 19, Lee wrote:

> Here Capt. D. Miller with 4 waggons, J. H. & W. H. Daniels with 4 do, S. Kent with 1 do, Benj Pendleton 2 do, J. Bean 2 do, M. Rank 2 do, J. Mayberry 2 do, W. G. Pain 2 do, D. N. Drake 3 do, left the co. & went on, said that was too soon for them to stop.

Most of these men are not listed in the official count.

They were nearly a week getting to Fort Laramie, the first house they had seen for some five hundred miles. Yet although they looked at it with some curiosity, as it sat like a wart on the landscape, a disfiguring outgrowth of the clay around it, they did not stop nor visit it. When the Pulsiphers had crossed the Platte a few days earlier, they had managed by raising the wagon boxes six inches and setting them on blocks of wood to keep them up out of the water. Lee reported only "good crossing," and added that as for the land, "the chief production is prickley pears."

They were on a steady climb day after day, over barren stretches strewn with the bones of dead animals and with the stinking carcasses of those more recently fallen. In one place Lee counted thirty dead; at another he pulled off onto the prairie some distance in an effort to get away from the stench.

At Warm Springs encampment on July 23, Brigham Young's company caught up with them, and here that night Louisa Beaman gave birth to twin boys, to the delight of their father, Brigham Young. Louisa long had been considered something of a heroine, being "the

first one to enter the Celestial Order of Marriage in this dispensation."
She had been the first acknowledged plural wife of the Prophet, and
after his death had been married to Brigham Young. The birth was
normal, and though a heavy storm of rain came up out of the northwest, the little fellows slept snugly beneath the wagon cover. It seemed
a good omen, this birth of twin boys.

The road grew steeper. Now all must walk, sometimes even push or
at least be ready to block the wheels with a large rock when the oxen
had to stop and rest. In many places they had to double teams. There
was one advantage, they were coming to trees, occasional grass, and
game, where the hunters could bring in sage hens and antelope, even
buffalo.

Here Lee was again taken ill. For a full week in mid-August he lay
in heavy fever, not knowing or caring whether they moved. When
Brigham Young's company caught up with him, the President visited
Lee's wagon bringing a bottle of syrup and promising assistance. This
came the next day in the person of old Brother Hughes with one good
yoke of cattle.

Lee was just beginning to mend when Abigail was stricken with
the same disease, mountain fever, soon becoming unconscious in her
suffering. She died on September 3, and was buried a short distance
from the road, a stone carved with her name and date marking the
place. Lee said there had been four other deaths here, but did not list
the names. Though he did not enter it in his diary, Lee here made a
cache of about five hundred pounds of his load, materials which he
could bury and return for during the next summer.

One day's journey took them from their camp on the headwaters of
the Sweetwater to Pacific Springs. En route they went through South
Pass, and were for a short time literally on top of the world. Now they
would be through with climbing for a while. So great was the relief
that they stopped the teams while everyone looked at the vista which
opened before them. The land fell away and stretched in all directions
over an endless sage plain, with occasional buttes and up-juttings in
the middle distance and dim, pale-blue peaks against the skyline. This
was not an encouraging or inviting view, to be sure, but at least it was
down hill. They were so weary with climbing.

At Pacific Springs John Pulsipher had written that "we found a large
flat of wet springy land & stopped 5 days on the best of feed and
rested our foot-sore cattle." Now nearly two weeks and twelve hundred
head of cattle later, Lee reported of the same place, "Grazing short."

The next day brought them to the "Dry Sandy," which was literally
true to its name; a dry, sandy wash. They tried digging for water, but
secured only muddy, alkaline seeps so unfit for use that the ox that
drank it died the next morning. The land here was barren, without

enough grass in all the area they passed in a day to fill a bushel basket, and not a tree or willow big enough to make a whipstock — just some stunted, brown shadscale and desert bramble.

At Little Sandy they found water, and at Big Sandy where they crossed the stream was six rods wide and about eighteen inches deep, with a clean gravelly bottom. They enjoyed the fresh running water here, though within a few miles the bed was totally dry, as though no water had run here since the first day of creation.

At the Green River they found a cottonwood grove in which to camp. Father Zera Pulsipher, they were told, had dragged his seine up the river a few days before and caught some very nice fish, but none in their own party caught any. The water was beautiful and clear, running sixteen rods wide and nearly three feet deep at its lowest, while earlier in the season it had to be forded. Some wanted to stay in this pleasant spot and let the teams rest, but the leaders insisted that they move on as the drives between water were short. When that very night a rain fell which raised the water, they felt that their judgment had been vindicated.

Finally, just as their teams were about worn out, help came. Sanford Porter and Harley Swartout from the valley brought a yoke of strong cattle and a good wagon to lighten their loads. They all felt that it was an act of divine providence.

They passed Batees Trading Post without stopping, and on to Fort Bridger, which Lee described briefly. "The fort consists of 8 block houses & a smawl Enclosure picketed in. Land exceeding rich, grass durable winter & summer, although there is Frost every month of the year."

Lee was now traveling with Father Morley and others of the Young and Kimball trains. The stronger teams had gone ahead as they could, some straight to the valley. The more faithful waited at the mouth of the Weber River for four days "that their leader might enter the valley in his proper place, at the head of this year's emigration."

From the crossing of the Weber on was the hardest part of the journey, partly because all were weary and partly because of the rough mountain road. There were now more than five hundred wagons to enter the valley as a group.

Here, almost at the end of their journey, they came near having their first serious accident. Rachel, walking beside the wagon on a narrow road, was so near that the wind blew her skirts into the wheel, and before she knew it, they were being wrapped around and around the hub. She screamed for help as she tried to extricate them, but in an instant they were drawn so tight that she could only grasp two spokes in her hands, her feet between two others, and make a complete revolution with the wheel.

When the wagon was finally stopped, she was almost right-side up, but firmly bound. How could she get free? It would not occur to them to cut her clothing off; they could not afford to do that. Instead, they unhooked her skirt, unbuttoned her petticoat, and by splitting the placket and taking off her shoes, they pulled her out as clean as though they were skinning the legs of a chicken. Lavina stood by with a blanket to wrap around her and her long underwear gave some protection, but all eyes could see that she was at least six months pregnant. Now the clothing was easily removed, and in the privacy of the wagon she shook them out and put them on again, climbing out again to walk.

Almost every writer complained of this stretch of road, of the rocks and underbrush and the steep, narrow places. Instead, they should have been grateful for what earlier travelers had done — James Clyman and Lansford W. Hastings and the Donner party. This last group had spent precious time here chopping through the trees, moving rocks, and cutting away banks, time which lost them their lives later. But for this delay, they could have been over the pass before the snow fell. Their own brethren of last year had also done some road work, as they themselves were doing now.

On this last night out, Lee's family talked of their journey, giving thanks for their safety and summarizing the trip. They had been a hundred and twenty-five days on the road, had travelled 1031 miles by their roadometer, an average of a little less than eight miles a day. They had crossed over desert and mountain and struggled through deep sand, but they had also rested in spots of indescribable beauty. Only one person had died; the mother of Aggatha and Rachel. Four of their oxen had died and one hive of their bees had melted down, but their two horses were in fair condition, the nine chickens and the dog still alive. They had no sheep, but their herd of cows and loose cattle had made the journey. After one more day all would have a chance to recuperate. Tonight they sang the songs of Zion with happy hearts.

1848-1850
Zion at Last

They had caught their first distant glimpse of The Place from the top of Big Mountain. From that point they could get only the general impression of a misty cove in a forest of peaks, a haven where they would be safe from all the world. They had gone down the precipitous slope with all four wheels locked, and men hanging onto ropes behind each outfit to keep the wagon from literally running over oxen and all hurtling into the canyon below. A short distance down, and they must double up Little Mountain, to skid again with stumbling haste into Emigration Canyon. Five more miles of twisting through brush and repeated crossings of the stream, then struggling up one short, steep pitch, and they emerged into the open valley. Zion at last!

They pulled to the side and stopped. The teams must have a breather, and the people wanted time to absorb the view. The valley stretched to the dim circle of mountains; the lake shimmered in the west. The blue-gray floor was marked by a few faint green lines where streams came out of the canyons. Straight ahead lay the cleared space with the pencil-line squares of the fort, toward which the string of wagons was making its way like a long, thin, jointed snake whose tail was still in the canyon.

As he looked, Lee paraphrased Nehemiah, the Old Testament prophet, in speaking of the Jerusalem about to be rebuilt: "Now the city was large and great, but the people were few therein, and the houses were not builded," and then added the familiar Mormon promise that "Zion shall be established in the tops of the mountains and exalted above the hills, and all nations shall flow unto it." One who had watched Nauvoo rise out of a bog, who had seen converts from Europe gather to it, could not doubt that here they should build a New Jerusalem to stand until the millennium. He should have a part in the building, he told himself.

The fort consisted of two full blocks, each forty yards square, and a half block, the same length, and all attached to each other. The solid rows of houses all faced center. The manufacturing of the valley was represented by an adobe yard, a saw mill, a corn-cracking mill, and Brother John Neff's flour mill on Mill Creek.

The tang of autumn in the air and the scarlet splotches blazing on the mountains reminded them all that winter would soon be upon

them. With characteristic dispatch Lee set about, first driving his
livestock and poorest oxen to good feed on Cottonwood canyon, and
then assembling rock and adobe for a house. He set two wagon boxes
onto temporary foundations for use as bedrooms, and to leave the
running gears free for hauling wood.

When the first snow fell on November 28, it caught some of the
settlers with their houses uncovered, but not John D. Lee. He had
worked to such purpose that he had two homes finished, one on the
lot in town and another at the site of his farm, eight miles out. By
February 11, he noted that "J. D. Lee from necessity removed Sat.,
10th Rachel his 6th wife & her child to his Farm till the weather would
get more mild; his team being so much reduced that he was unable to
haul wood for 2 fires in the city & 2 on his Farm."

Aggatha and the children had moved to the farm early, for here
they had fuel near, feed for the cows, which meant milk and butter.
The hens had a snug coop and a small run, and in early spring Lavina
would exchange a handmade basket for a rooster to assure baby chicks.
The two brood sows meant pork for another year; with luck, the one
beehive would provide honey. Only the dog seemed a luxury, but he
was almost one of the family, a warning at night, a help with the
cattle, a companion for the children.

Never once did the Lee family seem short of food. On the plains
they had entertained the messengers who carried the mail and invited
several chance visitors to eat with them. On February 21, after noting
that he had finished another cabin on the farm, assisted by Rachel and
Lavina, and covered it with mud and clay, he reports that he entertained at dinner the surveying committee of which he was chairman:
Amasa Lyman, J. M. Flake, William Crosby, John Brown, and Randolph Alexander. Three days later at his house in town "Pres. B. Young
& Emoline, his Wife, Dr. Willard Richards & Amelia, his Wife, took
supper with J. D. Lee and spent the evening."

In the meantime, winter had come early. The snow was six inches
deep, the creeks were frozen, and the mills could not run. The problems that arose from these conditions show most clearly the importance
of the Council of Fifty, or the ᴛᴛꜰɪꜰ, in helping the community to
survive. Lee was the secretary of the organization, and though only
scraps of the minutes are preserved in his diaries, they show clearly
the problems and how they were met. Brethren had been urged to
help those whose houses were unfinished and to make temporary room
for them in their own homes, that none should suffer.

At the meeting on December 9, the ᴛᴛꜰɪꜰ considered first sending
a petition to Congress asking for territorial government, then turning
to local affairs, decided that something must be done about the cattle.
During mild weather they had been turned loose to pick their living,

but with this deep snow, they would either starve to death or fall prey to the wolves or Indians. A committee of three, Porter Rockwell, John D. Lee, and George D. Grant, was appointed to round the cattle up and drive them toward places where they might find browse enough to keep alive. Although some people objected to having their cattle taken into a community herd, the council overruled them, saying there was no other way to prevent wholesale losses.

Next they considered the "destroyers" in the valley and decided to make war on them — wolves, wild cats, polecats, minks, bears, panthers, catamounts, coyotes, eagles, hawks, crows, and ravens. President Young nominated John D. Lee and John Pack as captains, and they were to choose up sides among the brethren and agree upon the way the contest was to be conducted.

On the evening of December 28, John Pack and Thomas Bullock met at John D. Lee's home in town and after supper made up their articles of agreement and listed the names of the participants in the hunt. They agreed that the count should be made on the morning of February 1, 1849, at ten o'clock, and that the side which had earned the most points should be entertained at a dinner provided by the losing side. They wrote out the list of points, ranging from fifty for a bear or panther skin down to two for the right wing of a hawk, owl, or magpie, and one for a raven. Isaac Morley and Reynolds Cahoon were to be the judges, or counters, and Thomas Bullock the recorder. And lastly, the man who produced the most points was to receive a public vote of thanks at the dinner. Later the YTFIF voted to give a reward of one dollar each in tithing for each wolf or fox skin, as "Pres B Y said that he wanted a Sleigh Robe made of Some of those cross Fox skins & trim it neatly & present it to Colonel Kane by Dr. Burnhisel, that he was of the opinion that the Col. would prize it higher than a thousand dollars."

Lee wrote carefully the list of participants in the order of their selecting — ninety-five men on a side, including all those in authority from Brigham Young down, as well as many who were only men of the streets. At the meeting of the YTFIF, on January 20, it was decided to continue the hunt for another month.

When the count was made on March 1, John Pack's group had won by about a thousand points, but Lee would not accept the decision because some of his hunters lived far out and he had not been able to contact them. On March 5, when the final count was made, the total in points was between 14,000 and 15,000, with Lee ahead 2043 "skelps." Now Pack would not accept the decision, because the rules said that the final count should have been on March 1.

Things were further complicated by the fact that the man who made the largest killing of all was Tom Williams. Though he was a good shot, Tom had an unsavory reputation in the community. Since the Nauvoo days he was known as being such a clever thief that he could steal anything from a hen on her roost to a steamboat engine. In addition, he had some connection with the bogus money makers whom Brother Brigham had denounced so vigorously. He had returned with the Mormon Battalion boys and had been one whose conduct was publicly condemned, so for him to receive a public honor at the hand of the Mormon leader was quite out of the question.

Though the program had been initiated by the YTFIF, and though they thought it had been beneficial, the bickering between the captains as to who had won, and the fact that the promised public celebration was not held, placed both Lee and Pack in ill repute in the town. This is shown most clearly by an entry in the diary of Hosea Stout. Writing under date of April 28, 1849, he said:

". . . One circumstance took place today which I never saw before. John Pack & John D. Lee were each put in nomination for majors by regular authority & both most contempestuously hissed down. When any person is thus duly nominated I never before knew the people to reject it. But on this occasion it appeared that they are both a perfect stink in everybody's nose. The reasons for which it is not needful to relate. . ."

But this was only a minor item in all the activities of the YTFIF. There was the problem of regulating prices, for the report came that the price of beef was exorbitant, and that those who had beef were robbing their poorer brethren. Brigham Young, however, objected to price control, saying "Let trade seek its own level." He did promise to do something about it, and spoke with such force in a public meeting against those who would pretend to be saints and yet rob their brethren that one man who had sold Lee a beef for forty dollars came later and said, "Kill the ox I let you have & weigh it & pay me what it weighs."

Another problem for consideration was the care of public arms. Brigham Young proposed that they build a small frame building to house them and appoint a man expert in the handling of guns to care for them. He at once named Thomas Tanner for that position, and then at the motion of Amasa Lyman that each man of the council donate one dollar toward the building, and the second of Willard Snow, each of whom placed a dollar on the table, the others followed suit until a total of thirty-two dollars was collected. The only two who did not contribute were Parley P. Pratt and Reynolds Cahoon, neither of whom had any money.

The problems of building a bridge over the Jordan River, of selecting and laying out a cemetery, of fencing the farming land, all were given consideration. But the most immediate and urgent was again the shortage of food. Each Bishop was ordered to visit every home in his ward and get a report of the actual amount of breadstuff on hand, as well as seed of any kind, grain, cows, and calves and bring the report to the next meeting.

On the fifth of February, the coldest day of the season to that time, the council met and heard the report of the conditions relative to the amount of food on hand. The committee reported a little more than three-quarters of a pound of breadstuff per person per day until the ninth of July. All felt that perhaps there was more in camp than had been reported, whereat Brigham Young declared, "If those who have do not sell to those who have not, we will just take it and distribute it among the poor, & those that have and will not divide willingly may be thankful that their Heads are not found wallowing in the snow." However, he promised to try persuasion first, which he did the next Sunday with gratifying results.

In the matter of public works and buildings it was decided that some kind of tax must be levied, about one per cent on land sales and improvements. Albert Carrington was appointed assessor, collector, and treasurer with discretionary power to pin down upon the rich and penurious and "when he comes to a Poor man or widow that is honest instead of Taxing them, give them a few dollars."

Other items decided by the council were the building of bathhouses at the Warm Springs, opening a street at 9th East, making a bridge over Canyon Creek immediately, and granting Brigham Young the right to build a mill. Amasa Lyman was given the right to name the committee to apportion the fencing on the South Farm, and he chose James M. Flake, William Crosby and John D. Lee. Brigham approved, provided Lee should be the chairman, because, said he, "When a man is taken out of this council to do business, let that man be chairman of whatever commity he may belong to. Thus the chairman can report to the council."

The most surprising case before the YTFIF was that of Ira West, one of the first captains in the organization as they left Nauvoo. No specific charges are entered in the record of amounts owed, girls seduced, or transactions of a doubtful nature, but it is very clear that he was no longer in good fellowship and that action against him was to be drastic. In the first appeal against him, made on March 3, it was declared:

Then can the members of this council suffer their sympathy to arrise to that extent that mercy will Rob Justice of its claims, Suffering infernal thieves, Murderers, Whoremongers & every other wicked curse to through mercy to live among us, adding sin to sin, crime to crime, corrupting the morals of the People when their Blood ought to flow to atone for their crimes. I want their cursed heads to be cut off that they may atone for their sins, that mercy may have her claims upon them in the day of redemption.

The case was held over until the next day, when it was clear that "The Council all agreed that he had forfeited his Head, but the difficulty was how he should be disposed of." Some suggested that he should be executed publicly, others thought that he should just disappear, then the people would know that he was gone, and other offenders would take warning. Still others put up a strong argument for a case in open court before a judge and jury.

Finally, Brigham Young said to the marshal, "Take Ira E. West & Thomas Byrns into custody & put them in chains, & on the day of the Election, there offer them for sale to the highest Bidder." He proceeded to say that he could execute sentence himself if the council should order, and then, relenting a little, ". . . but let those two cases pass until we have State officers & should Ira E. West be miss on the day of the Election, I motion that we forgive him the debt."

One might assume that perhaps this man did lose his life, but the diary of Hosea Stout, at that time not a member of the Council of Fifty, tells what happened. Writing under date of Monday, March 12, 1849, he says:

Today was our first political election which commenced at 10 o'clock A.M. A large assemblage of men convened where many subjects were discussed and among the rest the subject of Ira E. West who had been tried by the H. C. & cut off from the church & fined 100 dollars for lying, stealing & swindling &c — and afterward had attempted to run away & was now in chains. He was here offered for sale to anyone who would pay his debts & take him untill he could work it out. No one however took him & for a while the prospect was fair for him to loose his head — His brother C. West took him at last, I believe.

From such entries as this, it is clear that the YTFIF really was the municipal government, making the rules and laws, executing them, and passing judgment upon its members. In all its deliberations the welfare of the Kingdom was its whole concern, the food, shelter, and health of its members, the social needs, even the removing of undesirable elements. Primitive, yes, but not more primitive than other frontier communities of the period.

Perhaps we should not forget Lee's private life in the press of his public duties. On February 25, 1849, he wrote that:

> . . . then had some conversation with Louisa Free, his third wife; told her that he would give her a writing of releasement if she wished it. She replied that she had not asked for it, but to suit himself. He said that he knew that she never would be satisfied until she would learn by contrast, & as for the child, that he was willing to have her keep it at the present if she wished. The proposal was acceptable. She said that she had the best of feelings for him, & wished always to remain so. Then they parted.

Thus ended one of Lee's happiest love affairs, for this girl was beautiful, accomplished, and affectionate. For nearly three years she had been a favorite with him, and he always spoke with doting fondness of her little son. The trouble really stemmed from a dream which she asked him to interpret for her on March 27, 1847. Up to that time he had been known as an interpreter of dreams, and all his life long he placed great stock in them, but after this experience he sometimes declined to use his gift.

This dream almost made him weep, its meaning was so clear: Louisa would become dissatisfied and would "seek to disolve the union that is between us and that too without a just cause." Yet he felt sure that in the end he would be the means of saving her. He began by saying, "Louisa, the vision is plain and the interpretation thereof is sure. . ." He ended with the remark that, "My heart is pained when I think on the future."

During his time of trouble at Summer Quarters, Louisa was living with her parents, and though she herself made no criticism of him, her mother did. Lee visited her occasionally and played with the boy of whom he was very fond; on the plains, he called at the camp and took a small gift to his son. But while Louisa treated him well always, she did not make any direct appeal that he take her back, or offer any apology, or actively court his favor. She did give the impression that should he really court her, she might return to him. This, of course, he would not do. It would be beneath his dignity, and besides, he could not forget the prophesy he had made. Ten years later, on January 16, 1858, he wrote that "This morning Louisa W. sent me the portrait of her first child & herself, the child she had by me." Louisa was now the wife of Daniel H. Wells, and since, according to the *Confessions*, the boy died at the age of twelve, he was probably dead before Lee received the picture.

The winter not only came early, but continued long and cold, with snow almost every day during March. In all the valley the bread shortage became more acute, the cattle poorer. John Pulsipher, who at Winter Quarters spent much time helping others, now himself felt real hunger. His family had not been able to get anything but soft corn, most of it now so moldy that it was nearly black. They dried it out and parched it over the fire, "and if we could have got enough of it, bad as it was, we would have done very well. Father rode many a day to get a half a bushel & was glad to get it by paying a big price. In March we had a small grist mill running, with toll 2 quarts out of a bushel."

By mid-March Lee had rented his houses in town and had all his family at the farm. He had secured a variety of seeds for garden planting — beets, cabbage, parsnips, carrots, turnips, and pie plant. With all hands busy, work went on apace. By the first of April he had twelve acres of wheat planted; by mid-April he reported thirty acres. With any production at all, he should face the next year with a good surplus.

Early in May he wrote of his thrifty crops with pride, but soon the crickets began to appear. At once the family went out to fight them. Armed with bushy branches, they would line up along the side of the field and walk abreast through the knee-high grain, swishing the branches and driving the crickets ahead of them in a black horde to the wide canal which ran along the side. Into this the crickets hopped until the stream was thick with them, drowning them and carrying them away. Around the field and through it again went the workers, encouraged by the fact that the second ditchful was not so heavy as the first. By persistence, they might save a part of the crop.

Lee would not take any chance. He at once started plowing and preparing new land for corn. If the wheat crop were lost, corn would be next best, and the crickets would have passed before the seed was out of the ground. His family had lived chiefly on corn before; if they had to, they could again.

The Council of Fifty had met emergencies of many kinds, but here was one with which they did not know how to cope. The south fields had been attacked early in May and families there were all out at hands-grips with the pests. As reports came in, the Council considered surrounding all the fields with water on all four sides, but that was impractical. With the wheat just coming into head and last year's flour nearly gone, the prospect was dreary. The most optimistic estimate was that the flour would last until July 9; if flour must be freighted in, people would suffer bitterly. And they were totally helpless.

Mormon history echoes with the story, every family having its own version. The desperate struggle is told, the total surrender, prayers of faith, and then, the flocks of gulls so large that they darkened the sun, settling on the fields. They attacked the crickets, gorged themselves to capacity, drank at the streams, disgorged, and returned to the feast. The crops were saved! In every home there were tears of gratitude and prayers of thanksgiving. God had intervened to save the lives of his people. The Sea Gull Monument on the temple grounds at Salt Lake City depicts the incident more effectively than volumes of words.

Lee's account of the miracle on June 2 is brief: "Crickets by Millions Marched into J. D. Lee's farm, but luckily the gulls in numbers sufficient visited the fields & repulsed the destroyers." On the very same day he wrote that he went into the canyon for lumber. Assisted by his wife Rachel, and his neighbor, A. P. Doudle, in one week he cut and hauled to the mill ninety logs, which would make eight thousand feet of lumber. He planned to build a stone mansion, and he knew that an essential was plenty of well-cured lumber.

In addition, he had saved two cords of pine bark to be used in tanning. He knew that with a few hides and the material to tan them properly, he could be sure of shoes for his whole family. He had a good shoemaking outfit, and if he couldn't secure the heavy leather for soles, he could at least make moccasins.

By July 1, the first of the gold seekers began to arrive at Salt Lake City, ready to exchange their wornout animals for fresh ones and to trade bacon and groceries for milk, butter, and fresh vegetables. While Aggatha managed at home, Martha, Polly, and Lavina could get together such items as they had from the garden and dairy and haul them in to Main Street where they could market each day as much as they had. Lee took three ox teams, now fat and in condition, two horses, and a wagon, and started east as far as the Sweetwater on what he called "a picking-up expedition."

Rachel accompanied him on this trip as she had done on the one to the mountains for logs. There were several reasons for this: Aggatha needed to manage her own children and was also growing heavy with the son she would bear on October 11; she had already taken Rachel's seven-months-old baby girl to her heart, the only baby in the family since the death of little Heber John two years ago. Then too, Aggatha was not as jealous of Rachel as she was of the other girls. More important still, Rachel was young and vigorous and without the nausea which Martha was experiencing now for the first time, though both were at about the same stage in pregnancy. Besides that, Rachel could ride a horse, harness and drive a team, or do any type of outside work, while the other wives were expert in all the household tasks — fancy tailoring and embroidering, baking, cooking, making candles or soap. Each should do what she could do best.

Lee knew all about the great celebration to be held on July 24, but he chose to leave a week early. Perhaps the public rejection of April still rankled or perhaps he just wanted to be first on the way back so that he could get a better selection of things along the trail. His family could all attend the celebration in the light wagon, enjoy the program, the visiting and food, and tell him about it when he got back. He must not miss this chance to get what was better than money — tools, utensils and food.

They left the farm on July 17 with two yoke of oxen pulling a wagon empty except for the bed roll, a sack of grain for the animals, and hay to serve as a mattress while it lasted. Rachel drove the team, while he rode one horse, led another, and drove the extra span of oxen.

At the last crossing of the Sweetwater, they found a company that had camped for an indefinite stay while their teams recuperated. Dr. Hidden and Charles Stevens from St. Louis were in charge. Mrs. Hidden was impressed with Rachel and eager to visit about what lay ahead, while the men seemed to enjoy John D's talk. They camped together that night and shared their supper, and next morning Lee bargained to haul a thousand pounds of their freight back to the valley for seventy-five dollars in groceries and a wagon worth nineteen dollars.

Since they expected to stay here for at least a week, he made Rachel comfortable in the new wagon and arranged to have her remain while he went on in search of a stove. A few miles from the camp he found a yoke of oxen nearly starved, abandoned because they had diseased, sore feet. He stopped, fed them, brought them back to the camp, doctored their feet with hot tar, and left them for Rachel to care for until his return.

The weather was hot, the road lined with the wagons of emigrants headed for the gold fields, all eager for information. How many miles? What kind of road? Any supplies to be had in the valley? Sometimes he met women and children on foot, some carrying part of the load, dusty, weary, discouraged. Some teamsters asked for a map of watering places and offered to pay for it; others gave him their excess loading which they would have to discard anyway.

Four days' travel brought him to the fourth ford of the Sweetwater, where he met Charles Shumway's group on their way to Zion with ten thousand dollars which they had earned on the ferry at the Platte. This they would give in to the church, as they were assigned by the YTFIF on March 4. The project had been a financial success, and these faithful members of the YTFIF who operated it were dedicated to the cause of helping the needy to get to Zion. Here Lee left the ox team with Charles Stevens, while he went on with the horses to try to find a stove. About thirty miles before he reached Devil's Gate he found one to his liking, a fine large Premium Range No. 3 which would have cost more than fifty dollars to purchase. On the way back he started loading up with powder and lead, cooking utensils, tobacco, nails, tools, bacon, coffee, sugar, trunks of clothing, axes, and harness.

He also overtook a company led by a tall, spare Mississippian; a slow-spoken gentleman about thirty-five years old, of southern culture. This man and his wife also took a fancy to Rachel, giving her a handkerchief filled with coffee and another with tea, and nearly two bushels of dried fruit, saying they could not haul it further anyway. During her husband's absence, Rachel had not been idle, but had made a collection of items picked up within a radius of a few miles of the place.

When John D. Lee set out, he planned to bring home a good stove for Aggatha, but he knew also of other valuables. Stopping near Abigail's grave, he "reserected" a deposit which he said weighed almost five hundred pounds and consisted mostly of medicines. In this he picked up some of his own load discarded a year ago, now found "mostly safe."

At Pacific Springs he heard of the death of Samuel Gully, his most faithful adopted son. He had died of cholera and was buried on July 4, according to the report. This was a great sorrow for Lee, who remembered how Gully had always spoken up in his defense — to Jefferson Hunt on the Mormon Battalion trek, and against every opponent during the bitter days at Summer Quarters. A man would go through life and find few friends as loyal as Samuel Gully had been to him.

The road back was a desolation, strewn with dead animals that lay stinking in all stages of putrefaction. The land was as barren of feed as if it had been burned over. Lee sold his horses to a Mr. Provost for four hundred dollars, and traded one yoke of fat oxen for four poor ones. Surely, he reflected, God had been good to his faithful people, had preserved their crops by the miraculous power of His mighty hand, and had opened the way by which they might gain the necessities and a few of the comforts of life. This one trip had netted him more than he could have earned by two years' hard labor, not only by cash in hand, but in goods. Surplus tools were always an item of trade; powder and lead worth more than money, clothing of any kind priceless in the fingers of his skilled wives.

He had missed the celebration, true, but in his absence, Aggatha had hired the grain cut and stacked,and had taken care that the garden was irrigated, and the animals cared for. Now the corn was on, some to be cut from the cob when it was young and tender, dried and sacked for winter, but most of the crop left to ripen fully on the stalk. There was kraut to be made and pickles to salt down, and as fall approached a pit to be dug for potatoes, carrots, and cabbage. Sweet squash were cut in rings and threaded on heavy cord to dry. This winter would find them with food in plenty and variety.

At butchering time, the hams and shoulders would be salted and smoked, sausages made, lard rendered. Only the heart, liver, sweet-breads and spare ribs would be eaten fresh, everything else must be cured in some way. The head was halved, eyes and brains removed, and snout cut off, after which it was boiled down, seasoned with salt, pepper, and sage, and poured into pans as headcheese. When it was cold it set into a solid gelatin loaf, to be served as a delicacy for company or given as a sandwich filling to a hungry child. And almost as important as food, was the soap to be made from the fat stripped from the pigs' intestines and boiled with cottonwood-ash lye.

There was wool to be washed, pulled, carded, and spun into yarn for knitting shawls, stockings, and mittens. The homes must be rein-forced against storm, wood cut and ricked up, candles made. From the pick-ups on the road, clothes for all would be fashioned. The women cooperated cheerfully under Aggatha's wise direction, and each carried on for the mutual benefit with such skills as she had.

When President Young made his general official report to the saints in all the world, dated October 12, 1849, he painted a rosy picture. Without mention of the miracle of the gulls, he said the crops in general had been good except those that had been destroyed by early frost, assured that "with prudence" they should have a comfortable supply for all who had now gathered and for those on the way. He encouraged men of skills, men who owned machinery, all who could come to do so, for Zion was growing. Already there were settlements at Brownville to the north and Provo to the south and a colony would leave in a few days to settle in Sanpete County. All six of the apostles then in the valley had been called on foreign missions, all with com-panions of lesser rank. Parley P. Pratt's, however, was postponed until spring so that he could lead a group of twenty men to explore the area southward to the rim of the Basin.

Within the city building was moving apace. A brick assembly hall one hundred by sixty feet had been erected on the temple block; the walls of the council house were nearly to the square; bathhouses were under construction at the Warm Springs. He might have added that there were in the valley five grist mills, nine sawmills, and an adobe yard by way of industry. A mail service to the Mississippi River four times a year had been established.

Two things were perhaps more important than any of these: the fact that every home was a literal hive of industry, and that now a per-petual emigration fund was set up to help bring foreign Saints to Zion.

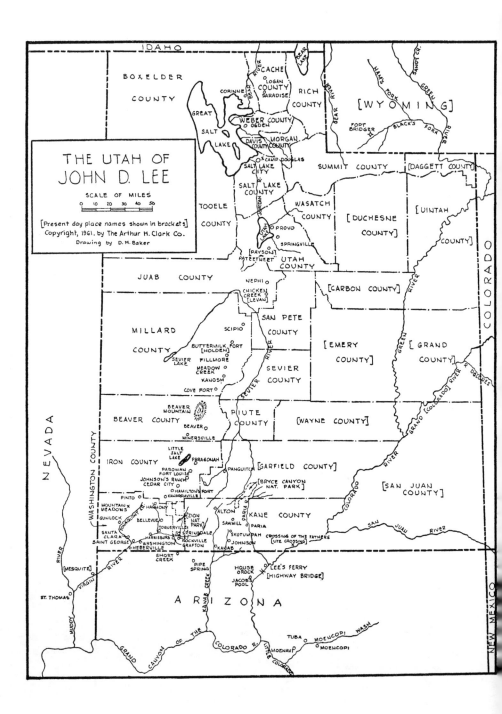

1850-1851
The Call South

After Brigham Young finished reading his annual report on December 2, 1850, other business was quickly disposed of and the meeting adjourned. John D. Lee listened with a glow of pride to the summary of the year's activities. It warmed his heart to hear that the new public bathhouses were finished and in use, that the Council House, which would be a credit to any city, also was practically completed. The prediction of new industry and expanded trade, of a possible railroad to the southern part of the state suggested new opportunities for himself. The order for the establishment of the first university west of the Mississippi and the appropriation of five thousand dollars to start the work also appealed to him. But at the boast that during the past year not one case had been reported for trial in the courts, he glanced around at the other members of the Legislative Council. They all sat in sober dignity, though he felt a wave like an electric impulse pass through the group.

The saints in Zion were the best people on earth, of that he was sure. But there were some rogues among them who had to be dealt with, either by the whipping post, by public humiliation at the election polls, or by means even more drastic. If it were necessary to emasculate a man who was corrupting the morals of the community, it would serve as a warning to others that such things would not be tolerated here, and it would guarantee that the offender should be harmless thereafter. Public courts had their place, but differences settled between brethren at the Bishop's Courts or before the High Council were not determined by legal technicalities but by the broad principles of human rights. So the president did well to tell the world that in Zion there was no need of civil courts.

There had been mention of opening up the iron industry in the southern part of the state, where Parley Pratt and his group had relocated the rich veins of iron ore with coal deposits nearby that Jefferson Hunt had found on his return trip from California. The *Deseret News* of July 27 had carried an article asking for volunteers to that area, urging men of skill and experience to move south some three hundred miles to help to work these mines and to set up an

outpost of Zion at the Little Salt Lake. Lee had read the article carefully and hoped people would respond to the call, but he did not think
it meant him. He was kept busy here, meeting regularly with the
council, acting on various committees, trading with California emigrants, and working at the new home.

As other members visited briefly and left the building, Lee lingered
over his minutes, expecting a word or two with Brother Brigham,
either by way of friendly exchange or assignment. He would not think
of leaving a meeting, walking away to his own business without first
speaking to President Young.

"John," Brother Brigham said without any preliminary as he put his
hand on Lee's shoulder, "when I talked about making the settlement
in the south, I meant you. If we are to establish an iron industry there,
we must have a solid base of farming to help support it. We need
men like you to produce food for the miners and mill workers. You
know our policy with regard to members of the council taking the lead
in forming new settlements. The kingdom cannot grow without men
like you."

Completely taken back, for an instant Lee could find nothing to say.
He had never refused an assignment; he had never questioned a call.
But this was different.

"I don't see how I can possibly leave now," he protested. Then
growing bolder, he blurted out, "The whole idea is repugnant to me!
If I could pay as much as two thousand dollars in money or goods, if
I could furnish and fit out a family to take my place, I would rather
do it than to go. My house is just up to the square, and I was bending
every effort to get the roof on before the snow comes. Some of my
family are not well. If I could even get the house covered and
secure. . ."

"Be of good cheer, Brother John," Brigham interrupted. "Brother
George A. has asked especially for you. He says he would feel safer
with you along, and I would feel safer to know that you are along.
Leave your city lot in my care, and I will sell it and settle your bill
with Livingston & Kinkead. You said it was about six hundred dollars,
didn't you? The lot should be worth that much. Accept this mission
and you will be prospered and blessed beyond your fondest dreams."

To that there was no answer. He would go, of course.

As he mounted his horse to ride back to the farm, Lee looked at his
surroundings with new eyes. He had come to love this place, sheltered
as it was by the mountains. The city was rapidly becoming large and
great; houses were being built everywhere; emigrants were gathering
from foreign lands.

If the kingdom were to become a reality, the iron industry should be fostered and new settlements must be established. Who should lead, if not the chosen Council of Fifty? Had they not worked as a unit to help accomplish what he could see around him?

In addition to the council house, there was the adobe hall of science ready to receive equipment even now on its way from France. Also coming from France was the sugar factory, its parts being hauled by two hundred yoke of oxen. There was the tithing office, the busiest center of town, to which people brought their tithes of grain, vegetables, butter, and eggs. These would be distributed to new arrivals in exchange for public work. Attached to the tithing office was the home of the *Deseret News,* a building so low that one visitor remarked that he could get on top of it as easily as he could get inside. The press was the same one that W. W. Phelps had brought to Winter Quarters during that bitter winter of 1846. Now here it stood like an awkward bug on its cast iron legs, its hand-operated press waiting for news.

Pole fences enclosed the blocks south along Main Street, while ditches and young trees edged the sidewalks. In another year or two there would be plenty of shade.

Lee rode slowly, considering what this move would mean. He would leave the decision to Aggatha as to which wives should go, knowing that she would be right. She encouraged him to accept the call, insisting that she could manage some way. Relieved, Lee wrote, "Let the writer here remark the Tender regard, kind, liberal & affectionate feelings manifested on the part of Mrs. Lee toward her husband with regard to this mission."

They agreed that none of the children should go on this winter journey. They could be snug and warm at home until the family should move early the next fall. Aggatha had two babies just a year and five days apart, John Willard and Louisa Eveline, the latter just six weeks old. Rachel's two little girls were just thirteen months apart, and Martha's daughter was ten months old. On the other hand, Polly and Lavina were now both pregnant for the first time, and would prefer to go than to face the ordeal of birth without the sustaining faith of their husband.

Lee made careful preparations, for while they had traveled through the summer to the valley, they must now be prepared for very cold weather, and the memory of the months on the plains of Iowa made him determined not to repeat that suffering. He reinforced every wagon bed with an extra layer of lumber to use in building his house when he arrived; he distributed the load to the best advantage. He waterproofed and painted his wagon covers and arranged blankets to hang behind the seat to shut out the cold.

There were only two buggies to go in the train, his and Brother George A. Smith's. Each of these was fitted with a small stove, the pipe of which passed through a tin reinforcement in the top of the cover. His contained also a wooden box with a hinged lid, the top to be used as a writing desk, with his writing materials, a candle, and the record books in a tin box just beneath.

Although there were more than fifty other stoves in the train, most of the others were not set up for use, the people using hot rock or portable heaters made of large buckets with a little sand in the bottom into which a few shovelsful of live coals could be placed as they left the campfires.

Looking over the list of those called, Lee was pleased to see the names of some old friends. One was John Steele with his wife Catherine and two children; the man who had refused to leave his family at Santa Fe was now bringing them on this winter journey, his wife driving one wagon. In Nauvoo, John Steele had shown his courage in defense of the city, and in Salt Lake City he had spoken boldly in justification of the Battalion boys, and he was one of the few who did not panic at the near-disaster of the crickets. Lee was glad to have this man along, and later would be even more grateful for his integrity and support.

Another was Zachariah Decker, twenty-two, now married to Nancy Bean and father of a young son by her. They had changed the name of Lee's daughter Eliza to Cornelia and were to protect her carefully from any knowledge of her real father. Also on the list were Bishop Elisha H. Groves, whose daughter would become Lee's wife in a couple of years; Charles W. Dalton who would become his son-in-law; William H. Dame, thirty-one; tall, big-boned, gangling Nephi Johnson, seventeen, and George Wood — all of whom would be involved with him in the blackest deed of Utah history. Joseph Horne was to be the gardener as also he would be later in the first cotton experiments. Going too, were the Lewis brothers, Tarleton, James, and Phillip; all of whom had known the Prophet and had lived through the days of persecution and trial.

Surely, thought Lee, this was a select company. But then it would take people well grounded in the faith to accept such an assignment; others would apostatize first.

Each man had fitted out his own wagon and got on the road by December 11, with the understanding that they would gather at Fort

Provo, forty miles out. There they would organize and perhaps secure additional supplies or needed articles.

Of his own fitout, Lee wrote:

> On Wednesday 1850 Dec 11 John D Lee started for Iron County, with 2 waggons 4 yoke of cattle & 3 yoke of cows & Heifers also one carriage & 2 horses & of his family Mary and Lavina wives, 2 teamsters, Hyrum Woolsey & Paul Royls a Frenchman. Took 400 lbs Flour to each person & some more making about 2200 lbs Flour. 100 lbs. groceries one barrel Pork, one of Crout, Pickles, Beans, Peas, Dried fruit, &c. . .

They traveled slowly, taking more than three days to go the forty miles to Fort Provo. There, on December 15, they had their first general meeting around the campfire, with their President, George A. Smith, addressing them from the running gears of an old wagon. Then they were organized according to the conventional Mormon pattern into two groups of fifty wagons, each with a captain and each subdivided into five groups of ten wagons under another captain. Elish H. Groves was made trouble-shooter to settle differences between the brethren; John D. Lee was clerk, and recorder; Henry Lunt, the camp historian. Anson Call was captain of the first fifty and Simon Baker of the second.

They had hoped to recruit at least twelve men at Provo, but were not able to get a single one to go. At Hobble Creek Settlement, now Springville, Aaron Johnson and thirty-five other men had built a fort which provided some shelter and a few supplies. At this point they decided that George A. Smith, John D. Lee, and Henry Lunt would ride ahead in Lee's buggy to Peteetneet, now Payson, where James Pace was in charge of another settlement. Lee's wives would follow in George A's buggy. The roads were so swampy that the wagons took four days to cover the ground which the buggy passed over easily in one.

To add to the difficulties, it turned cold on the second morning, and for the next two days snow fell steadily. In the meantime Lee and his companions were at the Pace home enjoying good food and warmth, and writing the reports, petitions, letters, and a history of their journey to this point. In addition they made a complete inventory of the contents of every wagon and of all the people and livestock, as well as provisions, tools, and materials for building. Lunt's report was very detailed, while Lee's presented only a summary; where Lunt gave every name, Lee said the company totaled 167, of whom 119 were men, 30 were women, and 18 were children.[1]

While the president and his clerks wrote letters and reports, the teamsters with their overloaded wagons struggled through the mud. One after another became so hopelessly stuck that he had to abandon his outfit until some of the leaders came back, unloaded the wagon entirely, and by means of shovels and extra teams were able to extricate it.

Fort Peteetneet was the last settlement toward the south. From this point they must make their own road, for the old Spanish Trail, poorly marked even in summer, was now erased by the snow. Had not Jefferson Hunt and his sandwalking train of last summer been forced to abandon most of their wagons in favor of pack trains? After the many troubles to this point, what wonder that their hearts should quail before what lay ahead? Their course lay across mountains where for days they must travel in snow, sometimes more than a foot deep. The men, heavily bundled, would have to walk most of the time, while the women and children sat wrapped in blankets, their feet at hot rocks or improvised stoves.

Polly and Lavina Lee busied themselves with knitting woolen stockings or crocheting lace for the bottom of baby dresses. Aggatha perhaps would have condemned this as extravagance, but if a girl has exchanged baskets of her own make for a piece of white cloth and some crochet thread, who would blame her?

On Christmas Eve they had reached Chicken Creek, just south of the present town of Levan. All day they had traveled in snow, and in the evening they waited while Brother Horne scouted to see if he could not mark out a new road on higher ground. He failed to locate

---

[1] According to Lee's summary, the company consisted of 101 wagons and carriages, drawn by 368 oxen and 12 mules, with 100 horses extra and 44 saddles for riding them. The live stock consisted of 146 milch cows and 20 head of beef cattle — with ¾ of a butchered animal yet unconsumed.

The personnel of the company totaled 119 men over 14 years of age, 30 women, and 18 children under fourteen, a total of 167. They carried along also 121 chickens, 14 dogs, and 18 cats.

Their military equipment consisted of 9 swords, 112 guns, 52 pistols, and 1 cannon, with 1001 rounds of ammunition. Their farming and building tools included 57 plows, 3 pitt saws, 4 crosscut saws, 137 axes, 45 common scythes and 72 scythes with cradles, 45 sickles, 110 spades and shovels, 98 weeding hoes, 3½ sets of blacksmith tools, 9½ sets of carpenter tools, and one mill apparatus, evidently a flour mill.

For constructing their homes they had 190 pounds of nails, 436 lights of glass, and 55 stoves to go in them.

Food supplies and seed included 54 bushels of seed potatoes (which were all frozen before they arrived at the place), 1269 pounds of barley, 2163 pounds of oats, 3486 of corn, 35,370 of wheat, 1228 of groceries and 46,922 of flour.

any better, so they spent all of Christmas Day getting the wagons across this one creek. Polly, Lavina, and Zilpha Smith cooked their evening meal together, after which they and their husbands gathered around the little stove and listened to President Smith read aloud from the "Narrative of Capt. Blakely 2 Mexican Ladies their two Brothers & the treachery of Capt Goren etc." Thus they were transported from the cold and snow to a land of true romance.

The journey was hardest on the animals. Day by day they wasted, their hides drawing a little more tightly over their bones. On the morning after Christmas, they found that President Smith's yoke of oxen had been driven off. After an all day search, Henry Lunt's company brought them in, both wounded, one fatally. With the oxen they brought an Indian and his brother, a boy about twelve years of age.

John D. Lee wrote in some detail of President Smith's reaction. Here were his oxen, the faithful team that had brought his family across the plains from Winter Quarters, with Indian arrows sticking in their hides. When one fell, the president kneeled beside it, talking to it as to a fallen comrade, offering it a handful of grain and some melted snow to drink. When he could see that there was no hope for its recovery, he told a man to shoot it, and walked away so that he would not have to witness the killing. Surely he would mete out a just punishment to the wretches who had done this.

He ordered the Indians brought to his tent, but when he saw how miserable and hungry they were, he offered them some bread. Finally he gave the dead ox to the older Indian in exchange for the boy, promising to feed and clothe him. The child was given to Adam Empey, who at once put a buckskin shirt on his back and tightened it with a belt around the waist.

The week following was even more difficult because they had to cross a high mountain range. The ground was too frozen to shovel, the snow was slippery, so they were often forced to move only one wagon at a time with from four to six men to keep it from tipping over. The rear axle of Brother Love's wagon broke, so they must abandon it and redistribute its load into already overloaded ones. When Brother Wood's wheel collapsed, they rigged up a sled runner out of a plow beam and dragged it the four miles to camp. Thus moving only two to four miles a day, they came to Meadow Creek in Millard County, on New Year's Day. There they decided to stop while the wagons were repaired.

The young people came in a group to ask if they might not have a dance, since it was a holiday. As soon as permission was given, they set about to clear a place in the brush and to collect wood for their fires. Lee spent much of the day reading the novel, *The Poor Cousins*, to Brother Smith and their wives.

At the sound of the fiddle, flute and drum, they all went to watch the party. Truly they were young folks, a dozen or more still in their teens. When the watchman called out, "Ten o'clock, and all is well," the dance was dismissed by prayer and the crowd dispersed to their wagons. Lee often mentioned the ten o'clock call of the watchman as he finished writing his account of the day's activity. With his comfortable arrangement of desk and light and writing materials he could take time to write in detail of the discussions, the sermons, the difficulties of the day, and the nature of the land and the weather.

Quite a number of the group were new emigrants from England and Wales, so when the president in one of his speeches spoke of the glory of the United States and its noble founding fathers, they protested emphatically. They had not come to this country to hear partisan, nationalist speeches, they said. Nor could the Welsh saints sing the hymns in English. So the good-natured leader apologized for his thoughtlessness by assuring them that all governments on the earth were corrupt, except one, and that was the kingdom of God. And he encouraged them to organize a choir of their own and sing the hymns in their native language.

With the snow as deep as two feet, the cattle had difficulty enough to exist, much less have strength to pull the wagons. It was decided to abandon any attempt to keep an orderly position, but to allow the horse teams and the stronger ox teams to move on as fast as they could that they might perhaps find less snow and more feed. President Smith and Lee remained behind with the last wagons to be sure that none might be left in trouble. After a grueling forenoon getting over Beaver Mountain, in the late afternoon they pulled onto Buck Horn Flat, where the sage was thick and luxuriant but there was no timber or grass. Here they stopped while two of the brethren went back to help a few wagons in the rear. While they waited, John D. was asked to read his journal of the few days previous aloud to the group for their approval or criticism. At the conclusion, the President remarked that they here were the weak, broken fragments of the company, and probably more in danger of Indian attacks than those who were ahead. Perhaps while they waited, they should get out the arms and inspect them. Edson Whipple was placed in charge of a bit of review drill according to military form, had the boys march and countermarch, and then fire a volley. This was great sport! Why not fire the cannon just once to celebrate their arrival over the mountains? Why not, indeed? They were so earnest and eager that the President gave his consent, and ordered John D. Lee to take charge. The men lined up and divided into six sections and marched to the rear of the cannon. At the signal, Brother Bastain fired the cannon, and then all the rifles were discharged.

At the camp six miles ahead, the sound of the guns caused great consternation. Had President Smith and his few wagons been attacked by Indians? In about an hour two horsemen came as an express to learn of the trouble, and immediately others were sent to report the meaning of the shots. Even the head camp heard the sound, though they were fifteen miles away, and twenty men started back to the rescue, to be met by messengers from the camps to reassure them.

They were now in the general area for which they had started, the long valley through which several streams drained from the mountains into the Little Salt Lake. The problem now was to decide upon a definite location for their city. Here the tact and quiet way of the leader served better than rebukes or scoldings would have done. He reminded them that they had traveled more than two hundred and sixty miles in inclement weather and over bad roads, and without one fight, or even a single quarrel so far as he knew.

"Now I suggest that we all move on to the next creek and there make a general camp, a safe corral, and insure proper care of our families and outfits, and then make a general exploration before we decide on the exact location of our city."

The suggestion was well taken, and John D. Lee was asked to prepare his buggy with four horses to draw it, to bring his writing materials, the thermometer, and candles, so that he could keep the records as he went. Just before they left, Brother Hall came to show them a silver watch which he had picked up as he cleared back the snow to start a fire at the old camp ground. It had evidently been left by some California emigrants, and seemed a good omen.

The mounted escort, consisting of eighteen men on horseback, were the ones who would do the real exploring. They had been out about an hour when they met Captain Jefferson Hunt with seven other men and a pack train of forty-two animals. President Smith asked Hunt to accompany them in the exploring party, while his men went on to camp. Captain Hunt had been very sharp and impudent to John D. Lee at Santa Fe, but their difficulties had been resolved and they met now as friends. The time would come when Lee could repay Brother Hunt in a very real way with good for evil, or good for whatever favors he should receive. For Captain Hunt took them to a cache where he had left secreted the year before many valuable tools including wagon wheels, a hand saw, planes, chisels, augurs, spades, and chains, and told them to take and use them, and if ever he was here and needed a tool, perhaps they would lend him one.

Perhaps the most important news that Captain Hunt carried was that Brigham Young's appointment as Governor of Utah Territory had been confirmed. Now that he was governor, legally as well as actually, they proceeded to organize Iron County, name its officials, and ask

Jefferson Hunt to represent them in the coming legislature. John D. Lee withdrew his name as recorder, saying that he did not plan to be here long at this time, and that they should select the recorder from among the permanent settlers. He nominated James Lewis for the position.

From the first there was dissatisfaction in the camp with the location. Some of the most successful farmers did not like the red soil; it was coarse and shallow, they said, and without fertility or humus. Others did not like the black soil of the bottom lands, because it was so deeply rooted with grass and rushes that their teams could not plow it. Argument led to argument, until personal insinuations and insulting words were exchanged. John Steele, unhappy about the situation and seeking solitude, returned to his own wagon. His bed was all made up and everything about it clean and quiet, so he lay down on his stomach, and raising on his elbows, looked out through the back cover toward the west. Suddenly his mind was illumined and it seemed to him that this was the place God had meant for the town, right here where the leaders had asked them to stop. He arose quickly, returned to the crowd, and spoke with such fervor and eloquence that he convinced them that this was really the place.

When President Smith, Captain Hunt, John D. Lee, and the other explorers returned, they found the company all satisfied with their first selection. This point settled, they named January 17 as election day, when every man cast his ballot for the ticket that had been previously selected. This was followed by a public dinner served on clean, white tablecloths spread in the center of buffalo robes. After grace was said, they enjoyed the fresh roast beef, the biscuits, sweets, and dried apple pie, and drank a toast in tea instead of liquor to the inhabitants of the new county.

As soon as the food was cleared away, the dance began and continued until the watchman called out the hour of ten. With a full moon and the four fires and the exercise of the dance, who could be cold? There was room for three quadrille sets at a time, John D. called the figures and danced as he did so. The town was here, though the land was not surveyed nor the fort laid out. When the mail left the next morning about one hundred letters went with it to announce the arrival and tell of the journey.

At a public meeting the next day the people decided that before they began on their homes they would build a public house — a house for worship, school, dancing, and council. They agreed that the most pressing needs were a road to the timber, the fort laid out, the meeting house built, homes, and fencing. They detailed some to build roads, others to cut logs, others to herd the stock, and a group to survey the land and the fort. That the selection of the site and laying out of the fort were grave responsibilities was shown by the fact that Lee twice wrote that he and Phillip B. Lewis were "of the Council of Fifty," that special group whose call to establish the kingdom came directly from Joseph.

The fort was laid out in a fifty-six-rod square, with a corral in the center of forty rods, around which was a street four rods wide. Two large gates opened from both north and south. The lots were two by four rods, which would give room for a small garden attached to each house. Next they must lay out a big field where each man could have his bread crops and hay. They must learn to cooperate, for in this company were blacksmiths, carpenters, shoemakers, tailors, stonemasons, bricklayers, even silversmiths and portrait painters. Eventually each could work at his trade as he chose, but for the present they must unite on public work. President Smith told Lee privately that he might count the hours it took him to write up the history as a part of the public work, since it was as important as road making or timber cutting.

Brother Williams and Joseph Y. Hovey each made a good grindstone to keep axes and tools sharp — the first manufacturing in the colony. Brother Francis Whitney, one of the blacksmiths, was detailed to do his part of the public work at his trade, as was Burr Frost. Now many wagon boxes were set off the wheels onto a base of rock to serve as bedrooms, while the wheels and running gears were used to haul in the logs.

In the meantime the Indians were camped nearby on their regular trip south to Mexico with children for sale or trade. Walker and his brother Sanpitch did a lucrative business at this exchange of children for horses, sometimes purchasing them from the poorer tribes of the south where every winter meant near starvation, sometimes raiding the camps and carrying them off by force. Now they had a boy for sale to the settlers of Parowan. He was a scrawny, starved little fellow whose black eyes looked out from the mat of hair like those of a trapped animal. He was tied to a bush by a rope of yucca fiber, where he waited for his food of bones and leftovers. As soon as John D. Lee saw the shivering bit of humanity, he felt that someone should rescue him from that miserable condition. Pointing to the child, he asked the chief, "How much?"

The chief pretended not to understand, but turned and spoke to another Indian who answered, "Gun. Two guns."

"No sell-em gun," countered Lee. "Sell shutcup. Sell beef."

The Indian relayed the message and then turned back. "Got gun, kill deer, kill much rabbit."

Lee knew the counsel against selling the Indians ammunition and guns, but he felt that he could not live with himself if he did nothing for this miserable child.

"I talk to my big chief," he said. "Purty-soon come back."

"You'd better get him if you can," George A. said. "I heard Dan Jones tell how they offered him a two-year-old child, and after they had bargained a while, and he didn't want to meet their price, the Indian became angry, grasped the child by the feet and in an instant had dashed its brains out against the wagon wheel, and threw the body at him. 'Take him for nothing, then!' he said. If you have shown an interest and started to bargain, you'd better pay what they ask."

Lee gave a rifle, some powder, lead, and caps, and the Indian untied the child, who realized all the time that he was being bargained for and ran at once to clutch his new father around the legs.

Lee squatted on his heels, pushed back the mat of hair and looked into the black eyes. "You Lemuel," he said, pointing to the boy and saying again, "You, Lemuel. Me," pointing to himself, "Father Lee." He repeated the names again, pointing. "Lemuel. Father Lee."

At the tent the child shrank from going in to face the women, so Lee stopped him just outside, and motioned for him to stay there — stand still.

"Look, you girls, give me a hand," he said coming in. "I've brought home about the sorriest little bit of humanity you ever saw. But I'm sure he's overrun with lice. One of you hand me the scissors, and look around for something to put on him, and the other get the little tub and some warm water."

At sight of the scissors, the child began to tremble, but Lee spoke to him reassuringly and holding his head steady, began to cut. It wasn't exactly an expert haircut, but soon nearly all the hair was off, and lying on the ground. In another instant the rags that were fastened on one shoulder were off, too, and hair and rags in a quick wad put under the black tub where Polly had the wash water ready for morning.

Then inside the tent and beside the small heater, he soaped the shaven head, and with a washcloth scrubbed the skinny little body. Finally dried and wrapped in a piece of blanket, the child was ready to drink a bowl of hot gruel. But what to dress him in?

"It wouldn't take long to make him something," Lavina said, "but there's not a thing that I can think of to put on him now."

"He'd be lost in any of your clothes, and I can't imagine giving him anything of mine," said Polly.

Looking around, Lee saw a fifty-pound mush sack that was almost empty. He poured its contents into a pan, turned it wrong side out, shook it hard until the meal was out of it.

"Now you watch me make him a shirt," he said. Folding the sack, he cut off the two sewed corners, and then cut an arc out of the middle fold. One quick pull and the child's head was through the center hole, a little maneuvering and his hands were through the sides, so that he stood like an awkward, cut-out paper doll.

Polly and Lavina looked at each other and smiled. Lee kept saying, "Good, *bueno*," but he didn't feel quite satisfied either until he had tied a short piece of heavy cord around the waist. Now clean and warm and fed, the child rolled up in an old quilt and lay on the ground near the stove. By morning they had made him a shirt from the bottom of an old heavy work shirt and a pair of pants from the little-worn backs of a pair of Lee's pants. Later a buckskin jacket protected him from the cold. They enjoyed seeing him eat; they taught him the names of the utensils about the house. Soon he became a sort of pet for them, responding remarkably to their kindness and food.

For two weeks the men worked furiously, for there was so much to be done and the weather was unusually mild and clear. They built the road to the timber; they organized the cutting and hauling so that they would not get in each other's way on the road. By the end of January they estimated fifteen hundred logs and as many poles hauled out. They surveyed a field which was to be divided into five-acre plots for each family, enough for vines, potatoes, and garden stuff. In the big field each should have ten acres more.

On February 2, they held a worshipping service at which the sacrament was blessed and passed to all in the audience, and John D. Lee was called to speak. He spoke of his weakness of sometimes losing his temper and speaking on an impulse harsh words that he later regretted. He hoped that this brethren would forgive him wherein he had erred or hurt their feelings, for he had only one desire and that was to do right and to help build up the kingdom. Altogether, it was a sort of confession and a different attitude than he had often assumed.

At the end of the afternoon session, names were drawn from a hat by Bishop Groves, each man taking a lot in the fort as his name was called out, and the clerk making a record of each. The new city was first named Louisa, in honor of Louisa Beaman, the first woman to enter into the order of celestial marriage in this dispensation, but it was later changed by Brother Brigham to Parowan, to correspond with the Indian name.

The mild weather of early February was deceptive, for on the thirteenth snow fell again, and for the next two weeks it was extremely cold, so cold that practically all their potatoes were frozen.

Lee's journal ended abruptly on March 1, with the notation that the records would be kept by James Lewis, whom he himself had nominated earlier for that office. Through late February he had worked diligently to get out logs for his home, for Lavina would soon be delivered of her child. The wife of Brother Whitney, the blacksmith, had given birth to her son on March 1, while the whole company was still in tents and wagons and the weather was bitter cold. He must have better protection for Lavina.

It was a matter of some pride with him that his home be well built. It was of hewn logs, notched carefully to fit so that there would be very little mudding to do between. The roof was of aspen poles covered with rushes and sod, the little foot stove set up and burning before the fireplace was done. The sawmill was not yet in operation, but he had brought a false bottom in each of his wagons, extra lumber boards under the flour and grain. Of these he made a solid door, and the window had six panes of glass.

The bed posts were smooth poles sawed off even with the eaves, two beds with aisle between them. Across these poles he braced others on which he put lumber to form a half-attic over the beds, a place for storage, and a warm corner where little Lemuel would sleep. With curtains across the bottom, the little new babies would be sheltered from drafts.

Lavina's son, John David, named for her husband and her brother who had died at Summer Quarters, was born March 19, 1851. On April 24 following, Polly's daughter was born. They named her Elizabeth for both her grandmothers.

In early May President Young, along with "many others" arrived at Fort Louisa for a week's visit. In the census which he ordered to be taken, the Lee family were listed as:

John D. Lee	37	Farmer
Mary	33	
Lavina	15	
Lemuel	12	
John D.	9	
Sarah	3	

Since plural marriage had not been announced, this was made to look as if there were but one wife and her children. Correctly done, it would have read:

John D. Lee	37	Farmer
Mary V. (Polly)	33	
Lavina	30	
Lemuel	12	(Indian child)
John David	9	weeks
Sarah	3	weeks

Polly's daughter, not yet christened, later records call Elizabeth.

When Brigham Young returned on May 16, thirty men went with him, some to get their families and others to remain in the north. John D. Lee was not with the group, for he wanted to stay until his home was completely finished and the crops all in. He must be assured of food for the winter.

He left on June 4, taking the wagons and oxen and his riding horse, and leaving the buggy and horse team here. He felt that Polly and Lavina were among kind friends, their babies were both well, Lemuel would care for the chores about the place. He himself must get his families together, since this was now to be his home. He felt that God's protecting care would be over the family of one whose first desire was to do His will.

1851-1854
New Frontiers

John D. Lee reached Salt Lake City on July 1, in time to profit by the summer emigration to the gold fields. Now he would trade for money or for items he could take with him to his new home or exchange with local citizens. Horses, oxen, or cattle were better than cash, and the weary or footsore could soon be restored by plenty of feed. His whole summer plan was to sell his farm, his half-finished house, and such items as he could not transport.

In the general conference on October 6, 1851, his name was among those on the list which was read from the stand for appointments to new missions. After an eloquent plea for settlers to volunteer to go south, George A. Smith proposed that John D. Lee establish a settlement at the junction of the Rio Virgin and Santa Clara, where grapes, cotton, figs, and dates could be raised. Anson Call who was not satisfied at Parowan, was asked to spearhead another colony in Sanpete County.

Lee was pleased at this public recognition. To be singled out as the father of a new community seemed an honor worthy of his abilities. He urged his neighbors and friends to join his party, but most of them were getting so well established that they were reluctant to leave the city.

Within a few days he was on his way, with a company of nineteen wagons. On October 26 the train was overtaken by President Young and his party en route to Fillmore to lay out a city and start building the state capitol there. This idea of placing the seat of government in the geographical center of the state pleased Lee very much. Now he would not be so isolated, he told himself, but actually much nearer the legislature than his friends in the north.

When he gave the parting hand to his adopted father, he thought that he would go at once to the site of his new venture. But he had not taken other plans into account. Brother George A. Smith had gone south ahead of him with orders to begin a town near the deposits of iron and coal, for the development of the iron industry would be important to the whole church. Brother Smith, with thirty-five men and Henry Lunt as their leader, was already on the site.

To complicate matters further, William H. Dame had been sent back in the other direction to Paragonah (the Indian name for Red Creek) to build a settlement there. He had twenty men with him, and their calling was to operate a tannery for all the southern section, and to produce leather for export north.

As soon as he arrived at Parowan, Lee wrote that "We made the journey in three weeks to the day, without the loss of a single animal." Considering that his company had stopped to do some important road work on the way and had still made the trip in less than half the time it took the year before, he had some right to boast. But he had brought with him only seventeen men, expecting that some of those already in the south would join him. His letter closed in a vein quite characteristic of him:

> I am now as I always have been in your hands and in the hands of the Lord, ready according to the best of my skill and abilities to do for the best. I have no hesitance in saying that I believe that I shall be able to accomplish whatever you in your wisdom may require at my hands, the God in whom I trust being my helper. . . I once was a proud spirited man — but shame, experience and reproach has softened my feathers. Should you feel to send me a word of instruction, it will be gratiously and cordially received. With feelings of reverence, I subscribe myself Your son and brother in the seal of the Covenant forever
>
> JOHN D. LEE

But mails were slow and this letter of November 5 was evidently set aside for some time before it was answered. In the meantime, Lee had rallied thirty-one able-bodied men who were ready to join him in a move south. The people of Parowan were holding a farewell party for them. The dinner was over and the dance in full swing when someone called out, "The mail is in!" Instantly all were eager for news from headquarters. Yes, there was the letter to John D. Lee from Brigham Young. Right in the midst of the company he opened it, but as he started to read, his face took on an expression of chagrin and disappointment. He had been ordered not to go on south this season, but to remain and strengthen the colony at Parowan.

It was a bitter pill, but Lee took it, reading the letter aloud to the company. He explained that since the president, through his Divine knowledge, was certainly wiser than he, there must be a reason unknown to them why the move this fall would not be safe. Here at Parowan there were houses empty, the fort was enclosed, and the gates hung. With so many very young children in his family, no doubt it would be safer to stay.

When Lee came south this time, he brought with him an additional wife, Sarah Caroline Williams, the girl he had baptized in Tennessee when she was ten years old, the same girl who at the age of fourteen had demanded admittance into his family while they were still at Nauvoo. Because she was so young at the time, she had received the sealing ordinance but had never been his wife, having gone to live with her aunt, Marcia Allen. Lee's journal entry of December 2, 1846, said that they had moved to the settlements in Missouri and "it was not, however, without feelings of sorrow that she left and went away, notwithstanding Sister Allen promised to be a mother to her and see that she had a good home."

On two other occasions Lee mentions that he had received word of her, but she did not cross the plains in his company; in fact, her name is not listed in the same year that Marcia Allen came across. Somewhere, in the meantime, she had married a man named Thompson and borne a son whom she named James. Now, at the age of twenty-one, she had asked to come back.

Lee accepted her and her boy, of whom he became very fond, always referring to him as "my stepson, James Thompson."

By the middle of January with his families all settled and comfortable, Lee decided that he should be busy with affairs of the kingdom. The mills were closed, the canyons blocked with snow. "Under these conditions," he wrote to the editor of the *Deseret News*, "I felt justified to spend a few days exploring the country, believing that the time thus occupied would be more conducive to the spread of the cause of Zion in the mountains than to sit by the fireside, reading, or otherwise passing off the time."

The plain fact was that he was bored with inactivity and tired of being cooped up in crowded, small cabins, with so many women and children. Then, too, he wanted to see this land below the rim of the basin and perhaps locate in advance the site for his new settlement. Some of the young men of the fort, also eager for activity and adventure, wanted to go. Among them were John Steele, Chapman Duncan, Charles Y. Webb, Lorenzo and William Barton, J. and Miles Anderson, B. Jones, Zadoc Judd, R. H. Gillespie (a Scotch brother), and J. H. Dunton.

They left on January 27 with four wagons, thirteen horses, and provisions for fifteen days. They made Lee their captain and traveled south to the Virgin River, keeping a careful log of distances traveled, the nature of the land and the streams. When he stood in the warm southern valley in February and found the grass growing in the scrub brush and the cottonwoods bursting into leaf, he wrote that "it was like a fire shut in my bones."

Back in Parowan in late February they all cooperated to "pitch a crop," working together on the big field and leaving the garden spots largely to the women.

During March the Piede Indians came into the area and drove off some of the cattle. In the pursuit which followed, two natives were killed. There might have been some serious trouble had not Chief Walker and his band arrived from the north. Walker had pledged his friendship to Brigham Young and the Mormons and had received so many favors and gifts that he was willing now to help discipline the Piedes. These bands he held in scorn, anyway. Sometimes he raided them and stole their children; sometimes when the winter was long and cold, he purchased little girls, giving a pony or an ox to the band for two or three. The white people too were afraid of Walker and his brother Sanpitch, keeping close watch upon their own young ones when the Indians were camped near.

Several other people of Parowan purchased Indian children about this time. John L. Smith paid wheat and beef for a little girl, Janet. Christopher J. Arthur bought a young boy, Samuel, a bright, willing child who became a constant companion to Arthur's son, who was about his age.

Many legends came to us of the traffic in Indian children. One tells how Ann Chatterly MacFarlane, a bride of a few months, was sewing carpet rags one day when an Indian mother burst into the house, thrust an eighteen-months-old baby boy at her, and fled in mortal terror out the back door. Knowing that the mother must be closely pursued, and at a loss herself as to where she could hide the child, Ann picked up her ample petticoats and put him underneath, motioning at the same time with her finger on her lips and a soft "Sh-sh-sh-."

She stood, holding her apron full of cut carpet rags before her when three young braves broke into the room. One spoke some English.

"Where papoose?" he asked. "Papoose here. Show where."

"No sabe," Ann looked him straight in the eye and shook her head.

Instantly one was on his knees under the bed, while another lifted the lid of the trunk. The half attic over the bed, the bottom of the cupboard, the wood box beside the stove all were searched, while Ann stood calmly or moved a few steps to keep out of their way. She could feel the baby's two arms tight around her leg as, quiet as a quail, he waited out his fate.

Soon the leader began to talk in a loud, angry tone and to brandish his club. Still Ann did not flinch, but walking to the back door, pointed to the willows along the creek, in the direction opposite to the one in which the mother had gone.

Not until the next night, after the Walker band had moved on, did the Indian mother return for her baby.

As midwinter had been the proper time to explore the southern country, so June was right to examine the mountain timberland. The crops were doing well, the grain would not be ready for harvest until mid-July. This time Bishop John L. Smith headed the expedition and

James Lewis kept the records, while John D. Lee and John Steele acted as pathbreakers, guiding the group up the canyons to Panguitch Lake, over the divide, and along Long Valley. They made, as usual, a careful record of distances and a description of the general terrain.

It was on trips like this that Lee was at his best, for he was a superb frontiersman, always taking time to climb to the highest point and get a perspective of mountain and valley and stream. Here he felt that he was exercising his powers and using his skills to the best advantage. In a letter to Brigham Young written on March 17, 1852, he said:

> . . . Brother Brigham Young, I am a thousand times obliged to you for sending me to Iron County, not that I wanted to be away from you and the Council, but that it has placed me in circumstances where of necessity I had to rub up my talent. . .
> I have waded through trouble and passed through dark and try-ing hours and through experiences I have learned patience, and many who should have been my friends in those days would gladly have put their feet upon my neck. But your words and Bro. H. C. Kimball's in particular afforded me more comfort than every other balm on earth. . .
> Then I had zeal but not according to knowledge, a desire to do good, but lacked patience and knew not how to bear with people and would gain their ill will by my own folly. . .

This seems to refer to his difficulties at Summer Quarters, and also perhaps to the contentions that grew out of the "scalp hunt." It is, for all its wordiness, quite a perceptive analysis of his own character and temperament, and the reference to the prophecy made by Heber C. Kimball shows how completely he trusted its fulfillment. In the same letter he continued:

> I believe that I have the full and entire confidence of the brethren here and at Cedar City, Presidents and all, and I know that they have my prayers and faith. When I preach to them my tongue is unloosed, and I enjoy the liberty of the Spirit. . .
> I have no fault to find with any person here. . .

So far as his white brethren were concerned, then, Lee was at peace. As for the Indians, he remembered the words of Brigham Young, as he discussed them on May 12, 1849: "This present race of Indians will never be converted," he said. "It mattereth not whether they kill one another off or somebody else do it, & as for our sending Missionarys among them to convert them, it is of no use. . ."

Early in August, an unfortunate incident occurred at Parowan,

which Lee reported in detail to President Young under date of
August 7, 1852. The brother of Chief Ow-wan-nop came into the Lee
home where Aggatha was alone and became very demanding and
saucy. When she ordered him to leave, he struck her across the head
with a board, breaking the skin so that the blood ran down her face.
She struggled with him until William Barton, hearing the noise, came
to her rescue.

The whole camp was much concerned by this, and President John
L. Smith, John Steele, and Henry Lunt met with the chief at the Lee
home, and made him understand that his brother must be punished
for this offense. Further than that, the punishment must be given by
the Indians, not the white men. The chief agreed, and the tribe
gathered. The culprit was to be stripped to his waist, tied to the
liberty pole, and given forty lashes. The chief himself was to use the
rawhide lasso.

By the time thirty-eight of the prescribed forty lashes had been
given, all the spectators cried out against any more, for the chief
grew more angry and fierce with each blow and said with a fiendish
voice, "You will not learn. This will teach you."

After the culprit was freed and lying on the ground half-senseless
with pain, the others gathered to smoke the pipe of peace. The chief
took charge, bidding them all sit in a circle, the white men at equal
distance from each other, an Indian between. When all was arranged
to his satisfaction, he stuffed some toquapp (wild tobacco) into the
pipe, pressing it down firmly with a dark forefinger. Then he deftly
lifted a red coal from the edge of the fire and placed it on top. When
the smoke began to curl upward, he drew himself to his full height
and lifted the pipe above him at arm's length, offering the first smoke
to Shanob (God) and calling upon Him to witness the pact of friendship that was being made. Then seating himself again, he slowly took
three long draws at the pipe, exhaling with satisfaction each time.
Very deliberately he passed the pipe to John L. Smith, who sat at his
right.

If Brother Smith hesitated just a little before he put it into his
mouth, he might well be excused, for the end of the stem had been
wrapped with a narrow band of tanned skin around and around to
form a knob thicker than a man's thumb and filthy with the accumu-
lations of many years and hundreds of Indian mouths. It was their way
to move with slow deliberation in this ceremony, but the white man
waited almost too long before he swallowed hard, and proceeded to
take his three smokes with long, deep sighs of what he hoped would
sound like satisfaction. So it moved slowly until every one in the circle
had his turn and the pipe was back in the hands of the chief. It would

not be good luck for him to smoke a second time, so he turned the bowl over and tapped it, emptying the ashes onto the ground.

The white men now brought bread and meat for the natives to take home, and all congratulated themselves that the incident would establish friendly relations. The Indian deserved to be whipped, and his own people did the whipping. Simple people like these must be trained by rewards and punishments, much as one must train a dog.

Then there came a day when a white man struck an Indian over the head with the butt of a gun. The chief came, demanding that the offender be whipped, and so numerous were the Indians that the settlers accepted the suggestion. Two years later, on December 14, 1854, Thomas D. Brown wrote:

> Brother Lee having returned, we were called early to decide on L. Harris' offense. Many Indians present. It was agreed that L. Harris receive 25 lashes for hurting Indian Joseph, and 5 more for whipping an Indian boy Lemuel. Jas Powell was appointed to whip him; this satisfied the Indians and the chains were taken off. They have mostly gone to see the whipping.

The people in the southern settlements were always interested to read of developments in Salt Lake City; the establishment in 1852 of a territorial library in the council house, with five thousand dollars appropriated by Congress for books which Representative Bernheisel might select, filled them with pride. They also were glad to read of the public announcement of plural marriage. Though it had been practiced openly since the arrival in the valley, it had not been announced to the world as a basic tenet of the faith. Now that Orson Pratt had read it in the general conference and spoken in its defense, it could be urged as a requirement of all who should be given responsible positions. With the publication of *The Seer,* word would go out to all the world.

In April of this same year, the Deseret Iron Company was organized in England, with local saints there contributing. This was a great encouragement to the sixty-nine families at Cedar City, most of them from England and Wales, who were trying to manufacture iron.

All the letters from the southern settlements spoke of the severity of this winter of 1852 and 53. The first snow came in October, and from that time until spring they had little respite. They were even menaced by wolf packs from the mountains; for that and other reasons they appreciated the protection of their fort.

At Cedar City the colonists had an especially difficult time. Their hopes of a great iron manufacturing industry here had resulted in disappointment; for all the promise they had only a few utensils to show. On September 3 there came a devastating flood which ruined their machinery and covered much of the village with rocks and debris. Those trusting saints who had taken the tires from their wagons to be melted down for machinery now had no wagons. The covered wagonboxes, put upon stone supports might serve as bedrooms, but the tireless wheels were stored and the useless running gears stood, cumbersome and in the way. Small wonder that five wagons of discouraged settlers joined the California emigration.

The summer of 1853 saw a great deal of travel through the settlements, and it is from some of these chance visitors that we get our clearest picture of them. On the first of August E. F. Beale, superintendent of Indian affairs in California, arrived at Paragonah. His recorder, Gwinn Harris Heap, wrote of the area:

Paragoona . . . contains about thirty houses, which, although built of adobes present a neat and comfortable appearance. The adobes are . . . made of pink-colored clay. The houses are built to form a quadrangle, the spaces between them being protected by a strong stockade of pine pickets. Outside the village is an area of fifty acres inclosed within a single fence. . . It is called The Field, and a stream from the Wahsatch Mountains irrigates it, after supplying the town with water. . .

We . . . rode to Parawan over an excellent wagon road, made and kept in repair, and bridged in many places, by the Mormons. We passed, at a mile to our left, a large grist and saw mill worked by water power. . . At all the crossroads were finger-posts, and mile-stones measured the distance.

Parowan is situated at the base of the mountains, and contains about one hundred houses, built in a square, and facing inwards. In their rear, and outside of the town, are vegetable gardens, each dwelling having a lot running back about one hundred yards. . . The houses are ornamented in front with small flower-gardens, which are fenced off the square, and shaded with trees.

The Field covers about four hundred acres, and was in a high state of cultivation, the wheat and corn being as fine as any that we had seen in the states. . .

Cedar City is a place of more importance than either Parawan or Paragoona, but it is built on a similar plan. . . The inhabitants are principally foreigners, and mostly Englishmen from the coal districts of Great Britain. . .

The kind reception that we received from the inhabitants of these settlements strongly contrasted with what we had been lead to anticipate from the reports of Mexicans and Indians whom we had met on the road.

He spoke of the number of Indian children who lived in the settlements, and the fact that they were not slaves, but members of the family, who called their foster parents "mother" and "father."

Another who wrote in detail of his trip over this road was Dr. Thomas Flint. He passed in October, and stopped at Parowan while the blacksmith, Mr. Whitney, repaired his wagons. From his account we get a summary of the companies on the road. He reached his destination with more than two thousand cattle and sheep. Traveling ahead of him most of the time was the Hollister train of eleven wagons, one hundred and fifty-four cattle and four thousand sheep. Still ahead was the Frazier train, though he did not give statistics, and behind were the White & Viles train and another group headed by Judge Burdick.

On February 6, 1854, Colonel John C. Fremont arrived in Parowan with a company of nine white men and twelve Delaware Indians, all nearly starved to death. The settlers were so generous to him that thereafter Colonel Fremont never would say an unkind word about the Mormons, no matter how his friends might ridicule them.

In April, 1854, President Young sent twenty-three young men south as missionaries to the Indians. Garland Hurt, the Indian agent, wrote to Washington that these boys "embrace a class of rude and lawless young men, such as might be regarded as a curse to any civilized community."

They were indeed young men, with twelve of them under thirty and the oldest of the group forty-six. Five were still in their teens; at least eight were unmarried. They were rude, perhaps; wild in the sense that they were good horsemen; men who knew the out-of-doors and who were hardy and resourceful. Most of all, they were so devoted to the church that they would accept this assignment. For the mission to which they were called, they were well prepared.

Their first duty was to raise food, not only to supply themselves but to share with the Indians. They had come in ten wagons with some extra horses and cattle, with tools and seed. They were to move south to the last settlement and there set up their headquarters. John D. Lee had in use all the tillable land on Ash Creek, so they pulled on some four miles to the northwest and selected a likely site on higher ground. At once they began clearing the land and building the main ditch. Fencing could come after the seed was in the ground; the dam could be put in when there was a channel prepared to carry the water.

They had organized when they left Salt Lake City, with Rufus C. Allen, president, David Lewis, first lieutenant, Samuel F. Atwood, second lieutenant, and Thomas D. Brown, clerk and recorder.

They had met some Indians en route, paid toll for passing over the Indian lands, and had seen the native runners lope through the brush

to notify their friends of this wagon train. They rested and visited at
the settlements, especially at Parowan, where they were impressed
with the cleanliness of the place and the general thrift and optimism
of the settlers. Nowhere else were folks so hospitable and generous to
them, so Christian in spirit.

Their experiences are preserved through the pen of the recorder,
Thomas D. Brown, lately of London, England. That he had some
education is shown by his occasional use of a Latin phrase, his vivid
description of the land, and his occasional verse. He was one among
them who was not prepared for the rigors of frontier life, who could
not use a grubbing hoe very effectively and did not like to wash out
his sox and underwear. But he did keep an accurate and vivid record.

On May 19 a horseman came to tell the missionaries that President
Young had arrived at the home of John D. Lee at Ash Creek. Meeting
would be held there at early candlelight in a clearing prepared for
that purpose. Since the president traveled with a group of "82 men, 14
women, and 5 children, traveling in 34 carriages and with 95 horses,"
there would be many more visitors than missionaries in the audience.

John D. Lee sat with the authorities facing the audience who were
seated on logs or rocks or squatted on the ground. From this position
he could study the faces in the firelight, for some of these men, he felt
sure, would remain permanently in the south.

Some of them he had known since his entry into the church. There
was Robert Ritchie, who had lived through the violent times in
Missouri and who had befriended him after he was driven from Far
West. There was David Lewis, who had walked away unscathed from
the massacre at Haun's Mill, a six-foot-one giant who weighed two
hundred pounds and was solid muscle. He had not changed much in
the last ten years, Lee thought. His skin was still clear, his blue eyes
steady and alert, his whole bearing full of vitality and moral fortitude.
He had always insisted that he did not run from the blacksmith shop
where most of the people were mortally wounded and a few waited in
mortal terror of the death which soon came. He walked out at an even
gait and was not hit, though the bullets fell thick around him as hail,
and five shots went through his clothes, three through his pantaloons
and two through his coat. Lee could not know that after he had his
call to this mission David Lewis wrote the account of the massacre at
Haun's Hill in all its horrible detail; nor could he foresee that in just
fifteen months he would be buried at Parowan. Tonight he stood out
in the group as a natural born leader and a man superior among his
fellowmen.

Another who caught his attention was a lanky boy, six-feet-two, Lee
would guess, as he folded his long legs and sat down. With hair and

eyes as black as any Indian's, this lad carried himself with an easy, confident air as if he had never been placed in a situation he could not master, as though he had no fear of God, man, nor devil. Lee had to remember a while to place him, he had grown so out of all reason. Then he knew. Thales Haskell, who lived with his mother in the home of his sister Irene and her husband, Francis Pomeroy. Pomeroy could speak Spanish, so had to do all the trading for the authorities in Salt Lake when the Mexican train came in; Charles C. Rich had taken him along to make the purchase of the ranch at San Bernardino. At Winter Quarters they had lived across the street from the store in one of the better cabins; Pomeroy had come into the Valley with the Pioneers, and his family had followed with Brother Pratt. No doubt that was the reason Thales had been called with this group. Lee did not know that the boy had already been on two long expeditions chasing Indian thieves in the north and that he belonged to the mounted division of the Nauvoo Legion.

Back in the shadows was Jacob Hamblin, already dubbed by the historian as "a quiet man" for he had settled disputes among the brethren on the road and since their arrival. Lee could not guess, seeing him there in the twilight, how closely their lives would be bound together in the future.

Lorenzo Roundy he had known at Nauvoo and Winter Quarters, and Elnathan Eldridge, and John Lott, though only a boy at the time, had been a part of the military group that defended Nauvoo.

But the one of whom he was most suspicious was the historian, Thomas D. Brown. He was older than most of them, well into his middle forties, a Scotchman who seemed to see things with a different eye than most. He had not gone through the persecutions in Missouri and Nauvoo; he had never seen the Prophet or known firsthand the magnetism of his personality. "That man will apostatize," Lee said in his heart that night, even before the discussion began. Later he repeated the statement to some of his friends, and they asked him "Do you say that in the name of the Lord as a prophecy?" "I do," Lee answered.

But now Brother Brigham was telling them that they should organize themselves for more efficiency. Instantly someone called out, "I nominate John D. Lee." "I second it," another said quickly.

Now it was this same Thomas D. Brown who got to his feet.

"If it is not out of place," he said, "I would like to state that is the opinion of the missionaries and my own feelings that we would prefer another president to Brother Lee. I would nominate Patriarch Elisha H. Groves."

President Young was a little taken back. "What do you say, Brother Allen?" he asked, turning to the youthful president.

"The feeling of the company is not to have Brother Lee as president," he answered firmly. "They would prefer to keep their present organization." The undercurrent of "yes," "that's right," made it evident that he expressed their unanimous opinion.

"Keep your present organization then," Brigham Young told them. "Let John D. Lee preside over this settlement and the Stake when there shall be enough people to form a stake."

He then went on to instruct the missionaries in their duties, outlining a course of action somewhat different from the one he had taken at Summer Quarters and during the first year in Salt Lake City. He told the missionaries that:

> You are sent not to farm, to build nice houses and fence fine fields, not to help white men, but to save red ones. Learn their language, and this you can do more effectively by living among them as well as by writing out a list of words. Go with them where they go. Live with them, and when they rest let them live with you; feed them, clothe them, and teach them as you can, and being thus with them all the time, you will soon be able to teach them in their own language. They are our brethren; we must seek after them, commit their language, get their understanding, and when they go off in parties you go with them.

John D. Lee, listening, did not feel hurt that he was not in charge of the Indian Mission now, for he did intend to build nice houses and fence and maintain a fine farm and collect flocks and herds about him that he might sit under his own vine and fig tree according to his earlier promises.

Parley P. Pratt was even more explicit in his instructions. He had been the first missionary to the Indians, having been sent out by the Prophet himself. Now he admonished the young men before him to:

> Give them a shirt, pants, and petticoats. Say not only "be ye fed and clothed." Language neither feeds their stomachs nor covers their nakedness, nor can words convince them of your friendship. Feed, clothe, and instruct them, and in a year they will more than repay you for your outlay. . . Teach them habits of cleanliness and industry "and many generations shall not pass away until they shall become a white and delightsome people. Win their hearts, their affections; teach them, baptize them, wash, cleanse, and clothe them. I should always have clean garments ready and clothe every one I should baptize. . .

This wrestling, jumping and gamboling in their presence sets them a bad example, of idleness. Get their good will by manifesting yours. . .

Lee listening remembered the whipping incidents, still firm in his belief that there are some offenses that should be punished, still feeling that as you punish a dog for what you do not want it to do and reward it when it obeys your commands, so you might have to use this practice in dealing with these savage people. President Brigham and Brother Parley had not seen as much of these Indians as he had. Treat them kindly, deal justly with them, but be firm in correcting any serious misconduct — that was his theory.

President Young the next day went up on the broad tableland and selected a site for the real Fort Harmony and marked it off two hundred feet square with gates to the north and south and a well or cistern in the center. Detailed plans would come later, he said, but for now they were to build a strong adobe wall on the two sides which would serve as the back wall of the homes. There could be some two-story places also, with the family bedrooms upstairs. Since they were quite comfortable where they were for this season, the work at the new fort could go on during the slack season in farming, but they should push it with all the speed they could without neglecting the crops.

Late in the afternoon as Lee rode with the president, Heber C. Kimball and others over the broad flat and from an elevation looked back at the jutting red bluffs glowing in the late sun, he said to himself, "This is my home, my permanent home of which I was told soon after I had joined the Church. How I hated to leave my place at Far West! Then at Nauvoo I hoped I had found it. Never again until I reached Cottonwood did I have a feeling that I could put down roots. But now I know. This is Home."

1854-1856
Sow the Wind

After the return of Brigham Young and his company, Lee devoted his time to the building of the large, new fort and the breaking up of land for crops. His holdings on Ash Creek he would leave for the Indians. All through the summer he labored, directing the group, moving a family at a time as the rooms were finished, until by February, 1855 all the inhabitants were living at the new site. That did not mean that the fort was finished, but it did mean that they were where they could work more effectively. More than a year later, in 1856, they were still trying to rally all hands to complete some of the public works, the end walls and gates, the guard house, the cistern in the center of the square, and the privies just outside.

Since Lee was not assigned as a missionary to the Indians, he assumed little responsibility toward them except as they came to trade or beg. He made no special effort to call them to meetings or preach to them or baptize them.

The missionaries, on the other hand, took their assignment very seriously. They must learn to communicate with these savage people, must gain their confidence and good will, must help them to distinguish between the Mormons and the "Mericats." The Mormons were their friends, come to live among them and help them, while the Mericats only traveled through with big herds of cattle eating off the grass. The Mericats would shoot at Indians just to see them jump.

The missionary group was somewhat divided in their loyalty. In the first place, they were ordered to plow and plant that they might have food both for themselves and their Indian friends; in the second, they were told to go and live among the natives. They tried diligently to do both. They worked desperately to get their crops in the ground and then they set out to do missionary work.

One group went as far south as Las Vegas to explore the country and to establish friendly relations with the tribes there; another remained on the Tonaquint, or Santa Clara Creek. Here they learned some Indian words and tried to teach the natives a few English names. They prayed and preached and sang, though they realized that their audience had little comprehension of their message other than a general idea that these men were their friends (heap tickaboo), and that they had come to help them raise much wheat and many cattle, so that they would not be hungry when the cold moons came.

Some natives were baptized, and each received a new shirt as he came up out of the water, until soon the rite became popular, some even asking that it be repeated so that they might get another shirt. The recorder left many vivid accounts of these natives as they were upon their first meeting with the white man. One at least deserves to be included:

> We went over to their Wickeups after our supper and found their women grinding seeds by the light of the moon, and boiling a large potful of pottage — in a conical dish made from clay and sand, thin and hard. This mess seemed of a darkish grey color with like chunks of bacon in it. We tasted the flour which the women were making from the seeds of grass — by rubbing them between two rocks. It tasted much like buckwheat flour or bean meal. What we fancied to be pieces of bacon, I have been told were bunches of matted ants. One of the brethren tasted this food and said, these clusters tasted very oily but knew not the cause; this porridge the female stirred with a large spoon or ladle, like the water gourds of the states made from the horn of a mountain sheep; with this the mess was divided on wicker baskets, flat, in the shape of wood turned dishes, about 1 quart to each — the elders served first — this was soon cleaned out by bending the forefinger of the right hand inwards around the point of the thumb for a spoon — the same dish handed back and filled and passed around. They supped this up greedily, and with the head of a roasted porcupine, brains and bones, added to an entire roasted sand lark, seemed, added to what we gave them — to about satisfy. Then like hogs with little or no covering they huddled together in the sand. Oh! how Ephriam has fallen!
>
> After prayer, we too were soon asleep — on our buffalo robes — not far from our friends.

After a few days, all the party returned to Harmony except Jacob Hamblin and William Henefer, who were to remain and continue the work. Everywhere they saw squalor and filth and barbarism. They witnessed a wedding in which the braves fought for a young squaw until they almost tore her apart literally, each trying to drag her to his own tepee. They saw the old and sick abandoned. They saw children sold into slavery to Sanpitch, brother of Chief Walker.

The recorder also told in detail of the antics of the Indian medicine man in curing the sick, and of their customs of healing one by causing another to suffer. For example, when Chief Walker, the Hawk of the Mountains, became ill, he ordered two Piede children killed in order to alleviate his pain. At his death in mid-January 1855, his tribe killed two Pah-ute squaws, three children, and twenty horses to accompany him to the Happy Hunting Ground, and buried a twelve-year-old boy in the same mound with him to act as special guide and valet to the old chief.

The missionaries became much discouraged with their inability to change any of these basic customs. Then when they returned to Harmony and found most of their crop dead for lack of water, they felt that they must leave to earn foodstuffs. Some stopped in Parowan and found work, others returned to the north to winter with their families, and only four or five waited out the winter in the Santa Clara area. These built a number of small cabins from the cottonwood poles that grew along the creek bottom, covering them with willows and dirt. The next year they enclosed the cabins in a rock wall about nine feet high, two feet thick, and a hundred and twenty feet square. To this they brought the first families south in early 1856.

This was to be a crucial year in southern Utah, even as it was in most of the territory. On January 1, five Indian agencies were formed in the territory, and John D. Lee was placed in charge of the one in the southern district, the Iron County agency. He was to receive a fixed salary of fifty dollars per month and was to represent the government in distributing tools, seeds, and supplies and helping the natives in their farming attempts. While not in competition with the missionaries, he did have now an extra power, for he was the "Indian Farmer" representing the Great White Father in Washington.

On January 4, 1856, the citizens of Washington County sent a petition signed by thirty-two men — the total male population — asking for an autonomous county government, with the county seat at Harmony. The petition was granted and the government set up on February 7, with John D. Lee as probate judge, clerk, and assessor.

The first business of the court was to try a case against Enos, an Indian, upon a complaint signed by Robert M. Dickson, who stated that Enos had killed and carried off two sheep and some flour. The sheriff, Charles W. Dalton, was ordered to take Enos into custody and to summon "twelve judicious men, residents of said county," to serve as jurors.

The court went through the legal procedures. The meeting was duly called to order by the crier, the case stated, and a defense provided for the Indian. The defendant claimed a jury, but objected to Rufus C. Allen's serving. After another had taken his place, the court proceeded to call the witnesses, two Indians, who both swore upon oath that Enos had committed the crime of which he was accused. The two attorneys each questioned the witnesses and tried to impress them with the need of giving true testimony.

Through it all, Enos sat expressionless and stolid, understanding enough of the proceedings to be concerned with what his punishment might be. The jury was finally delivered over to the bailiff with instructions to put them in a private room where they should have no conversation with anyone during their deliberations. The court had convened at 10 a.m., and the verdict was not brought in until 4 p.m. The jury found the accused guilty and sentenced him to three months of hard labor, during which time he was to wear a ball and chain.

The first divorce was issued within the first week. John Wardall and Sarah, his wife, had mutually appealed to the court for it and for a division of the property. After due consideration, the court decided that it would be to the best interests of all concerned to grant the divorce. The bill stipulated that the father should take the two older boys and the mother the two younger children, a girl and a boy. Then every item of the property was listed: bedding, utensils, stone jars, sacks, wash tubs, down to "1 tin cullinder, 1 sive & 2 Baskets." Following the division, the bill was granted "by which they are made free from each other; and they are at liberty to marry whomsoever they will as though there had been no Marriage contract previously ratified between them."

In 1854 President Young had talked to the people upon the law of consecration, and urged them out of loyalty to the church to deed all their property to it. Thomas D. Brown, himself not in sympathy with the principle, mentioned that "Consecration a bugbear," and the "people do not like it." Still he made out twelve deeds of transfer under the law of consecration on blanks provided by the church.

Now Lee began entering upon the pages of the county record similar deeds. Typical is that of one of the Indian missionaries, Richard Robinson and his wife Elizabeth, who "for & in consideration of the good will which we have to the Church of Jesus Christ of L.D. Saints, give & convey unto Brigham Young, Trustee in Trust for Said Church, his heirs & successor in office & assigns all our claims to the ownership of the following described property to wit: . . ." After which, they listed and evaluated the one underground room, corrals, horses, calves, sheep, swine, brewing apparatus on a small scale, one fouling piece, kitchen furniture & wearing apparel, totaling $855 in value.

Since fewer than a third of the members of the church ever signed such deeds, and since not one of those who did sign was actually required to give up any property, this whole practice was just another test of loyalty.

Thus, in early 1856, John D. Lee was presiding at the court sessions, exhorting his brethren to help with the public works, and managing his farm and cattle. At Santa Clara, the drought had caused the creek to dry up until the stream did not reach the fort, and some families had followed the water up to establish holdings on the site of Gunlock.

At Cedar City the people had experienced two serious setbacks in their work, so that the production of iron seemed as distant as it had ever been. There, too, the grasshoppers played such havoc with their crops that it looked as if they would face a tragic food shortage.

There had been some talk in the north of a general movement of reformation in the church, but the vigorous call to repentance, to cleansing and soul-searching which would lead to rebaptism and a renewal of covenants did not begin until mid-July. Actually it had been in action in the southern settlements several months earlier. For example, on April 26, Rachel Lee wrote in her minutes of the morning meeting of the blessing of four Indian children recently purchased. In the afternoon, they were visited by Isaac C. Haight, stake president, and his two counselors, John M. Higbee and Elias Morris. After a meeting in which several men confessed to slothfulness and neglect of duty, Isaac C. Haight baptized the following: Bishop W. R. Davies, Henry Barney, Amos G. Thornton, Elisha Groves, Rufus C. Allen, John D. Lee, William Young, Lorenzo W. Roundy and Charles W. Dalton.

These were confirmed in the evening meeting, and according to Rachel's account:

> . . . All those that ware Baptized spoke their feelings and resolution to be better men hensforth — When Bro. Roundy spoke he felt truly pentinent before the Lord and floods of tears Gushed from every Eye. I do here bare witness that never since Harmony has been Settled has there been such feelings of penitence and contrition and joy and thankfulness to God for his mercies and loving kindness toward us through all our Wickedness, and hardness of heart that have existed in this place one toward another. Yea every one Melted down in a flood tears with thankfull to thier God & Savour for giving us a chance before it was gone to late for us to repent, of our ways, &c
>
> Many of the brethren spoke and all rejoiced to gather. Prest Haight and council Rejoiced exceedingly and spoke thier satisfaction to see the true penitence of the Brthren in the course of the reformation and said that this was not a revival like had been sometimes of short duration but it would continue untill the deviding line should be drawn between the righteous and Wicked and the great struggle would commence between the two Kingdoms Benediction by Prest Haight ———

The home visits, the catechisms, and the baptisms on a large scale did not get under way until after midsummer, when additional material was sent out by the general authorities. Always, since the Nauvoo days, the sin of adultery had been considered second only to that of murder, and men who were convicted of corrupting the morals of the young women of Zion were apt to be seriously dealt with. There was much preaching of "blood atonement" and marital infidelity was one sin which might be so punished. In contrast, the men holding the priesthood were supposed to live the "celestial law" with regard to their relations with their wives, and never force their attentions upon any woman nor have sex relations with her except at her desire. Sometimes the instructions on this matter were very specific. Under this law, although a man might have more wives than one, his sex activity was supposed to be very much restricted. He certainly would not be fit to hold a high position in the eternal worlds if he could not control his carnal desires in this life.

Much has been written of the excesses of the Mormon Reformation, but in this field it is doubtful that there were more strict actions than there had been earlier or later. A case in point is the Braffit case in Parowan, which is recorded in the Iron County Court Minute Book B, page 8. This gives the minutes of a special session of the probate court held on July 19 and 20, 1854, in which George W. Braffit and his wife Sarah were brought into court and a grand jury indictment against them was read. The record did not include a copy of this, but the testimony of witnesses brought out evidence that one Lucien Woodworth had left his second wife, Margaret, in Parowan while he returned to Provo to get the remainder of his family and settle his affairs preparatory to his leaving for California. He had charged his friend Braffit to look after Margaret in his absence, to see that she did not want for food or fuel. He was evidently detained in the north longer than he had intended, and in his absence an attachment had sprung up between Margaret and her guardian.

Witnesses testified to this, and the boy who drove the wagon told how he had hauled Margaret Woodworth and her two children to Cedar City. He had accompanied Braffit and assisted in caring for the team, sitting in the seat with Braffit while the woman and children rode in the back under the wagon cover. Philip Klingensmith, bishop at Cedar City, then testified that Margaret Woodworth visited him at his home on the same night and asked if a woman was obliged to go to California against her will. She said that her husband wanted to go, but that she preferred to stay in the territory and raise her children among the saints. He told her that she was not obliged to go.

Now here was a fine point of conflict. The council was always against people leaving the territory unless they were sent, and from that point of view, the woman was to be commended. But here was Lucien Woodworth, who had always been a faithful man, a builder on the Nauvoo house, who had left his wife in the custody of a friend, and returned to find her alienated from him and wishing to marry another man — and, if current gossip were true, already violated by the man who should have protected her. Worse still, it seemed that Sarah Braffit had approved of this behavior and aided and abetted him in his schemes. She was older and her husband had no other wives, so she had assumed that she might assist him to gain his celestial glory by getting this young woman, of whom they both were very fond, to be his plural wife.

The strange thing about the procedure was that "the prisoners both plead Not Guilty, but said they had done what they had, and offered their lives to pay the debt, but should not take steps in the case. Wanted to go to Brigham, confess, and have their heads taken off." From this, it would seem that they assumed that to be the logical punishment. But the court insisted upon hearing the evidence and deliberating for two days before they brought in the verdict, which was that Sarah Braffit was found "not guilty."

The Judge then gave decision in the case of George W. Braffit as follows: — that the prisoner be imprisoned twenty years at hard labor and pay a fine of one thousand dollars. The Court then authorized the Sheriff to take all the property of the defendant into his possession to pay the fine, also to keep the prisoner in safe custody until he could be taken to Salt Lake City. . .

John D. Lee says that he took the prisoner into Salt Lake City himself, where after some persuasion he succeeded in securing a pardon for him from Brigham Young. Braffit secured work in the city and remained there, his wife joining him later.

No word was said regarding the guilt or innocence of Margaret, the idea being that women were weaker vessels, and that a man who really honored his priesthood would live above the wiles of any woman who could not legally become his wife. If Braffit and Margaret had waited until her husband's return and made their appeal to the proper authorities, this might have been settled amicably.

Several years earlier, in 1849, Lee recorded that he had presented the case of one John Holt who had been his convert in Tennessee, and who in the course of the long trip across the plains had courted a girl and taken her to wife without going through the proper procedure. With some little reluctance, Brother Brigham agreed to let the matter pass, provided the couple would now be legally married and conduct themselves as saints.

Likewise, a number of years after the Reformation was spent, Lee and Bishop Davies were called to go to Grafton and investigate a case where a married woman accused a married man, not her husband, of seducing her and trying to get her to leave her husband. Lee and the bishop talked privately with the woman, and then privately with the accused man. She said he was guilty; he insisted that he was not. So a bishop's court was held in which both were brought to testify before five men — the local bishop and his counsellors and the two visitors. The result was the same, with the man stoutly denying all accusations. There seemed nothing to do but excommunicate both from the church and let the matter rest.

But Lee did not like this. The man was a long-time associate and friend, and should be absolved if he were innocent. Lee went back again to the woman and:

> said to her that I feared that (she) had laid a plan to destroy an innocent man & that an act of that kind was nothing more or less than assenting to the shedding of innocent blood, which sin is worse than all the adulterrys that she could committ, but this she could not get forgiveness for in this world nor the world to come & how would she feel in the day of Judgement to meet a Man who through her falsehood, had been sacrificed & his Blood caused to flow. . .

She burst into tears and said that she had lied and asked forgiveness.

Mormon diaries give ample proof that sexual immorality was considered a serious crime, indeed, always punishable by excommunication from the church, but quickly forgiven if the people repented by making public confession and being rebaptized. For nonmembers of the church who got Mormon girls "into trouble," it was still more serious, especially if it involved more than one girl. Esaias Edwards told how his son-in-law wished to take a second wife but did not merit the approval of the authorities; so when the girl was found to be pregnant, she was given all his possessions to repay in part the injury she had sustained. This left the wife dependent upon her father for housing and support. When the young husband became involved with a second girl, he left the area in all haste, "knowing that his life would be forfeit."

Since this attitude extended from at least the Nauvoo period until the turn of the century, it is not likely that the reformation made any change in the punishment for it. There is no doubt, however, that the local authorities became more vigilant and more strict in demanding that members conform to the requirements. Nor is there any doubt that there were cases where this supervision was carried to an extreme. Sometimes the stories were told later by the participants as jokes, though at the time they were not humorous for the backsliders.

Two such stories come from the town of Springville, where the fires of the reformation burned most brightly. One had to do with a Brother Warren who was considered something of a "Jack Mormon" in that he did not always attend to his church duties regularly, and did not always accept counsel without question. One night when the visiting teachers came to his home, Brother Warren had just arrived from a hard day's work tired and discouraged, and was just sitting down at supper. The visitors noticed that the family proceeded to eat.

"Brother Warren, do you allow your family to eat food without asking the Lord to bless it?" the elder asked.

"What little we got here aint worth bothering the Lord about," Brother Warren answered, going right on with the meal.

Now the proper thing, if Brother Warren had manifested the right spirit, would have been to acknowledge the correction, apologize, and say a tardy grace. Since he did not, and did not seem to accept them in the proper spirit, the visitors soon left.

A few nights later, just as he was ready for bed, Brother Warren was surprised by a knock at the door. He himself answered it, lifting the latch and opening the door to greet five armed, masked men.

"Come right on out here without any fuss," the leader told him in a deep muffled voice. Two of the men instantly took his arms, pantless and shoeless as he was, two stepped behind him, and they followed the leader around the house, down the walk, past the corrals, down the road toward the fields, all the way in utter silence. Arriving at last at his own watermelon patch, Brother Warren stood between his guards while one of the men in the rear, taking plenty of time, thumped one melon after another until he found one to his satisfaction. Then drawing a long blade from its sheath, he sliced it open with a cracking stroke. All the group kneeled around it.

"Brother Warren, will you please ask the blessing on the food?" the leader asked.

Brother Warren's tongue was loosed so that he offered a long and eloquent prayer, asking God to bless the food that it would nourish their bodies and brighten their minds and warm their hearts, that they might have his Spirit which was the spirit of love and forgiveness, to accompany them, that they might ALL henceforth spend their full strength in carrying on His work.

The melon was sliced and served around to them all. When it was finished, the visitors escorted Brother Warren back to his door, opened it, and saw him safely inside, without another word being spoken.

The second incident happened later, after the arrival of the army, and was also reported in Lee's Diary as well as in the *History of Springville*.

It seems that Jackson Stewart had spoken out against some of the excesses in Springville, and as a result felt that he was under suspicion to such a degree that it might not be safe for him to remain there. So he decided to try to make it over the high mountain to the east of town and perhaps join the army forces. Leaving home without any word to his family, he set out in the night up Hobble Creek Canyon. All day he traveled, climbing the high mountain and doing well until he was enveloped in a heavy snow storm and became confused as to direction. Passing over a ridge, he came upon a sentry who turned out to be, instead of a soldier, a Mormon sentry placed to stop any who tried to leave. He was held prisoner here until word came from the authorities to bring him in.

When finally the guard brought him down to the road at the mouth of the canyon he was met by a mounted posse with flags and a band. Accompanied by the guard, he was escorted through the town, marching in the rear, while the band played a funeral dirge. He did have a chance to present his case to the stake officials and was promised that he would not be molested. He lived in fear until the next summer, when he went with some emigrants to California.

These cases represent the aberrations or the "lunatic fringe," perhaps, of the Mormon Reformation. It was a call to repentance truly, and an effort to separate the wheat from the tares and to make the faithful more conscious of their duty and more determined to live up to their covenants, especially those which they had made in the endowment house. An entry from the diary of Rachel Lee under date of March 10, 1856, gives in some detail the requirements of those who would receive their endowments.

> The Bishop then arose . . . said that [he] held in his hand a Letter Addressed to Prest J. D. Lee but that he would read it as it concerned all the Saints which reads thus Dated March 2nd, 1856 To Presidents, Bishop, and brethren in the counties of Iron and Washington: I write to inform you that the persons who can get their endowments must be those who pay their tithmony from year to year, who live the lives of Saints from day to day; Setting good examples before their neighbours; Men and women, boys and girls over Sixteen years of age who are living the lives of Saints, believe in plurality, do not speak evil of the Authorities of the Church, and posses true integrity towards their friends, can come up after their spring crops are Sown, and their case will be attended to.   BRIGHAM YOUNG
>   HEBER C. KIMBALL
>   J. M. GRANT
>
> P.S.   Send us word ten days before you send your company, that we may have the Rooms vacent for them.

This makes it very clear that only the faithful would be allowed to receive this ordinance, and that those who did must conform strictly to every tenet of the church including a firm belief in "plurality." The covenants which this includes will be discussed at some length later.

The fact was that the reformation spread to all parts of the church during the last months of 1856 and the first half of 1857, and no ranch or hamlet was so far away or isolated that it was not subject to the catechism. For example, John Pulsipher had been one of twenty missionaries sent to the Indians in the neighborhood of Fort Supply in a combination farming and preaching assignment. They left Salt Lake City on May 17, 1855, to labor for two years. In the spring of 1857, he reported fifty wagonloads of apostates leaving the territory to return to the states because they did not wish to accept the rigorous demands of the reformation. Even in that outpost every settler was examined, or catechized. Although the items are not in exactly the same words or order as some which have been quoted, they include the same requirements. As he gives the questions, they are:

Have you committed murder by shedding innocent blood — or consenting thereto?

Have you betrayed your brethren or sisters in anything?

Have you commited adultry by having connection with a woman that was not your wife or a man that was not your husband?

Do you pay your tithing promptly?

Have you spoken against any principle contained in the Bible, Book of Mormon, Doctrine & Covenants, or any principle revealed through Joseph the Prophet or the authorities of the Church?

Do you wash your bodies & have your family do so as often as cleanliness requires or circumstances permit?

Do you teach your families the Gospel of Salvation?

Do you preside over your family as a servant of God & is your family subject to you?

Do you fulfill your promises, do you pay your debts, or do you run into debt without prospect of paying?

Have you taken anything that did not belong to you without the owner's knowing it, or giving consent?

Have you found lost property & not returned it to the owner or used all diligence to do so?

Have you lied about or maliciously misrepresented any person or thing?

Have you branded any animal that you did not know to be your own?

Have you taken up strays and converted to your own use with-
out accounting to the proper authorities?
Do you work 6 days & go to the house of worship on the 7th?
Have you taken the name of Diety in vain?
Have you been intoxicated by strong drink?

Following the questioning, which was done privately to each individual, the whole group gathered to renew their covenants by
rebaptism that this experience might really represent a newness of
life and a determination to do better. While in general this was a
stimulation to improvement, there were some who actually confessed
to sins that they had not committed and others who magnified their
own faults to a point where they lost their sense of proportion. Still
others were disgusted and alienated by the whole procedure.

For the saints on the Santa Clara, this summer of 1856 would be
remembered chiefly for of the drought and the Indian troubles. There
were no early rains, so the water failed. The Tonaquint, which the
two years before had carried a good irrigating stream, dried up until
it failed to reach the fort, and the women were forced to follow up
the wash and bring water down by the bucket for use in the homes.
Now they would have to bundle up their dirty clothes and take tubs,
washboards and soap up the valley a couple of miles, build the fire
there and do the washing, spreading the clothes on the bushes to dry
and waiting to carry them home, clean and folded, in the tubs.

Then the old Chief Agarapoots came into the area, angry and
threatening to drive the white men out. Jacob Hamblin, now the head
of the mission, had tried kindness with him, always insisting that the
Mormons were "tooche-e-weino Tick-a-boo," or very good friends who
had come to help the Indians. With ugly defiance, Agarapoots killed
an ox belonging to the settlers, skinned it, and divided it up among his
band.

The other white men, Dudley Leavitt, Thales Haskell, and Zadoc
Judd among them, thought that Agarapoots should be punished;
whipped, perhaps, or forced to pay for the ox in horses or skins.

Jacob insisted upon handling the affair in his own way. He went to
talk to Agarapoots, but was greeted with signs of disdain and scorn —
the thumb on the nose, the wrinkled nose and shrugged shoulder, the
pantomime of vomiting. "Mormon *poogi* no good," he said repeatedly.
"Mormon poogi no hurt Agarapoots."

"You will make your own bad medicine," Jacob made him understand. Indeed, it seemed so, for the very next day the chief sent post
haste for the Mormon leader. His little son had become severely ill
and now he wanted some Mormon medicine or poogi.

Jacob, looking at the child, could see that it was past human aid, so refused to pray over it, saying that the parents should first wash it and clean it up, as he had been trying to teach them.

Agarapoots refused, and the little fellow breathed his last as they argued about it. Now the chief accused Jacob of allowing the boy to die by not doing his poogi, while Jacob tried to make him see that the sickness was his own fault in the first place. Did he not promise him that he would make his own evil medicine? Did he not deserve this?

Did he forget the time when the women and children were out of the fort, how he and his men had charged down upon them and almost run their horses over the Mormon papoose? Did he not force himself into the Mormon fort when the men were away and frighten the women and children? If Jacob's own little boy, Lyman, had not scrambled over the back wall, caught the mare that was feeding among the willows, and ridden up toward where the men were working on the dam, who knows what Agarapoots might have done? Jacob did not need to remind the old chief of his fear when Lyman blew the cowhorn signal that echoed all along the valley. This hideous sound was what really scared the marauders out of the fort and sent them galloping away.

Next he had killed the ox. Would he pay for it? No. So now his boy is dead. See, Agarapoots made his own evil poogi.

Agarapoots and his tribe moved toward Pine Valley for the burial rites and to be near the head of the stream and out of the heat. But he left swearing vengeance against the settlers. Then the friendly chief, Tutsegavits, came to report that Agarapoots was going on the warpath; the white men wanted to prepare to fight. But Jacob would have none of it.

"You pray him dead," Tutsegavits begged with childish faith. "Him heap bad man. You pray him dead."

Jacob asked for volunteers to go with him to the Indian camp. The men sat silent for a long minute before Thales Haskell said, "I guess that means me."

The two men rode toward the Pine Valley camp of Agarapoots, but the Old Chief would not come out of his wickeup to talk to them. Jacob distributed some bread among the braves who stood about and made them understand that he really wanted to be a friend to them all. Then, stepping to the door of the wickeup, he said, "Agarapoots make his own katz-at poogi" (evil medicine) and turned to ride back to the Santa Clara.

When a few days later Agarapoots died, all the Indians believed it was Jacob's curse that killed him. From that time forth, he had a much greater influence over the southern tribes than he could have won in any other way.

Not long after they all learned that Jacob's medicine could not cover every emergency. Thales Haskell had adopted an Indian boy who was now coming into his early teens. One day while all the men were at work on the dam and ditch, this boy took Thales' gun from over the mantel, evidently wanting only to examine and experiment with it. The girl wife, Maria, did not dare remonstrate and before either of them knew what was happening, the gun was discharged, the bullet entering her body near the hip on the left side, passing through the abdomen, and lying just under the skin on the right side. Maria was more than six months pregnant, which meant that the child had been killed also.

It was a great tragedy, not only for the loss of the mother and child, but for the suffering which she had to endure in the dying. It was tragic for the youthful husband, who adored this girl almost to worship, and for the six other teen-age wives who had come to look upon Maria as an ideal — playing her concertina and leading them in singing each evening, love songs, nonsense songs, or hymns. How much she had meant to them all!

How could God have allowed this to happen to her? If it must be someone, why not one of the others? And all because she was too kind, too tolerant of this Indian boy, who ran as fast as he could to Jacob, insisting he didn't mean to — the gun just barked out loud when he touched it — and begging Jacob to do his poogi so that Maria could be well. But Maria could not be well; hers was the first grave on the lonely hill.

In August, John D. Lee visited the settlement with President George A. Smith and other local authorities. Truly this was a hot, hopeless place, where the thermometer must have registered a hundred and ten in the shade. Yet when Brother Smith puffed and fanned and mopped his face and neck, Jacob said, "Why, the weather is fine today. You ought to come sometime when it is really hot!"

Now Lee was glad that he had not been allowed to settle farther south. Brother Brigham certainly was inspired when he canceled that order, for his location at Harmony was a thousand times better than anything here — more water, much, much more land — a place for expansion. He noted the primitive wash-dish beside one cabin; a scooped out stump of a tree with an augur hole low down and slant-ing to drain the water out, and a cork to hold it in. At least it was stationary. He noted also the number of gourd cups and dippers in use, with the ripe shell cut around, the seeds scooped out, the inside polished with river sand, and then the whole thing baked at a low, slow heat. Light, serviceable dishes they made; adequately good for children and Indians.

As to Hamblin's methods of dealing with the natives, they were all right perhaps for a man who expected to spend his whole life living among them, associating closely with them, and adopting as many of their ways as they did of his. That was Jacob's mission.

As for himself, while he would continue for a while as "Indian Farmer," he felt that his real calling was to help build the kingdom through helping to develop new industry and establish new settlements. Right now he had been assigned to push the work of the reformation and awaken the saints to their duties.

1857
Reap the Whirlwind

New Year's Day, 1857 was exciting in the Lee household, because that night Mary Adoline was to be married to Don Carlos Shurtz. They were very young, to be sure, she fifteen and he not quite twenty, but they had been keeping company for nearly a year. This would be the second marriage in the family; the oldest daughter, Sarah Jane, had been a wife of Charles Dalton for nearly four years. She was a third wife, however, and her husband a well matured man.

The crowd gathered early. There was a program of song, speech, and toasts, then the ceremony performed by the father, followed by a wedding dinner and dance. It was a time of general rejoicing.

Throughout the winter the reformation continued. On January 18, in the evening priesthood meeting, the subject was family relationships. "The men should govern their wives in Love, and their children in Love, and that the time had come that men must not cohabit with their wives out of season but that all must keep the Celestial Law as regards these things. . ." The next week the bishop encouraged people to return the things they had borrowed or taken, that all things in every home that did not belong there should be cleaned out and returned ". . . and he appointed a place to put such lost property in the night that folks was ashamed to bring in the daytime."

When the stake president, Isaac C. Haight, visited, they could be sure of a powerful sermon. Rachel took the minutes and transcribed his speech thus:

Sunday morning Feb. 15, 1857. (Pres Haight)

He then explained how the marriage relations aught to be entered into legally, thus. — any man (good) that is worthy — has to go and ask the Parents of the woman first also his Prest, then ask the girl or woman herself Again if a man Desires a 2nd or third wife he must first get permission from Prest Brigham Young then proceed and ask the Parents, and then the woman herself, thus is the legal way and only honourable way And again said he thare is no woman having received her Endowments can marry a man that has not received his Endowments; But a man that has received Endowments may marry a woman that has not received her Endowments, thus the matter was plainly set forth.

— he also said that the Gentile custom of Sparkification was done
away so that the passions may not be aroused and undue advantage taken of the chastity of the Daughters of Zion by these
pernicious habits &c.[1]

On May 15, 1857, the Indian agent, Mr. Armstrong, arrived with
presents for the Indians; a straw hat, a shirt, and a pair of pants for
each man, also a spade or a hoe for each. He counted out the number
and left them for Lee to distribute while he went on to Santa Clara to
meet with Tutsegavit and his band.

On May 21 Rachel wrote that some twenty-one wagons passed by
going to settle on the Rio Virgin in order to raise cotton, etc. This
was the company of colonists who settled the town of Washington
where John D. Lee later was to have rather extensive holdings and a
very fine home.

July 4 was always the day for a great celebration, and this year it
was very elaborate. President Haight and many of the people from
Cedar City, including the brass band and choir, were in attendance.
An escort of ten mounted men went out three miles to meet them, one
carrying the flag of the Union and another the flag of Deseret. They
formed a procession and marched once around the fort before they
stopped at the place of meeting. Here the band played, the Cedar City
choir furnished music, and President Haight delivered the oration.
Then there were toasts and more music by both band and choir.

A whole beef had been barbecued for the occasion and long serving
tables spread out of doors, with plenty of homemade malt beer and
lemonade compounded of cream-of-tartar and lemon extract, with
dippers tied by strong string to the barrels and plenty of extra tin cups.
Competitive sports and the afternoon dance, according to Rachel,
were entered into with "great zest and hilarity."

The real celebration in the Mormon towns was July 24, the anniversary of the entrance of Brigham Young and his pioneers into the
valley of the Great Salt Lake. This, the tenth year, was made a very
special year in all Zion. Now the people of Harmony went to Cedar
City to share the activities there. The program recounted the history
of their mobbings and drivings, the martyrdom of their Prophet, the
tragic, unsettled years, and the arrival in Zion. A town dinner was
served in the bowery, and sports and dancing completed the day.

Little did the family of John D. Lee realize as they rode home in
their wagons, singing and laughing, that forces had been set afoot in

---

[1] Rachel Lee's diary is yet unpublished. The original is in the Henry E. Huntington Library at San Marino, California.

the East and in Salt Lake City which would shape the destiny of every one of them. For on that same afternoon two weary, travel-worn horsemen had interrupted the celebration at Big Cottonwood Canyon with momentous news for Brigham Young. All mail contracts East had been canceled and an army was en route to put down the rebellion in Utah!

How prophetic now seemed President Young's statement of just ten years ago: "If our enemies will give us ten years in these valleys, we'll ask no odds of them." Well, the ten years were up today. "We shall never run from them again," he had boasted. Now they should see.

Early in the year the Nauvoo Legion had been reactivated, with Daniel H. Wells named commander-in-chief. Word now went out declaring that "Utah is about to be invaded by a hostile force," and a full muster was called to resist such invasion. People must not dispose of a kernel of grain to any gentile, nor should they use grain to feed their own cattle. War with the United States of America could be a sudden, devastating affair or a long seige. Yet Brother Brigham had said that "with the help of God, they shall not come here," and every man was ready to support him.

Public speeches became more and more inflammatory; private gatherings rehearsed past indignities, and particularly the martyrdom of the Prophet and his brother. Word had come that Parley P. Pratt, their beloved apostle, author of so many of their pamphlets and songs, had been stabbed to death in Arkansas.

The first move was, of course, to call all the legion members into immediate readiness to march and to fight. The next was to call home the saints in scattered places, the colony from San Bernardino, those from Genoa and Ragtown and the other Nevada towns, the far-flung missions. Scarcely less important was the order to "conciliate the Indians and make them our fast friends."

George A. Smith brought the word to the southern settlements, and everywhere he went he spoke in terms of repulsing the approaching army, of defending their homes and firesides, protecting their wives and children against such persecutions as many had suffered before. When he reached Parowan, he found the militia already out on the public square drilling, making preparation to strike in any direction. At Cedar City also he found the battalion on parade awaiting eagerly direction for action. At Harmony, after the men were drilled by Adjutant Martineau they listened to a discourse by Brother Smith which pointed up the "hostility and virulence" which had actuated the United States in its dealings with this people.

On August 23, William H. Dame made a report of the Iron military district with nine units, the total arms and ammunition being 99 muskets, 190 rifles, 17 colt's revolvers, 192¾ pounds of powder, 335 pounds of lead, and 24 swords. He closes thus:

> The field and Staff officers are not enumerated in this return, but are well armed.
>
> The command feel calm, quiet, and willing to act upon any command that may be given and any orders from Head Quarters will be cheerfully obeyed. We can place 200 effective men in the field if necessary. Every effort is being made to secure the grain in every settlement, and your previous orders are being strictly carried out. Every inlet of the District south of Beaver is now being guarded. If a hostile force is found to be approaching us, we shall immediately express to you, and await your further orders; Unless attacked, in which case we shall act on the defensive, and communicate immediately with you.
>
> WM. H. DAME

So it was in every village and hamlet. The men were drilling and inspecting arms and preparing for battle. In the north Lot Smith was burning the army supply wagons and stampeding their animals; at Fort Bridger and Fort Supply the Mormons burned the grain, hay and buildings so that they would not fall into the hands of the enemy. Detachments were fortifying Emigration Canyon, preparing to start activities there where the army would be forced to pass through a narrow pass. The saints were determined like the Spartans at Thermopylae to hold the fortifications at any cost.

In the meantime the regular tide of emigration through Utah had started in early July and would continue throughout August. Those who arrived early took the more direct northern route and secured ample provision in the Salt Lake City area, but those who came in after the order was issued to sell no grain at any price met great difficulty. One of the first of these was the Fancher Train. It was a loosely knit group of several independent elements who had joined forces here in order to travel in greater safety.

Captain Charles Fancher had crossed the country in 1855, selected and made arrangements to buy a large tract of land, and returned in 1856 to recruit his family and friends to join in settling it. It was reported that he had with him four thousand dollars in gold coin to make the down payment, and a large herd of cattle and horses. His company consisted of eleven families with twenty-nine children and fourteen adults, a total of sixty-five people, with eleven well-stocked wagons. Traveling with him was a group of horsemen with their supply wagons, a rough and ready set of fellows who called themselves the "Missouri Wildcats."

This group all arrived in Salt Lake City on August 3 and 4, and mindful of the fate of the Donner Party in 1846, decided to take the southern route. They followed a few days behind President George A. Smith on his journey south ordering the people to keep their grain and not to sell a kernel to any gentiles. This, of course, was hard on travelers who faced the desert and had expected to replenish their stores in Utah. The Fancher train was well-to-do; they had cash to pay or goods to trade, but no one would sell. The attitude of the Mormons all along the way was one of belligerence and hostility, aggravated by the attitude of the group of "Missouri Wildcats," who spoke of the Mormon leaders with scorn, boasted of what they had done in Missouri and what they would do when they got to California, about bringing an army back from that direction to help put down the rebellion. It was time, in their opinion, that Uncle Sam took steps to subordinate this group.

In the meantime, the southern Indian chiefs had been taken into Salt Lake City for an interview with the Big Captain. Jacob Hamblin, newly appointed head of the Indian mission, had been told in his letter of appointment to conciliate the Indians and make them fast friends, "for they must learn that they have either got to help us, or the United States will kill us both." [2] Hamblin, wanting the natives to get their orders first hand, started north with Thales Haskell and the local Indian chiefs, picking up others along the way until he had ten in his company.

They held their interview with President Young on September 1. No interpreter is named in the record, but Dimick B. Huntington submitted a voucher on September 11, 1857, for lodging for Indians on a visit to the Superintendent of Indian Affairs at Salt Lake City on various dates from August 8 to September 1. Nor does the record give details of the conversation, but it would seem that the purpose was to make sure that the Indians were to be their active allies in the coming conflict. They would be back in the south to overtake the Fancher train at Parowan.

With the Indians now conscious of the impending war and eager to help their Mormon friends, and with the mounting tensions between the settlers and the emigrant train, the situation was explosive. When people would not sell provisions, the emigrants would sometimes use their long whips to pop off the heads of chickens in the streets; they would call their oxen "Brigham" or "Heber" or "Joe Smith" and berate and curse them through the streets, just to annoy the people.

---

[2] This letter is found in the "Church Letter Book, No. 3," pp. 737-738. The original is in the family of Jacob Hamblin, Mrs. Mary H. Beeler having had it in 1948. It has been published many times, but in a sharply edited form, the sentence here quoted being omitted, along with the entire paragraph which follows.

Reports of this came from two non-Mormon sources: One George Powers of Little Rock, Arkansas, who was following the Fancher train, described the Mormon preparations for war and their anger at this particular train. The people of Buttermilk Fort (Holden) had not only refused them any provisions but said they were sorry they had not killed some of them there and "that they were holding their Indians in check until the arrival of their chief (he was in Salt Lake City with the others), when they would follow the train and cut it to pieces."

Mr. P. M. Warn, another traveler, made a similar report:

They were very free in speaking of the Mormons, their conduct was said to be reckless, and they would commit little acts of annoyance for the purpose of provoking the Saints. Feeling perfectly safe in their arms and numbers, they seemed to set at defiance all the powers that could be brought against them, until they were cut off from all hope of relief.[3]

The worst accusation against them was that they had poisoned the springs near Fillmore so that many cattle and some Indians and at least one white man died. This had lacked documentary proof so that it seemed a fabrication to help justify what happened later, but recently a handwritten journal by Thomas Waters Cropper gives more weight to it. Mr. Cropper who was fifteen years old at the time, wrote the account when he was eighty-four, so that time and retelling might have colored it somewhat. Since it has not been published, it is included here:

. . . The balance of that summer I was herding cows. In company with several other boys I was up on the benches when we saw the unusual sight of an emigrant train. We ran down to where they were and accompanied them about two miles in to Fillmore. They dared us to ride one of their wild steers and I got on it, and it dashed into Cattelin's Mill Pond, which caused them a lot of merriment. They moved on down to Meadow and camped just west of town.

There appeared to be two companies of them joined together for safety from the Indians. One company which was mostly men called themselves the Missouri Wild Cats. I heard one of them make the brag that he had helped to mob and kill Joe Smith, and he further said, "I would like to go back and take a pop at

---

[3] *Daily Alta California* (San Francisco) October 27, 1857. From a letter by its Los Angeles correspondent dated October 24, 1857.

Mr. Powers traveled with the Matthews and Tanner freight train, which brought the first news of the massacre into California.

Old Brig before I leave the territory." They moved on over to what was known as the Big Spring on the Corn Creek Sloughs. A lot of Kanosh Indians came to their camp to beg and trade. One man insisted on examining an Indian's bow and arrows but the Indian refused and jabbed an arrow into the man's breast. The man whipped out a revolver and shot the Indian dead.

They poisoned the spring and a number of cattle died around the spring. The Indians ate some of the meat and several Indians died from the effects.

I went over and saw the cattle dead around the spring. Proctor Robinson, son of Joseph Robinson, had been skinning some of the cattle. He went back with me as far as Meadow and insisted on my going on to Fillmore with him (I was staying at Barrows). He was on a poor rhone mare and I was afraid she would not carry us both, but we started for Fillmore about eight miles distant. When about 2 miles out it began to rain. He complained of his eye and kept rubbing it. It swelled shut and the rain came down in torrents. I slipped off from behind him and told him to whip the old mare through and get home, for his face was getting very swollen.

I trudged on until I finally reached Fillmore. I was almost perishing with the cold and rain. I stopped in to warm and got something to eat at Theodore Rogers. Bro Rogers went part way home with me and I succeeded in getting home all right.

Next morning early I went down to see Proctor. He was so swollen and bloated I would not have recognized him. He died that night. Next day I went on the range and saw a lot more dead cattle.

This same company moved on South and met a sad fate at the Mountain Meadows.[4]

The fact that the cattle probably died from eating a poison weed rather than from drinking poisoned water was not so important as that the people believed the latter, and it gave them one more offense to add to the mounting list.

At Beaver the company had further trouble. One of their men who was out hunting rabbits was fired at by an Indian, whereupon he hurried back to his camp. William B. Ashworth wrote an account of the trouble in Beaver, describing the Indians that were following the train.

The Bishop then advised the emigrants to protect themselves as best they could, as the town could not help them on account of

---

[4] Typescript of the Cropper Journal is at the Brigham Young University. Original in the hands of Mrs. J. W. Tippetts, Orem, Utah.

all the women and children whose safety often depended on the friendliness of the Indians. He urged the men not to come up into town, as that would jeopardize, not only themselves, but the people of Beaver. I was at my father's side while all this was going on, and listened to every word with interest. . . The Indians all disappeared the day after the company left and it was surmised that they had followed the emigrants. This was at the time of great bitterness among the people against the Mormons. Buchanan's U.S. Army was even then on its way to Utah for no good purpose. . .[5]

At Parowan, the gates of that fort were closed and the company passed by the town. Here one man, William Leany, recognized a member of the company, William Aiden, as the son of a man who had befriended him while he was on a mission. He gave Aiden some vegetables from his garden, knowing well that he was acting in direct opposition to the official orders. A few days later he was called out of his house and struck over the head by one of the local police on the charge that he had rendered "aid and comfort to the enemy." He was left for dead, and indeed never did recover fully from the blow.

At Cedar City, the last place on the road where they could get provisions, the conduct of some of the Missourians was such that the local police tried to arrest them, only to be laughed at with scorn. Since the people would not sell nor trade any foodstuffs at all, some of the emigrants proceeded to help themselves; thus as they left the town, a trail of hate and resentment remained behind them.

In the Sunday service at Cedar City on September 6, President Isaac C. Haight spoke with bitterness of the coming of Johnston's Army, which he called an armed mob, and made pointed reference to the Fancher train which had left only the day before. The ward clerk reported his speech in some detail, a part of which was as follows:

> They (the Missourians) drove us out to starve. When we pled for mercy, Haun's mill was our answer, and when we asked for bread they gave us a stone. We left the confines of civilization and came far into the wilderness where we could worship God according to the dictates of our own conscience without annoyance to our neighbors. We resolved that if they would leave us alone we would never trouble them. But the Gentiles will not leave us alone, They have followed us and hounded us. They come among us asking us to trade with them, to help them, and in the name of humanity to feed them. All of these we have done

---

[5] A typescript of the William B. Ashworth "Autobiography" is in the files of Brigham Young University.

and now they are sending an army to exterminate us. So far as I am concerned I have been driven from my home for the last time. I am prepared to feed to the Gentiles the same bread they fed to us. God being my helper I will give the last ounce of strength and if need be my last drop of blood in defense of Zion.

Following the regular service, a special priesthood meeting was called at which the problems connected with the Fancher Train were discussed. Were they mice or men that they should take such treatment? Should they let such braggarts come into their midst and boast of the indignities they had heaped upon them in Missouri and Nauvoo? Should a man who would boast that he had the gun that "shot the guts out of Old Joe Smith" go unpunished? What had their vows to avenge the blood of the Prophet amounted to? Now the saints were at war with the United States; these emigrants were not the army, true, but they were enemies in a very real way, and should be treated as enemies.

Finally a resolution to the effect that "We will deal with this situation now, so that our hands will be free to meet the army when it comes," was presented and passed.

After it was passed, Laban Morrill, big and fearless, arose slowly.

"Brethren," he said, "I think we should clarify what we mean by dealing with this situation now. Exactly what do you propose to do?"

"Go out and arrest the group of troublemakers and force them to come back and stand trial and pay their fines," one answered.

"But that would mean food to feed them and men to guard them, and we can't afford either," another volunteered.

"I think they should be done away with, at least the one that bragged that he carried the gun that shot the guts out of Old Joe Smith. I think that we are all bound by our covenants to see that he does not live to do any more damage."

"There were others just as bad as he was."

"But how will you get them? They are all well armed, and we would lose more than we would gain. Any attempt to take one of them would mean the lives of the posse that went after him."

So the discussion went on, some in favor of "doing away with" the men who had been the chief offenders, others preferring to let them all go in spite of their insults and offenses, and husbanding their own strength for a real war when and if it came. At last another resolution was presented to the effect that they should send an express to President Young laying the case before him and asking for counsel. This was passed, with the provision that the rider should be allowed a hundred hours in which to make the trip. A third resolution was that a messenger go to the home of John D. Lee at Harmony and ask him to come and manage the Indians. Since Jacob Hamblin had not returned from his trip north, but had taken time out to go on over to Tooele and court himself another wife (the sixteen-year-old Priscilla Leavitt), John D. Lee as "Indian Farmer" would be next in command.

Thus events followed one another, leading inexorably to the final tragedy. Horsemen hurried back and forth between Cedar City and Parowan, and between the Meadows and Cedar City. Strong hatred, deep-seated beliefs, and greed were all combined in the drama. That this was a wealthy train with good wagons and ox teams and horses; with a large herd of cattle; and with loads of household goods and necessities was without doubt a factor with some who were involved. Their own deep religious convictions increased in potency — that "the blood of the Prophet should be avenged" and that by their own covenants, taken in the Nauvoo Temple or in the Endowment House, they were bound to help to carry out God's will.

One cannot read the diaries of the time without sensing the depth and fervor of this feeling. Consider a few examples, each from a handwritten account.

> David Lewis: (Describing the Haun's Mill Massacre) Sutch groans of the dying, sutch strugeling in blood, I hope that none that reads this account may never have to witness, unless it is in avenging the blood of those that was slain, for truly they shed innocent blood, which must stand against them until it is avenged. . .
>
> John Lott: I hope to see the day when the blood of martyrs will be avenged, and these damnable rebels make restitution. . .
>
> David Lewis: My brother Benjamin was killed in Missouri, and I am alive to avenge his blood when the Lord will. . .
>
> Allen Stout: Their dead bodies were brought to Nauvoo, where I saw their beloved forms reposing in the arms of death. . . I then and there resolved in my mind that I would never let an opportunity go unimproved of avenging their blood upon the heads of the enemies of the Church of Jesus Christ. . . I hope to avenge their blood, but if I do not I will teach my children and children's children to the fourth generation as long as there is one descendent of the murderers on the earth. . .

If they had wanted to, and some no doubt did, they might have found justification in their own *Doctrine and Covenants*, Section 98, verses 23-32. Here they are admonished to forgive their enemies, to bear all things in meekness and not retaliate, but after they have been driven four times, though they would still be more blessed if they could again forgive, "Verily, thine enemy is in thine hands, and thou art justified." There were those among them who had been driven more than four times, and who did not mean to be driven again.

Perhaps no example could be more eloquent of the power of this belief than the patriarchal blessing given to William H. Dame by Patriarch Elisha H. Groves on February 20, 1854, in Parowan. Near the end of the regular blessing is this very significant paragraph:

> Thou shalt be called to act at the head of a portion of thy brethren and of the Lamanites in the redemption of Zion and the avenging of the blood of the Prophets upon them that dwell in the earth. The Angel of Vengeance shall be with thee, shall nerve and strengthen thee. Like unto Moroni, no power shall be able to stand before thee until thou hast accomplished thy work. . .[6]

At this time William H. Dame was thirty-five years old, a mild-mannered, kindly man, but still appointed to be colonel commanding of all the Iron County military. To one who took a promise seriously, the blessing would seem not only prophetic of what might happen, but a sacred charge to be carried out. Might this have had some connection with the orders that were finally given at the Mountain Meadows?

On this sunny Sunday afternoon in September the Fancher party was camped near the lower end of the Mountain Meadows, a lovely location near a small, clear spring and in the midst of luxuriant grass. They had purposely stopped in a clear place where there were no scrub cedars nor underbrush to shelter skulking Indians. Now that they were almost a full day's journey from the Mormon settlements, they felt an ease and security. Here they would rest perhaps two or three weeks to give their cattle a chance to recuperate and to prepare for the barren waste ahead.

At Cedar City, James Haslam was preparing to leave for his long horseback ride to Salt Lake City and back, and the messenger had reached John D. Lee at Harmony with orders to come immediately to hold conference with Isaac C. Haight. Lee's hired man, Benjamin Platte, wrote that an Indian had come to Harmony earlier in the week and tried to persuade Lee to go with him and lead an attack on the train, but Lee had refused, saying that they had already killed one good man, meaning Captain Gunnison. But an Indian messenger was one thing and a call from his superior in both the church and the military was quite another.

Lee reached Cedar City after dark, and he and Haight took their blankets and rode out of town to the old ironworks, where they could

---

[6] The original patriarchal blessing is in the hands of Mrs. Lillis Spencer of Cedar City, Utah. Photostat at the Brigham Young University.

talk without danger of being overheard. The Indians were already
angry at the emigrants and some bands had followed them from
Holden; the other chiefs had returned from their conference with
Brigham Young ready and eager to enter this war on the side of the
Mormons. They could attack the emigrant train, drive off the cattle
and do what damage they could, then perhaps the Mormons could
save the survivors and salvage the outfits. But the affair was to be an
Indian raid.

There is reason to believe that as Lee heard the accusations against
this company and thought of the impending war, he would have fallen
in with the plan. On his way back home the next day he met several
local bands already gathering. They urged him to join them, but he
said that he must go home and get his guns and ammunition and set
affairs in order there. He would come back the next day, Tuesday.

The Indians, however, were ready for action, so without waiting for
Lee, they charged down the hill toward the emigrant camp before
daylight on Tuesday morning, yelling and shooting. Taken entirely by
surprise, the emigrants needed a little time to collect their forces, but
they were well armed and fearless, and they soon put the Indians to
rout. In the fight several emigrant men were killed — Lee said seven —
and a number of Indians were killed or wounded.

When Lee returned on Wednesday, he found the savages in a high
state of excitement. They had been given the idea that if they were
fighting for the Mormons, the Mormon God would protect them so
that the bullets of the emigrants would not hit them. Now the Mormons could either help them get revenge on the 'Mericats, or they
could pay with their own men for the Indian losses. Since Lee was
the only white man there, he was in a dangerous situation. He had to
persuade them that he, at least, was their friend and that he would
try to see that they had their revenge; or such revenge as they were
entitled to.

He finally persuaded them to let him leave and go south for help.
A few miles out he met a group of about ten Mormon men from the
Santa Clara and Washington settlements, and about a hundred more
Indians. The natives hurried on to camp with their own people, while
the white men made camp at a small spring about a mile from the
emigrants. They decided to send a messenger to Haight at Cedar City,
telling him of the situation and asking permission to pacify the Indians
and let the emigrants go.

The messenger was on his way by 2 p.m., but later that evening the
Indians decided to attack again. Lee, John Mangum, William Young,
and Oscar Hamblin persuaded them to stop the attack until the word
came from headquarters. It was at this time and on the day following

that Lee earned the title of "Yawgetts" or cry-baby, because he wept as he pled for the lives of the emigrants.

At Cedar City, the bell was rung, the signal to summon the militia, and the members gathered. A statement was read to the effect that the emigrants had been killed. Would not some Christian-hearted men come out and help to bury them? This was the story that several of the participants told.

Nephi Johnson indicated that the deception was Haight's, not Lee's. He was working in the harvest field, when two men came and told him that Isaac C. Haight wanted him to come in to Cedar immediately. When he arrived, he was told to go to the mountains and "settle a difficulty between John D. Lee and the Indians, as the latter had threatened to kill Lee." Haight also said that ". . . Lee had suggested that they withdraw and let the emigrants go, and Haight sent word to Lee to clean up the dirty job he had started, and that he had sent out a company of men with shovels to bury the dead, but they would find something else to do when they got there."

The military unit from Cedar City arrived in camp in the evening. During the night, on Wednesday, three of the emigrant men decided to slip out on horseback and go to Cedar City, report the Indian attack, and appeal for help. Young William Aiden, who had lived in Utah for several months and who had joined this group at Provo, was one of them. He insisted that the Mormons were essentially a good people and would surely protect white men against Indians. Had not William Leany already given him vegetables from his garden?

As they stopped to let their horses drink at a little creek, they were shot at from ambush by Mormon pickets. Aiden fell, mortally wounded, but the other two escaped, one wounded in the wrist, and turned to go toward California on the Spanish Trail, evidently feeling that their chance for survival would be better on the road than at the camp.

When word of this attack reached the Mormon leaders, it stirred them to more immediate action. Again the men met in council, this time praying together for guidance or for some sign of the Divine Will. Again a messenger was sent to the local leaders for orders. John M. Higbee went this time to Haight, who rode in the night to Parowan to Colonel Dame. In his account written years later, Higbee wrote the message which he said that he carried to Lee:

> Compromise with Indians if possible by letting them take all the stock and go to their homes and let the company alone, but on no conditions you are not to precipitate a war with Indians while there is an army marching against our people.
>
> As Indian Farmer and Major in the Legion, I trust you will have influence enough to restrain Indians and save the company.

If not possible, save women and children at all hazards. Hoping
you will be able to give a good account of the important duty
entrusted to your charge   I call upon all good Citizens in that   of
the district to help you carry out the above orders in helping to
make peace between the two parties

     by WM. H. DAME Col Commanding Iron Military District [7]

This was the dilemma. They were *not* to precipitate a war with the
Indians, yet here they were, outnumbered by red men demanding
vengeance. What, exactly did that order mean? Lee insisted that he
had written orders to the effect that the emigrants must be decoyed
from their shelter and all who were old enough to testify slain. His
wife, Emma, repeatedly told that the original orders were pinned into
the diary which was taken from her home at Lonely Dell soon after
his arrest. Later, in court, Klingensmith testified that "Lee's instructions came through Higbee from Dame at Parowan," and that Higbee
said in the hearing of the men, "Orders is from me to you that they
are to be decoyed out and disarmed, in any manner, the best way you
can."

Yet here on the ground, faced with the actual problem of Indians
and orders and vows — and a group of emigrants which included
women and children — with some about him urging action and others
in silent disapproval, how is a man to know what he *is* to do? Again
the group prayed for guidance. Lee insists that only after he had with-
drawn from the others and pled for strength, only after Brother
Hopkins had come and encouraged him could he nerve himself to
carry out his orders. Having accepted, was it he who had to build up
the morale of others in this war?

The final understanding was that each member of the militia should
kill but one man, the emigrant who would walk beside him. Those
who objected or did not want to carry out the assignment should shoot
into the air and then sit down quickly, lest the Indians or the Mormon
pickets should kill them by mistake. The Indians would be responsible
for the women and older children. Diabolical as the plan was, it was
perfectly carried out. Accompanied by William Bateman carrying a
white flag, Lee walked toward the emigrant camp. Three men came
out to meet them and negotiations began.

The argument was that if those who had committed offenses at
Cedar City would come back and face the charges, they would all be

---

[7] John M. Higbee's account, which covers seventeen pages in an ordinary note
book, is written in a clear hand and gives the story of the massacre as necessary
to appease the Indians. He says that no matter who gave the orders, it was Lee
who executed them. The account is signed "Bull Valley Snort," but there is no
question as to its authenticity. A typescript is in the Utah State Historical Society.

AN EXCERPT FROM THE PATRIARCHAL BLESSING GIVEN TO
WILLIAM H. DAME BY ELISHA H. GROVES, FEBRUARY 20, 1854
See text page 209. Courtesy of Mrs. Lillis Spencer, Cedar City, Utah.

given protection. But they must first show their good faith by giving up their arms. Had Captain Fancher been killed in the first attack? Or did he give the Masonic signal of distress and receive an answering promise? Some have argued that he otherwise would never have consented to this arrangement.

When Lee came out, Higbee, who was commanding on horseback, ordered the wagons to come up. Into the first, driven by Samuel McMurdy, were loaded the guns of the emigrants, mostly Kentucky rifles, and eighteen children, all of those in the camp under the age of ten, except a babe in arms that the mother preferred to carry. This wagon moved a short distance away and stopped while the next was pulled into position and the wounded were lifted into it. Some said that there were two men and one woman in this wagon, others that there were some children also. The signal was given to start.

The second wagon, driven by Samuel Knight, followed the first; John D. Lee walked between the two. Behind them about a quarter of a mile came the women and older children in an unorganized group, while a half-mile behind, each emigrant man stepped up and took his place beside an armed Mormon "guard."

The first wagon had passed from sight over a knoll, the second was some distance behind it, and following it the women and children were going through a low swale where the road led through heavy underbrush. Somewhere near the marching men the signal was given, "Do your duty!" Instantly all the guns were fired, and at the same moment the Indians leaped from their ambush and fell upon the women and children.

Everything worked according to the plan, and all accounts agree that it was quickly over. Most of the men fell at the first volley and, shot as they were at close range, died instantly. Those that escaped were picked off by a second firing, for these Mormons were skilled marksmen. The Indians seemed everywhere at once, there being so many more of them than there were of whites that they almost got into each other's way. The teamsters with Lee and their assistants killed the ones in the second wagon and threw the bodies out into the brush beside the road.

In the first wagon the children, hearing the shots, huddled together and cried in fear. When a stray bullet struck little three-year-old Louisa Dunlap in the elbow, shattering the bone, they all became hysterical. Meanwhile the horses reared and pitched in fright until it seemed that they were in as much danger of being killed by a runaway team as by the weapons of the Indians or the guns of the white men.

Just then Philip Klingensmith rode up on horseback. The team was quieted and the children somewhat reassured as they moved on up the valley to the Hamblin ranch.

Here Rachel Hamblin had heard the shooting, and her Indian boy, Albert, had hurried home with word of the massacre as he had seen it from a distant hill. In her wagon-box bed in the yard, Caroline Knight lay tense and frightened. She had come up two weeks earlier to escape the heat at Santa Clara and to be where Rachel could help her through the delivery of her first baby. She had had a difficult time and was still weak and nervous. When her husband drove up with the load of crying children and she saw blood on his clothes from his attempts to care for the wounded arm, she began to cry and wring her hands. The more her husband tried to comfort her, the more she screamed for him to go away, sobbing and crying hysterically.

Rachel at once took the children over, directing them to wash up a bit before supper, and asking the older ones to help those younger, while she cared for the child with the wounded arm. Her kind, motherly way soon reassured them, and before long they had all been fed some hot mush and milk and put to bed close together on quilts spread over hay on the ground. In the meantime, she dressed the wounded arm, then sat in the rocking chair holding and cuddling the child. Finally she told them that if they would be quiet for a few minutes she would say a prayer for them all. So she asked God to help them to sleep well through the night and to bless especially little Louisa so that her arm would not pain so much and would heal quickly without any trouble.

That seemed to have the desired effect. Before long the children were breathing deeply. After an hour or more, Louisa fell asleep too, so Rachel laid her carefully on her own bed and went to the wagon-box where Caroline Knight still sobbed. Perhaps a little rubbing and a prayer would help quiet her, too.

At the Meadows, John D. Lee had seen the wagon of children on its way and then walked back toward the emigrant camp. Some of the Indians were already stripping the bodies of the women and children, while others were at the camp throwing clothing and dishes out like gleeful children. One was racing about swinging a pillow around his head and scattering the feathers far and wide.

Lee at once ordered Nephi Johnson to take two others with him and guard the wagons. "Let the Indians have what they have already taken, but don't let them take any more," he said. "Tell them to go back to their camp where there is beef for their supper."

The other men gathered and stood while Higbee, Lee, and others made speeches to the effect that each had done his duty in helping to defend Zion, and to protect his own family and fireside. God had been with them, and they had helped to carry out His purposes.

Then they were ordered not to leave the place until morning, until after they had buried the dead. The bodies of the men had already been searched for money or valuables, the shoes removed, tied securely in pairs and piled together, and the bodies carried to the barrow pit.

Lee and Higbee rode to Hamblin's in silence. When they arrived, the place was quiet and dark except for the candle that burned under the wagon cover where Rachel's shadow moved about. Sam Knight sat dejected on the wagon tongue; Klingensmith came to meet them from the shadow of the haystack. In low voices they discussed where to sleep, and decided to spread their blankets on the hay.

A new moon hung low in the sky; the breeze smelled of balsam and sage. Soon the sound of approaching horsemen broke the silence, and they knew their commanders-in-chief were arriving, but as by common consent the three who had participated in the afternoon's bloody business lay quiet, feigning sleep. They heard the wave of fretfulness that stirred the children, the renewed cries of little Louisa, Rachel's sharp voice ordering the men to be off, to keep away and not disturb their rest. There were intense, low, angry words between the officers. Clearly neither wished to assume responsibility for what they found here.

Finally all was quiet again, except that from a distant hill came the eerie call of a coyote, its wavering notes seeming to catch the loneliness and sorrow and futility of life, like an echo of the voices of those who now lay so still at the Meadow.

1857
Aftermath

Stories of what followed that night and the next morning come to us from many sources: from the affidavits of various participants, from the testimony of witnesses at the Lee trials, from family legends. All agree that Haight and Dame arrived at the Hamblin Ranch during the night, and that Dame was appalled at the sight of the orphaned children, especially the one with the shattered arm.

When Klingensmith made his statement before Peter B. Miller, clerk of the court in Lincoln County, Nevada, on April 10, 1871, he made a point of the fact that "on the evening of the massacre, Colonel W. H. Dame and Lieutenant I. C. Haight came to Hamblin's where I had the said children, and fell into a dispute, in the course of which said Haight told Colonel Dame, that, if he was going to report the killing of said emigrants, he should not have ordered it done. . ."

After a brief, silent breakfast, the men started back to the scene of the massacre, six on horseback, while the seventh was detailed to drive the McMurdy wagon back to the camp. Sam Knight remained at Hamblin's with his wife, who now slept feverishly, and when she roused alternately called for him and then sent him away because he smelled of blood.

According to Lee, the officers galloped along in the blue mist of dawn, drawing rein near the first unburied bodies. They were women and children in distorted positions of violent death. At the sight, Dame grew ghastly pale.

"Horrible! Horrible!" he kept saying to himself.

"Horrible enough," Haight said clearly, "but you should have thought of that before you issued the orders."

"I didn't think there were so many of them — "

"It's a little late for that now. The fact is, it *is* done. And by your orders. Now what do we do next?"

From where they sat they could see the men at work burying the dead. Knowing their task, they had begun long before light. They worked in pairs, two to a body, carrying the men to the rifle-pits of their encampment, now somewhat enlarged and cleaned out to hold more. To the right a short distance from the road, another group was busy at a steep box wash, clearing an approach and digging out the brush. As the work of moving the women and children began, the horsemen rode down to where Nephi Johnson and two others were guarding the wagons and cattle.

"What do you suggest that we do here, Brother Johnson?" Haight asked the youthful giant.

"Do you really want to know my feelings in the matter?"

"Of course."

"Well, this is what I think. You have made a sacrifice of the people, and I think we should burn the wagons and turn the cattle loose for the Indians, and go home like men." Nephi spoke firmly as though he had thought it all out.

Such a suggestion was not reasonable, of course. True, they had found no money on the bodies to speak of — only a few watches and pocket knives, and the trivia men usually carry in their pockets.

"We must report this to President Young," Dame was saying.

"How will you report it?" Haight wanted to know.

"I will report it just as it is, a full report of everything."

"And will you say that it was done under your orders?"

"No."

Haight was furious with rage.

"You know that you issued the orders to wipe out this company, and you cannot deny it! You had better not try to deny it! If you think you can shift the blame for this onto me, you're fooled! You'll stand up to your orders like a man, or I'll send you to Hell cross lots."

"Come, brethren, this will get us nowhere," Lee broke in. "The deed is done. Now how do we proceed? I suggest that you delegate two men to each wagon, to catch a team and hitch it up and drive the wagons in a train back to Cedar City, as we talked of earlier. Bishop Klingensmith is in charge of the children, and must have help in placing them in good homes. Johnson and his men can keep an eye on the loose stock or we can let them run for a few weeks and then round them up. Many of our people are poor; you know what a hard season it has been. We can issue material to the needy in exchange for public work, or give them quilts and bedding, and perhaps some clothes. But, see, the sun is up and it is getting late. This is the time for action, not for contention. We can hold another council later to decide upon making a report."

The burying squads were working frantically, feverishly to finish this most distasteful task, and as soon as word came that when they were through they should gather at the spring a short distance from the wagon circle, many did not take another shovelful, but set out. A few, more conscientious, continued to shovel and to tamp down the soil to try to make the graves more safe from the ravages of wild beasts.

At the spring there were provided towels and soap, and each man washed himself thoroughly in what was a more than symbolic rite, soaping and lathering his hands and arms to the elbows, and his face and neck.

When all were ready, they were called to stand in a circle, where they were addressed by Isaac C. Haight at the request of William H. Dame. He told them that they had been privileged to keep a part of their covenant to avenge the blood of the prophets, and suggested that if the army came into the state, or if the one that was threatened marched upon them from California, they would likely be called to fight under much different circumstances.

Now the most important thing was that they should not talk of what happened here yesterday, not to anyone, not even to their wives. Nor should they discuss it among themselves. They should blot it from their minds and from their memories and leave God to accept of their actions in the light of their loyalty to His cause and the establishment of His Kingdom upon the earth. Then they closed in the circle, so that each man placed his left hand on the shoulder of the man nearest him and raised his right hand to the square. In the center stood Dame, Haight, Higbee, and Lee, facing them at the four points of the compass. Haight led the pledge, as highest in ecclesiastical authority, and they repeated it after him. It was to the effect that each of them promised before God, angels, and their companions in this circle, that they would never under any conditions speak of this action to anyone else or to each other, and that if any did so, he would suffer his life to be taken. This was done in the name of God, and for His glory.

With the "Amen" they all relaxed and stood at ease, while Higbee assigned two to each wagon and told the others their duties. They would all go as far as Hamblin's, where they would halt but not break formation nor leave their wagons until another brief council could be held to make decisions regarding the children. In the meantime, if any of them would care to take one or more of these orphans, he could make his desire known at that time.

It was Sunday morning when Lee started back to Harmony on horseback, just a week from the day he left. Deep in his innermost heart he knew that this had been the most momentous week in all his life, for he had been called by God's authority to lead and manage this horrible deed. He did not yet know what it would be like to live with himself as a murderer, when his dreams would sometime echo with such sounds as his ears had heard but once before. He was determined to keep the pledge of silence wholly; he would try to blot from his life all memory of the affair and to go on as though it had never happened, or had been a nightmare. And until the day of his death he would never again pass over the Mountain Meadows.

As he left the creek bottom, he came upon the local Indians under Queetuse, stopped to let their horses drink and feed. They called out greetings to him in loud, friendly voices, "Yawgetts! To-wich-a-Weino Tickaboo!" They were arranging their loot, stringing tin cups or buckets on yant ropes. One placed a brass bucket on his head with the bail hanging behind, another a kettle, with the handle behind, like children dressing up for a Hallowe'en party.

They started out, with Lee riding in the center, all on a sharp trot, but as they neared the fort, the Indians broke ahead in a gallop, rattling their cups and striking their pans, or pounding their headgear with knives or spoons, at the same time uttering their wavering, eerie cry which died in a long, minor wail. Through the fort gates they dashed, rode single file three times around the inside with their calls, and finally gathered for a last long, piercing cry. At a word from Lee, they passed just outside the gates and waited until some of the men carried out melons and served them. Still in great good humor, they called their goodbyes as they started single file for their camp.

The next week was busy. Lee returned on Monday to Cedar City and met his appointment with the other leaders. The first item of business was to decide what to tell Brother Brigham and how to do it. But Dame and Haight had figured that out during Lee's absence.

"We don't think we should write it," Dame said. "The written word is too apt to fall into the wrong hands, and it is too easily misunderstood. We think you should go, Major Lee, and make an oral report, since you are closer to Brother Brigham than anyone else, being an adopted son. You can make him understand how it was with us here, and the state the Indians were in and all. It would be better all around. And to him you could do it without breaking your covenants of yesterday, since it is his right to know of everything that goes on in this church."

This time when Lee returned to Harmony, he drove a wagon with a fine team and with some goods in it. But most important, beside him on the spring seat rode little Charley Fancher, a bright ten-year-old who had Lee to thank for his life. So far as he knew, it was Lee who turned the Indians back and would not let them go to the wagon loaded with children. He was their savior and benefactor, by whose command those who lived were spared. The boy sat close to him and talked freely of his parents and home and the experiences on the trip.

When they arrived at the fort, Lee gave the boy to Caroline with the charge that she was his new mother and he was to obey her and care for the three little children or do whatever chores she asked of him. She was instructed to treat him kindly.

"Show him what love and affection you can," Lee told her. "He is an orphan child, remember, and deserves all the kindness we can give him."

In her diary on September 20, Rachel Lee noted that her husband left that morning for Salt Lake City. She made no mention of his mission or business, if indeed she knew of it herself. The brethren in the south knew that President Young had likely heard of the massacre before this time, for the mail had passed going both ways, and Indian runners had carried the word to their camps. After the visit of James Haslam asking for instructions, the Mormon leader would certainly know that something vital was afoot down south.

Some legends persist regarding Lee's trip. One comes from the family of James Gordon, a neighbor of Lee's on Mill Creek and a member of his team during the scalp hunt of 1849. Lee stopped at the Gordon home en route to the city, told them of the Indian massacre, and brought into the house the loot which as Indian Farmer, he had taken from the Indians. He carried it in a high-topped black silk hat, and poured it out onto the table for all to see: watches, jewels, and silver items.

Could this eventually have been handed in to the tithing office? The General Tithing Office and Perpetual Emigration Fund receipt book No. 2 gives a list of jewelry collected in December 1857, and valued by J. M. Barlow, (Salt Lake City jeweler) at about $150, including: gold chain, silver watch, silver tongs, gold watch, gold ring, looking glass, etc.

Lee was nine days on the road, for his interview with Brigham Young was written in detail on September 29 by Wilford Woodruff, who also heard the report. Lee told of the offenses of the emigrants, their hostile and insulting attitude, their poisoning of the springs, and their threats to return with an army. The Indians were entirely responsible for the massacre; no white man was named, not even those who came only to bury the dead. Other parties on the road would have met the same fate if Lee had not sent interpreters to save their lives.

While Lee was away, other large trains passed through southern Utah, but all were so frightened that they placed themselves in the hands of the Mormons, upon whom they depended for guides and interpreters. The first of these, the Duke train, got along very well until they reached the last crossing of the Virgin where a band of Indians and a few Mormons stampeded their cattle on October 7 and brought some three hundred head back to Santa Clara "according to instructions" from Jacob Hamblin. It was all a part of the Mormon war pattern, the same thing that Lot Smith was doing at the eastern approach to the state.

Even after the sudden descent of winter had stopped the army at Ham's Fork, the leaders knew that nothing was settled. Should they offer resistance when the roads were open next spring, or should they

move out before the enemy? Whatever the final decision, they must
keep out guards at every entrance to the territory.

In this atmosphere, the leaders in the north could do nothing about
an investigation of the massacre at Mountain Meadows. In the southern settlements whisperings continued. No one knew exactly what had
happened, or how it had happened, who was responsible, or how any
individual man conducted himself. They could see the results, and
they could conjecture.

But the war was still on, even after the brethren were allowed to
come in from their defenses in Emigration Canyon. Everywhere the
people were singing their new battle song:

> On the necks of thy foes thou shalt tread
> And their silver and gold, as the prophets foretold
> shall be brought to adorn thy fair head,

with the refrain of, "O Zion, dear Zion, land of the free!" and the
promise that "the Gentiles shall bow 'neath thy rod."

Returning from his trip north after he had made his report and
handed over what he had of the valuables, Lee felt that he had indeed
done his duty toward the building of the kingdom. That President
Young himself was not above taking advantage of the government
which was sending an army against him, is shown in a number of
ways in his accounts in the Records of the National Archives; Indian
Department. For example, one voucher presented by Levi Stewart,
dated September 30, 1857, and paid on December 31, 1857, with a
draft on the Commissioner of Indian Affairs, was for "articles furnished
sundry bands of Indians near Mountain Meadows (320 miles south of
Salt Lake City) on superintendent's order." The articles included 171
pairs of pants, 135 shirts, 566 pipes, 39½ pounds of powder, 109 pounds
of lead, 14,000 firing caps, and many other things. They were invoiced
at $3527.43. Levi Stewart testified that the articles "were furnished for
an expedition to the southern Indians," and D. B. Huntington and
John D. Lee certified that they "were present, and saw the articles
mentioned in this voucher distributed to the following Indians:
Tat-se-gobbits and band, Non-cap-in and band, Mo-quee-tus and band,
Chick-eroo and band, Quo-na-rah and band, Young-quick and band,
Jackson and band, and Agra-pootes and band." These were the Indian
chiefs of the area, and whether or not the goods were distributed on
the date specified or the guns and ammunition before the massacre
and the clothing later, there is no way now to know. But President
Young approved and signed this voucher on the very day *after* Lee,
in Salt Lake City, made his report of the massacre. Huntington was

also in the city at the time. There seems little doubt that the amounts of all the articles listed were greatly exaggerated.

But Zion was taking its stand against the United States, and a part of any war is outwitting the enemy. If they could collect more than $3,500 from the government to use in their war against it, they were just good strategists. Later they would make out vouchers for the care of the orphaned children.

During these weeks immediately following the massacre, the people of Cedar City became so profoundly affected as to be almost in a state of shock. The extra wagons in the tithing office yard and the orphaned children in so many homes made them all acutely conscious of the tragedy at the Meadows. Although John D. Lee had one at Harmony, Jacob Hamblin three at Santa Clara, Richard Harrison one at Pinto, and Philip Klingensmith two, one of whom he gave to the Birbecks since they had no other children, there were still eleven others to be placed, all with only the explanation that their parents had been killed by the Indians.

There were now on the tithing office shelves many pairs of shoes, tied together and arranged by size; there were quilts and blankets, cooking utensils and dishes, and some clothing. There were muted whisperings of bloody shirts and dresses that were soaked in many waters, washed in suds, and ironed ready for wear, and of women who became nauseated or turned faint over their task but remained tight-lipped and stoic.

It was as though a pall of darkness lay over the little community. Brethren passed each other on the street without looking up or speaking, neighbors avoided each other, wives who had the constant reminder of an extra child remained home from church. Isaac C. Haight now moved one of his families to Toquerville; Philip Klingensmith took his farther up the Virgin River, Nephi Johnson moved still farther up into what is now Zion National Park. Though the military law forbade any to leave the territory or to make any move without the consent and direction of their leaders, those involved in the massacre did move to ranches and outlying settlements.

1858
Business as Usual

His business finished and his report of the massacre accepted, Lee returned at once to Harmony. On his arrival, he learned of some new developments regarding the massacre. Before he left, he had learned that all three of the men who had attempted to escape from the massacre had been killed: Aiden at the spring before the massacre, the second by Chief Jackson at the Santa Clara crossing, the third at the last crossing of the Virgin, nearly a hundred miles south. The Indians had committed the murder, but white men had carried the report back to the settlements.

The new evidence lay in a book which Chief Jackson had taken from the body of the man he killed, a record which outlined the travel of the murdered group and listed the names of all the company. Jacob Hamblin took the book from the chief, but not before John Hunt, the mail rider, had seen and examined it. A few others knew of its existence also.

Hamblin later told that Lee took the book from him and destroyed it; Lee never admitted seeing it or made any mention of it in his writings that are available. Suppose he did secure it. Would he have destroyed it, or would he have taken it in to President Young on his next trip to the city? This question may never be answered, but such a record, if found, would be most valuable.

Early in December Lee went to the city again, this time to attend the legislature. George A. Smith would represent both the southern counties in the council, while in the house, Lee and Haight represented Washington and Iron Counties respectively. They traveled in the same wagon.

There were many long weekends and early adjournments which gave time for pleasure as well as business. Lee visited his daughter, Sarah Jane Dalton, who now lived here; he also courted a new wife. His diary and family legends tell the story.

On his second Sunday night in the city he was called to the stand in the Fourteenth Ward and asked to offer the opening prayer. As the meeting progressed he noticed a fine-looking girl sitting beside a middle-aged woman. He looked straight at her and smiled; she caught his glance and dropped her eyes. At the end of the meeting she disappeared.

The next Wednesday he was invited to attend an evening sociable at the home of his old friend, Brother Dot. Here he met this girl, Emma Batchelor, lately from England, a lively twenty-two-year-old with a clear complexion, ruddy cheeks, and a delightful accent. He learned that she was working at the home of another friend, Brother Rollins, so the next day he called there and elicited an invitation to dinner.

If he had thought her attractive at first, she seemed doubly so now in her neat dress and white apron. Her biscuits were like none he had ever eaten before, and he had always thought Aggatha was a good cook. The roast not only was perfectly done, but there was a new, teasing flavor, a something added. When he asked for her company to the dance that evening, she blushed to the roots of her hair. He borrowed Brother Stoddard's fine team and closed buggy, secured a soft buffalo robe to go over their knees, and drove her through the snow to the ward house, where he waltzed and schottisched and went through the intricate changes of the quadrille with the ease of much practice.

The next morning he took Emma and Sarah Jane to the city to shop. They were almost the same age, these two, and were as much at home with each other as though they had been sisters. He let them have their pictures taken together; he had his own done too, but alone. He bought each of them a pretty fascinator to go around her shoulders and a lacy handkerchief to carry. He took Sarah Jane home first, for though it was early afternoon, her two children would need her. Nor did he make any other appointment with Emma, but as they rode the last blocks to Brother Rollins' he put his arm around her and pulled her close, tucking the robe about her.

"Cold?" he asked.

"Not very."

"A pretty girl like you must have had plenty of chances to marry here in Zion."

"A girl doesn't take every chance she gets, though, remember that."

"I will." And he fell into a long silence.

"With you it's different, though," she confessed at last. "You know that night at meeting. I knew you were the one for me as soon as you started to pray. You had such a good voice. Then I opened my eyes and I watched you all the time. I wondered how long it would be before you saw me in the audience. I thought you would; I tried to make you."

"Yes, and you would never look up again. You knew I was smiling at you, and you wouldn't look up. And when it was over, you ran away."

"I guess I was a little scared. I thought maybe you could find me if you really wanted to."

So being assured that Emma loved him and would be willing to cast her lot with his regardless of other wives and children and the life on the frontier, he told her that he would talk it over with President Young and let her know his decision within a few days. For right now, she must go back to her evening duties as cook and housekeeper for Brother Rollins' wife and he would attend the theater where *The Lady of Lyons* was playing.

He did not see her until Tuesday. On Sunday he preached in the Eighth Ward to an attentive audience where he was "full of the Spirit and had good Liberty."

Monday he attended the legislature, where the whole subject was the spirit of the people in California, the nonMormons angry and excited, the saints returning to Utah and leaving behind all they could not load into their wagons. "All hell is in commotion; government intends sending ten thousand troops by the South rout & as many by the North rout. . ." he wrote. In the evening he had an interview with the governor with regard to his marriage to Emma, and "I also Signed quite a No. of vouchers, as claims against government for Servises amoung the Indians." These last were to be as a thorn in his flesh all his life, and to stand in judgment against him many years later.

On Tuesday he took Emma in a borrowed carriage to the home of President Young for a personal interview. She had never met this great man personally, so was rather awed at the prospect. Brigham Young held her hand and looked at her searchingly. She met his gaze without flinching, though the natural color deepened in her cheeks and flooded her neck.

"So you came with the Martin Company, Sister Bachellor," he said after he had invited them to be seated.

"Yes, sir."

"And you have not suffered any permanent effects? Your feet and ankles didn't get frozen?"

"I always was one of the first to wade the streams," she said, "but I took off my shoes and stockings and carried them across, so I could have them dry afterwards. And I always scrubbed my feet hard with my wool neck piece. And I asked the Dear Lord to help me take care of myself, since there was none else to look after me, and promised that if I should come through whole, I'd not complain at my lot, no matter what it was."

"But you were sealed to Brother Kippen, weren't you? Have you not complained at that?"

"That was something different. I was sent to his house to live, and I earned all I got by washing and ironing and scrubbing and waiting on the first wife. I was as a servant maid to her. I thought that the sealing was as a protection to give me a home, and then I could choose my husband."

"And do you think that you have found the man you want now?"

"Oh, yes, sir."

"You understand the order of this kingdom. You know that he has other wives, and you are willing to take your place among them."

"Yes, sir."

Brigham rose and took her hand, motioning for her to stand, also.

"Sister Emma, I bless you in the name of the Lord. You are free from any bonds with any man previous to this hour. You will find Brother Lee a kind husband, who does not expect any one woman to be subservient to another, but each to have her own place as a wife by his side. Be faithful to him through all adversity and you will find him a pillar of strength to you. Make your preparations and meet us here at 12 o'clock tomorrow noon and we will perform the ceremony."

So it was that, on January 7, Emma Batchelor was sealed to John D. Lee in Brigham Young's own sealing room. After the ceremony he took her to his boarding place at Brother Ezra T. Benson's and introduced her to the other members of the legislature who also ate there. Sister Benson had prepared and decorated a wedding cake, John D. brought some cherry brandy and other liquors in honor of the occasion, and they celebrated with a fine dinner.

Through the next week his work at the legislature kept him busy, for he was a member of the committee for herding and herd grounds and also of that on Indian relations. There were discussions of ways and means for doing away with the government tax, for the running of the mail, and other public works to be done through the bishops and the tithing office. They also decided to organize a bank by which they might control their own finance. The army was now in winter quarters on Ham's Fork, living in tents, where they would have to stay for two or three months longer. By April the saints would either have to keep them out by force, move away ahead of them, or back down from all the war talk of the autumn.

The legislature adjourned to meet in Parowan, or such other place as might be convenient, since plans for the general move had not yet been formulated. There was some discussion of a wholesale, permanent evacuation, but a canny holding off to see if there might not be some other way to save face short of actual combat.

President Young had a long, private talk with Lee, counseling him to encourage the manufacturing of powder and the getting out of lead. He should also wake up the people to their duties, for perilous

JOHN D. LEE
From a photograph taken December 26, 1857,
just after the Mountain Meadows affair.
Courtesy of Edna Lee Brimhall, Thatcher, Arizona.

times might be facing them. Since Israel must be self-sustaining in the mountains, he was sending Joseph Horne and a group of twenty-two young men to experiment with the raising of cotton at the confluence of the Virgin and the Tonaquint, or Santa Clara Creek. He had received samples of that grown at Santa Clara earlier. As a member of the Council of Fifty, Lee should go with the group and help them select a good location, and lay out the fields and ditches.

At last they were ready to leave. They had four mules on the wagon, but what with the new stove Lee had bought, Isaac C. Haight's new wife and Emma and their boxes of clothes and knickknacks, they were heavily loaded. At Provo they picked up two of Richard Woolsey's boys to take along so that they might bring back teams and move their whole family south. They were destitute and wanted to get where Lee could help them.

They were ten days on the road. At no time did they camp out, for they planned their stops so that they would have shelter and supper and breakfast with friends. Lee accepted these hospitalities as freely as he gave them, for most of the people with whom he stopped had stayed at his home previously. Or he left a gift of sugar or a ham or some other item at least equal in value to the cost of his food.

By the time they reached Buckhorn Flat near Paragonah, the team had become so fagged they could hardly travel. Richard Benson came along with an empty wagon and a fresh team and offered to take part of their load, so Brother Haight and Elizabeth and one of the Woolsey boys took their luggage and went with him. They invited Emma to go too, thinking she would like to get in out of the cold and mud, but she refused, saying that she preferred to stay with her husband. That night Lee wrote in his diary:

(Reflections). Emma is the 1st English girl that was given me in the Covenant of the Priesthood, & a more kindhearted, industrious, & affectionate wife I never had. She covenanted to follow me through Poverty, privation, or affliction to the end of her days & I believe that her intentions real & integrity true.

They arrived at Harmony on the night of February 5, and were warmly greeted by the family. Emma looked around the large kitchen with its premium range and shining teakettle, its coal-oil lamp and its loaves of fresh bread cooling on the sideboard and knew that she was to be one of a large and busy family. For a temporary arrangement, she was to sleep with Mary Ann Williams, the girl who during the reformation period of 1856, had been sealed to Lee, but was then only thirteen years old, too young to be his wife. According to the celestial law, a man must wait upon the desires of his wife, and the older Mary Ann became, the less she wanted Lee as her husband.

The next morning John D. called all the families together that they might meet Emma and she might get acquainted with them. He also wanted to report on his trip and to hear from them what had gone on in his absence. They met in the large upstairs hall.

For Emma this was a real experience, though she accepted the doctrine of plurality as the highest, holiest order of marriage. Everywhere it was being preached and young women came to believe that it was better to bear children to a leader in the church, though he had other wives, than to marry an inferior man. The number of his wives and the caliber of his children were something of a measure of a man's worth, a matter of great pride. No man was expected to hold a responsible position in the church who would not live this celestial law.

Here were seven mothers, each with at least two children, all living within the fort or nearby in the village. The wives ranged in age from Aggatha, who was forty-four, down to Mary Leah Groves, who was twenty-two, just as Emma was. Then there was Mary Ann just past sixteen, who was not yet a wife in fact. As for the children, Alma was eighteen, Joseph fourteen, and Willard nine — then there were *seventeen* little ones eight years old and younger. Add to these James Thompson, Lem, the Indian boy, and Charlie Fancher all about ten years old, and you have a total of twenty-three children in the household, and every one present at the meeting, sitting on chairs, on benches, or on the floor.

They sang several songs, hymns with which they were familiar. Lee offered prayer and then addressed them, advising the mothers to continue to teach their children the songs of Zion, to sing these in their private homes until, when they came together, they could really put the spirit into them. All who were eight years old should be memorizing the Articles of Faith and the Sermon on the Mount and other scriptures, so that when they met again they would give each a chance to see how well they could recite them, either alone or together. They should be also taught other good poems and stories, that their minds should be trained to gather and store gems of truth.

He would make a full report of his trip north in church tomorrow to all the adult congregation, and would talk over the matters of the farm with the older boys and the hired men. As for the wives, he was proud of every one and held each in love and respect as he hoped they in turn did him. Just as soon as possible he would finish the apartment for Mary Leah so that she could move into the family hall, and Emma could probably share it with her until they could do better. As for him, President Brigham Young had charged him to go with Brother Joseph Horne and the boys to lay out the cotton farm, which would take most of the next week. It was not an assignment he had asked for, but he realized how important the raising of cotton would be to the welfare of this people and the building up of the kingdom of God on the earth, and he hoped that he would never shirk any assignment or fail to do whatever was required of him in building and strengthening the kingdom.

Only two days at home, and he must go south with Brother Horne and his boys. The women, accustomed to his long absences, had learned to manage without him, the older boys doing the chores, feeding the stock and entertaining themselves with target shooting, horseback riding, or calf roping. Since the younger children were forced to stay indoors much of the time, the mothers tried to teach the girls simple cross stitch handwork or mending, or entertained them with games and songs.

Lee and Brother Horne and others decided on the site for the cotton farm, surveyed for the ditch and located the place for the dam. On his way back, Lee stopped at the struggling little community of Washington and purchased sixteen acres of cleared land that he too might support the cotton-raising project. He also secured a two-roomed rock house on a lot in the town. Later he could move two of his wives there.

Through the next week, he worked at roofing additional rooms at the fort in Harmony, and with the help of Elias Morris at plastering, had them snug and tight and ready for occupancy, a place for Emma and Mary Ann and Terressa Chamberlain, who had refused to go back north with her husband.

Now the late winter storms set in, with snow so deep that travel was impossible, and the whole village was isolated. The business of caring for cattle and keeping fires occupied full time.

Brother Brigham had charged Lee to stir up the saints to their duties and to carry on the work of the reformation. Since he could do nothing financially profitable, he had as well be about the Lord's business. So he rode to the outlying ranches, to Pinto Creek, and finally to Brother Ritchie's at Pine Valley. At this high altitude it was snowing steadily, but so persuasive and zealous was Lee that Brother Ritchie and family were willing to renew their covenants by baptism. "I baptized them in the storm. Snow 2 feet deep. Confirmed them & made a record. The Spirit of the Lord was with me and blessed my labours," he wrote. Certainly these were not "warm water saints," these people who would count at naught the discomfort and the danger of taking cold as compared to being counted clean before the Lord and in full fellowship in His Kingdom.

When the storm continued into the last week of March, Lee decided to take a part of his family and go to Washington, where it would be real spring and planting time. He took Polly to do the cooking and care for the house, and Terressa Morse Chamberlain. Though she was forty-five years old, she was in excellent health and a willing worker, either outside or in. Alma and the Indian boy, Lem, made up the company, which traveled in two wagons and took along seeds, fruit trees, and grape cuttings to set out, besides food and provision, with a milk cow tied to the back of each wagon.

The women were soon established in the solid rock house and for ten days all hands worked to enclose the lots and plant them to trees and vines. Here in this mild, warm climate it was pleasant to work in the earth.

In the midst of it all came an express from Salt Lake City carrying a secret circular to say that the policy was now to move out of Salt Lake City and leave it ready for the torch should their enemies attempt to take possession of it. The saints from the south must lend teams and outfits to help with the move.

During the next two weeks they were in a flurry of uncertainty. The plans were now to move out ahead of the invading army. Where should they go? To Mexico or the isles of the sea? They had always been taught that this is a land choice above all other lands; why then should they leave it?

Yet on March 10, Haight recorded that he had received a letter from President Young ordering them "to send a company to explore the White Mountains to find a place for the saints to hide from their enemies." Four days later came another letter calling for fifteen men with the necessary animals and supplies to go on the expedition. Lee himself made an entry which shows the temper of the times:

. . . Spent the night at Pres. W. H. Dame, who had just re- turned from G.S.L.C. with instructions from Pres. B. Young to raise a co. of from 60 to 70 men, 20 wagons with 4 mules to each wagon 2 teamsters & a horseman, with seed grain, tools &c to penetrate the desert in search of a resting place for the saints. Said that he hoped the Co. could find a desert that would take them 8 days to cross but was affraid that it would take them only 3 days to cross it, counting this is the 4th attempt & if you cant find the place I will go myself when I get to Parowan.

Scouts were sent out, but returned to say that while they found plenty of desert, they found no place that would support human life. Finally, writing to Lee for wagons and oxen to help with the move, President Young said on March 24 that "It is at present expected to make Headquarters at Parowan for a time, when we arrive there." It was a great relief when the decision was reached that all those south of Provo would not need to move at all.

Writing under date of April 11, 1858, Lee said that the saints from the south were sending fourteen wagons with from two to four yoke of cattle to each and some fifteen yoke of extra oxen. "Of that no. I furnished 2 waggons & 18 yoke of oxen. I also sent up 75 head of beef catle, cows, & calves to meet my obligation with L. Stewart & W. H. Hooper G.S.L. City."

It would seem that this contribution was largely from the booty from the Mountain Meadows massacre. Now that the people of the south had made their contribution, they could go on about their daily tasks and wait to hear of the army marching through their beautiful city, now deserted except for a few men ready to set fire to every home and improvement should the invaders try to take possession.

On June 14, Governor Cumming issued a proclamation that peace was restored to the territory and offering his sincere congratulations for "the peaceful and honorable adjustments of recent difficulties." The "full and free pardon" which had been issued by the President of the United States was also made public to the Mormon people, who refused to admit that they had done anything that deserved a pardon.

During all this spring of 1858 Lee was busy enlarging and improving his farm. He now had employed permanently several hired men, while he himself moved from one holding to another. His trips included the farm at Washington in one direction and the mills at Parowan in the other, besides taking a part of his family up to the spring to wash the wool, another part out to gather dock-root for tanning leather, or to the canyons for posts. Always he took at least two of his wives along and some of the older children, rotating the turns among them.

One incident shows the faith his family had in Lee's uncanny insight, or his following of either hunches or inspiration. On the afternoon of May 16 Caroline missed her three-year-old son, George. She had thought he was playing with the other children, so no one knew exactly when he left. She raised the alarm and the full community turned out to search; around the corrals and haystacks, through the fields, in the ditches, and finally out in the rocky, wild country toward the canyon.

Boys and men on horseback, women and older children on foot worked their way through the brush and thickets calling and searching for signs. Darkness fell and most of the group came in, but the mother stumbled through the brush with a lantern until she was exhausted.

Finally, Aggatha persuaded them all to come in and unite in asking God's direction in their search and His protection over the child during the night. Before light the search was resumed. When James Lewis left with the mail at six o'clock, they told him of the tragedy and asked that he carry word to the child's father at Washington. Caroline, beset with fear lest George had been carried off into slavery by some passing Indian bands or had been devoured by a cougar or other wild beast, felt that she must have the support of her husband.

Lewis arrived at Washington in the early evening, and, before he took the mail in, he stopped to tell Lee, so that he might perhaps ride to Harmony during the night. Word of the child lost for fourteen hours quickly spread through the village, with neighbors offering to form a posse.

Lee asked his family to go about their evening chores and to leave him in solitude, that he might inquire of the Lord and act according to the direction of His spirit. He must have quiet and time. At first he was in confusion, even beset by a neuralgia or "nervous toothache," which he thought was the power of evil trying to distract him. "At length the vision of my mind was opened & I saw that my child was found & returned to his Mother unhurt," he wrote.

When the neighbors saw him out working about the yard the next morning, they asked if he had received word from his lost child. He answered "Yes, but not from any earthly source. The Lord made it manifest to me that the child was safe and well."

Before noon another messenger arrived from Harmony with word that the evening before, about the time Lee had gone to inquire of the Lord, little George had been picked up by an old Indian, Toot-le-pah, and returned to his mother little worse for the experience. His wives sent word that they felt sure he knew that the child was well, or that he would have been warned had he been in danger. This message of trust from his women warmed Lee's heart.

So often during this season Lee wrote of visits from Indians, some begging, others asking for beef, others to report raids in the north, and still others with captives to trade. Within a week he purchased four Indian girls — Alice, Mahala, Annette, and Alnora. Two of these he evidently traded to other families, for he mentions only Alice and Alnora, both of whom died, Alnora of lung consumption in October, 1860. The boy Lem had lived in the family for six years and was now a young man. After he had tried to gain his freedom and been brought back by his own people, Lee gave him a pony, some clothes, and food, and told him to go and find himself a wife and a living in his own way.

During this season, Lee seemed to be courting the girl, Mary Ann. Although she was never alone with him on a trip, she was usually included. In March he took Caroline and Mary Ann; during planting time it was Caroline, Emma, and Mary Ann who usually dropped the seed; and also these three who went to the spring to clean and wash the wool.

On July 14, "for some reason then unknown to me, I was constrained to visit the settlement at Quich'up'Pah." He had heard from the Indians that some animals had been stolen at Beaver, and that some of the band were coming south. Lee took with him Lavina, Mary Ann and Doc, an Indian. When they reached the place they found General Jefferson Hunt with a part of his family and C. Crisman's sons and their families standing off an Indian attack on their cattle.

Lee heard their story, and sent his Indian, Doc, to the camp to ask the chief to come in and talk to him. "They replied that I could come to their camp, but they would not come to the Mormon camp." Lee went to them. At first the chief refused to shake hands with him. "I expressed astonishment & said like which signifies: What is up? Or, what does this mean? What have I done to merit such treatment? Have I not been a Father to you? At that he handed me his hand with a Friendly grip, continueing You have been a Father and a friend to us. We are not mad at you." Then they explained how the big herd of cattle had eaten their grass and ruined their grain, and the owners refused to make any compensation. Lee promised that he would "fix it" by morning, and accordingly they all went to bed instead of standing guard.

"I then knew the cause of the impression that was made the evening before leading me to this Place. . . I believe that blood would have been shed if I had not of went & moderated their anger," he concluded. This was all the more a source of satisfaction to him, since he had felt that Jefferson Hunt had been insulting and disrespectful to him at Santa Fe, when he went to carry out the orders of Brigham Young and bring back as much of the soldiers' pay as he could.

For the twenty-fourth of July that year, Lee took five of his wives — Rachel, Caroline, Mary Leah, Emma, and Mary Ann — to join with Polly and Lavina, who already lived at Washington, to share in the community celebration. Aggatha and the children could take care of things at Harmony; Martha Berry's little girl was in such poor health that she did not care to leave. She was dissatisfied, anyway, and getting ready to separate from her husband. She would take the children to her mother at Kanarra and leave them, while she married Dennis Dorrity as his third wife and moved with him to Kanosh.

Mary Ann, though she joined in freely with work and play and was loved by the other wives, still would not be a wife to John D. Lee. She even wrote two letters of protest to Brother Brigham, which he answered to her husband, but offered no solution. They should settle these things between themselves or should discuss them with their local authorities.

For a time her name does not appear, and then on January 18, 1859, all the difficulty was resolved. Lee's account is graphic:

> She for some cause became dissatisfied. I told her that if I could not make her happy that she should have her liberty, and if there was any other man that she could be more happy with, to say so & I would use my endeavors to have her seald to that man. She replied that she could love me and respect me as a Father but not as a husband, and that she wanted my oldest son for her companion & that she loved him more than any other Man she ever saw. Upon reflection I answered that her request should be granted. . .

Having settled the matter, Lee invited the entire population of the fort, ordered a large wedding cake made and decorated, and a sumptuous feast prepared.

When Lee saw how Mary Ann sparkled, how she ran first and kissed Emma and hugged her, then clung to Aggatha and kissed her, he wondered if he was perhaps the only one who was not conscious of the little drama that had gone on right under his nose. Emma had encouraged it, he could see; Aggatha had also known. He had been away a great deal, and had not realized how much these two had been thrown together; at the corral where Mary Ann often helped with the milking, in the kitchen where she washed the family dishes and scrubbed floors, on the trips where they often rode horseback together.

But when he saw the love and happiness in their faces, he put aside all resentment. A boy not quite twenty and a girl seventeen-past could face anything together when they look at each other like that. As a father, he was pleased. This thing, he could see, was right.

1858-1859
Uncertainty

Now having witnessed the marriage of Mary Ann Williams and John Alma Lee, and being assured that she remained the faithful and *only* wife of this young man, we drop her from this account and return to pick up the significant events of the year 1858 and 1859 as they would affect the destiny of John D. Lee.

As on the previous year, he was host to a large group from Cedar City on the Fourth of July. For more than a week in advance he had kept a crew of twelve men busy painting, papering, laying new rag carpet, and generally renovating his home in the fort. This time he made three hundred gallons of malt beer early enough that it would carry a real kick; he butchered two fat beeves and two goats; for days ahead his wives made pastries. The general program followed rather closely the one of the year before, only with a little more flourish. The twelve mounted men from Harmony met the twelve "Equestrians" from Cedar City five miles out on the road, and while the color bearers stood at attention, they gave a military salute and did some fancy figures to the music of the band. There was the same orator of the day, the same band, and choir, and an equal abundance of food and drink.

But while Isaac C. Haight and his associates celebrated at Harmony, most of the citizens of Cedar City remained at home with no special activity to mark the day. By this time discontent had increased until people were voicing their suspicions to one another. It was more than ten months after the massacre, and the war hysteria had burned out. The army had marched through the city of the Great Salt Lake; peace had been declared; the citizens of Utah forgiven for their rebellion; the "move south" a thing of the past. Then why was the discipline still so rigid here?

They would ask Brother George A. Smith about this. He arrived on August 3, accompanied by Amasa Lyman, Erastus Snow, and Charles C. Rich of the Twelve Apostles, and a number from Parowan, all with their wives. Strangely, neither William H. Dame nor Isaac C. Haight was along. The company had gone down by way of Pinto to Santa Clara, Heberville, and Washington, stopping at Harmony on the return trip.

They each had five meals at the table of John D. Lee, and fed their cattle at his stacks. At the meetings they counseled thrift, but they also "droped the reigns & told the People that they were at liberty to go where they pleased from one Setlement to another, where they thought that they could better their condition, Etc." This marked the end of the military restrictions of the "war."

Brother George A. was especially friendly, as he recalled some of the experiences they had shared during the trip to Parowan; the novel they read, the excitement they caused by firing the cannon. Lee recorded that Brother Smith had his clerk, Brother McKnights "take the No. of my family, the Progress of this Fort &c. Spoke of their kind reception & in his Journal called me the Master Spirit of this Place, &c."

They invited Lee to be present at a special meeting to be held the next day at Cedar City. Complaints had come in to Headquarters regarding President Haight, they said. Lee was flattered, but went with some misgiving. He did not know that en route to Harmony, George A. Smith, with James McKnight and Nephi Johnson, had left the others, and following the abandoned road through the Meadows, had passed over the ground of the massacre. The scars of the rifle pits were still clear, scattered bones lay bleaching in the sun, masses of human hair still clung to some of the bushes, and remnants of faded sunbonnets were seen; everything spoke too eloquently of what had taken place. Brother Smith could guess by whose order this was done and what the group to whom he had preached a year ago were in the humor to do.

Though he could see clearly that the women and children had been farther from the camp than the men, he still wrote that "the men must have run away and left the women." In the first report he made the massacre entirely an Indian affair, with the Mormon interpreters returning to Cedar City and leaving the Indians to carry it out alone. Besides his own observations, he must get his information from Nephi Johnson, the Indian interpreter, who was sworn to secrecy.

The private meeting at Cedar City lasted for two days. During his stay there, Lee slept at the home of John M. Higbee, his associate on that tragic afternoon at the Meadows. Sharing his bed and board was Erastus Snow. Minutes of the discussions are not available, but Lee remarked in his journal that the people were at liberty to move as they pleased and that in the end Brother Smith, "reproved all, gave good council, blessed and dismissed."

Lee was released to go home, while Haight was asked to go with the visitors to Parowan. On that night, August 6, James McKnight and George A. Smith wrote up the result of the investigation. From evidence on the ground and from what they had learned they concluded that:

1. The Indians attacked the train on Monday and the massacre occurred on the following Friday.

2. Nephi Johnson and some other white men arrived on the ground on Wednesday, but finding the Indians angry and threatening, returned to Cedar City.

3. For some reason not explained, the emigrants left their wagons, the men and women traveling separately.

4. Isaac C. Haight and William H. Dame arrived together at the scene on Saturday morning after the massacre.

5. The white men buried the bodies in shallow graves, from which the wolves had dragged many of them.

6. There were some two hundred Indians present.

The date was first given as September 22 to 25, but a note at the end in the handwriting of George A. Smith corrected it to say that the massacre occurred some fifteen days earlier. Brother Smith knew of James Haslan's ride and of the fact that Brigham Young's answer reached Cedar City on September 13. To place the massacre later would be to implicate Brigham Young. George A. Smith knew the temper of the leaders involved; he could guess and respect their pact of silence.

Complaints against the rigid military rule could be corrected, but cases where the police had used their clubs too freely could not. Bishop Dame had written that his men were armed with "small" canes about the size of a rack stake. Of heavy oak, these were deadly weapons, and the injury which William Leany had suffered from one would trouble him all his life.

Whatever the details, the visitors found plenty to criticize. At the conclusion, Isaac C. Haight wrote in his journal, "Much good counsel and instructions were given, and some severe chastisement by Elders Smith and Lyman."

At Parowan they opened a second private court, this time without Erastus Snow and Charles C. Rich, who had gone to investigate the iron works. That the court investigated the Mountain Meadows massacre and that William H. Dame was able to clear himself of responsibility is shown by a handwritten paper found in his personal collection. Evidently in the hand of James McKnight, it is signed by all the men present. It reads:

PAROWAN,   August 12, 1858

We have carefully and patiently investigated the complaints made against President William H. Dame, for four successive days, and are fully satisfied that his actions as a Saint and administration as a President have been characterized by the right spirit, and are highly creditable to his position in the priesthood; and that the complaints presented before us are without foundation in truth.

Geo. A. Smith	S. O. White
Amasa Lyman	F. T. Whitney
James H. Martineau	M. Ensign
James Lewis	S. S. Smith
C. C. Pendleton	John M. Higbee
Charles Hall	Samuel West
H. M. Alexander	Tarlton Lewis
Job P. Hall	Elijah Elmer
John Steele	Wm. Barton
I. C. Haight	P. Meeks
Nephi Johnson	Orson B. Adams
	J. N. Smith

This is a most significant document. On the ground, Isaac C. Haight had insisted that "nothing has been done here except on your orders." Now he meekly signs a statement clearing Dame. Nephi Johnson also exonerates Dame, as does John M. Higbee, though only after a four-day debate. If Dame is without guilt, who then was responsible? Who, indeed, except John D. Lee? As Indian Farmer, he could be held to account for the conduct of the natives, in some degree at least. Not being present, he had no defense.

The list shows that the men were mostly from Parowan, some of them officers in the military but not participants at the Meadows. James H. Martineau was adjutant to Dame, Calvin C. Pendleton, surgeon, James Lewis, major, and Charles Hall and Francis T. Whitney both second lieutenants. The others were only privates, if indeed they were members of the militia at all. Perhaps the contradictory nature of the orders was the subject for the long controversy, some insisting that "under no condition are you to precipitate an Indian war while there is an army marching against our people" meant what it said.

Now George A. Smith and James McKnight made a second report of the massacre, dated Parowan, August 17, 1858. It was much longer than the first and listed the offenses of the emigrants in Missouri and Illinois and as they passed through the state, until the Indians became incensed and attacked them. "For the citizens to have attacked and killed the Indians in defense of the emigrants would have been little else than suicide, as you are well aware of the exposed condition of the Southern settlers. . ."

The damning part was the sentence that "It is reported that John D. Lee and a few other white men were on the ground during a portion of the combat, but for what purpose or how they conducted or whether indeed they were there at all, I have not learned."

The whole proceeding evidently made an impression upon the secretary, James McKnight, for whatever was said, he had walked over the ground and seen the evidence; he had listened to the witnesses and taken the minutes and written the reports. This man who had been baptized in Australia by Charles W. Wandell, served as bishop of the Minersville ward from 1866 until his excommunication from the church for "apostasy" on December 19, 1875, soon after the first trial of John D. Lee. His experiences here evidently contributed to his attitude.

As for Lee himself, he had returned from the meetings at Cedar City to take up his fall work. To him, a part of the building of the kingdom meant improving his own surroundings. As others in responsible positions had fine homes, so he wished to have one in which he could entertain his guests in a suitable manner. He purchased lumber, hired skilled labor, and had a crew making adobes, in an attempt to have food and shelter for the winter travelers. He bought other houses in the fort; Lavina and Polly had been moved to Washington, and Martha Berry had left, so he had extra bed rooms available.

Because of the long desert stretch to the south, the overland travel was made during the winter months and most of the wagon trains stopped at Harmony. At thirty-one cents a meal and the same per head for a night's feed for cattle, Lee took in from twenty to seventy-five dollars a night, depending upon the size of the train. There were nights when Aggatha, Emma, Rachel, and Terressa cooked most of the night to serve travelers. Ten horsemen who had their feet frostbitten stopped several days; then hired Lee's wagon to take them as far as Washington at a cost of thirty dollars for the group. One large train stayed so long that he took in a total of one hundred and seventy-five dollars.

In November, 1858, Lee purchased several pieces of property in the new town of Washington: a stone building and two lots from J. B. Regions and a double adobe building, three lots, corrals and fifteen acres of land from John Couch. With Polly and Lavina stationed there, he could also take in travelers at that point. In fact, he started a new home which was to be his "mansion," the finest of all the houses he built in his life. It was of cut stone, two stories above the ground, with a full basement. Because of the mild weather, winter was an excellent time to build and by keeping fifteen men steadily employed, he had the walls up and the roof shingled by the end of March, though it would take more than a year longer to complete it fully.

Amasa Lyman came again in the spring en route from San Bernardino, and was entertained first at Washington and then at Harmony, where on March 19, 1859, he sealed Terressa Morse Chamberlain to John D. Lee. She had lived in the home for more than a year now and wished to become a member of the family.

Of her background we know only that she was married in 1848 to Solomon Chamberlain, a man thirty years her senior, and their only child, Sariah Louise was born October 8, 1849, at Salt Lake City. The census for 1850 listed the family as:

Solomon	Chamberlain	aged	62	b. Conn
Terressa	"	"	30	b. Ohio
Charles	"	"	17	b. Mo.
Robert	"	"	16	Ohio
Louisa	"	"	1	b. Deseret

This group came south with John D. Lee's train in November, 1851, and on to Harmony later. When her husband moved north, he took the daughter, but Terressa refused to go. Later Louisa returned to Harmony and became a plural wife of Lemuel H. Redd. Charles Chamberlain also returned and worked along with John D. Lee's sons, at whatever farm tasks were assigned him. Lee often spoke of him as Charley Chamberlain *nee* Charley Wilson, as though he were not actually a son of Solomon.

In April word came that Judge Cradlebaugh was on his way to investigate the Mountain Meadows massacre, accompanied by a force of two hundred soldiers. Jacob Forney, the new Indian agent, came ahead to gather up the surviving children that they might be returned to their relatives in the east. They took Charley Fancher from the Lee household, although he was reluctant to go, and in line with the policy followed by all who had kept any of the children, Lee made out a bill to the government for his care.

Although Lee had corresponded with Forney, he had never met him and had no wish to do so now until he was sure that there would be no writ served for his arrest. Accordingly, he remained in the field until Aggatha signaled him that all was safe. Jacob Hamblin introduced the two men, after which they had a long conference. Lee denied knowing anything about the massacre or having had anything to do with goods that had belonged to the emigrants. Then he went on to really unburden himself by recounting the mobbings and drivings which the Mormons had endured, accusing the President of sending an armed mob to Utah, and praising Brigham for permitting them to enter. The saints had committed no offenses for which they needed pardon, he insisted; if the President had been sincere in issuing the amnesty, why did he send officers with soldiers at their heels? Forney evidently heard him out, though Lee's account ends abruptly in the middle of a sentence.

The next day, Lee mounted his fine horse and started toward the upper Virgin, avoiding all roads, and following the stream to Klingensmith's home at Pocketville. The two men decided to go into hiding together, and chose a place from which they could see the house and the all clear signal of clothes hung on the line. After dark they would come down for a warm meal at the house and return again to spend the night at their hideout, secure until morning.

Lee was too restless to remain there, so they followed the LaVerkin Creek up and climbed to the plateau, exploring the tableland with its vivid colors and numerous jagged cliffs and buttes. After three days of riding they came to the brow of the mountain and found that they were about six miles due east of Harmony. From here, with his field glass, Lee could see his homes at the fort and his fields, where his sons and the hired men were busy plowing, planting, building a fence, and irrigating. He could also scan the road and tell the identity of the travelers. He was so impressed with the scene that he wrote:

Sat. May 14th. Pleasant. I stood on the summit of the mountain east of Harmony about 12 noon and with my spy glass looked over the whole valley. . . . From this point I could overlook the whole country, from the tops of the mountains down to the base, and a more lovely and beautiful landscape I never saw before: the snow caped mountain on the south with the lofty pines on its summit clothed in their green foilage . . . tinged with red and blue down to the slopes of the mountains; the vale covered with green vegetation intermingled with shady groves of cedar. . . . My residence and farm appeared more dear and lovely to me than ever.

He could not resist slipping down the mountain, following ravines cut by erosion, to the home of his brother-in-law, Sam Groves. Through him he sent word to Patriarch Elisha H. Groves that he wanted to visit with him, and then to his wife Rachel to bring him some provisions, pen and ink, and a pint of spirits. Both were to meet him at the east end of the pasture fence.

Brother Groves arrived first and told of the doings up state and of the threats that were made against all who had been implicated in the massacre. After an hour or two Rachel arrived with the items he had asked for and with food. She ate with him and then accompanied him back across the valley and up the steep mountain where she spent the night with him, slipping away at daybreak to return home.

Now he could spend his time writing up his journal, reading, and exploring the country. Through it all he was very humble and prayerful, depending upon God to direct him and following his hunches in moving his hiding place. He recorded that when he lost his pistols and could not find them, he prayed earnestly and arose to walk directly to them.

The following night two other wives, Aggatha and Caroline, joined Rachel meeting him at the fence. They brought an excellent hot supper, embraced and kissed him and wept with joy that he was well and at liberty. After the meal he sent Rachel and Caroline back with a tender farewell and took Aggatha with him up the mountain. The following night it was Rachel, Mary Leah, and Terressa who came with the hot supper, and Mary Leah who stayed. They brought him a letter from Emma, who was awaiting confinement, so was unable to come to him. He was so touched with the message that he copied it into his journal. She said in part:

> . . . My dear Companion — It affords me joy that I cannot express to know that you are alive and have been safely delivered from the hands of your enemies. . . My prayers for your deliverance and safe return to the bosom of your family who loves you dear, has been unceasing. And although I cannot be with you in person to share your sorrows, yet the Lord knows that I am in spirit and I also bear testimony that your spirit visits us. May God speedily permit you to return home, for I feel as though I could not stay from you much longer. I am sometimes tempted to try to climb the mountains in search of you. God bless you, my dear, to live long to bless and enjoy the society. . .

Here the page ends with the last of the letter missing.

Judge Cradlebaugh and his group had arrived at Parowan on May 4, and within a few days set up their permanent camp in the big field, about a mile and a half out of Cedar City. He had a double assignment — to collect and bury the bones of the slain emigrants, and to arrest as many of the participants in the massacre as he could catch.

The judge brought warrants for the arrest of a half-dozen of the leaders, and he wanted information concerning others who were involved. He found the local people reluctant to talk, for none knew anything for a certainty, and if they did, they would not betray their brethren into the hands of the enemies of the church. A few did want to talk, but feared the consequences. At least one participant came to the judge secretly late at night and told the story of that tragic day, giving some names and details, and begging for protection and anonymity. The burden of the crime was more than he could bear.

Like the others, Jacob Hamblin would not give any information nor

Parowan August 12. 1858.

We have carefully and patiently investigated the complaints made against President William H. Dame, for four successive days, and are fully satisfied that his actions as a saint, and administration as a President, have been characterized by the right spirit, and are highly creditable to his position in the priesthood; and that the complaints presented before us are without foundation in truth.

Geo. A. Smith

Amasa Lyman

James H. Martineau

James Lewis

C. C. Pendleton

Charles Hall

W. H. Alexander

Job P. Hall

John Steele

J. C. Haight

Nephi Johnson

J. D. White

F. T. Whitney

M. Ensign

S. S. Smith

John M. Higbee

Samuel West

Tarlton Lewis

Elijah Elmer

Wm Barton

P. Meeks

Orson B Adams

J. N. Smith

CLEARANCE CERTIFICATE OF WILLIAM H. DAME
See text page 244. Courtesy of Mrs. Lillis Spencer, Cedar City, Utah.

would he help to capture any of the guilty. Jacob claimed to have the facts from Albert, his Indian boy, and also from Lee himself, but this was not the time to tell them. Jacob knew all about the capture of the cattle from the Duke train; he had walked over the massacre site within a few days after the killing and could see what had gone on. But he knew, too, that the men who committed the crime did it out of mistaken zeal for their church, and as yet they were sustained by the authorities.

The enemies of Hamblin say that he was as deeply dyed as any of the participants because he made money out of the massacre. Records of the General Accounting Office at Washington, D.C., show that he received a total of $2,961.76 for his part in collecting and caring for the survivors.

. . . From September 10, 1857 to April 18, 1859, Mr. Hamblin was paid $600.56 for the care and supervision of Sarah, Rebecca, and Louisa Dunlap, who were children saved from the 'Mountain Meadow Massacre.' He was also paid $318.00 for expense incurred while conducting a search for the purpose of finding a child said to be among those saved in the 'Massacre.'

Subject man was paid $350.00 for the period from December 1, 1858 to June 30, 1859, for the care and supervision of children saved from the 'Mountain Meadow Massacre'; and $1,693.20 for the period from August 1, 1858, to April 18, 1859, for the board, clothing, and schooling of children saved in the 'Massacre.' . .

At any rate, Judge Cradlebaugh was not able to apprehend a single person. After spending almost a month in the area, he gave up the project.

For all its seeming failure, Cradlebaugh's trip south was important. His men searched out all the scattered bones, gave them burial, and erected a stone cairn over them about twelve feet high. On top of this they placed a large, handhewn cross upon which were inscribed the words, VENGEANCE IS MINE, SAITH THE LORD, I WILL REPAY. From all the evidence they could gather, they put together their version of the tragedy. About this time someone made it into a ballad which was sung to the strumming of a guitar or banjo in a sort of chant ending on a minor note. Although seven or eight variants have been found, all relate the same story, telling how the emigrants were attacked, how they were promised safety if they would give up their arms, and then were killed:

They melted down with one accord, like wax before the flame Both men and women, old and young — O Utah, where's thy shame?

Most significant is the assignment of the responsibility in the last verse. It would seem that each singer made his own conclusion. One, for instance, which would represent the Mormon version, ended:

This life will soon be over and another coming on
And the perpetrators of the deed must suffer for the wrong,
'Tis true they do deny it, and the crime they will disclaim
To get out of it the best they can, the Indians bear the blame.

Another is very pointed in placing the responsibility:

By order of Old Brigham Young this deed was done, you see,
And the captain of that wicked band was Captain John D. Lee.

A third closes thus:

By order of their President this bloody deed was done
He was the leader of the Mormon Church; His name is Brigham Young.

While this was not sung openly in Mormon circles; indeed, after a hundred years some who will furnish the words or sing it privately will not allow their name to be used; it went the way of most folk songs, being passed from one to another by memory. The fact that every version mentioned the name of John D. Lee helped to fix the total blame later and added to the score against him.

All of the southern leaders remained in hiding until the judge and his company returned to the north. On May 28, 1859, Lee noted that he had eaten his first meal at home in more than a month, while Haight recorded the date of his return as June 3. The Indians, intrigued by this game of hide-and-seek, crowded to Lee's home to tell him of the bribes they had been offered for his scalp — money, horses, guns — but he was their good friend, Yawgetts, and they would not help the "Mericats" catch him. Actually, the sum offered for any of the leaders, Dame, Haight, Higbee, Klingensmith, or Lee, was $5,000.00.

After the preaching of last August, many people began to move from Cedar City. Part of this was because of the failure to produce iron in commercial quantities, after all the sacrifices and labor. But almost every man who had been at the Meadows that day, took his family or families and left, some north to Cache Valley, some south to Arizona, a few to the desert outposts, but all with the desire of getting so far away that their children would never even hear of the massacre, and would never connect their fathers with it. Thus it was that this community which was to have been the great center of commerce and industry and in 1857 boasted 857 families, now less than two years later had only 386, less than half its earlier population.

During this time of stress, hard feelings developed between Lee and Haight, with each saying bitter things of the other. Brother Charles Hopkins, who had helped Lee to go ahead with his assignment that horrible day, tried to get them to talk it over. Finally Lee told him:

> If Elder Haight wishes to be friendly and drop the past, he must not turn a cold shoulder or wear an air of scorn thinking that I will bow to him, for I never will. I am the injured person. If I had injured him, I would readily make restitution. I have been seriously wronged, but I am willing to bury the past and say no more about it provided he will show signs of friendship. Let him come to my house and be friendly as he used to be, and I will receive it as a signal of peace.

That evening Haight, Hopkins, and two other brethren from Cedar City came to the Lee home for supper. The others left immediately after the meal, but Haight made the place his headquarters for three days while he hunted for lost cattle.

In mid-July George A. Smith and Amasa Lyman came again with their wives and another group from Parowan. It was almost a year since George A's last visit, but only three months since Amasa Lyman had been in Lee's home. This time their attendants were Jesse N. Smith, E. Brown, James H. Martineau, and Orson B. Adams, all of Parowan. They stayed two days before they moved on to spend July 24 at Washington. Lee took five of his wives and several of his older daughters and accompanied them.

While the guests visited the other settlements, Lee prepared to entertain them on their way back. Aggatha had purchased two dozen dinner plates and two dozen cups and saucers, with serving dishes to match, in a fine quality of queen's ware so that she could seat twenty-four at one table with china that anyone could be proud of. For the next ten years these dishes were kept carefully packed except for special occasions, and hauled from one home to the other whenever the leaders came down.

On the return trip, Apostle Smith invited Lee to bring Aggatha and go with him as far north as Parowan, where his wife Zilpha would be glad to entertain them. At Cedar City they held a meeting at which they disorganized the stake, so many of the people having left, and released Isaac C. Haight from his office as stake president. Philip Klingensmith was also released from being bishop, and Henry Lunt sustained in his place. "the presant change is satisfactory I believe to

the entire settlement," Lee wrote, showing that those responsible for
the massacre could not be sustained by the people.

Throughout the trip the apostles had been entertained at Lee's
home; they had invited him to join their company and to sit on the
stand with them in meeting. Surely, he told himself, they did not hold
him responsible for what happened at the Meadows.

That they did discuss the matter is shown by Lee's entry telling that
he had a private talk with Amasa Lyman on very special business,
after which "I wrote a letter to G. A. Smith & H. Stout, Lawyers to
defend my case, providd I should be arrested & brought before the
Destrict court upon the charge of aiding in the Massacre at the
Meadows. Although I am innocent of the crime, yet I am compelld to
employ council to direct the case in the proper channel," he noted.

On October 12, Patriarch Isaac Morley and his wife Alnora, sister of
Eliza R. Snow, the poetess, arrived at the Lee home. This was a joyous
meeting, for Brother Morley had given Lee his first patriarchal blessing, had worked with him and sustained him at Summer Quarters,
and had crossed the plains in the same company.

"Why, Brother Lee," he said. "I am astonished at what you have
done. You have houses and land, flocks and herds, wives and children.
I marvel at what you have accomplished."

"The Lord has only helped to fulfill the promises you made to me
in His name twenty-four years ago," Lee answered. "At that time I
had but one wife and one child. Now I have forty children and have
had seventeen wives, with homes to shelter them and land to support
them."

Well might Brother Morley be impressed with this hive of industry,
for Lee had many hired men at work besides the members of his
family. He noted that some were harvesting, one team had gone for
salt, another for dock root to be used in tanning, still others hauling
lumber and shingles. Other workers were installing a new boiler at
the molasses mill. The number of children interested him also, for
though Brother Morley had married four wives, only seven of his
children had grown to maturity.

For two weeks the Morleys were guests at one Lee home or the
other, during which time they drove his buggy and team to travel
among the various settlements.

When travel began in the late fall, the Lee home became a tavern
with a large sign above the door. Among those he entertained were
horse thieves, with officers following after them a few days later.
Within two weeks the officers returned bringing part of the group,
having permitted some to give up their stolen cattle and go on to
California. A traveling show put up here. The long wagon train that

was moving the goods of Brothers Lyman and Rich from San Bernardino rested here a day. Brother Lyman had been here so often that he
seemed almost a regular, free boarder.

On December 3 when he left, he shook Lee's hand and said, "Brother
John, I bless you, and I ask God to bless you and yours forever. You
are one of his true servants."

This, with a final blessing from Brother Morley, helped to dispel the
cloud that had hung over Lee much of this hectic year. Now he felt
that 1859 left him still firmly established in the hearts of the church
leaders and in the kingdom.

This was a fleeting hope, for the shadow of the massacre hung heavy
over every man known to have been on the ground. Of them all, only
William H. Dame officially cleared himself (see pags 243-244).

The diaries of Joseph Fish, who lived in Parowan, show Dame as a
high-strung man, given to long, impassioned tirades. These support the
folk-tale that at that meeting Dame declared: "You can NOT lay this
onto me! I will not take it! If you dare try, I'll just put the saddle onto
the right horse, and you all know well who that is!"

It could be no other than George A. Smith himself, sitting at the head
of the table. Isaac C. Haight had also traveled with him; Jesse N.
Smith, teamster, and James H. Martineau, recorder, all sitting in the
circle now, had accompanied George A. Smith on his southern tour. At
each settlement he had stirred the people to get revenge for past
suffering, and to resist the "Cursed Americats" with the last ounce of
their strength.

So it was that Dame was cleared, but it still seemed proper that he
go on a two-year mission to England. That would remove him from the
area. Haight was released from his position in the Church and with his
son-in-law, John M. Higbee, went into hiding in Arizona. Haight took
the name of *Horton*, his mother's maiden name, and died in exile. Higbee did not return to southern Utah until after the execution of John
D. Lee.

1860-1861
Prosperity

The fall of 1859 found Lee better prepared than ever before to care for the traveling public. Both the homes at Harmony and Washington were well stocked with cured meats, cheese, crocks of butter, sacks of dried fruit, and pits of carrots and potatoes. He had made thirty 50-gallon barrels of molasses for himself, besides what he made up for his neighbors. He also cooked whole clingstone peaches in some of the molasses syrup, boiling them together to a thick consistency. Packed into crock jars and tightly covered, this was a delicacy for his own table or a good product for sale or exchange.

On January 15, 1860, Lee reported that the whole area was shaken by an earthquake. It was not felt in Washington, but at Cove Fort people reported loud booms along with the quake, as though there might be a great explosion somewhere in the direction of Camp Floyd. At Cedar City and Parowan, dishes rattled in the cupboards and some chimneys fell. Most serious damage was at Harmony, where part of the fort walls were cracked so badly that they had to be torn down. People here were troubled, wondering if it were an evidence of God's displeasure. Could it be a bad omen, or a warning?

As before, Lee spent much of the winter in Washington working on his stone mansion. Carpenters were putting in doors and windows, floors and ceilings, and building mantels, cupboards, and closets. Stone masons were putting up a large stone granary behind the house, and when it was finished built an outhouse with a shingle roof. One evidence of a family's status was the quality of toilet facilities it provided, and Lee wanted his to be of the best.

It was characteristic that he should build a stone fence from the smaller rocks that could not be used in the walls. Solidly laid up in mortar, two feet wide at the bottom and one at the top, three feet high to the long, smooth capstones, it would be a splendid finish to the mansion. He worked at this himself, with the help of his wives, some of the younger boys, and the two Indian girls. In addition, he had a crew of men fencing, setting out trees and vines, or digging a pond for his private spring, that he might have fish, perhaps, or at least ducks and geese.

He also entered into community activities, urging the people to make their meeting house large enough to be a credit to them, a building in which they could take pride. They finally accepted his suggestion that it be at least twenty-four by forty-four feet and solidly built. It stands today, with a beautiful stone addition.

Later, he persuaded the people to donate one day's work each to the bishop, who was forced to spend so much time in public service that he could hardly get his house built. Accordingly they agreed upon a day when some of the men hauled stone, others cut it, and still others worked at laying up the walls. The women prepared a town dinner, and a dance finished off the "bee," while the bishop had more done on his house than he could have done alone in weeks.

On February 27, Brother Philo Dibble arrived with two pictures to display, one of the Prophet addressing the Nauvoo Legion, the other of the martyrdom. He held the program in Lee's hall, keeping the pictures covered until the crowd had gathered. Adults paid fifty cents each, children twenty-five. Brother Dibble gave a life sketch of Joseph Smith from his childhood as a farm boy to his peak of power as the mayor of Nauvoo, commander of the legion, and Prophet of God. Then he showed the legion picture. After he finished the story of the death of Joseph, he unveiled the second picture.

At the conclusion, he asked his host to supplement the program, which Lee did so effectively that Brother Dibble invited him to go along to Santa Clara and the other settlements and give the whole lecture. This Lee was glad to do, for he always welcomed an opportunity to speak of this man, who to him was second only to Jesus Christ.

Lee attended church regularly and preached often, but his greatest influence was among the sick. He was sent for so often and prayed with such evident results that many thought he was blessed with a special gift of healing. Nathan C. Tenney was one of these. For example, on February 4, 1859, Lee was at his home in Washington when word came that "N. C. Tenny Very Sick & sent for me to come to Harmony imediately & lay hands on him & Pray for his recovery, Stating that if I would come that he would be restored. . ." This word came late at night and Lee did not get his affairs into shape to leave until the next day. On February 8, he noted that "This morning Bro Tenny fast recovering. He stated the Eving before when I layed hands on him & Prayed for him that now he would get well & that if Bro Lee could have been here before that he would not have suffered so much. . ." In August of the same year when Lee visited Pocketville . . .   "At the close of the meeting I was called to lay hands on N. C. Tenny who was attacked with the Pleurisy in his side & when we had anointd & Prayed for him, he was instantly restored. The glory I ascribed to God the bountiful bestower of all Perfect gifts."

On January 18, 1860, there was a more spectacular event, which he recorded thus:

". . . About 10 m. a shocking occurrence hapened. Wm. Slade shot from one of my doors at a crow. The ball glanced & struck one of Br. Wm. Wood litle girls above the fore head, Shot away the Scull, leaving the brain Pan bare. The alarm was given, the Neighbors flocked to the Scene. The child lay in its gore, apparently lifeless, the Parrents almost frantic. I called them to order, laid hands on it, with Elder Freem & others, rebuked the Powers of Death, & asked the Lord to raise it, & the child imediately came too. This gave confidence to all presant, & I hope it will be a warning to all carless shooting. . ."

This faith in Lee's prayers was especially strong in his own family. His wives wanted him to stand by during the ordeal of childbirth, though his only help was his sustaining faith. Often he was asked to administer if the delivery was especially long and hard. Such a case was with Rachel on March 9, 1860, when he promised her that "she would be deliverd of a living & a lovely offspring, & that it would be a proper child & the express image & likeness of its Father, which should become a great & Mighty Man in the Kingdom of God here on the Earth. . ." They named this child John Amasa, after its father and Apostle Amasa Lyman who had so often been a guest in the home.

Lee often carried this same idea of Divine approval and help into his business ventures. Early in 1860, he conceived the idea of building a flour mill at Washington, with a lumber mill attachment that could be run by the same power and used when there was no wheat to grind. In his responsibility to help build up the kingdom and his calling as one of the YTFIF, he should be able to see and take advantage of anything that would promote the general good. Here was potential water power going to waste. As he traveled along, he pondered the matter in his heart, he prayed earnestly for guidance, asking God to send him the needed help if this project were in accordance with His will. He arrived at Washington to find three men waiting to be hired, a fact which he interpreted to be a direct answer to his petitions. Since the kind of mill he had in mind would be a large stone structure, which would take more than a year to finish, he would continue to operate the small burr mill that he had purchased earlier from Brother Theodore Turley.

In June of this year, the town of Kanarraville was settled on the stream where old Chief Quonarah had his headquarters, and families from Cedar City and Harmony moved onto the site. This meant that additional property was for sale in Harmony, and true to his custom, Lee bought it. During the time he was in hiding the year before, when he had been able to look over the whole terrain from the cliffs across the valley, he decided that he should build a new home high up near the mouth of the canyon, a little below the lone pine which they all used as a landmark. Here he would have a magnificent view of all his orchards and fields below and the blazing red cliffs, "the finger bluffs" to the east.

With this in mind, he started an adobe-making project, for he planned to have a mansion here that would equal the one in Washington; not of rock, of course, since that was not so readily available here. But Brother Brigham had spoken with great enthusiasm of adobe buildings and promised that when properly built, they would harden with the years and become more durable, providing perfect insulation against both heat and cold. There was just the right kind of clay at Harmony and plenty of it. Lee set up a mechanical mixer drawn by a horse, with molds that would hold four adobes at once. With a large, smooth drying field, his crew soon turned out four thousand adobes in three days. They let these dry, turned them once, and then stacked them loosely so that the air could circulate between them. Later they might even enlarge their drying yard.

The mid-July celebration of that year was a family affair rather than one involving the two communities, or even, indeed, the one. But Apostle George A. Smith did come, bringing a group of more than twenty-five people, among them his wife Zilpha and her three children, twenty-year-old George A. Jr., his sister Mary, and brother Charles, both younger. They all remained two days and nights, enjoying the melons and fruit which Lee had brought from Washington, the excellent meals, and the malt beer. For the twenty-fourth, Lee returned the compliment by visiting at Parowan with a group of his family.

Through all this, the center of attraction was young George A. with the spirited gray mare which he had trained to do so many tricks. The boy loved to demonstrate his own horsemanship and the skill of his mount. Already he was trying to persuade his father to let him go on some of the longer exploring trips with the seasoned frontiersmen, certain that instead of hardships they would be glorious adventure. Both Lee and his father tried to persuade him to wait a year or two at least.

Upon his return to Harmony, Lee met a young man on the opposite end of the social scale, and his treatment of this outcast is eloquent evidence of his willingness to defend the underdog. Young Nephi Stewart was there, much discouraged and depressed. In a public meeting the Bishop of Beaver had accused him of stealing horses and deserting his wife and asked the congregation to withdraw the hand of fellowship from him. In a Mormon community this meant that no one would employ him, no one would invite him into a home or have any dealings with him whatsoever. Lee listened to his story, asked him many questions, and decided that he had been dealt with unjustly. After some discussion, they agreed that Stewart should take charge of some of Lee's property at Washington for a year, during which time Lee should give him board, room, seed, and other assistance in return for a portion of the crop.

At once the Bishop protested, saying that any man who had been driven out of Beaver should not be accepted in Washington. Reporting his speech in church, Lee wrote: "He [the Bishop] said that all such Men ought not to get a Night Lodging & that no honest man would Suffer him & that he ought to be drove out from us to the Piutes Indians on the Muddy & he would be one to help doo it, & if any man wanted to Shoot him, to Shoot & be Damed."

The Bishop then took his seat and requested that John D. Lee speak to the people on polygamy. Since this was always a topic for exhortation and Lee believed in the principle so completely, it ordinarily would have been a good subject for him. But today he was of another mind.

> I replied that I did not wish to be circumscribed or fettered in my feelings, that the Subject in consideration engrossed my attention the most at the presant time. The Man alluded was a stranger to Me as well as to the most of this community. Reports says that he is a bad man. But I am not authorisd to believe & credit all reports, Especially where the character & Life of a man is at stake. I would certainly be unwise to Judge a Mater [without] hearing both sides & investigating it carefully.

He spoke not so much in defense of Stewart as against the harsh and hasty judgment of him. At the close of the service he was asked to meet with the ward bishopric to discuss the matter with them. One suggested that if Lee harbored such a character in their midst, he should be responsible for anything which he stole. Lee replied that he would vouch for the conduct of Stewart, but that there were people among them in good standing who sometimes stole, too.

The second counsellor, Collins, then said that he had lived in Beaver a year and had never heard of Stewart's stealing anything; on the contrary, he was a good fiddler and sang songs and used to make lots of fun at the parties. As for himself, he had no objections to Stewart's staying there. Thus Lee defended the young man to his neighbors on

the one hand and urged the boy to better living on the other. The fact
that for several years Stewart continued to work for Lee would seem
to justify this defense.

Early in March of 1859, the Washington County Court was moved
from Harmony to Washington, and James D. McCullough was appointed probate judge. Lee gave as the reason for the change the fact
that Washington was now the largest town and the county seat, but
his association with the massacre was without doubt the reason for his
dismissal. He turned over the records without question and became on
such friendly terms with the new judge that they often invited each
other to family dinners and shared in entertainment of various kinds.
Judge McCullough seemed to respect Lee and almost to court his
friendship.

The Washington County Agricultural and Manufacturing Association decided to hold its first annual fair on September 6, 1860. Word
of this was published nearly a year earlier, and throughout the settlements people had looked forward to it and prepared for it. In the
handwork department there were samples of weaving, of finished
clothing from baby dresses to men's coats, braided straw hats, moccasins made of the backs of men's pants or from tanned deerskin,
knitted mittens and stockings and shawls, and various kinds of home
decorations from cross-stitch samplers and crazy-patch cushions to
hair flowers. There were samples of indigo plant and the blue cloth
colored by it, madder root and the purple-red cloth or straw that it
had stained. There were cotton stalks with the most bolls, and stems
displaying the largest; there were melons and squash and vegetables
of all kinds, all displayed at out-of-door booths.

Best of all, there was the chance to visit. People came in their
wagons, carrying foodstuffs enough to feed their own families or to
contribute to the tables of those who invited them in. There were not
homes enough to accommodate all the visitors in Washington, but
visitors could sleep in their wagons or on the ground or atop a friendly
haystack.

John D. Lee had worked desperately to have his mansion finished —
window glass in, the plastering done and as much of the carpentry as
possible. He even worked all day Sunday to clean the street in front
of his place and to bridge the ditch where the water entered his lot.
His family from Harmony arrived the day before, bringing their contributions for display and driving stock for the exhibition. In another
wagon was the band consisting of four violins, banjos, bass drum,
triangles, combs, and clapsticks. As they arrived in the evening, they
unfurled their flag and drove the length of the street and back, playing
all the way. The next morning they were out again serenading the
town, stopping to play before individual homes and accepting the treat

of malt beer or pie or whatever the host brought out, or waving and calling friendly greetings to those who had nothing but their thanks to offer.

John D. Lee listed his family "firsts" proudly — the best each of mare and colt, heifer, half acre of cotton, man's straw hat, homemade shawl, piece of patchwork, and a special diploma for excellence in crochet work. Characteristically he did not mention any second places or any first awarded to anyone else, though there were, of course, many others.

On October 11, Jacob Hamblin and his group of missionaries arrived on their way to the Moquich Indians. Four of the men expected to remain for a year to learn the language and do missionary work; the others would become acquainted with Indian customs and try to establish friendly relations. There were two wagons, one carrying the boat and the other supplies. The company was composed of nine men, among whom were Ira Hatch, Thales Haskell, Jehiel McConnell, A. J. Thornton, and Isaac Riddle. There were also two Indian girls — Jacob Hamblin's Indian wife, Eliza, and Ira Hatch's Indian wife.

The one of them all who took Lee's eye was young George A. Smith, who came to put up with him. George A., Senior, was a dear friend with whom Lee had traveled, and this boy was an open-faced, fearless lad, good-natured and high spirited. He rode his fine gray mare and had another horse in the band to carry his pack outfit. So elaborate were his bridle, saddle, and other equipment that the "Journal History" noted that his outfit cost $319, including two horses.

The next morning when the company pulled out, the horsemen with twenty head of horses and mules, the wagons bringing up the rear, this young man on his prancing mount seemed like an aristocrat among country bumpkins. How little did Lee anticipate, as he returned the farewell salute, the tragedy which lay ahead for this boy.

Work went on with increased intensity throughout the fall. Lee had iron rollers made for his molasses mill and found them much superior to the wooden ones in use by his neighbors. This mill netted him forty dollars a day during the molasses harvest.

On November 9 word came of the death of young George A. Smith at the hands of the Indians. According to the report, the natives were angry because of some killings by American soldiers and were waiting for revenge. At the camp across the Colorado, George A.'s mare ran away and joined a band of Indian ponies. Jumping on another horse, heedless of his own safety, he went in pursuit and found that an Indian had her caught and was leading her away. Without stopping to argue, the young man grabbed the rope, when he was shot with several arrows. By that time, the natives had surrounded him; one had taken his gun and put four bullets into his back.

His friends found him and got him onto a horse, but it was torture for him to travel. Still they could not leave him, nor did they dare to stay, since the natives had demanded that two more men be given up to settle their score. Except for Enos, the thieving Indian who had given the settlers so much trouble, they would all have been killed. But he used all his knowledge of Navajo and all his influence in getting them away. Young George A. breathed his last about sunset, and they were forced to leave his body unburied among the rocks. No use now to remember that Brigham Young had blessed the boy just before he left and promised him that he should prosper. No use now the expensive outfit and the fine horses. There was no explanation except that he did not obey the counsel so often repeated that no man should leave the camp alone. The tragedy cast a gloom over all the southern settlements, though there was deep gratitude also that no others were harmed.

Throughout the fall and winter, Lee continued to work on his mill. He had planned carefully how he would supply his machinery and sought for ways and means to get materials. He expected to use the native mica or isinglass for the windows, and hired a man to get it out for him before the walls were up; he hauled his lumber from Parowan; he located millstones in the mountains, one of which took nine yoke of oxen to bring in. He kept a crew of from eight to ten men busy at one phase or another of the work.

On the last Sunday of the year, he asked the Bishop to announce in meeting that he would serve a dinner and provide a dance on New Year's Day for all who would help him haul stone for his mill during the forenoon. His wives spent days cooking to prepare for the event, and he had everything organized. On the morning of January 1 he wrote that they arose before daylight, dressed and washed themselves and "then invoked the blessings of God to be with us & all Iseral to guide our footsteps through this day & coming life to his Praise, to increase our faith & confidence in him.   . ."

There was such a good turnout of the brethren that by three o'clock they had deposited fifty-two loads of stone near his mill. He then had dinner served to some eighty people, including his family and regular hired men. The afternoon was spent in sports and visiting, and at early candlelight the dancing began. Later, refreshments were again served and the dance continued until two in the morning "to the entire satisfaction of all." On January 4 he gave another free dance with the understanding that those who participated would help him on his floor when he was ready for it.

By February 23 he was pleased to record that "Today the wall of my Mill was completed & cornish on. Some 600 loads of rock and 10,000 adobies were in it. Present cost is 2000$."

In the meantime, community and church activities went on as usual. At a conference held on January 20, they decided to set up a system of home missionaries or an exchange of speakers among the wards, that would give variety to the audiences in each and provide new opportunities for men who appeared regularly before their own small groups. They numbered each town and worked out a scheme whereby once a month each would receive visiting preachers from one of the others. By going to a different ward each month, the missionaries could make the rounds of all in eight months, when a new set would be appointed.

All through the month of March Lee pressed work on the mill, with some hands building the flume and others working on the millstones and other machinery. Although the walls were up, he kept the masons busy building a big stone oven, the foundation for a barn, and a stone corral, while he and Bench, his Indian helper, planted out a vineyard of a thousand grape cuttings.

On April 1 he went back to Harmony and set all hands at work on his new location. His wives had a bee of their own, putting on two quilts at once, inviting all the women of the community to help quilt, and serving dinner to them and their families, with a party at night.

By this time Lee decided that the best way to manage would be to sublet some of his land. Accordingly he made up an agreement with Nephi Stewart to run his twenty-acre farm at Toquerville.

Early in May word came that President Young and suite would visit the area for the first time in five years. Lee now doubled his efforts to have everything in order at both his places that his "father" would appreciate his diligence.

Lee received word from Cedar City that the president and his suite would go to Santa Clara via the Mountain Meadows and meet him first at Washington. He set out in such haste that he did not go properly prepared. At the Grapevine Springs he met his son-in-law, Henry Darrow, whom he dispatched post-haste to Harmony to bring back the queen's ware china, the fine cutlery, and also some provision from the storehouse there. He would go on to Washington and see that a beef was killed and chickens dressed and ready.

Brigham Young rode first in his train of twenty-three wagons along the old Spanish Trail. When he came to the stone monument at Mountain Meadows, he pulled out and stopped. Everyone else stopped and all gathered around to hear what he had to say about this. At first he walked a short distance away and up the incline as though he wanted to look over the whole valley and visualize what had happened and where and how. Then he came back to the pile of stones, built into a rude pyramid some twelve feet high and crowned by a hewn cross of cedar upon which were painted the words VENGEANCE IS MINE

SAITH THE LORD, I WILL REPAY. A flat stone at the bottom bore the inscription, "120 men, women, and children murdered in cold blood early in Sept. 1857. From Arkansas." And on another slab, "Erected by Company K, 1st Dragoons May, 1859."

Brigham Young walked around the monument, studied the inscriptions, and then raising his right arm to the square, he said impressively, *"Vengeance is mine, saith the Lord, and I have taken a little of it."* Without another word, he returned to his wagon and rode on. Riding with the company were horsemen from the south who thought they understood what he meant. One immediately threw a lasso rope around the cross, and turning his horse suddenly, jerked it down and dragged it a short distance. The others dismounted quickly and began tearing down the stones, scattering them in every direction, until before the wagon train was well on the road, the monument was demolished. Both Wilford Woodruff and John D. Lee wrote of the President's quotation, but neither mentioned the destruction of the monument.

Three years later, in the spring of 1864, Captain George F. Price of Company M, 2nd Cavalry, while en route from Camp Douglas to Fort Mojave stopped here and rebuilt the monument, putting the cross back into place. It was still standing as late as 1870, after which it was again torn down.[1]

President Young preached at Santa Clara on Sunday and sent a messenger to Washington setting the Monday meeting at 4 p.m., as he was going to the lower settlement to preach in the forenoon. This was really his experimental farm where a company had been working at the raising of cotton and other semitropical crops. While the wagon train stayed on the road toward Washington, he went with some of the mounted group through the bowl-shaped valley between black hills on the west and red hills on the north and east. He noted the spring that ran down through the western part and was told that one of equal size ran through the eastern part.

James G. Bleak's account says that he stopped his carriage and said with a sweep of his arm, "There will yet be built, between these volcanic ridges, a city with spires, towers, and steeples, with homes containing many inhabitants." This prediction, made in May, would be put into action the following October.

---

[1] Lorenzo Brown, passing the place on July 1, 1864, wrote a detailed description of the marker after it had been re-built:

It is built of cobble stone at the bottom and about 3 feet high then rounded up with earth & surmounted by a rough wooden cross the whole 6 or 7 feet high & perhaps 10 feet square. On one side of the cross is inscribed Mountain Meadows Massacre and over that in smaller letters is vengeance is mine & I will repay saith the Lord. On the other side Done by officers & men in Co. M Cal. Vol. May 27th and 28th 1864. Some one has written below this in pencil, Remember Hauns Mill and Carthage Jail.

John D. Lee rode his best horse out to meet the president, just beyond the town of Washington. He was greeted warmly and invited to ride in the carriage, while one of the others took his horse. As they rode along, they visited about conditions in the south in general, and Lee pointed out his stone mill, which the president would take time to look at more carefully after dinner. The company drove to Lee's home and corralled, and of the seventy people, forty put up there, while the others scattered among other families in the village.

Lee was proud that the president, with his wife, sons, and teamsters, Daniel H. Wells, John Taylor, Wilford Woodruff and George A. Smith, should all remain with him, as well as Albert Carrington, J. Fox, Dr. Sprague, Levi Stewart and wife and Bishop McCullogh. They ate dinner, supper, and breakfast at his table, from a well-set board.

From Washington the visitors would stop at Toquerville, Grafton, and Pocketville, though most of the wagons would go directly back to Harmony with the preachers traveling on horseback because of the bad roads. Lee packed his china and serving dishes and set out about dark, traveling nearly all night to arrive in time to make preparations. The next day he butchered a beef and two sheep, and the family all cooperated to cook.

Just at noon, the company came in sight. Lee hoisted the flag in honor of their approach and rode out to meet them. Dinner was waiting and since the group had added a few leaders from each village there were about a hundred and twenty-five in all instead of seventy. Again Lee fed them three meals, though his wives had to stay up cooking nearly all night in order that the visitors might be on the road early the following morning.

President Young invited him to join the train as far as Beaver, so Lee took a light carriage and, with Bishop Davies for a companion, went along. At Cedar City the citizens had prepared a public dinner for them; at Parowan they scattered to private homes. At each place the President preached, exhorting and encouraging and criticizing. At Minersville, Lee took leave of them to return home.

For Lee this had been a rewarding experience indeed. The President had expressed approval of his mill and praised him for his industry and foresight as it was shown in his homes, yards, corrals and fields. Best of all, he had seemed to approve of his efforts. Referring to the massacre, he lamented the death of the women and children, though "under the circumstances this could not be avoided." "The men merited their fate," he said. As for the people who would have betrayed their brethren into the hands of their enemies, he had not language strong enough to express his scorn.

"For that thing they will be damned and go down to hell," he thundered. "I would be glad to see one of these traitors, though I don't suppose there is any here now. They have run away."

On his way home, Lee hired Brother Grundy to go to Washington to set his mill in operation. The wheat was almost ready for harvest and he wanted everything to run smoothly when the grinding started.

Late in November the new colonists began to arrive, a Swiss company to settle on the Santa Clara and a company of three hundred families to found St. George. They had been called at the conference in early October and were given a month to get on the way. Having a city so near was good news for Lee, because his lumber mill and his flour mill would now be much in demand, and in the four months since Brother Grundy had taken over, everything was in good running order.

Lee spent most of the fall at Harmony, where he was determined to get some of his families moved from the fort to the new location. He had the excavation made for Emma's house and the walls started, and had plans for a mansion a short distance away. This time, instead of building a fort, he hoped for a comfortable cottage for each wife, where she could have some privacy and maintain her own flower and vegetable garden, and have chickens and pigs as she chose.

On December 22, the people were called together and organized into a Branch, with Lee appointed as presiding elder. He was sustained by a unanimous vote, and in honor of the occasion he invited everyone in the settlement to come to a dinner on Christmas Day. Everything went off so well that he felt that surely the hand of the Lord was over him for good, and that his faults had been forgiven and his sacrifices accepted by his Father.

1862-1869
Disaster

The rain that had threatened all of Christmas afternoon began to
fall before the dinner was finished, so most of the guests hurried away
at once. A storm always complicated evening chores and meant that
there should be an extra supply of wood inside. They had learned to
expect some snow and rain at this time of year; they welcomed it, in
fact, for it meant water for next summer's crops. But they were not
accustomed to rain that continued day after day for a week and then
for another week. Lee closed his journal for the year with the statement, "Through the week the storms still raging; prospects dark and
gloomy; the Earth a sea of water and thus closes 1861." The next day's
entry is equally eloquent. "Jany. 1st., 1862 Begins with a storm. The
face of the country is deluged with water."

Well might Lee have regretted the ten days he took during the
pleasant fall weather to follow Brigham Young and his party to Washington, back to Harmony and on to Beaver. Perhaps even the time he
had spent on the mill at Washington could have been put to better
use here, where he knew that the fort was not in good condition.
Perhaps now he lamented that he had not used more straw in the
adobes in the first place, when Thomas D. Brown and others complained that he was not building to specifications. But they had no
straw, or very little so far away that it did not seem worth it to slow
down the work while men went for it. It was the earthquake that had
done the most damage, cracking some of the walls full length.

Whatever his regrets, he was now faced with a bitter reality.
Throughout the next week the rain fell steadily, and then turned to
cold and snow, which continued until the fourteenth, when the rain
began again. By this time much of the fort had actually been reduced
to a pile of mud, and none of it was really safe. During the summer
he had built the basement room for Emma's dwelling at the new
location, and she had moved into it, but now the water began to seep
in so fast that they could not bail it out. Working in the rain, Lee fixed
up some lumber shanties in which they took temporary refuge.

On January 15, the barn fell, the side foundation having been
washed away earlier. Lee moved all his family into the west side of
the fort, which was better preserved than the east — and not too soon,
either, for within a few hours they heard the whole side fall with a

sickening roar. Nor were they safe here, for the north wall was melting away like sugar.

On January 18, the storm slackened a little, and with the help of two neighbors, they moved three wagonloads of furniture, food, and children to the upper site. The mud was axle deep, so that it required eight yoke of cattle to each wagon to drag them at all. Everything was wet; clothing, bedding, fuel. Once the big range was set up, with the fire going, they could keep it alive with the boards and timbers of the fallen barn, for by keeping some stacked on end behind the stove to be drying out, they could manage a circle of warmth.

Surely nothing like this had ever happened before. On the morning of January 31, they had their first glimpse of the sun for twenty-eight days, but before noon it was clouded again and snowing, piling to a depth of ten inches in the next two days. By now all the family was moved out of the fort except Sarah Caroline and her children. She insisted that, since the roof was off the second story and the rain had ceased, she was safe for a while longer. She did have four walls around her and a big fireplace, where they could keep warm, also two beds with dry bedding, and she dreaded to leave it when she had no other place of shelter.

For days Lee had been dogged by the fear that he was not going to get them all out of the fort in time. The grownups and older children were all kept busy with the moving and with helping to get fuel and shelter. There were six wives living here; Terressa lived with Emma, and between them they could care for Emma's year-old son. Aggatha's youngest was six, and his older brothers and sisters helped to see that he was kept warm and dry. But Rachel had two little boys, aged one and three, while Mary Leah and Sarah Caroline each had four younger than eight. It was these two families that remained longest at the fort.

At last all were moved to higher ground except Sarah Caroline and hers. She had a web of cloth in the loom, which kept her occupied, and she maintained that she would like to finish it before they moved. It represented so many hours of work, that she wanted to take it out completed. With her at the time was Terressa, the two changing off at the loom and caring for the children. After all, the entire group of little ones had crowded into this one room the night before while the storm raged outside. One night more, and they would get out too.

The children were in bed, five-year-old Margarett Ann beside her brother George Albert, just a year older than she, at the head. The two older boys were up, and Terressa had little Sarah Ann. Suddenly the mother had an impulse to get out and hurried all through the door in her first fear, without disturbing the two sleeping children. Whether it was already falling or whether the draft from the opening door made a difference, no one could guess, but the partition wall from the upper floor crashed, coming through the ceiling, the heavy weight killing the two children instantly. At least it seemed that they must have been instantly killed, for there were no cries except from those who had escaped and were calling for help. By the time anyone could get there with a light and remove the debris, there was no hope for the children.

This was truly a sad affair, even more so because both parents had known that they should leave the fort, and both had delayed because of the rigors of wet and cold to which the children must be exposed if they left the shelter and fire. Now the little bodies could hardly be buried properly, with the rain unceasing and the soggy graveyard in a location where it was almost impossible to dig a decent grave. The meeting hall was gone and there was no other place to hold a public funeral. During a brief lull in the storm they gathered at the graveyard. A hymn was sung, a few words of comfort offered to the weeping mother, a dedicatory prayer, and then the mud was being pushed into the hole, plumping onto the boxes with a reverberation that reminded them of the wall which had snuffed out the young lives.

These people did not know that the storm was general. In California, city streets were inundated; in northern Nevada towns had each its own private tragedy. All they knew was that in the cotton mission of southern Utah there was destruction everywhere. The little hamlets on the upper Virgin all were washed out. Philip Klingensmith lost his home at Pocketville, and his cane mill, blacksmith shop, stored food, hay and grain, furniture — everything he had at that place. The same was true of many of the other settlers.

On the upper Santa Clara at Gunlock, the families of Dudley Leavitt and William Hamblin had to abandon their houses, take shelter under makeshift tents of wagon-cover or tarpaulin, and watch their possessions go down the stream. At Santa Clara everything went before the flood — the burr flour mill, molasses mill, threshing machine, and the orchards and vineyards. The rock fort, which had sheltered missionaries and later settlers, caved off in great hunks into the stream, until, when the water subsided only one corner was left perched precariously on a ten-foot ledge.

Stories of this forty-day rain and the resulting floods have become legend in Utah's Dixie. At Santa Clara, Jacob Hamblin was standing too near the bank when a piece of land almost as big as a cabin slid into the water. He was left with his footing melting away under him like sugar and no way to scale the sandy ledge. Just as the last of the ground disappeared and he was about to slip into the muddy current, a lasso rope whirled over his head and fell around his body. His

Indian boy, Albert, had seen his predicament and had come to his rescue. The rope firmly under his arms, Hamblin clung with his hands, braced his feet against the bank, and climbed to safety.

One end of this same lariat was now tied to a post at the foot of the hill and to another at the tree near the corner of the fort. By holding firmly to it, men went back and forth through water above their knees to carry bedding and grain from the fort to the hill. A woman who had given birth to a baby after the flood began was carried out in this way.

One elderly lady sat under her dripping shelter on the hill and rocked back and forth, saying over and over, "It is the end of the world. It will never come daylight again. The end of the world. The end of the world. . ." Beside her a Swiss sister prayed aloud in her native tongue.

Lee's former hired man, Benjamin Platte, and his wife, Mary, were living at Pocketville and all that they had was lost in the flood. After the waters subsided, some people followed down the stream bed to see what they might salvage, for a few things were bound to lodge wherever a tree was stuck in the sand. At one home Mrs. Platte saw a barrel with the corks still securely in. "That is my barrel of molasses," she announced. "See, Ben, it's that barrel that Brother Forsythe made, solid as a nut. See the oak willow hoops! That's our barrel, all right!" But the man who had found it meant to keep it unless he had more proof than that. Instantly, Mary loosened the cork and pulled it out. There around the bottom was a piece of plaid cloth. Opening it triumphantly she fitted it into the bottom of her husband's shirttail, from where the piece had been cut. The plaid matched perfectly. There could be no denying that evidence!

Lee was given to seeing the hand of God in everything that happened, either good or bad. However, he felt that in this case the death of his children was his own fault for not following his promptings in spite of what anyone else said or did. Had he done that, their lives would have been saved. He could not change things now; he could only repent deeply and resolve that in the future he would be more responsive, quicker to do what he was prompted to do. In the light of this great loss, all others he suffered were as nothing.

At Harmony, his families were homeless but the land remained unhurt, and he knew that within a short time he could rebuild homes. The fort was ready to be abandoned before the storm began and the momentary discomfort of rain, cold, and mud soon would be forgotten, as Brother Brigham told them after their move from Summer Quarters in the rain. The new settlers, three hundred families at St. George and twenty-three of the Swiss colony at Santa Clara, had been forced to wait out the storm in their wagons, without even a general shelter. Lee had lost much, but some people had lost everything in the storms.

All through February and March he worked to build houses with all available help, though he had been forced to let many of his hired men go. He took Mary Leah and her four children to stay with her parents at Toquerville until he could build a place for her. Rachel and Aggatha occupied one cabin; Caroline, Emma, and Terressa another.

Lee dreaded to visit Washington, for he had learned that the mill on which he had spent so much of both time and money was washed away, the machinery buried deep in the sand. The molasses mill with the iron rollers was gone also, and one piece of land. When finally he did go, Lee found his fruit trees bursting into bloom, his mansion well-kept, and his young sons working at the garden. He took heart. He would have to lease out the field land here however, because his responsibilities at Harmony were so great.

Though he worked very hard, still it took Lee more than four years to build back to his status before the flood, so disastrous had it been. He kept up his regular pattern of life, attending always to his church duties and helping with the sick. When the Harmony ward was asked for outfits to help bring the poor saints across the plains, he donated as much as all the others put together. In spite of everything, however, his prestige kept slipping. Apostle Erastus Snow would come to his home, eat with him and consult with him on matters pertaining to the Indians, but would not give him any public recognition. On March 5, 1864, on the suggestion that he do so, Lee resigned as bishop of Harmony Ward, and James H. Imlay was appointed in his place.

By 1866 Lee had all his families in comfortable homes and the mansion which he had planned before the flood almost finished. He had also taken another wife — his last. She was Ann Gordge, eighteen, who had come with her mother and brother David from Australia in 1856. Her father had been drowned and her mother, Merabe Hancock Gordge, had married John Phillips as a plural wife. They lived at Beaver.

Aggatha had been failing for some time until by the spring of 1866 she was on her death bed with a lingering malignancy. She knew that she must die soon, and not wishing to leave any bitterness behind her, asked for all the wives to come to see her. During long hours in bed, she had thought often of the past and of her experiences when her husband had accepted the celestial law of marriage. It had been hard to see him with other women; especially young, beautiful, accomplished ones.

She had never really accepted the principle until John D. took her to call on Brigham Young. He was kind and understanding as he reminded her that, after all, she was Lee's first, the bride of his youth. No one could ever take that from her. Then Young had told her that, as the first wife, she would set the tone of the household; she even more than her husband would be responsible for maintaining love and peace and cooperation. Plurality was not easy for the young wives, either, he said. She must help them through their times of discouragement and be kind to their children. If she did this, in the end she would reap the blessing of their love and respect. Moreover, she would help to bring her husband into the highest positions here on earth and to eternal exaltation hereafter.

Aggatha had accepted the counsel and the charge, and felt that she had in part succeeded. She reminded herself of the answer given by one other sister in the church when she was asked, "Doesn't it almost break your heart to have your husband take another wife?"

"If my heart stands between me and the Kingdom of God, it *ought* to break!" she said.

So it was that she did not interfere when she could see that Mary Ann Williams was in love with Alma rather than his father. So it was too, that she could meet Emma with such poise and cordiality — Emma, so young and fresh and full of vitality, but also impulsive and sharp of tongue. With her skill in cooking and the household arts, she had already taken Aggatha's place when it came to putting on banquets for the authorities or managing town dinners.

Now here was the last one, the buxom girl, Ann Gordge, who had helped to plant corn and wash wool, who had stayed through the night and held John's hand as they waited and watched at her bedside. Living as she did with Emma, Ann would have little chance to demonstrate any skills beyond washing dishes or scrubbing.

Dear Emma, Aggatha thought, how wonderful she was in spite of her lively tongue and quick temper. Now she was pregnant again, heavy and miserable. She had lost her first baby soon after its birth, and her little boys, Billy and Ike, were now six and three years of age. At every birth she had hoped for a daughter, and three times she had had a son. With Rachel, it had been just the opposite — she had wanted sons and then had four daughters before she got a baby boy. They had been discussing it one day.

"Well, if this one is another boy I'll give it to you, Rachel," Emma said, jokingly.

But to John D. such a remark was not a joke.

"You should never say such a thing, Emma," he said. "You should be ashamed. If it were a boy, you might be called upon to keep your word. But this time it is not a boy that you are carrying, it is twin girls. You shall name one of them Rachel Emma, the other you may be called upon to give back to the Lord in punishment for your heedless tongue."

Now that her husband had said it, Aggatha knew that Emma would bear twin daughters. If she could only live long enough to see them!

Her suffering grew in intensity, and with it her desire to see her children and all the family. Perhaps if this wish could be granted. she could relax and die in peace. A horseman was sent to notify them all and call them home — not Sarah Jane who lived now at Beaver, not Polly and Lavina who were at Washington, since they were all so far away.

She had lain in a state of semiconsciousness for several hours, but when word came that the children had arrived, she aroused and seemed to revive.

Joseph, now twenty-two, came in with a bucket of snow which he had climbed to the top of the mountain to find. How could she put into words her tenderness for this boy who had been her baby in Nauvoo during those most difficult years, who had always been most considerate of her.

"Thank you, Joseph," she said. "You are always so good to me. This snow is so cooling. Let me eat some more and then I can talk to you all."

"Alma," she cried, "I'm so glad you could come. And Mary Ann and the babies. Alma, you are a married man with a family of your own. Pray with your children and bring them up in the fear of the Lord. Be humble and prayerful and live the life of a Latter-day Saint."

To each she gave a private word, commending the two little boys, Samuel and Ezra, into the care of her sister Rachel and their older brothers and sisters. Then to them all she gave the same advice.

"Honor your father and listen to his counsel. He is a man of God, and he will never lead you astray. Turn to him in your sickness and trouble, and stand by him in whatever he may be called to endure."

The wives came in a group — Rachel, her beloved sister, Caroline, Mary Leah, Emma, now heavy and misshapen, Terressa, and the girl-bride, Ann.

"I love you all," she said. "If I have ever hurt your feelings in any way, I ask your pardon. I hold no ill will against any of you. Learn to bear and forbear and to be charitable with one another. Let your love for our husband bind you together and not tear you apart. I shall hope to meet you in a better place, where I am free from pain."

There was weeping and broken words of goodbye as each wife passed the bed.

"Let them all go," she said to her husband, "all but you and the older boys. I want you to dedicate me to the Lord."

This ordinance was used only in rare cases, and usually only upon the request of the sufferer. The teaching was that each should bear his lot with fortitude and await God's own time for his release. However, when it was evident that death was inevitable, the prayer would include a request that, in mercy, the time should be cut short and the patient released from his pain.

Three days more Aggatha lingered, though she did not speak again. At last she relaxed, her muscles losing the rigidity of suffering, and a faint smile settling on her face with the last exhalations of her breath. To the watching family standing in silence around the bed, it was as though they had witnessed a miracle as her spirit took its flight. It was just at midnight.

The funeral service must be held the next afternoon, for it was June and mortification had set in even before the breathing stopped. Some of the wives hardly got to bed at all, for the body must be washed and dressed; the burial clothes could be put on more easily now than later. For days the coffin boards had been ready, fitted, planed and measured. By daybreak they were put together, and others of the women were busy with the lining and decorating of the casket.

The meeting was held in the living room of the home in which she died. Neighbors and friends all came to speak of the virtues of this sister who had been as a mother to them all, and whose children could in reality "rise up and call her blessed." She was buried in the cemetery beside little George and Margarett, where even today the cut stones mark their places.

The year, 1866 was one of general unrest among the Indians of the south, so that people on the ranches and smaller settlements were counseled to gather in larger units for safety. When Apostle Erastus Snow came with this counsel, Lee protested, saying that he had no fear of the Indians because they were his friends. His homes were placed so that with a minimum of labor he could enclose the spaces between with a high picket fence that would provide a large central space. This he was permitted to do.

His sons now constituted a good working crew. Every day he recorded the activities of each, always listing among them Charley Chamberlain "nee Wilson," the son of Terressa, James H. Thompson, son of Caroline, and William Orson Lee, son of Martha Berry, who until his own marriage worked with his father.

His records show something of the family management and economy. That season there were four hundred and fifty pounds of wool to be divided among the wives in proportion to the number of their children. On one trip north, he took two hundred pounds of butter and cheese to exchange for cotton yarn, tea, coffee, groceries, and tinware. On some of his trips to Parowan for wheat, he took whiskey to exchange.

On one of these trips Bishop Lunt at Cedar City asked him to sit with a group in judgment upon George Wood, who was brought up before the bishop's court for disturbing meetings, precipitating fights, and threatening the brethren. The question was: Should he be cut off from the Church and cast out? Lee pled for leniency, asking that they give George a chance to make a confession and to be rebaptized as a pledge that he would try to do better. Though some of the council protested at first, Lee's judgment was finally accepted.

On July 22, Lee wrote that "Emma B. . . was confined & according to previous promises that I made to her, brought fourth a pair of twin Girls, one of which was Named before its birth, that is, the first Born was called Rachel Emma & the other was called Ana Eliza. . ." for Ann Gordge, Emma's companion wife in her home, and the girl friend with whom she had crossed the plains. The first weighed 8½ pounds, the second 8¾, making a total of 17½ pounds. Of the incident Lee recorded, "I further said to Emma, the mother of the twins; you have obtained the promise, a Daughter to bear your Name and an other to comfort you. . . I now promise you that if you will be on your guard, live humble & Faithful, the atonement will be made without the loss of your Litle Girls. I pray the Father in the Name of the son to give you Faith, firmness, and Fidelity, that Satan may not move you from the pathway of your duty. . ."

For many years, Lee had felt that he had a definite prophetic power in so far as his own family was concerned. It was the right of every good man to have the inspiration of God in his private affairs, he believed, and such incidents as this strengthened his own faith at the same time that it impressed his wives.

Among the people at Harmony, on the other hand, he was in general disrepute. Whisperings about the massacre continued; the stories became more numerous and highly colored. In many ways his neighbors showed their disapproval — by turning their cattle into his grain fields, interfering with his water ditches, and making snide remarks to his wives or children. He always attended church, he was first to fill the assignment made by Brigham Young to get out poles for the new telegraph line, he was prompt in paying his tithes. At Parowan and Cedar City, he was often called upon to speak at church, and at Kanarra he was held in high esteem. Perhaps his very industry, his driving use of his family and hired help, his shrewd trading, his ability to amass property and to live well made his neighbors all the more critical of him.

Certainly he carried on a brisk trading program. Late in 1866 he recorded that he had purchased for trade thirty-two guns; he was always exchanging produce or cattle for the things that he needed. On Christmas Day he entertained all his children and grandchildren as well as several of the families of Lemuel H. Redd and Sam Worthen. The dinner was prepared by Emma at her home "& had the applause of all who Participated in it." On the morning of New Year's Day he wrote that "We hale the New Year with a firm determination to live nearer to the Lord this year than I did the past year."

During spring the company of Simms, Matheny, & Felshaw came into the town with a load of goods to trade for cattle. They stayed at the Lee home, boarded and fed their stock, and he traded with them and also took goods for their expense. He set up a private school at his home and hired Charles St. Clair to teach it.

Later in the spring, his two sons, Willard and Joseph, were called on missions, so Lee rounded up some cattle to drive in to Salt Lake City to meet the expenses of their transportation and clothes. He carried with him a letter from Bishop Henry Lunt of Cedar City to the effect that "Bro. J. D. Lee is a staunch, firm Latterday Saint, seeks to build up the Kingdom of God & live by its Principles & is in full Faith & Fellowship." This would be an important document for him to present wherever he stopped to do business.

En route to Salt Lake City he met President Young and his company coming south.

"I had hoped to meet you at Harmony before you left," Brother Brigham told him.

"I am on my way to the City with my sons who are called on missions, with beef cattle to pay their expenses. But if you wish, I can go back with you."

"No," said Brother Brigham. "If you are driving stock, you will just have time to get there before the company leaves. By the way, we are sending a group to the Southern States and had considered sending your boys with them. What would you think of that?"

"Since you ask me, I will tell you," Lee answered. "Young, inexperienced boys like these can do little in the Southern States. Men of experience are needed there."

"We will send them to England then. God bless you, Brother John. I will see you in the city before you leave."

As they passed through the various settlements, they traded molasses for butter, six pounds to the gallon, a horse for a cow and a year-old calf, and got an order for a stove on a past debt.

Emma was along, going up to meet her sister, Fanny Gilbert, a widow who was supporting her family by taking in washings. The two women had years of visiting to catch up on, and the children at once fell in love with their new Uncle John.

Lee was much impressed by the reception which President Young received upon his return to Salt Lake City. A parade consisting of the military in uniform, the brass and martial bands drawn by matched horses from four to eight to the vehicle, marching children attended by their teachers, each group carrying banners and mottoes — a total of twenty-five thousand passed before the home of President Young, where he stood for more than an hour and a half bowing and waving to them as they marched by. "These marks of kindness he has won through Faithfulness and Fidelity to his calling as a man of God," Lee wrote.

Joseph and Willard left for their mission to England with $110 each and a full outfit of new clothes. During their stay in the city they had shopped, had their pictures taken, attended the endowment house during the day and the theater at night. Now they were to have their first travel experience, crossing the plains to the Mississippi River on freight wagons. From there on they would be able to go by rail and boat.

Lee and Emma took three of Fanny Gilbert's children home with them, Henry, Joseph and Elizabeth, with the promise that he would bring them back in the fall when he came up again, this time to bring President Young's herd of goats.

At Fillmore, a young woman, Jane Woolsey, proposed marriage to John D., saying that she loved him more than any other man and that she wished to become a member of his family. He reminded her that he was an old man while she was still a very young girl who might have many chances for marriage. When she insisted that she had never loved anyone else, he promised that if she still felt the same when he came up in the fall, he would take her in to Salt Lake City and have her sealed to him.

He arrived home in mid-June to find his farm in excellent condition and his crops doing well. During the summer there were the traditional celebrations, with the daily business of work between. Young Henry Gilbert, who had come down with him, had spells of insanity wherein he ran over the hills, sometimes foamed and roared or brayed like an ass, until they were hard put to know what to do with him.

In mid-October Lee started to Salt Lake City, driving Brother Brigham's goats, with a new wagon well fitted up. This time he took his wife Rachel to accompany him, the three Gilbert children to return home, and little Tom Woolsey to help with the goats. They spent eighteen days en route, in order that the animals might feed along the way. From Kanarraville, he took Julia Huntsman, who asked to go to Provo to see her mother; at Fillmore he picked up Jane Woolsey. But the girls were so giddy and giggling, so irresponsible and silly, that by the time they reached the city he was so thoroughly disgusted with them both that he would not marry either.

He delivered the President's goat herd without the loss of a single animal and received for all his labor a hearty thanks, the feed for his team and horses, a suit of fine cloth worth forty-four dollars, and a long visit with his adopted father.

When he arrived home early in December, 1867, he was disturbed by the bad management of the farm during his absence. With Aggatha gone and the two older boys away on missions, there had not been the same industry in preparing for the winter or the same care in storing the feed for the cattle that they usually had. By the next April he was constrained to write that:

A darker time I have not seen for many a year to sustain a large family with Bread. About 50 Mouthes to fill daily — yet my trust is in god. I have all my Bread, Meat, & vegitables to bye till after harvest & but few cows to give us Milk as yet. My Promise is by the Prophets of the Lord . . . that I shall never lack, nor my Own beg Bread & in the times of Famine I shall be fed & that Means Shall flow to me from unexpected quarters. This saying has been verified in Many instances. I have always found room when I had made one step to Make an other. So when one 100 lbs. of Flour was about gone, there would be another one come — so that we always have Bread & have the Name of setting the best Table in the Place & as a general thing our store House is well supplied & in this time of Scarcity I acknowledge the hand of the Lord in it that we may be more Frugal in taking care of what the Lord has blessed us with. . .

Now he rented out his farm land at New Harmony for one-half the crop divided in the field, keeping only his garden lots and orchards for himself. Since their cabin leaked badly he had need to build now another house for Emma and Ann.

About this time the first open trouble developed with his neighbors. While he was away at Washington, his wife Emma received a "fictitious" letter from the post office, purporting to have been written by an officer at Camp Douglas, in which Lee was warned that he had ten days in which to escape or he would be hung up on Old Fort Harmony for his participation in the Mountain Meadows massacre. Emma at once decided that the message was of local origin, for it was the third such letter that had been delivered through the mail, though without the proper postmarks.

Emma accused George Hicks and John Lawson of writing the messages in the hope that they would frighten her husband into going into hiding again. Always before, he had been warned by special messengers whose loyalty could not be questioned, and who came direct from Brigham Young or others who understood the secret code. On the face of it, the letter was false, and since both Lawson and Hicks had had differences with the family over the ditch or the fence line, she suspected that one of them had written it.

"You are nothing but a poor, sneaking, pusillanimous pup, always meddling in other men's business. You had better sing low and keep out of my way or I'll put a load of salt in your backside," she told Hicks.

One word led to another until at last he preferred a charge against her for un-Christian-like conduct, and had her brought before the bishop's court. Here the whole situation was reviewed. She maintained that he had provoked her to say what she did by a long train of outrages, while he insisted that she took advantage of the fact that she was a woman to abuse and slander him. In the end, the bishop and his counsellors decided that both were in the wrong, that they should make amends to each other and that both should be rebaptized as an evidence that they had repented and would try to do better.

Lee advised Emma to submit, for even though he felt that she had given Hicks no more than he deserved, still the bishop represented the authority of the town and had made the best decision that he knew how to make. Besides that, he was a very young man and would probably gain wisdom with the years.

Emma hesitated a while before she could bring herself to accept the terms, then rising she said in a clear voice, "Very well, Bishop, I accept your decision upon one condition — that I may select the man who is to baptize me."

Glad to see that the matter might thus be settled, the bishop consented.

"Very well, then. I am much obliged to you," she said with a fine sarcasm. "I demand baptism at your hands, since you are so inconsiderate as to require a woman to be immersed when the water is full of snow and ice — and that only for defending the good name of her husband. Maybe if your own backside gets wet in ice water, you'll be more careful how you decide next time."

At this the spectators burst into gales of laughter.

"Good for you, Emma!" one called out.

"Stick him to it! He deserves it!" cried another, and in general everyone seemed to think it was all a good joke.

But Hicks would accept no such decision. He had done nothing for which he should be rebaptized. Nor would he shake hands with Lee or with Emma or make pretense that he considered the matter settled. The bishop postponed action, since he had an appointment at Kanarra, he said, and the whole affair was dropped.

This was but one of many irritations. The Lee children, especially, when they were humiliated, would retaliate by fighting. One of his daughters was abandoned in the center of the dance hall floor when her partner learned who she was. He would not dance with a girl whose father was a murderer, he said, whereat one of her brothers slapped his face and told him he could at least have been gentleman enough to show the lady to a seat. This incident called forth another session with the bishop's court.

Perhaps the most spectacular bit of trouble with his neighbors came that fall when John Lawson brought his son-in-law, George Dodds, and began cutting down the young trees and willows that grew along the creek where it ran through Lee's property, just behind the house occupied by Emma and Ann, the two youngest wives. They both went out and protested, saying they needed the shade for their ducks and chickens, and they did not want him in their yard. Lawson disregarded them entirely so they sent for their husband. He and his son Willard came at once and ordered Lawson off the place. Tempers flared and there were threats of shooting, but Willard remained calm, suggested that they just take Lawson's ax away and send him packing. This they did, each man swearing that he would issue a complaint against the other.

The next morning early, Lawson returned with four others and began again at chopping along the stream where it ran through the Lee yard. Now the young wives had no time to send for help or to wait for it to come. Ann filled a pan with boiling water and, when Lawson paid no attention to what she said, threw it at him. It had little effect, since she was too far away, so he laughed as he went on with his work.

Angered, she hurried back to the house and returned with Emma and a pan of hot water each. Now Lawson stopped, held up his ax, and told them to stand back. Emma threw her dose and, when his attention was diverted, Ann threw hers and sprang at him, catching the arm that held the ax. In the scuffle they both fell, Ann on top. "When I with several others reached the scene of action, found them both on the ground & Ann with one hand in his hair & with the other pounding him in the face. In the mean time Emma returned with a New Supply of hot watter & then pitched into him with Ann & they bothe handled him rather Ruff. His face was a gore of Blood. My son Willard finally took them off of him. . . ."

Lawson went at once to Kanarra and swore out a complaint against the girls for assault and battery with intent to kill. The sheriff served the papers and the court was handled according to the law, with Bishop Lorenzo W. Roundy acting as judge. The decision was that Lawson pay the costs of the court and twenty-five dollar fine for trespass and for deliberately stirring up trouble. The spectators were called upon for their reaction to the verdict, at which they were unanimous in sustaining the judgment.

"Thus showing a difference of oppinions in 2 setlements, Harmony & Kannarah. Harmony would have Justified an apostate in spreading desolation to a man's door & deprecate the Idea of defending even a Person's private Rights," Lee wrote.

In the spring of 1869, Brigham Young and company, traveling in eight wagons or carriages, set out on another regular visit to the southern settlements. At Fillmore they encountered a heavy snow storm, quite out of season for April, which held them road-bound and threw them off schedule. Understanding that they did not intend to visit Harmony, Lee rode to Cedar City and then on to Parowan to meet them, in the hope that he might have a chance to visit with President Young.

They all greeted him warmly. Brother Brigham even addressed him publicly in meeting. "John D., did you ever know me to Preach what I did not Practice? I answered in the negative, No, nor neither did anybody else Ever know me to Preach what I did not Practice," Lee recorded. It was a little thing, true, but it was a recognition and it lifted Lee and set him apart as someone special.

As they left town the next morning, President Young called Lee to the carriage and asked him to tuck the foxskin down firmly as an excuse to tell him in private that they planned to be in Washington on Friday. Would he go ahead and make the necessary preparations? Lee would and did; with dispatch.

On Thursday afternoon, word came over the telegraph wire that the president would spend the night at Harrisburg or Washington. A day early! Lee passed the word to Captain W. Freeman, and together they secured an escort of twenty mounted men, rode out a mile beyond Washington, and waited an hour on an eminence, watching the road for any sign of dust. By dusk they had convinced themselves the President had stopped at Harrisburg. The roads were bad, the trip strenuous, and he did not like to travel at night. The other members of the posse overruled Lee's suggestion that they ride ahead another mile or two.

About half an hour after they had disbanded, the company arrived. Lee hurried immediately to the home of Bishop Covington to make his apologies.

"Where is your escort?" President Young asked sharply. Then without waiting for any explanation, he went on, "You know that I need an escort especially when I am traveling at night and in Indian country."

But the president was so worn out with the trip that he wanted to dispense with formalities and get to bed. He agreed to eat his supper — he ordered only a bowl of mush and milk — with Bishop Covington, but said that he would sleep at the home of John D. Lee and take breakfast with him. Since Lee had a sumptuous meal all prepared, the other members of the company came to his home and enjoyed it, some of them joking good-naturedly about the fact that Brother Brigham was so put out at having to enter the town without an escort that he would deny himself such a meal as this. When he finally came over, he went immediately to bed, saying that he would do his visiting on the morrow.

Before sunrise he was serenaded by the local band, while many of the townspeople gathered. The school children came marching in double file, grade by grade, each bearing a banner honoring their beloved President, the leading one being: "WELCOME BRIGHAM, THE FRIEND OF MANKIND." Everyone was eager to see and hear the famous man, the representative of God upon the earth.

After the meeting, the armed escort of the night before rode ahead with the flag to the outskirts of St. George, where they were met by the brass bands from St. George and Santa Clara and the military group in full uniform. As they entered the main part of town, they found the streets lined with people; little girls in white dresses scattered green branches and flowers before them or tossed them at the carriage as he passed.

One young mother, heavily pregnant and holding a restless eighteen-months-old child, had waited so long for the procession that she was almost ready to drop. As the carriage passed, the horses stiffly reined in and prancing, Brother Brigham removed his hat and bowed to one side and the other smiling.

"Well, is that all there is to it?" she asked a little petulantly.

She was very quickly and sharply rebuked by an elderly lady who had overheard her remark.

"Young woman, you have had the privilege of looking upon the Prophet of the Living God," she said. "That should be reward enough if you had to stand here all day."

Most of the people shared this feeling.

As for John D. Lee, he was not a part of the procession. When they met the group from St. George, Brother Brigham motioned him close to the carriage.

"You are going back now?" he asked, but it was as much a statement as a question. It was a dismissal of him and his, a way to tell them that their services were no longer needed. They returned to Washington to get their teams and wagons loaded with wives, children, and neighbors so that all could hear Brother Brigham speak in the basement of the Tabernacle, now under construction at St. George.

This might have seemed a small thing, the expected thing, really, to the other horsemen. To Lee, it was a distinct let down. It was the first time he had not been invited to be one of the official entourage, to travel as an equal to those of the retinue next in rank to the president himself. It was the beginning of the end, Lee felt vaguely. Since the cotton mission had been established seven years before, since the flood had destroyed his mill and the fruits of all his labors, things had been different. Erastus Snow, the man in charge here, had never seemed to appreciate Lee. He had not been given any important stake assignments. Lee expected coolness in St. George, but he did not expect this pointed slight from his adopted father.

Still he forgave it, attended every meeting of the two-day conference, and took extensive notes on the sermons of Brother Brigham, which he transferred with great care into his diary.

1870-1871
Excommunicated

For some years there had been a growing discontent among members of the church with the policy of the leaders. This found voice in the *Utah Magazine,* the first issue of which appeared January 17, 1868. At first Lee subscribed to it and sold subscriptions to his neighbors. When on November 3, 1869, the *Deseret News* wrote that: "Instead of building up Zion and uniting the people, it would destroy Zion and divide the people . . . therefore *The Utah Magazine* is not a publication suitable for circulation among or perusal by them, and should not be sustained by them," Lee immediately canceled his subscription. "I would not support a circulating Medium that tended to apostasy," he wrote.

In the same way, he would listen to no word against his leader. On July 4, George Hicks delivered the oration and sang a song which he had composed to tell of the hardships of the southern mission. The whole tone was light and rather disrespectful; in fact, Hicks had once said openly that "Brigham Young was led by Green Backs & not by the Spirit of the Lord." At the close of the program Lee refused to join in the dance, and when urged to do so, he answered "that I did not strike hands with the enemies of this kingdom, neither make merry with those who defamed the Character of the Prophet Brigham."

The unrest in the north now resulted in the excommunication of some of the most brilliant and vocal members of the church, most of whom were loyal to its teachings, even to the celestial law of plural marriage. They resented only the fact that President Young presumed to dictate to them in their financial affairs. They had invested in mining, railroad, and mercantile businesses and claimed the right to use their own judgment, and had no desire to injure the church.

Among the group were W. S. Godbe, E. L. T. Harrison, T. B. H. Stenhouse, Eli B. Kelsey, Henry W. Lawrence, Edward W. Tullidge, and W. H. Shearman, each of whom had a circle of followers. Their original complaint now broadened into an accusation that Brigham Young condoned murder and kept in office men who should be brought to justice. Some mysterious deaths in Salt Lake City should be explained: Dr. King Robinson was assassinated on October 22, 1866; John V. Long, former secretary of Brigham Young, was found dead in a ditch on April 14, 1869; S. Newton Brassfield was attacked and killed on one of the main streets in April 1866.

Worse still, they said, Brigham Young gave public recognition to men who had participated in the Mountain Meadows massacre. *The Utah Reporter*, published in Corrine, ran a series of open letters addressed to Brigham Young, demanding that those guilty of that outrage be brought to justice. If the authorities had not specifically ordered the massacre, they were accessories after the fact by shielding the guilty. The articles were signed by "Argus," who claimed to have lived in Southern Utah and learned the facts from some of the participants.

During this time Lee was actively defending Brigham Young in the south. He spent the winter of 1869-1870 visiting all the settlements as far north as Fillmore, preaching in every one on the folly of the Godbeite faction and "on the subject of the apostasy, showing the weakness of Godbeism."

On February 24, 1870, Brigham Young left Salt Lake City with a caravan intending to visit the southern outposts of his domain. Lee met the group at Beaver, where he was greeted warmly and invited to sit on the stand. In a private conference Brother Brigham advised Lee to move, but with all his farms so prosperous and his plans so promising, Lee did not act upon the advice.

In early September the President came south again, this time with a small group, to explore the area east of Kanab for an approach to the Colorado River. Lee named the members of the group as Daniel H. Wells, Brigham Young Jr., Gen. R. T. Burton, Bishop Musser, Dimick B. Huntington, Bryant Stringham, J. Winder, J. Hinkley, J. W. Fox, Orson P. Arnold, and Joseph W. Young. Lee was appointed a "road commissioner" to locate the road and select the camp sites. William H. Dame and John Topham were in charge of the "traveling tavern," from which they served sumptuous meals three times daily.

Their path lay up Clear Creek Canyon to Panguitch Lake, over the divide, and up the Sevier River to Panguitch. Here they found the town deserted, and took shelter in some empty log houses. Now they discussed the prospect before them. They would move into an area unexplored, except that Jacob Hamblin had made his way through a part of it, coming in from the opposite direction, and Peter Shurtz had spent a winter somewhere in its wastes. Why not cross the divide at Roundy's Station [where the town of Alton has since been established] and skirt to the south and east rather to the west to Kanab, only to have to turn at an acute angle back? It would save them at least seventy-five miles of travel.

Late in the evening Brigham Young and John D. Lee had a private talk in which again the president urged that Lee move.

"I should like to see you enjoy peace for your remaining years," the president said. "Gather your wives and children around you, select some fertile valley, and settle out here."

Lee hesitated. "Well, if it is your wish and counsel. . ."

"It *is* my wish and counsel." The voice was firm to sharpness.

They were interrupted by the guard, but Lee knew that his future was set.

The next morning, after traveling a short distance, the group stopped to reconsider. They had notified Levi Stewart that they would be in Kanab tonight; they asked him to have supplies ready. If they were to take this new route, who would go back over the mountain with word to Levi? Who, indeed? Since it was an unmarked way over a high mountain, no one responded to the call for volunteers. Finally Joseph W. Young said that he would go.

Lee protested instantly. "Brother Young is a sickley man," he said. "I will go in his place."

Someone else suggested that it was a trip for a younger man, but Lee was firm. "I am a good woodsman, and can make the riffle as well as anybody," he said.

Mounted on a good horse contributed by Major Powell, who had joined the group, and accompanied by Wilbur Earl, Lee set out, arriving at Kanab just at sunset as the people were all out watching the road for President Young. He delivered his message, asked Levi Stewart to have his load of provision ready as soon as possible, ate a part of the banquet that had been prepared for the official party, and was on his way east within an hour. He and Levi rode together in a buggy, while Earl and a teamster took the baggage wagon.

At midnight they stopped a few hours to let the horses rest and feed, and were on their way again before daybreak. After they left the twelve-mile-place where the road turned north to Johnson, they were in unbroken country, but they kept the general direction and by eleven o'clock intercepted the official group. It was a fortunate meeting, considering that neither party knew just where they might find the other.

They stopped for an early noon camp, feasted on melons and fruit and Mrs. Stewart's box of food from what was to have been last night's banquet. All afternoon they traveled over terrain growing more and more barren, along sterile clay formations where nothing could grow, over ridges dotted with scrub cedar and desert brush. At the stream they found a small field of green corn that the Indians had cultivated and a patch of squash. The corn was just ready to eat — sweet, good ears of small kernels; but the stream was a shallow trickle and of tillable land there were only uncertain patches close on the bank.

"What do you see here that would be of any benefit to us?" Brother Brigham asked Lee.

"Nothing," Lee answered promptly. "I wouldn't bring a wife of mine to such a place as this."

Nor was he impressed with the Peter Shurtz fort of which he had heard so much. The story was told that Peter had brought his wife and two children here and had found this large, overhanging rock. He dug underneath it, walled up the sides, made a fireplace, and then walled in a small yard which enclosed a spring. He gathered some fuel inside the enclosure and had food enough to see them through the winter.

With the coming of cold weather some unfriendly Indians had attacked them. Though one of the oxen was driven off and killed, Shurtz and his family were safe. By spring the Indians were so hungry they were ready to be friendly. Peter met them for a "talk," and explained that since they had killed his oxen, they must all go hungry, for he could not plow the land and plant seed. The old chief had his men pull the plow, four at a time in relays, and they cooperated to plant corn, wheat, and squash; enough to see them all through the next season. The third year, Peter secured another ox and moved on to new frontiers, arriving eventually on the San Juan.

After one day of exploration the company reached the general decision that there was little here with which to build and returned to Kanab, where Brother Fox surveyed and laid out the town and Brother Hinckley tried for water with a forked stick. After the lots were numbered, the settlers each drew a number from a hat to signify his home. Levi Stewart was set apart as Bishop, his first injunction being that he should set up a portable sawmill and get out lumber for building.

"I should be glad to try it," he told President Young, "if I could have Brother Lee to help me. He understands machinery. We have worked together before, and between the two of us, we can get the lumber out."

After some discussion as to the price of the mill, they came to an agreement: Lee was to return to New Harmony, sell out and get back as soon as possible. This was a bitter pill, but so deeply rooted were his loyalty and habit of unquestioning obedience that he took it in silence.

As they started back, they needed no pathmaker or vanguard. Lee remained behind to travel as far as Pipe Springs with Levi, and from there he rode ahead of the company, aloof in his wounded pride and nursing a heavy heart.

At Harmony he set about to harvest his crops, make his molasses, and care for the late fruit. He offered all his holdings for sale. Since he was obliged to leave, he had to take what he could get for his property. Lemuel H. Redd bought the new brick house and most of the farm, making the first payment in horned stock and wheat, the annual payments on the remainder to be in wheat at tithing office prices, other produce, or cash.

Lee worked with such dispatch that within three weeks he was ready to start to his new location with the first unit of his family — four loaded wagons and about sixty head of loose stock. Some of his older boys drove the cattle ahead, while two sons-in-law and two hired hands made up the team personnel. This trip was devoted to Rachel, her children and belongings. She had along her fourteen-year-old daughter, Amorah, and the four younger boys: Ralph, twelve; Amasa, ten; Frankie, seven; and Willard, two years old.

If Rachel grieved to give up the new home, the society of family and friends, the abundance of fruit and garden, she made no complaint. Her husband had been given an assignment, and she was glad to stand by him and do her part. She organized her wagon for the greatest efficiency in cooking and camping; she had a box of sewing, mending, and knitting at hand in order not to waste her time en route.

It took them ten days to travel the less-than-one-hundred miles from Harmony to Kanab; ten long, laborious days for man and animal. The wagons were heavily loaded, and though the first lap from Harmony to Kelsey's on Ash Creek was relatively easy, from that point on to the top of the plateau it was a series of doubling teams over the steep places. By keeping two wagons together they could move two at a time and then go back for the other two, and thus make Toquerville on the second day and Rockville on the third. Here they must stop for a while, for the lift from the canyon floor to the top of the plateau was some fifteen hundred feet in a distance of five miles, over such short, hairpin curves near the top that only one wagon could be taken up at a time, the process taking a full day for each.

Rachel stayed with the chuckwagon at Rockville, while all hands made the first trip up, Ralph and Amorah going ahead with the cattle. On this type of road, not more than two yoke of oxen could be used to advantage because of the many short, sharp curves. But all were taken along, and when one set was worn out, it was taken off the wagon, given a chance to rest and eat a handful of grain or a bait of hay, and the other two yoke were put in for a few miles. At best it seemed it was moving a foot or an inch at a time; still, there was no way to hurry it, for there was so much weight to be lifted to such a height by ox-power. Many years ago Lee had learned that consideration for his teams was most profitable as well as most humane.

The loose cattle fared well on the plateau, for there was good

natural feed, and the three-day rest left them ready to move on. The
country was now comparatively level, with a fair road bed except for
the deep sand near Short Creek, where again they had to work in
relays.

The log and lumber fort at Kanab seemed a haven. There were
people, someone to talk to and to listen to — a chance to sing together,
to pray together. Rachel could compare handwork, exchange recipes,
discuss remedies for croup or canker. She had never before appreciated so much the having of neighbors, other women with whom to
talk of women's interest and problems.

They left this isolated village reluctantly. Their way would lead
them east twelve miles, then north four or five more to Johnson's,
where one or two families lived. From there on, they must go two long
days' travel north and east, again a steady climb to lower Skutumpah,
their new home. This was a wide, grassy valley with rolling hills to
the east and west, watered by a meandering stream, a wonderful location for cattle and horses. Eighteen miles to the north, another climb,
to the base of the pink cliffs, would be the sawmill location, near the
timber on the high lands above. For the present they would go on to
the sawmill, which Levi Stewart had sent ahead.

For two days Lee rode over the upper valley, determining the best
location with regard to the timber, water, and yard space, and having
selected it, began at once with clearing and leveling the yard and
getting some logs stacked on it so that as soon as help came the sawing
could begin. He also selected and cleared a spot for Rachel's cabin.

It was now mid-October, the weather clear and fair, the time when
the mill should be running full blast. But until help came from Kanab,
he could do nothing more than he was doing. Finally, on the last day
of October, the engineer and the surveyor arrived. They set up the
mill, adjusted it, filled the boilers, steamed up, and sawed about five
hundred feet of lumber when a valve blew out. This repaired, they
started again and had run just long enough to get interested when the
mandrell broke. Now they were really stopped. Someone would have
to go all the way in to Parowan to get this item repaired before anything further could be done.

Knowing that winter would soon be upon them and that at this
altitude it would be rigorous, Lee persuaded the mill hands to help
him put up a block house for Rachel, with thick, solid walls and a roof
of lumber covered with grass and sod for insulation. There was lumber enough for doors, storm windows, shelving and benches, and with
the stove set up they were ready for any weather.

October wore away with nothing done so far as the lumbering
project was concerned; by mid-November Lee could stand it no longer.

He mounted his horse determined to go to Kanab, leaving Rachel and her children with a son-in-law, Henry Darrow, and Caroline's son, Jimmy Thompson. Finding Bishop Stewart not at home in Kanab, Lee rode on toward Pipe Springs. On the flat near there he met some of his own family en route to Skutumpah — three loaded wagons and about thirty-five head of loose cattle, in charge of William Prince, a son-in-law. In the group were Aggatha's two youngest, Sammy and Ezra, and Rachel's married daughter, Nancy Dalton, who was driving a team because Sammy was coming down with measles and too ill to sit up.

They brought word that Levi had been detained by a death in his family, but most important of all, they delivered a number of letters, "one of them from A. Carrington, Notifying me of the action of the 12 &c. but did not state the cause. . ." This was word of his excommunication from the church, but Lee made no mention of the fact to his associates as yet. Although he kept telling himself that he would borrow no trouble about the matter, he knew that nothing for him would ever be the same again. He had seen too many cases, among them that of Nephi Stewart, wherein a man was ruined financially and his life endangered by a public announcement that he had been cut off the Church.

He started back for Skutumpah with his family. After a hot "whiskey-sling" Sammy's measles came out and he felt better. They stopped in Kanab only long enough to arrange for storage of two tons of flour and two barrels of molasses, to lighten his loads for this last hard stretch.

When they arrived at Lower Skutumpah, they selected the site for the permanent homes on top of an elevation near the southern end of the valley. Here was a good view of all the surrounding country, and good drainage in stormy weather. They would set up a tent here and proceed at once to build a house or two, but first he and Nancy must ride up to the mill site to Rachel's cabin. Now for the first time he produced the letter from headquarters, handing it in silence to Rachel. How good to have a wife who could take such news without weeping or scolding or making a great demonstration!

"Rachel Andora received the inteligence of my expulsion from the Church with firmness," he wrote, "and reminded Me of a Dream or Night vision that I had related to her about the time, about the 8th of Oct., 1870, which was the date of My being droped from the Church."

He knew that President Young had lost no time in taking this action, so soon after their trip together and their long, confidential talks. And this entry of Lee's is the only written evidence to date of his excom-

munication, for the official records have been searched in vain for it.
Now, being reminded of his dream, he wrote it at length in the diary
and concluded with his own reaction:

> The impression is that the apostates & Godbeites are trying to
> implicate Prest. B. Young in the Mountain Meadow affair, on the
> grounds that he houlds Men in the church who are reported to be
> in it &c. . . I borrowed no trouble about the Matter. My
> concience is clear. I have not done any thing with an Evil intent.
> If I have Ered it is in Judgement & not of the Heart & one con-
> solation is, I know that my Redeemer lives & that My reward is
> Sure. Joseph the Prophet once Said that he would rather have
> every Man on Earth against him then to have his concience acuse
> him. It is Just so with me. I would rather have a clear concience
> than to have the Smiles & Goodwill of all Men. My love for the
> Truth is above all other things & is first with me, & believe that
> Prest. Young has Suffered this to take place for a wise purpose &
> not for any Malicious intent. My prayer is, May God bless him
> with light & with the inteligence of Heaven to comprehend the
> things of God & discriminate between truth & Eror. . .

Thus he wrote his formal statement of faith, that his descendants
might have his attitude from his own pen.

His sons-in-law liked his location so much that they stayed long
enough to haul in a large pile of logs, that they might have lumber
with which to build when they returned in the spring. Early in
December help came from Kanab, the mill was repaired, and sawing
began in earnest; so effectively did they work that teams began to
come in groups of three and four, to return loaded with freshly sawed
boards.

Just when things were going at their peak, word came on December
13 of a disastrous fire at Kanab — the whole fort burned and six of
Bishop Stewart's family with it. Most of the hands at the mill were
relatives; all were friends. They must go back and share in this trouble
and mourning. That same evening there was a heavy snowfall.

Lee knew that further work at the sawmill this winter would be
scarce. He would take a load of lumber as far as Kanab, pay his
respects to his old friend Levi, and send the younger boys with the
two ox teams back to Harmony, while he took the horse team to
Washington. He felt that he must see President Young and plead his
case in person. In justice to himself, he could not take this excommunication without a protest; he must have an opportunity to clear
himself before Brother Brigham. Rachel, with Nancy and the younger
members of the family, would be here alone for several weeks, perhaps

for more than a month, but this trip must be made. He would bring others of his family back with him.

At Washington he found his eighteen-year-old son, John David, very ill following a relapse from the measles. David was so fond of his father and had so much faith in him that his very presence was a tonic. Yet for all the warmth of his son's welcome, Lee sensed a coldness in his wives. Without much difficulty, he learned that the word of his excommunication had gone out and they had heard it here; Lavina had consulted Brigham Young as to what course she should follow and had been told that she could suit herself. She could leave him if she wished, but she could not sell his home or any of his property.

This was a blow to Lee. He had expected his wives to be loyal to him, at least, giving him a chance to explain. He gave Lavina a severe reprimand, reminding her of his past kindness, of this lovely home and the comforts he had provided. "You should have been the last woman to have gone to Prest. Young before seeing Me, at least," he told her, "or to have waited & known for yourself that I had transgressed & cut myself off from this church. You have never heard Me speak a word against Brigham, Nor against this church, But to the contrary, have always been a stanch defender of its Principles. . ."

Thoroughly hurt, he refused to enter the house to eat his meals or to sleep, although it was December 19. His daughters tearfully begged him to forgive them and come inside.

The next morning, "on a fasting stomach," he rode to St. George to call upon Brigham Young. He reported their interview thus:

> I asked him how it was that: I was held in fellowship 13 years for an act then commited & all of a sudden I Must be cut off from this church. If it was wrong now, it certainly was wrong then. He replied that they had never learned the particuelars until lately. The Truth & the whole Truth was then told to you; with the Exception of one thing & that was that I suffered the blame to rest on me, when it should rest on Persons whoes Names that has never been brought out, & that if any Man had told to the contrary, his informant had lied like Hell. I declared my innocence of doeing any thing designedly wrong; what we done was by the mutual consent & council of the high counsellors, Presidents, Bishops & leading Men, who Prayed over the Matter & diligently Sought the Mind & will of the Spirit of Truth to direct the affair. Our covenants & the love of Righteousness alone prompted the act. My concience is clear before God & I know that I have a reward in Heaven & I desire a rehearing & if I am denied I will appeal to My Father in Heaven. You can have a rehearing, & continued, I want you to be a Man & not a Baby; I have no feelings against

you, & continued, we will Go to the office & see Bro. Snow & Set
a time for a New hearing. . .

Lee had a conversation with Erastus Snow: "Privately Bro. E. Snow
asked me some questions which I answered & told him the facts in
the case. He seemed Much astonished &c, We set the following Wed.
to Meet & I returned to washington. . ."

During the next week Lee visited Harmony, where he was called
upon to speak in meeting and "bore testimony to the onward progress
of this Kingdom & of Prest. B.Y." He spent a happy Christmas with his
wives Caroline, Emma, Terressa, and Ann, and his married children
and their families. He returned to Washington expecting to have his
rehearing the next day, but was greatly disappointed to find instead
an unsigned note in the handwriting of Erastus Snow. It read:

To J. D. Lee at Washington
    If you will consult your own safety & that [of] others, you will
    not press yourself nor an investigation on others at this time least
    you cause others to become accessory with you & thereby force
    them to inform upon you or to suffer. Our advice is, Trust no one.
    Make yourself scarce & keep out of the way

In the meantime, the attitude of his family at Washington had
changed; his wives and children all became cordial and affectionate.
David's health was better. He of all of them, had held his father as an
ideal. However, such was Lee's pride that, while he brought gifts for
them all and stocked the home with groceries, he would not stay in
the house overnight.

Returning to Kanarraville on New Year's Eve, he attended the social
there. The next day he prepared to return to Skutumpah. This time
he would take with him Caroline and her eight children, ranging in
age from Harvey Parley who was eighteen years to Walter B., who was
only three months old. Four others were younger than eight. Her son,
James Thompson, was now almost twenty-one, a steady, reliable young
man who was a great help to her.

The trip out with Rachel had been difficult, but the return trip was
doubly so. Instead of clear, crisp, dry weather, the winter storms had
set in. Just as they were ready to leave it began to snow. The heavy
loads and the slush and mud combined to make some of the teams
balky, until it seemed as if not only were the elements in league against
them but the spirit of Satan had entered their teams. Of necessity,
they made short drives and long rests, taking fifteen days to reach
Skutumpah.

The first necessity was to build a shelter for the family of young children, all hands cooperating. While Lee and some of the boys were getting out additional lumber, others had started with the sleepers, the two-by-fours, and the roof beams. They set up the shingle mill inside, where Rachel, Nancy, and Amorah could operate it, turning out eight thousand shingles which were being nailed onto the roof as fast as they were finished. With such organization, the dwelling was soon ready. The fireplace, the shelves, even a part of the floor were put in after beds had been set up for the younger ones.

Throughout February all hands continued to work at building, finishing Caroline's 17 x 34 house with partitions and some built-in conveniences, and pulling down Rachel's blockhouse up at the mill site, transporting it down, and setting it up again.

By the first of March they had started the third dwelling. They all had a surprise when Emma without her children or any of her household goods arrived with one of the teams. The bishop and some of the neighbors had been trying to persuade her to stay in Harmony, separate from her husband, and make her own way. She was young, capable, and attractive; she could manage or she could marry someone else to better advantage. But Aunt Kisiah Redd had counseled her to listen to her own heart, to go and look the situation over, talk to her husband, and consider well before she made such an important decision. That was exactly what she had come to do.

It was by then, March, the valley rousing to the first touches of spring, and annual flowers beginning to appear. The sawmill was running at full blast, turning out about five thousand feet of lumber daily. Teams were coming in a steady stream, loading, and going back. Everything looked promising. More than all this, Emma was thrilled with the love and affection she received from her husband. He was so genuinely happy to have her come; his face had lighted with a surprise and joy that warmed her heart. She had known that he was her man that first night long ago, and she had covenanted to stand by his side through sorrow and adversity. She would indeed come back.

Now that the mill was running perfectly and everyone was so pleased with it, Lee decided to sell his interest. He knew too well the frustration and delays when anything at all went wrong; he sensed also the uncertainty of his own future. He did not offer to sell but waited until one of the men asked about buying it. Since he had lumber enough on hand for his own buildings, and logs stacked in the yard, he sold at a reasonable figure, even taking a little loss. His judgment was borne out when, about ten days later, the engine got out of repair again, and the company pulled out, taking with them what they could salvage to start operations at the Kaibab Forest.

On April 20 the two older sons, Joseph and Willard, arrived with their families, and Emma returned with all her belongings. In addi-

tion to her own four; Billy, eleven; Ike, eight; and the twin girls aged
four, she brought Ann Gordge's two older children, Samuel James,
four, and Merab Emma, three, with the word that their mother had
taken the three-months-old Albert and gone north.

The news was a tragedy, especially for the two deserted babies who
were to grow up, often feeling extra and unwanted, always faced with
the story that their mother was a bad, wicked woman who had deserted them and left the church. Lee knew that a part of the trouble
was his own inability to give Ann the kind of attention she deserved
and needed — but the basis of it all was that his excommunication had
forced this move to another frontier. The story came that Ann had
wasted and sold of his substance, that she had been unfaithful, and
had gone off with another man. There is family legend to the effect
that just before her last child was born, she tried to get into the potato
pit, but was so large that she got caught in the hole in such a way
that she could get neither in nor out. Two of the boys, seeing her,
laughed themselves almost into hysteria trying to extricate her, which
so angered and humiliated her that she determined to leave. Her
actual reason for leaving was probably much more complicated. First,
there were neighbors and friends ready with advice that, since Lee
was cut off the church, it was her religious duty to separate from him.
She was still young — only twenty-three — and she could do better by
herself. Then there was the fact that, although she had been in the
Lee family for five years, she had never had a place of her own, but
had always shared Emma's.

In general, the two women had adjusted well after the one serious
difficulty which John D. had been called in from the field to settle.
They had learned to cooperate on household tasks and had stood
together in the fight with John Lawson. They had taken turns with
one managing all the children while the other went on a trip with
their husband. Emma's twin girls were eight months old when Ann's
first son was born, and she bore a daughter and another son before
Emma had another child. Living as they did all in one house, her
children hardly knew which woman was their own mother; Jimmie
and Belle were almost as fond of Emma as they were of their own
mother.

Ann took the nursing baby, Albert, with her to Beaver, where her
brother, David Gordge, lived. She left the child there with his family
while she went on north to find work. Though Albert joined his mother
when he was eight years old, the two older children never saw her
again until they themselves were married and had families of their
own.

In June Nancy came out bringing word that some neighbors had
taken seven head of Lee's cattle and refused to let his sons have them,

AN EXCERPT FROM LEE'S DIARY REGARDING HIS EXCOMMUNICATION
See text page 294. Courtesy of the Huntington Library, San Marino, California.

saying that they were holding them against debts owed them by a
third party, to whom Lee was in turn indebted. Lee was outraged. He
set out at once for Parowan, and sent a messenger to Ammon Tenney
to meet him there in all haste.

When he arrived, he found that the court was dismissed and all the
people involved had returned to their homes. Undaunted, he rode to
St. George, where he went directly to Erastus Snow, the president of
the stake, and demanded that the brethren be brought in for a church
trial before the high council. At the suggestion of Erastus Snow, he
wrote out a formal complaint stating his case and asking that the
offending parties be tried for their membership in the church. The
trial was set for July 25, 1871, since all would be in town to celebrate
on the day before.

During the month which intervened between the complaint and the
hearing, Lee returned to Skutumpah, taking with him his son John
David from Washington.

The trial lasted for three days. Lee wrote in detail of the procedure,
and the clerk of the council also kept careful minutes, which corrobo-
rate Lee's as closely as minutes taken by two people could. The final
decision sustained Lee, ordered the offenders to return his cattle to
him and to pay the cost of the court.

One statement is interesting. Quoting the chairman, Joseph W.
Young, Lee wrote:

> . . . A great deal has been Said on the subject, yet I feel it My
> duty to say a litle more . . . these men would never have
> durst to attemp such a thing if Bro. Lee had not been droped
> from the church last April conference. He was cut off by My
> Peers as well as yours & it is none of our buisiness & have no right
> to Judge in the Matter. But they Supposed that he durst not come
> in to bring them to Justice. . .

This bears out the fact that any person who was cut off the church
was legal prey. The statement that Lee had been publicly cut off is
interesting because it is not recorded in the minutes of any conference
held in St. George. Other men were excommunicated and their offenses
named, two for adultery and one for total inattention to his duties,
but nowhere is the name of John D. Lee mentioned.

At the close of the trial, Lee made small presents of either cash or
tea to several of the brethren who had spoken in his defense. "The
Brethren took these little presants as a token of my good feeling
towards them &c. They gave Me a copy of the Decision & Many
rejoiced at my Triumph," he wrote.

Lee now set to work to move his wives at Washington out to the new location. He helped the boys with the harvest, sold the home and land to A. R. Whitehead and Benj. Paddock for two thousand dollars cash, stock, goods from the factory, and a set of blacksmith tools. By August 10 they were ready to start with the last load. As they were pulling out, word came that Mary's little daughter at Kanarra was not expected to live. Lee himself had contracted malaria, but he went at once.

> Found the Mother & Friends a weeping over the child. I told then that the child would Recover; administered to it, both Faith & works, & in a few hours the child was sitting up, calling.

At Johnson he found Isaac C. Haight also in hiding. Together they went to Kanab, but waited in a secluded spot out of town for Jacob Hamblin and John Mangum to bring them food and news. They learned that action was starting against all polygamists, and were advised to transfer all their property to their wives.

Lee proceeded at once to make out the necessary deeds and distribution, naming Rachel Woolsey, Polly Young, Lavina Young, Sarah Caroline Williams, and Emma Bachellor as recipients. Most important, he was ordered to take one or two of his wives and move down to the Colorado River crossing. This would be his greatest test.

1871-1872
Lonely Dell

Skutumpah seemed a quiet haven, a valley where cattle and horses would thrive and some crops would mature. Because of the success of the sawmill, they had four comfortable homes with lumber floors, shingle roofs, and glass windows. The thought of moving down on the Colorado River to a new frontier troubled them all.

To complicate matters, Lee himself was in poor health. After a severe illness, he noted on August 10, 1871 that "My Fever & ague turned to 3-day chills," which meant that he could work as he could on two days and go to bed with a chill on the third. Occasionally after that he mentioned that this was his "chill day," a fact to which his shaking pen gave mute evidence. At various times during the winter he made such entries as:

> Dec. 1 . . . Here we were without bedding or grub & the wind North high & I with my chill on. . .
>
> Tues Evening Encountered a desperate wind storm. We took shelter by the side of a high clift & was reasonably comfortable considering I had a heavy ague & fever.

His last mention of his sickness was on the first of February when he noted that "My Fever & ague Still Stick to me, like Poverty which Stands by when all friends forsake." After that time, he seemed to be in good health again, but during this most difficult move he must endure the regular chill.

November was the best season to visit the lower lands along the Colorado. The Indians had known this for centuries and Jacob Hamblin had learned it through his recent trips. The weather was clear and mild, the river at its lowest, and the sands not too hot for daytime travel. There was, as yet, no wagon road beyond Hogans Well or the Navajo Springs, and the one that far turned back to Johnson. Beyond the springs, pack trains had followed the trails marked out by Indians over aeons of time. They crossed over precarious trails around cliffs and traveled through arroyos where a wagon could never make its way.

There were other problems as well: Which families were to remain at Skutumpah and occupy the houses? Which wives would go to live on this last frontier? Caroline and Emma were both heavy with child, should either make the trip? The instructions were to take two wives. The question was; which two?

Rachel at once claimed her right as first wife since Aggatha's death. She would accompany her husband wherever he went. Caroline was equally devoted. She would like to go, and she felt that she had a better claim than anyone else because her babies were so young. She now had eight children (two had been killed by the falling wall); six under the age of ten, and she was to bear another, her eleventh, within two months. She needed her husband, her children needed their father — but none of them needed Rachel's dictation. Between these two there was a mutual jealousy.

Emma, too, loved her husband with a depth and passion which gave him first place in her life. True, she was impulsive and sharp-tongued and apt to flare into sudden anger, but it was like a match to rabbit brush, one quick sputter and it was out, without heat enough to start a flame anywhere else. Then she would be doubly affectionate, generous, and kind to all around her, willing to include in her circle all who were dear to her husband. She would prefer life with him under the worst conditions to life without him under the best.

The first contingent to pull out of Skutumpah in November, 1871, consisted of three wagons, one of which carried Caroline and her family, and fifty-seven head of loose stock. Some of the older boys were driving the cattle, others in charge of the wagons. At their first camp out, just above Johnson's, Jacob Hamblin joined them and held a long consultation with Lee, for he had been over this trail and on across the river at least a half dozen times. He told Lee that the cattle would do better if they traveled down the Paria Creek than they would over the long, barren road which the wagons must take, where there would be neither feed nor water. The reasoning sounded logical so Lee went, taking with him only the fourteen-year-old Ralph, leaving the teamsters to find their way past the junction to the Hogan Wells. There, some of the brethren sent to work on the road would act as guides.

At the Paria village, Lee found the problem of driving cattle down the stream was much greater than he had anticipated. If John Mangum and Tom Adair had not volunteered their help, he could not have managed. The fall of the stream was so great that it had cut a chasm where for miles the water was bank to bank. Though it was now low water and the skies were clear, a storm above would bring a flood that would sweep them all literally to the Gulf of California. There would be no escape for man nor beast.

They spent eight days on the trail, much of the time in water. Two days and one night they traveled without stopping because there was no place to camp. When their provisions were gone, they shot a cow that had become hopelessly mired in quicksand and cut steaks from her, living for the next few days on a meat diet. Lee had started with a half bushel of corn in a sack behind his saddle, intending to grind some for mush as they might need it, but hoping to save most of it for early planting. This onerous burden was the straw that broke the camel's back, not so much in itself but it was simply more than he could manage.

"It was Baptized as often as I was & one place it was under water 24 hours before I could find it, & had passed the place some 10 miles," he wrote.

Along the lower reaches of the stream where the valley widened to grassy coves and meadows, he left a part of the cattle, bringing only twelve head through to his destination.

He was disappointed on arriving at Lonely Dell, not to find his wagons there. Surely they could not have been this long on the road! But there was no trace of any human having ever been there. Hoping to meet them, he and Ralph started back over what they thought would be the wagon road, while his friends returned via the Navajo trail to the Paria settlement. Now Lee got his initiation to this land which for the next years was to be his greatest threat and antagonist. Good frontiersman though he was, he became so hopelessly entangled in a succession of flats and gulches that at last he gave up trying to go any direction but north toward Skutumpah.

Late at night on the fourth day, they stumbled into Emma's home there, as she and Amorah and James were sitting up waiting to take some loaves of yeast bread from the oven. The warmth of her greeting, her great joy at having them there safely, the delicious hot bread, butter, honey, and cold milk, soon revived them until they could talk of their hardships. Young Ralph's throat tightened at mention of his horse lying about eight miles back exhausted on the trail. He felt he must get out early the next morning and go back with some grain for it if it were still alive.

Soon Lavina, David, and other members of the family came, for it had been twelve days since the wagons had first pulled out, and there had been no word. All were eager to know something of the new location.

The next morning they loaded Emma's belongings and, with her children, including little Jimmie and Belle, started with two other wagons to follow the tracks of the first company. About twenty miles out they found one wagon abandoned with a broken axle, much of its load of provision wasted by ravens and wild animals.

When they reached the fork of the road they learned that Caroline had decided to go to Kanab, where she could have help during her confinement and put her older children in school. She felt that she owed something to her children as well as to her husband. The contrast between the well-marked road west to Kanab and the indistinct trail to an unknown emptiness somewhere in the south and east had helped to make up her mind. One wagon had already broken down. Might not her own fail to reach its destination if she went that way?

Leaving Emma and the teamsters to go on for a day's travel, Lee rode to Kanab to be sure that Caroline was set up for the winter with food and arrangements for fuel. It was probably better for everyone that she should be safely and comfortably established. Returning, he overtook the wagons on the second night out, and was able to help them over the worst places in the road.

Rachel and her one wagon had reached the mouth of the Paria, where she set up a tent for a temporary shelter, and sent two of the boys back along the trail with an extra team to help the next wagons.

Family legends tell of their first night at this new location. The moon was in its first quarter, high and bright. Rachel had a generous pot of stew simmering, having seen the dust of the wagon from their lookout during the forenoon. The wagons were eased around the last spur of the hill and turned up the wash, dragging slowly through the deep, loose sand. They had arrived at last! Greetings over, hands were washed "Indian style" by having one dipperful of water poured through four pairs of little hands placed one above the other with a pause while each lathered with soap, then a general rinsing from the dipper, and all were ready. There was plenty of water in the creek, but nobody wanted to leave the circle to go after another bucketful.

All stood quietly while the blessing was asked upon the food and thanks given to God for the reunion and the good health of the party. Each person received his ladle of stew and a slice of bread and butter and retired to sit on a wagon tongue or to squat on his heels to eat it. He might come back for another serving and another, or he might have his tin cup of milk to finish his bread with butter and molasses for dessert. It was a tasty meal and an ample one, and when it was over, Amorah washed the dishes, while Rachel and Emma consulted together about the bedding arrangements.

It had been a long day; still it was such a pretty night and it was so good to be together that no one wanted to go right to bed. Lee viewed the group with pride; three men, three women, and thirteen children. His brother-in-law, William Woolsey, and wife were the only ones outside his immediate family. Rachel and Emma were the other women, himself and his son James Y. (by Polly Young) now twenty-one, were the other men.

Only four of the thirteen children were girls; Amorah, sixteen, Rachel's daughter; Emma's four-year-old twins, Rachel and Ann; and

the little motherless Belle, age, three. The boys included Aggatha's
two youngest, Sammy, seventeen; and Ezra T., fourteen; Rachel's four,
Ralph, fourteen; Amasa, eleven; Frankie, eight, and Willard, three;
Emma's two, Billy, eleven, and Ike, eight; and little Jimmy, brother to
Belle, five. Perhaps because they had no mother here and because he
felt that he owed them special attention, Lee put Jimmie and Belle on
one knee and Willard on the other, and brought the twin girls into
the circle of his arms close against him, one on each side, while the
younger boys sat in the sand at his feet, and all the older ones found
seats in the circle.

"Do you know what night this is?" Lee asked them all.

They looked at one another uncertainly for a second and then Emma
spoke up. "December 23. Why?"

"This is the birthday night of our Prophet, Joseph Smith," Lee told
them. He went on to talk of the importance of this wonderful man
and of the only true church which had been restored through him. He
told of his own experiences in listening to the Prophet speak and of
the times when the power of the Holy Ghost lighted his face with a
clear, transparent brightness. How noble he looked as he walked out
like a king and gave himself up voluntarily to save bloodshed among
his people!

He wanted Samuel and Ezra to hear of their mother's courage during those dark days; how she had urged her husband to go and defend
the Prophet while she remained on the farm, how she felt so sure that
God would protect her from the raiding mobocrats, and how he had
found her and her baby in the snow under an improvised shelter.

At the close, he bore his testimony to the truthfulness of the Gospel
as it was revealed to the Prophet Joseph Smith and taught by the
Prophet Brigham Young, and enjoined each of them to stand by the
church, no matter what might be ahead for their father. It was an
experience that each child remembered with deep emotion.

The next morning Emma got up and looked around at the rugged
lavender cliffs to the east, the river to the south and back at the long,
difficult road over which they had traveled. She exclaimed, "Oh,
what a lonely dell!" The phrase appealed to John D. "You have named
our home, Emma," he said, "We shall call it The Lonely Dell."
Through the years ahead, Emma was to learn how lonely it really
could be.

Soon all hands were busy, men setting the tents, teen-age boys cutting willows, and the younger children dragging them to the yard.
They must have a temporary shelter until a house could be built. But
it was Christmas Eve! Rachel and Emma made final preparations for
a celebration. That night they sang Christmas songs and had refreshments. Dried raisins and parched Indian corn were mixed together in

a large bowl. Also there was molasses candy pulled to a golden lightness, drawn into a long rope and broken into crisp sticks. Christmas morning each child received a gift; homemade rag dolls, mittens, stockings, a pencil, a knife, a slate or a mirror. There was one item each, for the spirit of Christmas must be preserved even at this farthest outpost.

The first days and nights were perfect, clear and bright, with just the right tang in the air. Then came a short, violent storm, with winds of tornado speed; rain, thunder, and lightning. The piled and drifted sand told them that such storms would come again. Lee decided to move on up into the valley "where the wind would not get so fair a sweep."

By January 12 they had finished building two small rooms. One was a dugout with its back and two sides set into the hillside. It had a flagstone floor, and a willow and sod roof. Later this would be a cellar, and a place where the children could sleep during the scorching midday hours. The larger room was of rock laid up with mud and lime mortar, and had a dirt floor and roof, but two small windows and a solid door. The chief concern was a shelter for Emma during her confinement.

Now the Woolseys returned to the settlements, taking one of the outfits, and Lee took Sammy and rode up the stream to check on the cattle. On his return, Emma greeted him from the bed, where she lay with a new daughter cradled in her arm. She named the baby Frances Dell — Frances, for her sister, and Dell in honor of their new home.

She had come out here so that her husband could be with her through the ordeal of the birth, however, she had managed quite well without him. Also, during the experience she had become better acquainted with Rachel, telling her between pains of life in England, of joining the church, the trip across the plains, her first year in the valley, and the courtship of John D. Lee. Rachel listened with understanding, and was gentle and considerate as an older sister.

The next day they saw their first Navajos. At the first sight of the group Lee wondered whether to bring them across or not, since he could see that there were twelve or fifteen of them, but they kept calling. He made them understand that he must work on the boat first. When at last the boat was ready, neither of the boys wanted to risk crossing on it. The river looked so deep and they could not swim well. Besides, the Indians on the other side looked rather formidable.

Rachel did not hesitate, though. She steered the craft while her husband used the paddle or guide pole. The natives called out encouragement and direction, and came running to help pull the boat to the shore. They were so heavily loaded with blankets, calico, domestic, linseys, and other items that it took three trips to get them all across.

The horses, however, refused to cooperate, and Lee finally convinced the natives that some of their party must take them up to the Ute crossing and swim them across there.

The next day Lee traded two horses, a mule, and a fine colt for blankets, broadcloth enough for a suit, eight yards of calico, and some heavy material for work clothes and pants.

By early February Lee had made a trip with a pack horse up the Indian trail to the Paria settlement with some of the blankets and cloth to trade for grape roots, shrubs, and seeds of various kinds. Early in March he had planted onions, parsnips, radish, lettuce, rhubarb, a field of wheat and one of lucern.

On the last day of March a messenger came with a letter to say that a large company of miners were on their way out. He could miss them entirely if he took the Indian trail to the settlement, then doubling back, he could follow behind them and set up claims to the water at House Rock, Jacob's Pools, and Soap Creek. He should ask John Mangum and Joseph Heath to go with him.

Lee left a few hours after the messenger arrived, and followed the instructions. Brothers Mangum and Heath respected the authority of the letter and went willingly to House Rock where they put up a small house and painted a sign to say that on this date the land and water were secured. At the Pools they started another, but since their provisions were gone, they left it unfinished.

Returning, Lee found the miners camped at Lonely Dell, but decided that instead of running away, he would go about his work and trust in God. He found that some of the men would work for their board or gladly exchange tools for supplies or meals at Emma's table.

Rachel returned with flour, groceries, potatoes, trees, vines, and seeds, and work at planting went on apace, for they must raise their own foodstuff if they expected to stay here. Miners came and went, and although there were some threats, Lee met little actual danger. He was able to entertain visitors with food and stories; in general, he impressed them as a man of high caliber.

In an effort to hold the water and to provide more range for his stock, Lee decided that they should operate two places, the one at Lonely Dell and one at the Pools, some twenty miles back along the road. This would divide his time, for he must spend the greater part of one day on the road between places if he went by wagon, and about a half day if he went on horseback. Emma would manage things at the Dell and Rachel at the Pools.

Here, in a very special way, their lives were determined and conditioned by their surroundings. Isolated by several days' travel from any settlement, they were now so separated that there was no way to help each other in emergencies or to share pleasures. During the winter the weather had been pleasant except for the occasional wild winds and one or two brief, torrential rains, but with the approach of summer, the place was no fit habitat for man or beast, except those which through the ages had been able to adapt to it by remaining all day deep in their holes in the earth and emerging only between twilight and dawn.

Even today, though some trees are established, Lonely Dell from the air is only a splotch of green in the midst of endless stretches of barrenness in various tones of red, an area of hogbacks dotted with sparse, scraggly brush with writhing gullies between. Then, there was only a faint streak of willows to mark the outline of the creek. There Emma and her children had the business of caring for cows, calves, a couple of pigs, a few chickens and of watering the trees and vines and garden — when the dam held and water was in the ditch.

But Emma's lot was better than was Rachel's. She did have one room with a willow shed beside it and a cellar dugout against the hill. A few buckets of water thrown on the floors and on the ground under the shed, a sheet doubled and wet and hung in an open doorway would cool the air somewhat, while the cellar was a real godsend. Emma's garden had been planted early. By mid-July she had green vegetables aplenty; green corn, summer squash, radishes, onions, beans, with melons just starting that would last until late fall.

It was early in May when Rachel moved. Her location lay close against the vermilion cliffs, with a southern exposure. At her back was a talus slope of vitriolic blue clay upon which not a blade of anything could grow, not even the hardy little shadscale. The dry floodway was bare sand rocks, and except for the bit of wire grass and willows where the water seeped out, there was scarcely shrubbery enough to shelter a lizard.

Lee's record makes little direct reference to the heat, other than to note that a calf "melted down" and died en route between the two homes, and that he himself had been ill from overwork in the heat. He always left for one place before daylight or in the late afternoon. Soon after their arrival here, he wrote that they must have "some shelter from the burning rays of the sun." Even in May, it beat against the red bluffs, which seem to absorb and throw it back until the humans between were literally in an inferno. There was nothing with which to build except stone, but they could not endure the heat for as long as it would take to build a rock house. So using the few willows that grew along the spring, they built a shanty little better than an Indian wickiup. With Rachel's help, he set the upright poles in an octagonal shape; James and the four younger boys cut and dragged the willows to the site, and Amorah wove them in and out to form the walls.

Bushy willows and their trimmed branches were placed on top, and over them a wagon cover.

Just a week later on June 2, 1872, Lee wrote that

> Professor Beament & Bishop (with Jo Mangram their waiter) of the Maj. Powel's corpes of tipographical Engeneers came up, & they were also from the Lonely Dell. They had intend to have gone into the NavaJo country, Photographing, taking landscapes & Mountain Sceneries, But the Colorado River was up so high that they durst not venture to cross it.

He adds that the weather is showery with the next day cloudy, but the visitors took a north view of his location. This picture was enlarged and, along with others of the trip, sold widely, even being made up for viewing through a stereoscope.

It shows the willow shanty with the various gear of the time; an ax, a pick, a pitchfork, an ox-yoke, a bridle hanging from a protruding willow butt of the roof. The people include Lee, bearded and a little stooped and thin from his ague, his two visitors, Rachel's three youngest sons, and Amorah, an attractive sixteen-year-old in a long dress. Dimly seen in the upper right are Ralph and the hired man with the horses at the stone corral. Most important of all is the background of barren hills and sterile talus slope.

Soon after this, Rachel and Ralph went again to the settlements, returning with supplies and mail, among it "a confidental Letter of More importance then all, Saying that if I continued faithful & true to that Mission, that I never should be captured by My Enemies, to take no further trouble on that Point, that I should have timely warning of the approach of Danger & that I should be remembered for My integrity & interest in the welfare of this People & Kingdom." The letter was received at the Pools on June 8, 1872; it was probably written from Salt Lake City. Whether this "confidential" letter was signed by Brigham Young or by his secretary made little difference. Lee considered it to be from his adopted father and referred to it later as being from Brigham Young. Certainly it gave him renewed hope.

By the end of the month he prepared to make a trip back to the settlements himself, had made his final arrangements at the Lonely Dell and was on his way, when he had a strong presentiment that he should stop. "Return back to the dell and Put in all the corn that you can, & you Shall have Bread before you can send to the setlements for it," it seemed to say. He told Rachel of this and she, having, as always, full faith in his prophetic powers, insisted that they go back. This was on June 30.

On July 6, "when the last of our flour was baking, Rachel Said where we would get any more she did not know. Little Frank Said, The Lord will provide more by the time we eat this. His Mother Said that he would have to do it soon, for they were then eating the last. The conversation had scarce ended when the Barking of the Dogs anounced the near approach of Some Person. . ." It was members of his family coming on a visit and bringing four hundred pounds of flour.

Throughout the summer they continued to plant, knowing well that corn planted here in mid-July would ripen in October, and that turnips and other root crops would do well all winter.

On July 13, Major Powell's boats landed at the Lonely Dell, out of supplies except for coffee and flour. His expedition arranged to furnish these items, and additional groceries when they arrived, if Emma would cook for them. This was a great advantage to all concerned, since she had fresh vegetables in great variety and plenty of milk and butter. Young twenty-three-year-old James Fennimore especially was grateful for Emma's care, as he had been ill for several weeks. He was the photographer of the party, as Lee said, "now in the employ of Maj. Powel at $100, per Month, became quite feeble through exposure, being of a delicate constituti[on], which rendered him entirely unfit for the laborious duties . . . involving upon him. . ." He remained at Lee's home for three weeks, and left full of praise for them.

On July 24, Lee decided to celebrate, so he sent a written invitation to the Powell group to join him at dinner. Although Powell himself did not accept, others of his party came. Clem Powell wrote that they had a good dinner and that "The Old Gent regaled us with sermons, jokes, cards, &c., &c., &c. . ."

Two weeks later, just as Lee was pulling away from the Dell, he met the company — Major Powell, Mr. Almon H. Thompson, his brother-in-law and geographer for the group, Mrs. Ellen Thompson, his wife, who had come out from Kanab to see the country and the river, Harvey C. DeMotte, professor of mathematics at Wesleyan University, and their camp hands. Lee at once pulled off the road, unhitched his team, and, leaving the outfit in charge of his boys, returned with the major to Lonely Dell, where he provided watermelons and vegetables which Emma served in her own superlative way.

The Powell group remained another day, while Lee went back to the Pools. He was pleased to note that "In return for the kind reception & affable Manner in which they had been entertained since their arrival at this place, they & Maj. Powel adopted My Name for the place, Lonely Dell & so ordered it to be printd U.S. Map[ped]."

On August 21 he started for the settlements, using the cutoff he had made to the House Rock Springs. On his way he met Jacob Hamblin who was headed for the upper Paria village, so they stopped and fed their teams for three hours while they caught up with their dealings and the news.

Jacob apologized for not being able to get the supplies and seeds out as he had promised, but said that he had forwarded three hundred pounds of flour that had not been delivered. He praised Lee for staying at his post in spite of difficulty and discouragement, saying, "& that I had done more on this Mission then all the rest & as a reward for My integrity, I have the promise of triump[h] & that I Shall never be captured by My Enemies & that I Shall come fourth in the resurrection of the Just & no Power Shall hinder &c."

Although Jacob Hamblin was only a lay member of the church, and without full authority to make such a promise, it was cheering to Lee to feel that his mission here was important and that he was appreciated.

Lee had Rachel and her children along on this trip, for she had no home at the Pools worth the name. He was taking three outfits, expecting to load back with flour, groceries, glass and window frames for the house he expected to build, as well as nails and hardware. He would collect his annual payment on the place in wheat or cattle, and exchange as he could for the items he would bring back. They took short drives, camping at Johnson's one night, and Skutumpah the next. Here they stayed two days, for Caroline was back in her home with her family, including her new son, Ammon Doyle, now eight months old and beginning to crawl. Polly and Lavina were also living here, with most of their children. From Skutumpah they took four teen-agers back as far as Panguitch to visit. Several of Aggatha's married children lived there; John Alma, Mary Adeline Darrow, Louisa Evalin Prince, and Harriet Bliss and her sister Thirza, daughters of Martha Berry.

Wherever they went, they were greeted with warmth and affection.

Though the Redd family were cordial with them when they reached Harmony, the place was so full of memories that it was in many ways a sorrowful homecoming. Harmony held the graves of Aggatha, little George, and Margarett. There too, were the fruits of Lee's labors for almost twenty years: the houses, the fish pond, the grape arbors now loaded with ripe grapes, the trees heavy with apples, the wide ditch full of clear, pure water. His time at the Colorado had given him a new appreciation of good water.

At Parowan, on his way back, he had a long interview with William H. Dame, but did not accept the invitation to eat dinner with him. Dame had cleared himself somewhat of the responsibility for the Mountain Meadows massacre, had filled a mission, and was living quietly here. That Lee felt some bitterness at being singled out for excommunication there can be no doubt, though he made no comment as to the subject of the talk. He had a "quite a lively time with the Probate Judge & Clerk. In the Meantime Marshal P. Duncan (U.S.) officer drove up. I Made Myself known to him & had quite a chat with him & took a glass to geather as a Matter of Policy," so it would seem that he took quite literally the promise that he should not be taken by his enemies.

On his return to the Lonely Dell on October 11, he found Emma and the children well and overjoyed to see him. As usual, he brought food and gifts of special goodies and trinkets all around, and took private time with each child to show that he had a special interest in the welfare of each. He was disappointed to find that the floods had cut away the dam again so that part of the crop was lost. A band of hostile Indians had stolen most of Emma's flour, but a friendly brave hearing of it, brought her a venison, saying that he did not want Yawgett's children to have to cry for food.

During the fall months, some of his married children visited and considered moving out to the Lonely Dell. There, both water and land were available if only there were enough people to control the stream. Word had gone out that the authorities were going to open the route to emigration into Arizona. Brother Heath had already brought in one load of lumber toward building a boat and wharf, and on December 16 arrived with another load and the gunnels of the boat.

Lee had marked out his house for Rachel at the Pools, made most of the excavation for the cellar, and hired Elisha Everett to lay up the walls. The home was to be 30 x 35 feet, with a parlor, two bedrooms, and a family kitchen. Lee had assembled some stone and saw the work start, but had been forced to spend so much time at the Dell that the stone mason became discouraged and left. Lee rallied his hands and all set to work until on Christmas Day, 1872, he wrote that they had covered three rooms with lumber, put in two doors, and built some temporary cupboards.

The next day the Indian runner, Tocotaw, arrived with an express to say that President Young was on his way to St. George bringing with him Colonel Thomas L. Kane and wife, and that he wished to establish a ferry across the Colorado at this point. Affairs in the East made them feel that many of the saints might want to come this way to escape oppression. This news cheered everyone. A ferry here with good roads would mean that they would no longer be isolated, but would maintain the most important spot on a busy line of travel. They were excited just to think of it.

Immediately they began to prepare. Lee put up a blacksmith shop by building a stone forge and setting up his bellows. In his spare time he could hoop barrels, shape horseshoes, and help Uncle Tommy Smith with the boat.

They celebrated New Year's Day by a "bee" in which the men raised a log house for Heber and Nancy Dalton, the boys worked on the corrals and yard, and Emma cooked the family dinner.

On January 11, the boat was ready for launching, so they made a formal celebration of the event. They gathered together, twenty-two in all including the children, ready to share the picnic and the first boat ride. The larger craft, which they called "The Colorado" was "26 by 81½ feet, strong, A Staunch craft & well constructed & a light Runer. The Party presant all crossed on her to Christen her & take a Pleasure Ride. We crossed over & back twice, Uncle Tommy Smith & son Robt Rowed her over & I Steerd. Set down a good Post & fastened her with a cable chain & reached home about Dusk." The skiff they called "The Pahreah," evidently a much smaller boat.

From the first, Lee had gathered driftwood from the stream beds, using the smaller branches and saving larger pieces and logs for building purposes. He had brought the shingle mill down from Skutumpah, and now proceeded to make up some dry logs into shingles, running out some eight thousand, which he took back to cover the house at the Pools. If President Young did come down here, Lee must have a good home in which to entertain him.

This trying to operate two places so far apart and in this country, posed many problems. One time as he traveled toward Lonely Dell, he met his eleven-year-old son, Billy, coming on foot after him. Emma, alone for some time, had become despondent because another flood had taken out the dam and because some passing man had suggested that her husband must have deserted her. So she sent this child on a twenty-six-mile hike over a road where there was only one watering place.

Lee assured her of his love, but explained that he was tied by circumstance.

Now begins the Tug of War. A Dam 8 foot deep & 7 Rods long to make besides heavy repairs on the ditch before the water can be brought to revive the now dyeing crops, vines, & trees. However, imitedely we went to work. This Point Must not be abandoned. The probable Salvation of Iseral depends upon it, temporal if not Spiritual. I with my 4 litle Boys & what assistance Emma could render with a young Babe at the Breast, we continued our exertions for 21 days, watering the fruit trees & some vines by hand & by the grace of God we finally conquered & brought out the water & began to revive our Dying crops & while doeing so the Heavens smiled from above & Sent down gentle showers to aid us.

He felt that he was an integral part of an overall plan, an important person in a vital position. Let the emigrants come; he would be ready for them. "You shall be remembered for your integrity and interest in the welfare of this people and Kingdom," the latter had said. He would be worthy of the trust.

STONE HOUSE AT LONELY DELL
Photograph by J. Wes Williamson, Whittier, California.

The Old Fort at Lonely Dell

1873-1874
The Ferryman

The year 1873 opened with great promise. On February 1, Lorenzo W. Roundy arrived with twelve men on their way to explore the Little Colorado and select sites for settlements. They spent two evenings in the Lee home, where they ate and visited, to the great satisfaction of their host who wrote:

> After partaking of Supper we Spent the Evening in conversation, Singing, Speaking &c. Read Prest Youngs Letter of instruction & the Evening passed off so well that was 2 Morning before we went

Most of the men had been his friends long before the unhappy event for which he was now paying a heavy price. Lorenzo Roundy, who a few years later would lose his life in the Colorado, had been his neighbor. Andrew Gibbons and Isaac Riddle, whose homes he had visited often in southern Utah, had been his friends since the days at Far West; Ira Hatch and Jacob Hamblin were also close associates. Young Levi Smithson would become his son-in-law; James Jackson would live in his home as tutor of his children. Mosiah Handcock, rhymester and singer entertained as he so often did with frontier ballads.

Lee set the company and their animals across the river, but convinced them that they should leave their wagons. There was no way to get them up the opposite bank. Little Benny Hamblin should remain, too, as he was small for an eleven-year-old and would enjoy the company of the children at Lonely Dell.

After a mild, open winter, their first cold weather came in February. The snow melted quickly, but the wind from the Kiabab, where snow lay six feet deep, was bitter and cutting. Rachel's house at the Pools must be covered. Lee's shingles were not half enough, so he put a roof of willow poles, brush and sod on the kitchen, built in the gables and chimneys, cased the doors and windows, and built a mantel over the fireplace, and stone steps before the doors.

The exploring company returned on February 25 to report "snow from two to 6 feet deep, heavy range & fine timber in the Mountains. Litle Colerado wide bottoms & densly timbered with cottonwood, water rather Brackish." To Lee this sounded favorable. Better still, one of the men reported that he had heard Brother McDonald, Brother Brigham's clerk at St. George, say, "Brother Lee should be encouraged, for he was the kind of man that they needed, and that they knew he had not a treacherous hair in his head." This praise was sweet indeed.

On April 3 Joseph W. Young arrived with a company of twenty-five men who were sent to build a road and improve the approaches to and from the river. Brother Young chose the site for the road which Lee had marked out, rather than the one Jacob Hamblin recommended, saying, "We durst not trust Jacob's judgment in such things." Next he asked if Lee would sell the brethren milk, butter, and beef.

Lee answered that he would be glad to donate whatever they might need, or give it as tithing, if the church would accept tithing from him. They agreed to report the amount to Bishop Levi Stewart of Kanab that he might record it as Lee's contribution.

The first company of emigrants arrived April 22 with nine wagons and thirty-five horses. It took Lee two days to get them all across. He set his price at three dollars per wagon and seventy-five cents per horse, payable in produce or freight. On May 9 fifteen wagons arrived and were crossed; the next day twelve more. From them Lee received some dried fruit, soda, soap, sugar, matches, a scythe and snath.

He worked until ten o'clock getting the last of them across. Since it was a beautiful, moonlit night and they all had eaten a good supper Lee reported that:

> Some 15 or 20 of the co. took a Boat Ride on the river by the Silver light of the moon & while we were gliding over the Still waters of the Colerado, the music & the voice of the Songsters Made Melody. All felt well.

Two days later, May 12, he ferried eight ox-drawn wagons, and took the people for a pleasure ride on the river. "Had one Lady on Board with us, had Music by the constantina, Dancing & Singing. We had a splendid time."

When Henry Day arrived on May 18 with nineteen wagons, the stream had risen fully ten feet above the usual landing place and was swift and dangerous.

They were forced to tow the boat up at least a half mile higher and to cut a makeshift road along the rocky cliff.

> Nevertheless with care, perseverance & industry we succeeded in crossing 62 animals in all, 15 oxen & cows & 2 calves & 47 horses & mules & 19 waggons, 3 women, 1 child, & 28 men . . .

(all of which took the greater part of three days, and all safe)
. . . without any accident with the exception of braking two
oars, one Rough lock, & one wagon missing the boat as the
waggon was roled in & detained us about one hour, & one cow &
one horse jumped off the Boat & swam ashore all right.

The whole journey had been fraught with so much difficulty and
danger that Captain Day said a company should not have been called
into this country until a good road and ferry had been built. Lee
resented this, since he had crossed some fifty wagons and more than
a hundred animals. When Lee suggested that if he didn't like the
arrangements, he should try to do better, Day countered by saying that
he was not called to build roads or boats.

. . . I continued that Better men then he was Made Road,
Bridges & Boats from Nauvoo to Salt Lake without whin[in]g half
as Much as you at this Ferry. Brigham Young is the Man that
is at the head of this Mission, & he knows what he is doeing. He
does not expct you to be carried through to A.Z. on Flowry Beds
of ease, but to help prepare the way. The cos. that have gone
ahead had no roads or Ferries, only as they Make them & I do
not believe they will grunt ½ so much to make their Roads as you
do to cross after the Ferry is made.

Sunday, June 1, was Brigham Young's birthday. Lee and his family
decided to honor it by a special baptismal service. Lee himself could
not perform the baptism although he could speak at the meeting. Two
of his sons, one grandson, and James C. Jones, a visitor, were baptized.
By June 4 summer had set in on the desert, and on that day the first
of the Arizona emigrants returned reporting "that the litle Colorado
dried up & the country a Sandy Desert — nothing But Sand & Rock &
crooked cotton woods & that all the co. was turning back to water &
feed. Teams give out; wagons left. Provisions, stoves & implements of
husbandry left by the way."
Again Lee rebuked them, saying it was a trick of the devil to dry
up the water. The same thing happened in the early settlement of St.
George, he said.

the clarra dried up untill there was not water enough for stock.
The crops perishd, But the Mission did not Stop, although many
appostatised from their Mission. Prest. B.Y. Prophecied that the
Blessings of gold would follow the hand of industry, that the
water Should increace an hundred fold & springs of living water
should bust fourth & Rich feed would yet cover those sterile

Plains & yet a large city would yet be built on that ground &
Domes, steeples & spires would reach 250 feet in the air &c., &
the result was in a few Months a[f]ter a Flood came & washed
away a stone Fort & mill & Trees 150 years standing & the Stream
cut 30 feet deep & developed Springs of living water & ever Since
the Stream has increaced to thrice the sise & now sustains a
Population of Many thousand & a fine city is being build with
fine orchards & vine yards.

The fact was, however, that many of the company were returning
and the large group at House Rock Spring had decided to wait until
word came back from President Young before they made a move in
either direction. Then fate took a hand. On the evening of June 16,
1873, a storm blew up from the south with such fury that it blew a
large tree into the harbor, dashed against the ferryboat, tore her from
her moorings, and sent her on down the rapids.

Lee, who always saw the hand of God in every phenomenon of
nature, was much disturbed at the loss of the boat. Surely there was
evidence that further emigration to the Arizona mission would be dis-
continued for that season at least. Or was it proof that those who were
on the Little Colorado would now be forced to remain, and could not,
if they would, come back? The company at the House Rock stampeded
— poured out their molasses upon the ground that they might fill their
barrels with water, gave away much of their bacon and groceries for
transportation back as far as Kanab. Truly this seemed a waste to him,
or a lost opportunity wherein he might well have secured much needed
supplies for his families.

But now a greater trouble lay ahead. Two messengers from Kanab
carried an express to his home at the Pools; his daughter Nancy and
her little brother John Amasa brought it on to the Dell. It was to the
effect that six hundred soldiers with forty baggage wagons were approaching that place intending to establish a military post there, and
that they had sworn vengeance against him and all his family. Just as
he had convinced himself that life here might be at least more toler-
able, he was forced to leave. This time his source of inspiration
deserted him, or he would have been assured that the report was false
and that none of the group would approach this spot. But the advice
was for him to get away to parts unknown, and a dream of the night
before seemed to support the decision to leave.

With the aid of some friends and the skiff, he swam his horse across
the Colorado and headed south along the wagon tracks. At about two
o'clock that afternoon, he met twenty-two wagons of returning emigrants, also abandoning the Arizona mission. Here was a continuation
of the desert, not so broken as the one on the north bank but more

sterile and hot, with rare watering places and those "well mixed with Pollywogs and other insects." His horse was overcome by the heat and lay down, so that he was compelled to wait until the cool of the evening before he could move again.

On the forenoon of the third day out, he met Jacob Hamblin, who advised him to go on to Moencopi where he had planted a crop and left it in the hands of an old man named Winburn. That evening he came to the camp of Isaac C. Haight and his group, who were working on the road while hiding out in this desolate territory. From them Lee purchased a wagon with a solid box and a good cover to serve him as shelter, as well as supplies of food in exchange for cattle back at Skutumpah. Three stoves were left behind and a great deal of other gear, the people feeling that if they could get their animals and empty wagons back they would do very well.

With the road crew gone back, Lee was left alone with old Mr. Winburn. Both men worked to plant more vegetables, to keep the tiny stream of water busy on the garden already growing, and to fight off the wild animals and birds that were determined to devour the crops. Lee went on a one-day trip, exploring in the direction of one of the campgrounds of the company, where he gathered up sacks, tin cans, two pounds of coffee, a shovel, a keg, and some horseshoes, all useful items for him. He also visited the Indian farms at Tuba's domain where he was treated to green corn and melons, and where he learned something of the land to the south.

Toward the end of July Lee became quite ill, so ill, in fact, that he could hardly get himself a drink. He had sent Mr. Winburn to carry letters to his families across the river and to learn how they were. In his misery, he feared that he might die all alone. He took a teaspoonful of straight turpentine, then sensing that the cure might be worse than the disease, was forced to place his whole trust in God. He asked that he might be able to get a message to Rachel at the Pools, and seeing a little bird near, penned the following lines:

> Fly my sweet Bird to my House in the Cove
> & whisper this message to my loved ones at Home
> Tell her to come Quickly, My own Bosom Friend
> For I am alone in deep anguish and Pain.

He relaxed and was able to sleep, and the next day felt well enough to bring his diary up to date, including a full account of his dreams.

Two days later Rachel arrived, having returned with Mr. Winburn, crossing on the skiff herself and swimming her horse across the river. The same day Indian messengers arrived with letters that should have been delivered several days earlier. Now, comparing their experiences,

Lee showed Rachel the verse in his diary and told of the bird's flying off in the direction of the Pools, and she was ready with her story of a strange bird that landed in her yard and acted so tame that they put out crumbs for it. She at once interpreted it to be a messenger from him, told her children that their father was in distress, and began to prepare to come to him even before the boy arrived with the message. The story has become a family legend.

On August 24, John D. Lee and Jacob Hamblin agreed to trade places — Lee's home and holdings at the Pools for Jacob's claim at Moenave, near Moencopi. Lee was to give twenty-four bushels of assorted vegetables from the year's crop, a new harness, and a double barrel gun. Jacob was to assist Rachel and the children to move, and to take care of the cattle for one-fourth of all the calves from forty cows. They worked out the details to their mutual satisfaction, and Lee planned to have a permanent claim there.

All during August and into the fall Lee was busy at husbanding his crop. He dried much of his early corn by cooking it briefly, cutting it from the cob, and spreading it in the sun on a clean cloth. He also cut, scalded, and dried several bushels of green beans.

Lee visited with the Indians and entertained them at his place. He even wrote out a simple list of words and their Indian equivalents, so that he could talk to them in their own language.

In accordance with the agreement at the exchange of places, Jacob Hamblin returned on September 7, bringing a wagon with supplies and tools, and Rachel's younger children. With them were Heber and Nancy Dalton, the group numbering nine persons. Emma had sent Jimmie and Belle because she herself was hardly able to feed and care for her own five.

All hands were busy at farming, getting ready to build a house, and secure the crops. On September 30, young Lehi Smithson arrived on horseback, having swum the Colorado and made the trip all the way alone to court Amorah. They had met only a few times and had exchanged no letters, yet they had been attracted to each other and each had known that it was mutual. So he asked for her hand in marriage according to the best form, and her father not only gave his blessing but performed the ceremony himself. But the boy had come horseback. How could he take a wife and her belongings back?

This problem was solved when Heber and Nancy decided to make their home on the upper Paria. They traveled back together, the four of them in one wagon, Amorah taking her scant dowry of clothes and trinkets, a quilt top, and a pair of pillow cases.

Left with six young children, John D. and Rachel worked diligently in order that he could make a trip back to the Lonely Dell. They hauled in seven loads of squash and pumpkins and put away fifty bushels of potatoes, husked a great deal of corn and shelled five bushels. This crop was important, for it meant their very life. But they must also have a shelter before winter set in.

During the summer they had hauled up "house logs" three or four at a time, to have for use as roof timber or lintels. Earlier Lee had laid out the foundation of a stone building 34 by 17 feet, and they had worked at the walls as they could. When the first hint of snow came at mid-October, he hurriedly covered and plastered one room, finished off the fireplace and "made a cupboard & Mantletree, hung & cased the Door & windows of that Room & put up the clock. Also Made a Bedstead."

Lee knew that Emma would give birth to another baby in early November and wanted desperately to get to her, but everything seemed to conspire against it. Mr. Winburn became ill from an infected foot, inflamed and painful, and attended by violent chills and fever. Lee could not leave without first doing what he could to ease him. After the crisis seemed past, after he had the crop gathered and stored and sufficient wood cut and stacked against the house, Lee set out, accompanied by the two older boys, Ralph and Amasa. By traveling early and late, they reached the ferry at noon on November 8.

Their calls were answered by the children running to meet them, though Emma waited just outside the house. She had sensed that he would arrive today, so had a chicken simmering on the back of the stove, with dumplings ready to add to the soup, and steamed squash rings. She took him first to see his little new daughter, a well-favored little child. Then they would have dinner before he walked about the place.

She knew it would be a shock for him to see the complete desolation of what he had left green and thriving. A flash flood, the kind he knew so well, had created such havoc that she could do nothing to repair the damage. The garden, vines and most of the trees had burned to a crisp during July and August. The one apricot tree near the house they had kept alive by carrying water.

Emma could not tell John D. what she had gone through here alone, the memories of her childhood home, the dreams of her youth. She did report that Jacob Hamblin had hurt her feelings by suggesting that she had sinned to bear a child to a man who was cut off from the church. He didn't hint that her husband had asked him to get a midwife there to attend her, though she herself knew that would be impossible.

She explained how, when the preliminary pains began, she prepared and laid out everything within reach, how she had the teakettle boiling and the clean squares of cloth heating in the oven for the little navel, with scissors close by to cut the cord and string to tie it. She had sent Ike to keep the twins occupied at their playhouse under the tamarack bushes, and to see that little Dell was safe and happy. They were all too young to have to listen if she cried out toward the last. Nor was Billy to come in until she called him. He was to stay near, and say a prayer in his heart for her. When it was over, he must help clear up and bury the afterbirth.

She managed very well except for the last half hour or so. After the birth she had been so relieved, so full of pure joy and the sense of release, that the name Victoria, for the beloved queen of her homeland, came to mean "victory" in her mind. This the child was always called.

The name Elizabeth was added for Lee's mother, of course, but it was also for the girl friend who shared with her the experiences of that winter of 1856; to remind her of the pledge she had made with God. When she had tried to drive tent stakes into a ground frozen solid and watched people die of cold and starvation, and carried one little corpse to join twelve others in a common grave, she had promised God that if he would help her come through this experience whole, she would never again complain of the weather. During July and August, as she watched her precious garden and vines and trees literally burn up, she needed to remember her promise. Elizabeth, who had been with her from the day of their baptism until they reached the valley, had not been so fortunate; she had hobbled all the rest of her life on crippled feet, frozen so badly that they could never be restored. The very name would remind Emma of her own two sound ones.

Actually, the experience of little Victoria's birth was to become one of her greatest assets, for years later when she herself became a midwife, she understood better the fears of young women on lonely ranches and railroad stations. She was willing to go any distance through any weather to assist at a birth, or she arranged far enough ahead so that the expectant mother could be brought to her home. Not only did she carry healing in her hands, but she moved in an aura of optimism and confidence that was contagious. The ordeal just lived through; the heat, loneliness, fears, and ultimate victory was only one valley of despair. There would be others, but for the present, they must both consider what must be done and what could be done to prepare for the months immediately ahead.

Since the family had only a few pounds of flour in the house and little to go with it, Lee set out the next morning for the Paria settlement via the Indian trail. While waiting three days for the wheat to be ground, he had visited among friends and attended the church services, where he was asked to address the people. He never let an opportunity pass to bear his testimony to the divinity of the Latter-day

THE COLORADO RIVER AT LEE'S FERRY CROSSING

View looking south from Lonely Dell. Note the road leading right, uphill, to a sharp hairpin turn. Photograph by J. Wes Williamson, Whittier, California.

VIEW FROM LEE'S FERRY LOOKING UPSTREAM
The outbound road on the south bank runs along the center of the sloped area — see arrow. Photograph by J. Wes Williamson, Whittier, California.

work and of the importance of every little outpost in the overall plan for the kingdom. Father Thomas Smith, who had lived with Lee while he built the lost ferryboat, gave a special party in his honor, at which he was again asked to speak.

He enjoyed the association of his family, for Nancy and Amorah, his daughters, both lived in Paria, and he appreciated meeting friends who accepted him as though he were still in full standing. However, nothing gave him as much joy as a letter from Brother MacDonald, private secretary of Brigham Young at St. George, for he wept with joy as he read it

> He Congratulated Me upon the course that I was pursuing. Said that My love, loyalty & interest that I had for the truth & this People was a Marvel, Seeing that My Name was cast out as Evil. . . Also States that it was the intention of Pres. B.Y. to So Establish the AraZona Mission, the past May in a me[as]ure be forgotton. . .

Lee returned to Lonely Dell in a few days with nine pack animals loaded with flour, molasses, raisins, and other items. Two days were spent repairing his wagon and working around the place. Then, he must visit the Pools, round up and check the cattle there, brand the calves, and haul back the lumber and the cupboards which he had reserved when he made the trade with Hamblin. He sent Levi Smithson, who had come with him from the settlement, to help manage the pack train; Ralph, Amasa, and Billy rode ahead while he and little Ike followed in the wagon.

The place at the Pools looked as if no white man had been there for years. One of the large pigs was missing; the window glass, sash, and keg of white lead were gone, as was also his whole assortment of horse and mule shoes. The boys found and rounded up thirty-one cows, which meant that seven were missing, either driven off or killed. They separated the calves from their mothers, branded them, and started them toward the Lonely Dell to finish the winter where there was better feed.

John D. remained in the area for almost a month, but for Emma his visit was all too brief. Still she could not complain, for he would stay with Rachel at Moenave a little more than a month and be back with her on New Year's Eve. He had stocked the home well with food, killing and curing a young beef to add to the flour and groceries; he had repaired things in general and left everything in as good order as possible. Only the loneliness during his absence could not be erased, though she remained assured of his affection and devotion.

It was during this visit with Emma that the Lee-Hamblin feud really took root. Prior to this time, the two men had been very friendly, counseling together often, trading homes, planning work and crops. But now Lee felt betrayed, let down. The next time he met Jacob, on January 23, 1874, he wrote that they had some plain talk "about Matters of a delicate character, things that a man in his Position should be ashamed off. We, however, agreed to drop it as he pled innocence . . . , but was only one of his old tricks to Evade the Truth. I however treated him with the same kind respects as I did before."

Later other frictions developed between them, until each warned his children against those of the other, each issuing a solemn edict that none of his descendants should ever marry any from the opposite family. The net result, as might be expected, was a great many intermarriages, with mixed loyalties to the fourth generation.

When Lee had visited Emma in November he made no mention in his diary of any new boat, though McClintock says that John L. Blythe completed and launched a ferryboat on October 15, 1873, which was 20 x 40 feet, big enough to cross two wagons at a time. On his return, November 24, he wrote that he crossed his wagon, 6 horses and 5 cows, "but unfortunately in runing my waggon of the Boat, she Mired to the Exle & My team could not get her out till next day, when he unloaded every thing & doubld team."

On December 17th, Lee had word from a Mr. Echols that . . . "uncle Tomy Smith [came] with 5 men to finish the Boat, as it will be wanted soon." Lee was so interested in the ferry that he wrote to both the governor of Arizona and to Brigham Young through Brother MacDonald at St. George to see if he could get a license to operate it and upon what terms.

In the meantime, he went on two exploring and prospecting trips, keeping a careful record and making maps and "way bills" for the guidance of future travelers. He and Hamblin also had a serious difference with regard to the way the Indian affairs were being managed in this area, with Lee writing in his protest, and Hamblin going in person to make his report.

Then came a letter or telegram which changed all his plans. It was so important that he copied it verbatim in his record.

The Telegram was as follows (SS)

To Jno. D. Lee, Seniour   St. George, Jay. 28th, 1874
via Kanab
Dear Sir:
    Your letter to A. F. MacDonald was received by us with Much interest. We are Glad to hear you are still interested in the advancement of our Setlements. In reguard to the Boat, built by Jno. L. Blythe & Smith, our only obJect was to have a suitable Boat large Enough to cross with Safety & accommodate the

People. As to giving any one permission to cross without paying, we have never contempleted any thing of the kind. If you will see that this Ferry is kept up, you are welcome to the use of our Boat. You should charge a suitabl[e] price for your labour. When we come along with our company, we shall expect to pay you liberally for your Servises. We shall send chains so as to secure the Boat. See that your wife Emma gets a proper title to secure the Boat location, as probobly the Ferry May be valuable Some day & a support to your Family. We & our Families are all well & are doeing all we can to accomplish good.

Yours Respectfully,
Brigham Young

No. 184 Pd 11.25   G. A. Smith

Lee's joy knew no bounds. This official recognition of his worth and appointment to operate the ferry, signed by President Young and George A. Smith was something tangible, something to keep as evidence. Although it was six weeks between the writing and his receipt of it on March 7, that made little difference, for the exploring and prospecting trip that he had made needed to be done anyway.

He could not refrain from writing his reaction in his diary in a sort of paean of praise:

It was only an other Evidence of the high minded Philanthrophy that Ever characterize the Nobleness of his Character. Instead of doeing as some one horse Bishop, ready to take away our rights & Preveleges & Rob us of our hard earnings with impunity, he, Brigham the Prophet, counts the cost, weighs the disadvantages & inconveniences that we had to under go & Father like Says, You are welcome to the use of the Boat, only look after it & keep up the Ferry. . ."

He arranged his affairs and by March 14 was back at Lonely Dell, for this letter would tie him to the ferry. Here he met John L. Blythe and his wife for the first time, and found them to be "staunch & firm in the gospel & verry agreeable." They were now on their way into Arizona with ten families, to build a stone fort at the Moencopi fifty feet square and twenty feet high. Blythe had been a member of the High Council in Salt Lake City from 1861 to 1872. He was one of a group charged with the murder of A. King Robinson in Salt Lake City in 1866, had been imprisoned for a time, but released on April 30, 1872, and sent soon after to make the ferryboat in 1873.

Lee had it in his heart to visit Brigham Young, so taking Emma on her first trip back since her arrival at the Dell three years before, he set out on March 24, 1874. Lee knew that President Young would start back to Salt Lake City immediately after April conference, therefore, he planned his trip accordingly. They stopped at Skutumpah to call on the family there, and to trade their heavy wagon for a light outfit that would be more comfortable and easier to haul.

At Pipe Springs also he was met cordially, for Brother Brigham had already sent out a large cable chain with two locks and keys, instructing Brother Winsor to give them to John D. Lee. He would pick them up on his way back, but was cheered by the promptness with which the President had acted.

They stopped at Washington with Tom Clark, who had so often stayed in the Lee home. Here Lee bathed, shaved, dressed in his Sunday clothes, and mounting his horse, rode into St. George after dark. President Young received him graciously, "with the kindness of a Father," Lee wrote, introduced him to his family, and invited him to join them all at supper. After the meal, the two men withdrew into the private sitting room where they could discuss matters pertaining to the emigration into Arizona and the San Juan area. President Young listened patiently while Lee related a long dream of the City of Zion as it should be, where every person was busy working at the thing he could do best, and there was no poverty or crime.

They returned to kneel with the family at prayer, after which Lee rode back to Washington, with the understanding that he should join the official suite and travel with them as far as Kanarraville. He started early with Jacob Gates, but soon fell back with the company, where he visited at length with George A. Smith as they rode along. President Young had his wife Amelia with him, George A. his wife Bathseba, while James A. Young and Angus M. Cannon and their wives occupied another carriage.

As they passed the Lee home, where they had been so often entertained, they tipped their hats to Emma as she stood and waved from the porch. They spent the night at Bellevue, and held meetings at Kanarra the next day.

When Brigham Young took leave of John D. the next morning, he implicitly "enjoined it upon Me to See after the Ferry & not let the Boat get away, & not let it go into the hands of our Enimies or hire gentiles to tend it." He went on to say that reports had come that Lee associated with Gentiles, played cards, and drank with them, adding that once "he could trust me to do anny thing on Earth that was wanted to be done." Lee assured him that the reports were false, that he was as faithful to the church as ever. "John, you must be careful & stand by your integrity. Blessed me & drove on."

Lee did not realize that this was the last time he would see his beloved president; he knew only that now he was to be the official ferryman of a large boat at a crossing which was most important.

1874-1875
Captured

Lee hurried back to the ferry to prepare for the year's emigration, but learned that, after the fiasco of the year before, the plan had been temporarily dropped. Perhaps that would be to his advantage, for it would take time for him to get the place back into production. In the fall, as usual, he came back to the settlements for his winter provision, secure in the promise that he would not be captured by his enemies. The fall of 1874, however, was to be his unlucky one.

The story was written in some detail by Sheriff William Stokes, who came south from Beaver early in November with warrants for the arrest of eight men: Lee, Haight, Higbee, Wilden, Adair, Jukes, and Klingensmith. Strangely, the name of William H. Dame was not included. Because most of these men were out of the state, either in Arizona or Nevada, and since Lee was known to make annual visits in to the settlements, Stokes decided to get him first, even if he had to follow him all the way to the river.

He could hear nothing of Lee in the southern country, but at Hamilton's Fort he learned that, while Lee had visited Harmony and the other towns within the month, he was now on his way back to Lonely Dell. That meant that he might have stopped at Panguitch; so after some careful planning, Stokes and his group decided upon strategy. They camped for the night out of town, and early in the morning of November 7, 1874, dashed into the village, galloping at full speed up through the main street. At once people hurried out to discover the cause of the excitement, and when the posse turned and stopped in the center of town, they were immediately surrounded by curious questioners.

"I enquired of the citizens about Lee," Stokes wrote, "but could learn nothing from them about him. Some said they never knew him, others that they had never heard of such a man, had not even heard the name."

The crowd became so large that the officer began to fear for the safety of his men, so he resorted to the strategy of asking each citizen his name, writing it down, and ordering the man to assist in finding and arresting John D. Lee. Each man was ordered to go home, get his gun, and return in five minutes. This had the desired effect, for the men dispersed and not one came back to carry out the order.

Stokes found out where Lee's wife Caroline lived and began riding around the house and yards. Seeing a woman at the corral yard leaning over an empty log pen, he became suspicious. When she started away and turned back again briefly as though talking to someone, he was convinced that Lee was hidden in that vicinity.

Soon a young man of about twenty came along the street, and in line with his previous policy, Stokes ordered him to assist in the capture of Lee. It was Sammy, one of Aggatha's younger sons.

"John D. Lee is my father, sir," said the boy.

"It makes no difference to me if he is your grandmother," the sheriff answered. "I am going to search that house, and I want you with me."

The boy said he was going down to the threshing machine to see his brother Al, and started off, whereupon the officer drew his revolver and ordered him to stop. As the boy kept on going, the officer spurred up his horse and rode around to stop him.

"Shoot and be damned," Sammy said, looking him straight in the eye. "I'm not heeled, but I am going down to see my brother Al."

While they talked, Alma rode up and asked what was the trouble.

"This is the officer come to take father," Sam told him.

"Hell! Is that all? I thought it was a dog fight, I saw so many around," Al said with studied unconcern. After the boys talked together quietly a few minutes, Sammy came to offer his aid. While they searched the two houses, the boy was cheerful and willing, but when the officer suggested that they look through that pen he became very nervous and excited, and could hardly be persuaded to go to the corral. Henry Darrow, one of Lee's sons-in-law, followed.

It did not take long for Stokes to guess that Lee was hidden behind the log pen and covered with straw.

"Mr. Lee, come out and surrender yourself. I have come to arrest you," he said in a loud voice. No answer. No movement. The order was repeated a second and finally the third time. Then turning to his deputy, Stokes said loudly, "Mr. Winn, you go in there and disarm Lee, and I promise you that if a straw moves, I'll blow his brains out. My pistol is not a foot from his head."

"Don't shoot! Don't shoot," Darrow and Sammy both said at once.

Lee's voice came from under the straw, "Hold on, boys. I'll come out." He slipped the pistol which he held in his hand on his breast into the holster, came out, straightened himself, and brushed the straw from his clothes.

"Well, boys, what do you want of me?" he asked coolly.

He stood silently while the sheriff read the warrant, until he came to the part "charged with murder."

"Why don't you say wholesale murder?" said Lee. "That's what you meant."

He asked to see the officer's pistol, took it and examined it, and handed it back remarking that it was the queerest pistol he had ever seen.

Together they walked to the house. There some of the women and children were crying with fear, others talking at once with excitement. Lee quieted them, telling them it was time that he was brought to a fair trial. It would be much better to face up to it and be a free man again.

By this time the neighbors had gathered around until half the village was in the yard. Lee's sons took him aside and told him that if he didn't want to go to Beaver to say so and they would arrange it so that he wouldn't have to. But there were six well-armed men in the posse, and any attempt to break would mean death to too many people. When Stokes asked where they could get breakfast in the village, Lee apologized for his lack of hospitality and ordered his wives to feed the men. He also furnished the team and wagon to take them back to Beaver, with his son-in-law, Henry Darrow, to drive it.

Rachel went along, and knowing what was ahead, made a generous lunch for her husband and herself and took some wool blankets. The roads were rough, the country mountainous and travel slow. They were forced at last to spend the night out in very cold weather, in order to let the team rest and feed. Starting on again when it was nearly daylight, they arrived in Beaver about noon the next day. The whole town was thunderstruck that they had been able to take Lee alive.

Now began the long period of confinement. From November 10 until July 23 of the following year, Lee waited for his trial to open. In the meantime he remained cheerful and cooperative, and as Stokes wrote, "He never gave any trouble to me or his guards. He never tried to escape, but at all times assisted the guards to carry out the instructions they had received from the officers." Because of this, he made many friends among the soldiers and officers, and was allowed sometimes to have visitors inside and to come out of doors for a short while each day. Some legends come from this period, one of which is characteristic of Emma.

She had come all the way from the Lonely Dell to visit her husband. For the last part of the trip she had borrowed a buggy and team. Emma was thirty-nine, handsome, well dressed and poised, with a natural ruddy flush in her cheeks. She had carried her buggy whip in her gloved hand, the lash doubled back to the end of the stock. As she came out of the cell through the room where some of the guards were sitting, one man said to another, "Who is that handsome woman?"

"Oh, that is one of John D. Lee's whores," the other answered with a smirk.

In a flash he was struck across the face with the buggy whip, as Emma turned fiercely upon him. Surprised, he ducked to miss the next blow, and then turned and ran outside before the third.

No one raised a word or a hand in his defense. Instead, his companions all laughed heartily, while Emma, afraid lest she herself might be brought into court, got quickly into her rig, and used the whip to speed the team out of town.

William Ashworth wrote of visiting Lee in company with George A. Smith, and told how they sat on a bench outside leaning against the stone wall of the prison, while the guard walked back and forth in front a rod or two away. According to his account

> President Smith began by referring to Lee's early life in the Church, and to his activities in many ways in protecting the Prophet Joseph, and otherwise aiding the people in their troubles. . . . Finally he said, "John, you never turned a hungry person from your door, did you?" Lee nodded, and I noticed tears as large as peas running down his cheeks.

Had these two men met under happier circumstances, they might have reminded each other of the experiences of their long winter trip when they brought the first colonists to Parowan. They could have laughed about their reading a novel in order to forget the cold, or about the panic which resulted from the firing of the cannon. Now the shadow of that dark day fourteen years ago hung heavily upon them.

Lee could remember so many instances of the kindness of this large man, who couldn't stand to see an animal suffer nor treat an Indian cruelly even if he deserved it. Yet this same gentle man could preach rousing war sermons fanning into flame smoldering hates and passions. Each man knew that he himself shared a responsibility in the massacre, but each knew also that no man alone was wholly responsible for it.

When court opened and business finally began and the indictment was read, it included William H. Dame, Isaac C. Haight, John D. Lee, John M. Higby, George Adair Jr., Elliot Wilden, Samuel Jukes, P. K. Smith, and William Stewart. The jury selected, consisted of Josephus Wade, J. C. Hester, Paul Price, and John Brewer, all non-Mormons of Piute County; and Isaac Duffin, Toquerville, James G. Robinson, Paragonah, Milton Daley, Harrisburg, John C. Duncan, Cedar City, David Rogers, Washington, and George F. Jarvis, Joseph Knight, and Ute Perkins, all of St. George. Judge Jacob S. Boreman presided over the court.

The court room was crowded with spectators. Because of the cloak of secrecy which had shrouded the affair, it was impossible to find any participants who would testify. Only Philip Klingensmith of all who were at the massacre appeared in court, and he had made a written confession before Peter B. Miller of Pioche, Nevada, more than four years earlier.

The first witness called was Robert Keyes, who testified that he had passed over the ground on October 2, about three weeks after the massacre. He described the scene of nude and dismembered human bodies, in an advanced state of decay. From the condition they were in, he would conclude that they had been buried in a shallow grave from which they had been dragged by wild beasts.

He told a story which had already become legend, and which was to be repeated forty-six years later by John L. Ginn who had passed over the same route two months after the massacre. It was that there was one woman whose dead body was too beautiful to be attacked by wolves or vultures or spoiled by decay. Any person knowing the quick process of disintegration of the human corpse would sense at once the falsity of such a story, but it had a profound effect upon the audience.

The second witness, Asahel Bennett, testified that he too had passed over the ground early in December and had seen the unburied skeletons, some of them evidently children. From the masses of hair and bits of clothing and sunbonnets scattered around it appeared that others were women.

The one important witness, whose presence caused a visible thrill to pass through the audience, was Philip Klingensmith. He pictured the massacre as a military expedition in which the regiment to which he belonged was ordered to muster, "armed and equipped as the law directs, and prepared for field operations." He made it very clear that Isaac C. Haight had said that "he had orders from headquarters to kill all of the said company of emigrants except the little children," but did not know whether said orders came from the regimental headquarters at Parowan or from the commander-in-chief at Salt Lake City. He described the killing and told of the quarrel between Haight and Dame in which Haight accused Dame of ordering it done.

As a member of the militia Klingensmith was with the men, and thus saw only that part of the massacre. He admitted that he discharged his gun once, the inference being that he killed the man at his side. Then, in his capacity as bishop, he had proceeded to take care of the children.

Under cross questioning he insisted repeatedly that Higbee carried the orders, which he assumed came from Dame in Parowan. Higbee told Lee in the presence of the assembled military that, "orders is from me to you that they are to be decoyed out and disarmed in any manner, the best way you can." Higbee managed the militia as they formed with the emigrant men and gave the order to fire. Lee, he insisted, was ahead, walking between the two wagons, so that he, Klingensmith, had no knowledge of Lee's participation.

He further testified that Lee was not at the council meeting in Cedar City where the fate of the emigrants was discussed and the plan for killing them proposed. As to the emigrant cattle, he himself, assisted by John Urie, George Hunter, and Ira Allen had branded all they could find with the church brand, a cross. During the church conference in early October he had gone with Charles Hopkins and John D. Lee to visit Brigham Young, who told them to let Lee manage the cattle for the good of the mission, and "what you know about this, say nothing about it."

During the questioning many incidents were brought out to show the general temper of the times, the excesses which were the result of the marital law and the hysteria of the approaching army. But some things Klingensmith insisted upon through it all:

1. Lee was not at the council meeting, so had no part in initiating the idea.
2. After the first attack, Lee tried to call off the massacre; that he did all he could to stop it.
3. Lee received orders to decoy the emigrants out and disarm them, from Higbee, who carried them from Haight, who in turn got them from Dame.
4. That his own wife took a baby girl, nursed it at the breast and suckled it until it was old enough to wean, and then gave it to Richard Birbeck at Cedar City because they had no children.
5. That Brigham Young knew the essential facts of the massacre before they visited him at the October conference, and that he ordered Lee to manage the cattle, and enjoined upon all silence regarding the subject.

So the evidence piled up. The attorneys were eloquent in their recital of the lurid and horrible details, the defense insisting that while Lee was present and might have participated, he was there by command of his superiors, both military and ecclesiastical, whose orders in this time of military rule it would be death to disobey. While they admitted the facts of the massacre and all its unbelievable horror, they placed the responsibility upon the Mormon Church and its doctrine that men were justified in "avenging the blood of the Prophets," as a part of their duty to God.

For the Mormon audience, especially for the group of converts who had joined the church and emigrated to Utah later, this was a shattering and soul-shaking experience. Not having shared the Missouri and Nauvoo experiences or felt the "spirit of the times," they simply could not believe that the church with which they had become affiliated or any of the officers in it could condone such an outrage, much less be responsible for it.

In the end, the jury could not agree upon a verdict, the eight Mormons being for acquittal and the four gentiles for conviction. Now the whole thing must be gone over again, a most distressing and lamentable affair in all its implications. Since Lee would have to wait for the next term of court to be tried, the judge decided that he should wait out his time in the state penitentiary at Salt Lake City.

What of Lee's families in the meantime? Most of his older children were married and settled. Rachel left the Moencopi to come in to the settlements; Caroline and her young family were established at Panguitch; Lavina and Polly remained at Skutumpah; Emma and her little brood at the Lonely Dell. One of her experiences here has been often told and several times written:

Word had gone out of Lee's capture, so that even the Indians knew. One night soon after, a band of Navajos crossed the river and camped at the clearing not far from Emma's house, but contrary to their usual custom, they did not come up to trade or ask for food. From what her son Billy could gather, they were plotting mischief — either to take the horses and drive off a cow for beef, or to raid the house for food and loot. Emma also sensed a difference in their actions, but her mind ran more to knifings and scalpings until she was almost petrified with fear.

As night fell and she could see the Indian campfire glowing in the darkness, the braves standing and moving about as though restless and waiting, she became desperate. What should she do? She did not want the children to see how frightened she was lest they should begin to cry and make matters worse. So she called them all in for the evening prayer. It was a regular ritual in the home, this kneeling around the bed for evening devotion. But this time it was different. She prayed earnestly for guidance and inspiration to know what to do and asked for God's protecting hand to be over them. As she arose, she had her answer.

Instead of locking the house securely as she had intended to do, she told the children that they were going out to sleep at the Indian camp that night. She loaded Billy and Ike with quilts, gave Jimmie and Belle and each of the twins a pillow, and told them to follow her, youngest first. She picked up the tiny baby in her arms, and leading little 2-year-old Dellie by the hand, guided the little procession, past the corrals, along the trail through the scrub brush, to the clearing.

The chief, surprised, turned to meet them.

"I am afraid; very much afraid," she told him in her combination of Navajo and English and pantomime. "See all my papooses. Yawgett's papooses. They are afraid, too. You are a big, brave chief. You are Yawgett's friend. You will watch my papooses so they not be hurt during the dark hours. Let me make my bed down here, close to your camp, so that you can watch over my tiny papooses."

The chief was moved by her appeal. Pointing to a smooth place in the clearing, he motioned the boys to make the bed there. They spread it two quilts wide, reserving the long double blanket to open out for a common covering, and arranged the pillows.

Very quietly Emma placed them — Billy on the outside, then Ike and Jimmie close to him. She herself would sleep on the side toward the Indians, with the little girls between, some sharing pillows, all covered, for it was November and chilly.

She had planned to keep her vigil all night, but it had been a long, strenuous day, and before she knew it she relaxed and fell asleep. When she roused it was broad daylight. She remembered where she was, listened a minute to the quiet breathing of the children in the stillness, and raised up to look around. The Indians were gone! Down the trail as it wound over the hill she saw them pass single file on their way to Kanab.

The chief told the incident to Jacob Hamblin at Kanab, with the word that Emma was a "heap brave squaw." The authorities, sensing the danger of her position, called Warren Johnson to take his family and move to the Dell to operate the ferry. To Lee waiting out his time in the jail, it was a comfort to know that there was another family at the Dell and a reliable man to stand by with help and advice.

1875-1876
The Prisoner

Lee's diary of his experiences in the Utah State Penitentiary begins on August 9, 1875, as he was taken from Fort Cameron, Beaver, and ends on April 18, 1876, when the book was filled. This little volume is priceless because it gives such a closeup, intimate picture of life in the prison — the meals, the straw-filled bed ticks, the lack of sanitary facilities, the character of the individual inmates.

Basically it is, of course, a personal story. It follows the regular pattern, each entry giving place, date, weather conditions, and a summary of the day's happenings or his reaction to them. He puts meaning into the flight of birds, especially those he dreams about, and interpreting them as omens of his future. There is time now, to write about and analyze his dreams. He notes also, the first "tracking snow" with regard to the time of the moon as a sign of the number of storms ahead for the season. Most important of all, however, he names his visitors and tells of their discussions.

The first entry describes his departure from the Beaver jail at 9:30 P.M. Evidently the officers chose this unusual hour in an attempt to get away unnoticed, but Rachel and Caroline were both there to bid him goodbye, as were several of his children, and the streets of the town were lined with people.

His guards were Bill Hickman and Jack Kerby, who rode in the open carriage and Tom Wiem, who rode horseback beside it. Baer, the brewer, drove the outfit and George R. Maxwell, the U.S. marshal, sat beside him. Lee was very fond of this last officer, always referring to him as "General" Maxwell.

They spent the first night in the mountains, where although it was August, it was cold for sleeping. Lee was in bed with General Maxwell, but being uncomfortable, he got up before daylight, collected a great pile of dry cedar wood, started a fire, and called the officer to get up and get warm. "The General looking around seeing the guard all asleep, turned to me with a smile and said, I believe you are the best guard that I have. The Truth is, the whole party was past the Maredian in Liquor," . . . he wrote.

By long drives and short stops they reached Nephi by noon on August 12. Here Lee had his first sight of a train, which he called "grand, romantic, and sublime." He enjoyed the ride into the city all the more because General Maxwell still sitting beside him, pointed out improvements, new buildings, and businesses, and told him something of who owned them and what they typified.

Perhaps his initiation into his new home can best be given in his own words:

> The two young Men were very kind to Me indeed, & introduced me to the Warden, Mr. W. B. Burgher, who by the Bye appears to be a gentleman.
>
> Entering the Penetentiary I was searched, which is customary, then shown to a bunk with clean blankets and straw bed. The Prison is 40 by 30 feet, Made of sawn timber spiked togeather with 18 feet from floor to ceiling with 5-6-light windows within 3 feet of the ceiling & one double Door made of Iron Bars to admit air, besides an outer Door which is kept opend till 9 at night in hot hot weather & opened at light in the Morning. The inner Door is closed and locked at sunset.
>
> The wall is 4 feet thick & 18 feet high, 290 by 180 feet, built of adobies. The Prison floor is laid off flat rock & arround the outer wall of the Prison is a Table some 3½ feet wide, from two to 3 feet high according to the grade of the land; which affords a cool shady place to sit or lie down, as ½ of those are always in the shade.
>
> We are alowed two Meals a day. The grub is good, coffee Morning & Evning. The meals are 9m. & 4 p.m. A lunch is laid bye from each by those who are not content with 2 meals.
>
> There is 11 convicts & 3 more indicted awaiting trial. The Most of them are for murder.

A large lamp was kept burning all night, which made sound sleep difficult for one accustomed to the soothing effects of darkness. As a first impression of his fellows he noted that "My companions in tribulation are very Jovial & talkative, though some are rather rough and uncouth. Singing, Banjo playing, step dancing, card playing & swearing are the principle amusements indulged in."

One of the first of the inmates who appealed to Lee was Philip Shaffer, a freemason, who was being held awaiting trial for murder. He was a blacksmith by trade and was soon put to work building an iron cage in which the warden could lock any recalcitrant. Lee was allowed to work with him in riveting the parts together, and as they worked, they discussed the Arizona country and the future possibilities of the San Juan area. Shaffer made handcuffs and irons, and when later the warden suspected him of making a duplicate key, Lee answered the accusation in an open letter to the *Tribune*. Shaffer's case came up in late November, and he was released for lack of evidence.

Almost every day Lee was taken out to walk about the yard or to meet and talk to visitors. While he tried to remain aloof from his companions inside, he did interfere to stop a fight — or called the warden to stop it — and did attempt to remain cordial and cheerful, trying as he said "to break down the spirit of a Party division that is amoung my associates."

On August 31 General Maxwell came to visit him, having just returned from the south. He took Lee down into the city in a carriage drawn by a span of fine mares and allowed him to shop in different stores for items that he wanted — pills, hair tonic and a silk handkerchief among them — and bought him a box of cigars and a flask of whiskey with which to treat his friends. Best of all, he advised Lee as to his future, warning him that Sutherland and Houge had "an object to accomplish, aside from mine, which is more important to them than mine, hense they would use me as a tool & keep me lingering in prison from year to year. . ." Maxwell's chief argument was that Lee should make himself a witness against Dame and others, promising him that if he would do that, he could return to Beaver, have Rachel come to live with him, and get a trial within a month. Lee considered this and tentatively promised to comply.

During this time while Lee helped Shaffer at building the cage, the other prisoners were put to work at digging a well, and those who refused to help had their rations cut to two meals a day.

Lee spent most of his birthday, September 6, writing in his journal. At the age of 64 he was a prisoner "for the Gospel's sake," and sought comfort in the fact that "the apostles, Prophets & all the inspired of old in like manner suffered by persecutions." He had visitors almost every day holding out promises of freedom. Warden Burgher often invited him on the outside and walked with him around the grounds and through the orchard. He was even allowed beyond the walls where "I enjoyed the surrounding scenery with pleasure and delight, as the Penetentiary is located on a high Eminence, overlooking the valey & surrounding city & country until the Eye is lost in distance."

From September 8, 1875, he was taken out of the prison every day and allowed to do some work shoveling gravel, preparing peaches and prunes for drying, assisting Mr. Shaffer, the blacksmith, or Mr. Allen, the carpenter, or Mr. or Mrs. Ward, the cooks, with the fruit. These special privileges did not set well with some of the other inmates, who now began to make him the butt of their talk.

". . . Some of the inmates of this Prison are the most profane, vile, low, & vulgar & filthy that I ever heard speak in my life

. . . as was said of Lott, so I can truthfully say of myself, for my soul is vexed & tortured from day to day with their filthy conversation & profanity, & I pray the Lord to speedy deliver me from this sink of corruption, & den of foul & unclean spirits. . ."

This reference was to some of the prisoners who from his first day in jail, Lee had recognized as problems. One Jack Began knocked down a new arrival, James Kane, and a fight ensued which might have been fatal for Kane had not Lee intervened. From that time on, Began was in trouble often. On Saturday, September 17, in the midst of writing of other things Lee inserted the comment that "J. Began had his Irons taken of, having worn them 4 weeks." Time after time — a difficulty over a pair of boots, a spilt cup of coffee, a pair of blankets found torn into strips — one or the other of these boys was chained. At last they were chained and put together into the iron cage until Began became so ill that a doctor had to be called.

It was September 23 before General Maxwell came again, this time bringing with him Marshal Stokes, who promised to take Lee out immediately if he would tell his story in full. Both of these men had been kind to him and had shown such a real interest in his welfare that Lee knew them to be sincere. He had become so sickened with prison life that he determined to do as they asked. When it came time to do it, however, he said that he would need one more night to consider. After hours of melancholy soul-searching, he decided that he must . . . "do what is right, let the consequence follow., & I became perfectly resigned that if it was my Blood that they thursted for, let them have it — There is a Power that rules the destineys of Men that is more potent than the vindictiveness of the puny arm of flesh. . ."

The next day when Marshal Stokes came for his statement, he had made up his mind. He could not do what was asked of him.

I have weighed the matter over carefully & with resignation to my fate in the future, I have concluded to prefer to take up Winter Quarters in this Prison & there remain till I rot & be Eat up with the bed bugs before I will dishonor myself by bearing fals witness against any man, much less an innocent Man. . .

He set about to put fresh straw in his bedtick and to sweep and scald out the boards of his bunk in an effort to halt the march of the bedbugs, retired to rest early, and slept the sleep of a clear conscience.

October dragged along, with Lee in low spirits and poor health most of the time. Now some of his former kindness began to pay off. Early he had become acquainted with H. Edward Gaines, a boy of twenty, who was in prison for stealing a horse in Ogden. Lee listened to his story, sympathized with him, and wrote a letter to his father explaining everything. Learning the details of the boy's romance with a Mormon girl, Lee wrote a letter to her and arranged for her to come to the prison for a visit. Now young Gaines in turn nursed Lee, "with all the tenderness of a son." Later, Lee was able to get this boy employed as an assistant cook, with sleeping quarters outside the bunk room.

General Maxwell called on him again to tell him that "he had never tried to befriend a Man more than he had Me with as little success" and had decided to set him free as they did Klingensmith if he would only tell his story. Lee remained firm. He told them that he "chose to die like a man then live a villian, that the Truth they did not want & as for lies, they must call on some other person to tell them besides me." Having made up his mind definitely, he became more composed & rested well through the night.

Early in November the officers brought in other prisoners, one of whom, William J. Tracy, became a close friend of Lee. Tracy was waiting trial for murder. Lee found him to be "a man of a well balanced mind, possessing some noble, saving & redeeming qualities, — just such a man as I would select for a companion to associate with in adversity as well as prosperity." They discussed the Arizona and San Juan country, where Tracy hoped to go as soon as he got his freedom.

With the coming of cold weather, Lee was not allowed to go out of doors often, as there was nothing profitable that he could do outside. To add to this, a program of retrenchment was adopted by the prison officials, restricting the amount of food issued and cutting off the fuel. It seemed that the stock was exhausted and no money had been appropriated for more. The weather became so cold that ice froze in the buckets in their sleeping room. On November 13 Lee wrote that the men were burning the benches and bunk boards, breaking up anything that would give out heat. All their demands did not bring any coal. Instead, the supper rations were cut in half, putting most of the prisoners into a real fighting mood. Twice during that night, the lamp was knocked over by flying shoes. The warden evidently made the right connections and got supplies for on November 15 Lee wrote, "This morning we had a bouncing large Rations & all felt well, full bellies will satiate anger as well as hunger." But so much resentment had been engendered that some were actively working toward escape and many were vindictive toward the warden. When young J. Davis was ordered to help with the washing, he refused, saying that he was not a convict, but a prisoner awaiting trial. He was handcuffed and chained by the leg to the wall until he should comply. Lee wrote that during the night "the groans of Davis shivering with the cold arroused me. I closed the windows & covered him with clothes." The next day Lee was reprimanded for this action and ordered not to share his food with the boy. Davis was not released for ten days.

All this weighed heavily on the mind of John D. Lee. He arranged for an interview with the warden in which he asked to pay for the privilege of sleeping in the guard room. The warden promised to consult with Maxwell and give him an answer, but weeks passed and nothing was done.

One improvement was made inside the prison, however. The stove was moved into the center of the room with some 20 feet more pipe added, and a boiler of eighteen gallons set on it, so that the men could have warm water with which to bathe and shave. This was a real luxury.

During the time of shortage, Lee and Tracy pooled their food, supplementing it somewhat from the outside, and husbanding a little from each meal to ease the hunger pangs between meals. Occasionally Lee wrote letters for Tracy, Kane, and others of the prisoners; in fact, he seemed eager to do this service for any who asked. Now there were three other young men, boys he called them, brought in from Provo. They were Levi Vawn [Vaughn?], Joe Smith, a cousin of Lot Smith of Paria, and W. W. Phelps, none of whom could read or write. Still another young man for whom Lee had a genuine admiration was Charley Williamson, who was in on a charge of stealing horses. At first sight Lee said of him, "He doesn't look like a bad man." Later he spoke approvingly of his energy, industry, and spirit.

During the first week of December young Phelps asked Lee to teach him to write and to read, to which Lee answered that he would be glad to help him or any of the others who might like to try to improve their minds. This quickly grew into a regular school, with classes held every day, including Sunday. In the midst of a class on December 20, he was called to the door. There stood Rachel! His joy knew no bounds. The Warden said hastily that she could not stay, of course, for they could not entertain the families of the prisoners; if they started doing that, they would soon be overrun. Rachel accepted this cheerfully, saying that she would get quarters near enough that she could visit him each day, and would try to get work in town.

Lee continued his teaching:

Dec. 22 . . . Evening I went into the Prison to set copies for those that I had been teaching. The Prisoners & convicts were all glad to see me. I have More influence now in the Prison amoung the Prisoners then I ever had before.

He continued to have faith in his dreams. For two nights in succession he dreamed that he was playing cards with the warden, and both times he held the winning hand. Now he decided that Rachel was really his trump card.

Since he had become acquainted with her, Mr. Burgher was more willing to bargain. On December 23 the warden called Lee aside and offered to give him a room in the officers' quarters where he and Rachel might sleep, provided he would furnish his own stove and pay twelve dollars a month for her extra food and his liberty. She was to take over the responsibility of all the cooking. "The idea of going back into that prison is like death to me," Lee wrote, but he felt that all his wife's labor and $12.00 a month besides was a very dear price for what bit of liberty he would have. He was allowed to spend Christmas Eve in the room with Rachel, with the understanding that the final decision on his parole should await a conference with his friend Maxwell.

On Christmas morning no one responded to the six o'clock bell, the signal to start breakfast. Lee got up, found that it was raining and that no dry wood had been brought in, so he opened the outer gate, went to the barn and secured some, started a roaring fire and filled the vessels on the stove with water. The warden came in as he had finished and without a word of criticism asked him to start another fire in the dining room. This being Christmas Day when good will should be abroad, they made an agreement by which Lee was to remain outside the prison, living with Rachel in the officers' quarters in exchange for $5.00 a month cash and a three-year-old mare when he got out. Rachel was to take charge of the cooking and he was to milk the cow and do such other chores as he wished. He might go inside each day to teach the prisoners. Lee promptly paid the cash to seal the bargain.

From this day forth he went into the prison each day and held his school, working on the outside to build a table at which the scholars might work and making two benches for them to sit upon. The young men seemed to appreciate the time he spent with them, and he became fond of his "boys." When young Smith became ill, he dosed him, and reported that he dressed Smithey's foot with poultices.

The *Tribune* of January 5 took notice of his school with the following short article:

PENITENTIARY NOTES — John D. Lee's free school is progressing nicely & a number of the prisoners are rapidly learning to read & write. Lee is ahead of his old pal Brigham on the free school question at least, and is as good a man in other respects; — the only difference being that one is in jail & the other ought to be.

Lee reports his daily chores were milking, shoveling snow, sawing wood, cleaning out the barn litter, and currying the horse, in addition to teaching his school and writing many letters for different inmates. For nearly two months young Began remained very ill with a kind of flu as a result of his treatment. About mid-February Lee himself evidently contracted the same disease and was bedfast for a couple of weeks. He attributed his recovery to the careful nursing of his wife.

Lee became in arrears in the payments for his liberty. Rachel had done the laundry for some of the officers, but they refused to pay her. She borrowed three dollars from W. A. Smoot and got $3.50 more for washing the clothes of the prisoners, but that was not enough. Mr. Burgher accepted it and reluctantly granted them time to see what they could collect otherwise, for the thought of his returning to the jail sickened Rachel as well as Lee.

On March 4 he wrote a letter which he hoped would reach the hands of Brigham Young, Daniel H. Wells, or some of the other authorities who had so often accepted his hospitality,

> . . . urging the nessessity of repairing the Road at once near the Ferry & also near Lees Ranch before attempting to take portable mills & heavy machinery over it, as it is dangerous as it now is. Also stated my presant situation, that I was sick & that my liberty was liable to be forfeited & I shoved back in that loathsome prison unless I could raise $40.00. . . That I was no beggar, but tried to be independent, would always rather give than to receive, but circumstances that now surrounds me are beyond my controle. . .

He received no answer from anyone to this letter, and in spite of all her efforts, Rachel was not able to raise the necessary money.

For almost two weeks Lee had not been conducting his school, nor even after he could get out of bed and walk around did he go back. Conditions inside the jail had been growing worse. Mr. Burgher asked Lee one day if anyone had been to get an affidavit from him regarding the treatment of the men. Lee said that he had made none himself, but understood that some were being made and that some complaints had gone abroad. He warned the warden that there were desperate men there and that their feelings for him were such that he should beware and give them no opportunity for an attack.

About three o'clock in the afternoon of March 14, the opportunity came. Lee had walked to the barn and shelled out some redtop grass seed which he hoped to use for pasture on some of his land at the Lonely Dell, and becoming weary had climbed the stairs to his room and gone to sleep.

He was aroused by screams and yells and a commotion below. Hurrying to the window, he looked out to see a man lying on his face in a welter of blood, while downstairs Mrs. Ward shrieked in terror. The sound of running feet, crashing furniture and curses and grunts told of men in mortal struggle. It was Davis, Phelps and Charley Williamson after their fellow prisoner Gaines, in an effort to get guns and go after the key to the gate. Each had armed himself with as large a stone as he could force into the toe of a heavy sock, and swinging this full force had attacked Burgher, the warden, striking him nine times over the head and on the bridge of his nose and knocking him down unconscious. With one blow Davis floored Gaines and would have attacked Mrs. Ward had she not handed over the key. Seven men escaped.

Rachel bathed Gaines' head and chest until he regained consciousness. He jumped up at once, armed himself with pistols and mounting a horse, rode in pursuit. With the help of some men on the outside he rounded up and returned four of the escapees that evening.

It soon became clear that Warden Burgher was wounded mortally. Now Mr. Ward became eager for the help and support of John D. Lee. He began calling him "Uncle John," and asked if he would stay with him beside the dying man; it was so lonesome to sit there through the night alone. So Lee stood by and waited for the end, which came at three a.m., just twelve hours after the attack.

The next morning word came that young Phelps had been shot through the body by officer Holliday, and in the long hours of his dying had remained conscious, saying over and over that he did not resist the officer, that he was unarmed, that he had done nothing except to try to regain his freedom. When the next day Charley Williamson and Joe Smith were returned to prison, cross-handcuffed together, and heavily chained, Lee wrote that they "looked pitiful." These three had been his students, boys who had just got onto the wrong track. How many good qualities he had discovered in each of them! The thought of what was ahead for them made him almost sick. He filled two ticks with clean straw in an effort to make their stay in the cage more comfortable, but did not go inside to deliver them. There was little else he could do now. For his courage in capturing the four, Gaines was given his liberty, which meant immediate marriage to his faithful little girl friend.

The next two weeks were full of uncertainty and frustration — no letter from his family or word from his lawyers. Lee's one comfort was the fact that no one even suggested that he be put back into the prison or inferred that he should pay for the liberty he enjoyed. He had become "Uncle John," handyman about the place, too useful at milking the cow, cleaning the stables, sawing wood, shoveling snow,

and even shining shoes, to spare. The new warden had not even hinted
that he belonged in the jail. He was trusted with the keys, both inside
and out, and often was left to make the final lockup at night.

Now came perhaps his greatest temptation. Mr. Benjamin L. Durham, the new U.S. deputy marshal and second warden, suggested to
him that he go with some two or three responsible men to the Cen-
tennial in Philadelphia, and give public lectures. They would help him
write up a short story of his life, with his picture, to be sold for a
dollar each to the audience. In almost no time, they assured him, he
could take in thousands of dollars, which would relieve his present
straits, settle his bills, and help to provide for his family. Mr. Durham
himself would go along and would be responsible for getting him
released from the prison. Lee wrote to his lawyer, W. W. Bishop, asking his opinion on this plan, only to learn the next day that Bishop
had departed for Galveston, Texas, to conduct a lawsuit involving a
large sum of money.

Mr. Durham continued to encourage Lee, suggesting that it would
be good to be right out of the state and in the East for two or three
years, and then if and when he returned, he would be independent
financially.

But the more Lee thought of it, the less he liked it. He wrote in his
diary:

> .   .   .   I am loath to accept liberty & favours from those not of
> my religious faith. But what can I do. I am here in their hands &
> am powerless. Near 18 months have past since my arrest and
> confinement.   .   .   I have tried with all the energy of my soul
> & body to call fourth aid from those who should stand by me, but
> as yet have failed to elicit their sympathy.   .   .

He wrote in detail of the work and devotion of Rachel, of his letter
to Brigham Young and the other leaders, to which he had no response.

As spring arrived, he began to sort potatoes for seed, and was given
more and more liberty and privileges. The warden allowed him to
select three men from the jail to help, and the first day they planted
15 bushels of potatoes. Soon they brought assorted seeds of other kinds
and let three other prisoners out to help plant them. The warden "Told
the boys that I was boss, to work as I directed them & for me to take
my own course in gardening." In the afternoon he had different boys
out in order to give all a chance for exercise and air.

The last entry in the book notes that Warden Greenwood had returned the first diary he brought and exchanged it for a larger one,
price $1.65 — 400 pages, neatly bound. "Continued on Journal No 3
Since my Arrest and confinement."

Although this succeeding diary is not available at the present time, there is little question but that he kept it with equal care.

Less than a month later, May 11, 1876, Lee was released on a bail of $15,000, to reappear at Beaver three months from that date. Evidently he had finished planting the garden in the meantime, and the new officers had used their influence to get his freedom. William H. Hooper stood surety on his bond. William H. Dame was released on the same day under a $20,000 bond and George W. Adair on a $10,000 one.

LONELY DELL IN 1959
Photograph by J. Wes Williamson, Whittier, California.

THE GRAVE OF JOHN D. LEE AT PANGUITCH, UTAH
Photograph by J. Wes Williamson, Whittier, California.

1876-1877
The Scapegoat

When John D. Lee rode away from the penitentiary on May 11, 1876, he knew that he would return to court at Beaver in September for another trial, which he hoped would give him permanent freedom. In the meantime he would visit his wives and children again, and would do what he could to restore his business. It was a joy to just get away from jail, to leave behind him everything connected with it. If he could only blot from his memory the smell and filth of the common sleeping room, the lewd, profane talk of some inmates, the smoldering hates which resulted in violence and barbaric cruelties!

For three months he would move in the wide open spaces, sometimes with a wife or a friend, sometimes with a group, but often alone. It was summer even in May in the Colorado River valley, which meant he must travel through the late afternoon and evening, with a few hours' rest, and be on his way again before dawn. Innately responsive to nature, he enjoyed the recurring miracle of every sunset, each one different; always spectacular. As the brilliance faded in the west and the echoing colors along the vermilion buttes and the lavender cliffs melted to gray, peace like a benediction came upon him. Under the stars, luminous and low-hanging he felt all that had happened to him would somehow add up to his good. What was ahead of him he did not know. He knew only that in this landscape the span of man's life becomes so brief that his worth must be measured in honor and integrity rather than length of years.

He was more content to be alone because he sensed a difference in the attitude of so many of those who had been his friends. Men who had put their horses in his barn and their knees under his table without charge now walked away as he approached or greeted him coldly without an extended hand. Even some of his own family were bitter at the disgrace which had come upon them because of what had been revealed in court. Why did he not speak in his own defense? Why did he not clear himself as Klingensmith had done? Why did he not "put the saddle on the right horse" as Dame had threatened to do?

He had fought this out with himself in jail and found most peace when he kept his oath of silence. Now the open spaces seemed to sustain him, to make him even more certain that he would rather die a man than live a villain. Certainly his few remaining years would not be worth enduring in prison.

His sons tried to persuade him to cross the Colorado and go on down
into Old Mexico, where under another name he might secure holdings
and live out his last years in prosperity and peace. He would not go.
His word had been as good as his bond for too many years to change
now. Besides, to run away would be to admit a guilt which he was
not willing to assume.

He still had faith that Brigham Young might come to his rescue, in
spite of long neglect and of the warnings of his attorneys. Bishop had
advised him not to press for a second trial, especially at Beaver, in a
letter so frank that Lee copied it into his diary under date of March 11.

"said . . . that his opinion was that I would not be tried
in April next, that gover'mt was Making no preparations for a
trial & he is of the oppinion that they never intend to try me
again. If am released on bonds, I will Most likely ware out my
days & end the matter.

You ask my opinion, should we have a new trial, would we
have it before Boreman again? I say No! A Thousand times No!
Exhaust all we know of law, Management, trickery and curuption
before we permit the case to be tried again before one who is so
thoroughly opposed to the defendant as we know Boreman to be.
Any fate is preferrerable to that of failing, and that in the place
where you know the ambush is laid for you.

Whether or not President Young or his secretary wrote Lee that
he should escape we may never know. Emma told that in late
August a messenger arrived at Lonely Dell with word from the
authorities counseling Lee to jump his bonds and leave the country.
Rather than have this horrible affair rehearsed again, they would
assume the full responsibility to his bondsmen. The messenger arrived
too late. He came via Kanab, while Lee returned via Skutumpah, so they had missed each other and there was no way for them to
get together. Thus the hand of fate reached out to cast the fatal die.

Brigham Young cannot be too seriously criticized if he did consent
to sacrifice Lee. The fact was clear that Lee was caught, that he had
participated in the massacre, especially that he was the one who had
persuaded the emigrants to leave their wagons. This made him the
natural one upon whom to place the responsibility. If by executing
him the whole affair could be closed, why not make the sacrifice? The
action could be justified from an often-repeated story from *The Book
of Mormon,* where the youthful Nephi, commanded to secure the
records of his people, could not accomplish the assignment without
killing Laban, the ruler. Nephi hesitated to commit murder, but

was told that, "It is better that one man should perish than that a whole nation should dwindle in unbelief."

This was certainly a similar case, for to air this horrible massacre further would do damage to the church itself and to its leaders, since no one now could understand the smoldering fires of hate, the deep emotions of that fall of 1857; "the spirit of the times," the members of the Nauvoo Legion called it. When court opened it became quickly evident that since the last trial something had happened.

The opening statement of the prosecution left no doubt that this time the whole tone of the trial would be different. Now they themselves asked to insert into the record the statements of Brigham Young and George A. Smith which they before had gone to great pains to keep out. The Mormon Church was not on trial, they declared; the only man under consideration was John D. Lee. They would dispose of his case first, and consider others if and when theirs should come up. The question before the court was simply, Did John D. Lee commit murder at the Mountain Meadows? Did he not, upon his own responsibility, plan and execute this mass killing in defiance of the orders of his superiors, and in contradiction to the accepted teachings of his church with regard to the shedding of blood?

Lee, familiar with the Old Testament and the ancient law of sacrifice as it is given in detail in Leviticus, had often referred to himself as the "scapegoat," and the title now seemed more appropriate:

> And Aaron shall lay both his hands upon the head of the live goat, and confess over him all the iniquities of the children of Israel, and all their transgressions in all their sins, putting them upon the head of the goat, and shall send him away by the hand of a fit man into the wilderness:
>
> And the goat shall bear upon him all their iniquities unto a land not inhabited: and he shall let go the goat in the wilderness. . .

While he was at Lonely Dell and Moencopi, Lee was literally in the wilderness, in a land not inhabited, with the sins of the whole group upon his head. Now it looked as if he would be made the sacrificial offering as well.

The jury consisted of twelve men all in good standing in the Mormon church. A conviction by a jury of his peers would be more effective in that it would declare to the world the fact that the church did not uphold Lee nor approve of his action. That the conviction was predecided, that every man had pledged himself to bring in a verdict of "guilty," cannot be proved, though from many sources came statements to the effect that of the total list of jurors to be considered, twelve names were checked as being men who would convict Lee.

They were William Greenwood, John E. Pace, A. M. Farnsworth, Stephen S. Barton, Valentine Carson, Alfred J. Randall, James S. Montague, A. S. Goodwin, Ira B. Elmer, Andrew S. Correy, Charles Adams, and Walter Granger. Judge Boreman again presided.

The courtroom was packed. People stood along the walls and sat in the windows and crowded the stairs. Only seven witnesses were called by the prosecution, some of whom testified very briefly. They were all members of the Church, everyone now willing to speak out regarding John D. Lee but unwilling to mention the names of others except Philip Klingensmith, who had turned state's evidence, Isaac C. Haight, John M. Higbee, and men who were now dead.

The first witness called was Daniel H. Wells who had come down from Salt Lake City to be present. At the time of the massacre he was commanding officer over all the Nauvoo Legion in the entire Territory. He was on the stand only a few minutes. He admitted that he knew John D. Lee, but when asked what official position Lee held in the military in 1857, he answered, "He had been a major in the military. I don't remember whether he was at that time or not. At that particular time, I think not. I think he had been superceded."

One other point was asked Wells: Could Lee speak the Indian language? What influence did he have with the natives? Wells said he thought that although Lee probably spoke the Indian language imperfectly, he could make himself understood and was considered to have some influence with them.

This testimony seemed inoffensive enough, but it now removed Lee from authority in the military, so that whatever he did was without orders from or sanction by them.

The second witness was Laban Morrill, who still lived at Johnson's ranch in Iron County. He was not at the Mountain Meadows at the time of the massacre; had never been there in his life, he said. He had come into Cedar City on the Sunday night before the massacre, when the fate of the emigrants was under discussion. John D. Lee was not at the meeting. There were some who wanted to kill the company, but Morrill and others objected so vigorously that the group decided to hold action until a rider could go to Salt Lake City for orders from Brigham Young. Morrill did not see the letter nor did he see the rider leave, but he understood that the action of the meeting was carried out. He understood, too, that another messenger was to be sent the opposite direction, to Harmony, to order John D. Lee to come and manage the Indians, to hold them from molesting the emigrants until they should get word from Brigham Young.

Here again was a short, effective testimony, with only one point established: that Lee was to hold the Indians in check until word arrived from Brigham Young.

Joel White, the third witness, had come all the way from Cedar Fort north of Provo in order to testify. The questions asked by the attorneys established the fact that he had lived in Cedar City in 1857 and that, accompanied by Klingensmith, he was carrying a message to Pinto to instruct the leader there to hold the Indians in control and let the emigrants pass in safety. En route they met John D. Lee on horseback, and when they gave him this word, Lee answered, "I don't know about that," or "I'll have something to say about that," or words to that effect. This would be used to prove that Lee had acted in opposition to the wishes of the local military.

"Were you present at the Meadows at the time of the massacre?"

"Yes, sir."

Now here was a point where the attorney could well have asked what happened, what part White played in that horrible drama, who was responsible for the various groups. Here, without a doubt, was a point where further questions might have been expected. Instead, White was asked only regarding the date of the massacre, which he could not remember.

The fourth witness was Samuel Knight, the driver of the second wagon, a mild, quiet man who still lived at Santa Clara. At the time of the massacre he was staying at Jacob Hamblin's home on the upper part of the Meadows; his wife was not well and he had brought her up to get away from the heat of the Santa Clara river bottoms. He testified that he had seen Lee after the first Indian attack on the emigrants, and that Lee had pointed out to him the bullet holes in his shirt and hat. He had led the Indians in an attack and they had been repulsed. Klingensmith ordered Knight to bring his wagon to the camp; it had been loaded with arms and gear from the camp; also a few people. When he was pressed as to how many people, he said "two men, one woman, and, I think some children." He was so busy holding his team that he did not know for sure, but he thought the men were wounded — had been wounded earlier when the Indians attacked. He thought that Lee had killed the woman. He finally came to admit that he knew Lee struck the woman with an instrument like the butt end of a gun, but that his team was so fractious that he could not be positive what did go on. He knew no one else who was present; he had no idea whether or not others helped with the killing. He had tried hard not to see any of it. He had never seen Lee or anyone else driving the emigrant cattle. Under pressure he did admit that the Indians jumped out of the brush about that time and that they were killing people. He could not be too positive, but it was his impression that John D. Lee had killed that one woman.

"Do you know?"

"Yes, sir, I do."

But that was all that he knew that would benefit them.

Samuel McMurdy had perhaps come the longest distance of all to testify here. He had moved to the village of Paradise, Utah, south of Logan. On the witness stand, he testified that John M. Higbee had called him to bring his wagon and come to the Meadows, but that after he arrived, John D. Lee ordered him to drive up to the camp. Into his wagon were loaded the children. His team went first and walked fast, so fast that it was soon quite far ahead. Lee, who was walking between the wagons, ordered the halt. He did not see Lee strike anyone with a club or other object, but he saw him draw a gun and shoot, and saw a woman fall. Later he thought he saw Lee draw a pistol and shoot two or three in the wagon behind his, but he too was busy with his horses and he did not want to see anything. Strangely enough, he could not recollect the names of any who were there except Higbee and Lee. At first he said that he did not see any Indians around; then he did see them, but at the precise moment of time he could not say.

"You did not help to kill anyone?"

"I had nothing to do with it at all."

"Then you did not raise your hand against anyone at that time, or do any of the killing of the emigrants?"

"I believe I am not on trial, sir."

"I ask if you refuse to answer the question."

No answer.

The question was repeated, more pointedly.

"I do not wish to answer."

Furthermore, McMurdy did not know whether everyone was killed, or how many children were saved, although they were all in his wagon. The attorneys seemed not to press any point to the embarrassment of a witness, so long as he would testify that John D. Lee had killed at least one person.

Perhaps no witness showed less disposition to remember anything than did Nephi Johnson. He had come in from his hiding in the canyon east and north of Kanab. There, all mail was received by a special messenger. He claimed that he had gone up the side of the hill to catch his horse and saw the massacre from a distance. He got his orders from Haight, but after he arrived at the Meadows, he went to Lee for direction. He could not remember the names of any of the men who were there except John D. Lee, Klingensmith, Bateman, and Hopkins,

the last two of whom were dead. He saw Lee fire off, he said, and saw
a woman in the lead wagon fall. Later he saw Lee and some Indians
throwing the bodies out of the wagon. He couldn't swear to it, he was
so far away, but he thought he saw Lee going through motions that
would indicate that he was cutting a man's throat. Strangely, he did
not see anybody else do anything. Finally after repeated probing, he
confessed that, "I don't want to bring in any names."

Though the number of wagons was often given as eighteen, Johnson
said thirteen; he didn't know the number of cattle or horses. He had
seen one of the wagons later at John D. Lee's place in Harmony and
two of them at Klingensmith's in Cedar City. He could not recollect
anything that anyone except Lee said; he could not recollect names.
When pressed as to why Klingensmith, Haight, and Higbee all stood
back and gave Lee control he answered, "He acted like a man that
had control."

"Did he not have control?"

"I can't say."

"Did you not think at the time that John D. Lee had absolute control of everything there?"

"He acted like it."

"What do *you* believe about it?"

No answer.

The cross examination of Nephi Johnson continued at great length,
during which time it became clear that he would tell nothing to involve
any person except Lee, and he would tell just enough about him to
prove that he killed one woman and might have killed a man.

The seventh and last witness was Jacob Hamblin, by now well known
as a frontiersman and Indian scout with a reputation for honesty. He
was more composed than the preceding witnesses, perhaps because he
had not been present at the massacre at all and so had no oath of
secrecy to keep.

He began by saying that the next spring he went with his Indian
boy and gathered up the scattered bones and buried them. He estimated that the number killed was about 120 people. In the fall of
1857 he was at Fillmore on his way home when he met Lee who was
en route to Salt Lake City to make his report to President Young. Lee
told him of the massacre, but insisted that it was carried out according
to orders. Lee told him that in trying to hold the Indians back he had
earned the name of Yahgauts or crybaby.

Only after repeated probing would Hamblin admit that the orders
for the massacre came from William H. Dame. As to Lee's own personal participation he volunteered the story that there were two young

ladies brought out who had hidden in the brush and escaped the first massacre.

"By whom?"

"By an Indian chief at Cedar City, and he asked him what he should do with them, and the Indian killed one and he killed the other. . ."

"From where were these young women brought from [sic] — did he say?"

"From a thicket of oak brush, where they were concealed. It was an Indian chief from Cedar City brought them out."

"Tell us what he said about that."

"That the Indian shot one and he cut the other one's throat, is what he said."

"Who cut the other's throat?"

"Mr. Lee."

The attorney insisted that this story be repeated, with more detail. Did the girl cover her face? Did she pull her bonnet down over her face? Did she cry out? Did she promise to love and serve him all her life if she were spared? How old were the girls? Were they very beautiful? Always they came back to the statement that Lee confessed that he had thrown the girl down and cut her throat.

By the time the lawyers were through with Jacob Hamblin, the audience was in such a state of horror and shock, they were ready to believe the worst. Three witnesses earlier had testified that Lee had killed one person, a woman, and might have killed others. It did not matter that one said the woman was killed by a blow from the butt end of a gun; a second told that she was shot with the gun as Lee stood on the ground, and the third had her also shot, but said that she was in the lead wagon, in which only children were riding. Now Hamblin, who was many miles away when the massacre took place told the most convincing tale of all. No other white man was named as participating; the Indians were there, many of them, killing people. Now it seemed to the crowd that instead of one woman, Lee had killed at least four and there was a strong suggestion that he might have cut the throats of the wounded men in the wagon as well.

So carefully had the questions been placed; so patient and delicate had the lawyers been with the witnesses, that the combined sins of all the fifty men who were present were laid on the shoulders of John D. Lee. By the time the arguments were finished he had been made responsible for planning and executing the murder, in defiance of his superior officers and contrary to their orders.

Through it all Lee sat facing the court in silence. He called no witnesses; made no defense. After an hour's consultation the jury brought in a verdict: "Guilty of murder in the first degree."

That night Lee wrote a long letter to Emma at Lonely Dell, telling her of the outcome and asking for money that they might carry the case to a higher court. He insisted that he had been betrayed. He said:

> . . . My worthy friend and able attorney, W. W. Bishop, felt that we were sold; he . . . had the promise that all was right from the leading men of the church here in Beaver, and even went so far as to mark the names of each man to be retained on the jury. . . Six witnesses testified against me, four of whom pergured themselves by swearing falsehoods of the blackest character.
>
> Old Jacob Hamblin, the fiend of Hell, testified under oath that I had told him that two young women were found in a thicket . . . by an Indian chief, who brought the girls to me and wanted to know what was to be done with them. That I replied that they was to old to live and would give evidence and must be killed . . . that I then cut her throat and the Indian killed the other. Such a thing I never heard of before, let alone committing the awful deed. The old hypocrite thought that now was his chance to reek his vengeance on me by swearing away my life. . .

Immediately following the sentence of death, two identical petitions were circulated in southern Utah, one in Beaver and vicinity, the other in Panguitch, begging Governor G. W. Emery for clemency for Lee. They set forth the conditions under which the massacre occurred; the fear of the Indians, the excitement of the approaching army, the fact that a general amnesty had been extended. The crime had been committed nearly twenty years previous; Lee had grown old and was in poor health. But the chief argument was that "he is but one of many who are equally guilty with himself of the crime. . . Said Lee is thus made a sacrifice to atone for the whole crime . . . to suffer death upon the testimony, connivance and prosecution of those equally guilty or more guilty than himself . . . that the whole proceedings were more properly Military acts than personal deeds."

These petitions were signed by a total of 514 persons. That the Governor paid some attention to them, that he asked advice of the military is shown by the following, evidently the last page of a letter:

> Considering the age of the prisoner and the long time elapsing between commission of the crime and conviction, would recommend clemency only on condition of his making a full & explicit statement of all the facts and circumstances attending the com-

mission of the crime, substantiating his statements by proofs, and
fixing the responsibility of his acts upon the proper person or
persons . . . and disclosing the names of his accomplices,
with a full substantiated statement of the extent of their participation. This I have been informed the prisoner can do, and if he
will do so, would recommend that his life be spared and his
sentence remitted or commuted.   N Douglas
                                              Lt Col 14 Inf
                                              Comdr Ft. Cameron

Lee did not make the public confession that would have spared him;
however, he did start to write the story of his life. He began at his
birth and followed his activities to the summer of 1847, when he was
at Summer Quarters raising corn for the church. When he had written
thus far it became clear that he would not be able to finish it all before
his execution. He laid down his pen and, encouraged by friendly
officers, told the story of the massacre to stenographers who took it
down in shorthand. Hurt at his own betrayal, he told other instances
of misguided justice and unjustified murder. The manuscript was
given to W. W. Bishop, who published it later that year.

On March 23 in company with officers and soldiers, Lee walked
over the ground where the massacre had taken place. The hills and
the general contours of the land were familiar but instead of grassy
meadow land, there was a gravelly waste as though the curse of God
actually had fallen upon the valley. Wagon wheels had cut through
the sod, overgrazing had stripped off the grass, and the floods of 1861
and 1873 had drained off all that had been a meadow in 1857.

The morning was cool, the breeze sharp enough to call for an overcoat and muffler, for even though he was soon to be shot, he might as
well be comfortable while he lived. Bringing him to the Meadows was
either a publicity stunt or a sadistic attempt to break his morale. They
could as well have stood him against the prison wall at Beaver; he
would have died as quickly, but this made better news copy.

The photographer, ironically enough, was James Fennimore, of
whom Lee and his family had become so fond while he lived with
them at Lonely Dell. He set up his tripod and took pictures of the
wagons, the officers, the general terrain. Lee obligingly posed for him
sitting on the edge of his coffin.

The phrase, "Nothing in his life became him like the leaving of it,"
certainly seemed to apply here. Lee remained calm and resigned. He
had written a farewell message to his wives and children the night
before and when given a last chance to speak declared his innocence

in a clear, strong voice, faltering only at mention of his wives and children.

"I have but little to say this morning. Of course I feel that I am on the brink of eternity, and the solemnities of eternity should rest upon my mind at the present," he began, and after declaring that he had tried to save the emigrants and that he was being sacrificed in a cowardly, dastardly manner, continued, "I am ready to die. I trust in God. I have no fear. Death has no terror." Finally he closed with the words, "Having said this, I feel resigned. I ask the Lord, my God, if my labors are done, to receive my spirit."

He shook hands with those around him, removed his overcoat, hat, and muffler and handed them to his friends. Only one favor he asked of the guards, that they center his heart and not mutilate his body. He was blindfolded, but at his request his hands remained free. At the signal "Ready! Aim! Fire!" Five shots rang out, and John D. Lee fell back into his coffin without a moan or cry or a tremor of the body except for a convulsive twitching of the fingers of his left hand.

The coffin was closed and the body delivered to two of his sons who placed it in a wagon and by making a forced drive all night arrived at Panguitch early the next morning. Knowing of Lee's desire to be buried in his temple robes, friends opened the coffin briefly laid the robes on top of the body, and replaced the lid. Burial was in the local cemetery, where a simple monument now stands.

"Unto the Third
and Fourth Generations"

John D. Lee lamented the fact that he must bequeath to his children a legacy of shame, but even he could not guess how this burden would grow with the years. The Old Testament edict that "the sins of the fathers shall be visited upon their children unto the third and fourth generation" was in this case fulfilled. Since Lee was declared the only one responsible for the massacre and his execution made proof of it, people found it easy to lay other crimes at his door. The list grew in horror as it grew in length, stories of rape and murder in many forms.

In southern Utah, especially, folk tales multiplied. The Lee home in Washington became a haunted house where mysterious personages moved in the shadows, and shrieks and moans disturbed the night air. No one would live in the house, even after the mysteries had been explained away — the movements those of a squirrel nesting in the attic, the groans coming from a beer bottle which propped up a window in such a way that the wind blew into it and produced the eerie sounds. After the house was used as a granary and store room, boys did their chores there before dark. Finally the house was torn down, and the stone used to help build the dam in the river. The fig tree on the lot, said to have been planted on the grave of a murdered child, was allowed to die because no one dared eat of its fruit.

More damaging than the folk tales was the report that Brigham Young had cursed John D. Lee and predicted that his posterity would live in poverty and ignorance. Small wonder that his grandchildren suffered slights and slurs, that courtships were quickly terminated and engagements broken off when young men learned that the girls they had thought so desirable had the blood of John D. Lee in their veins.

There were, of course, some loyal friends. Lemuel H. Redd would never allow a disparaging remark about John D. Lee to be made in his home; George Decker defended Lee's reputation publicly. Nathan Tenney listed him as one of the few who would enter the Celestial Kingdom. Evidently the five hundred people who signed the petitions asking that his life be spared felt that Lee was not so black as he had been painted. Yet in the strong tide of public sentiment their voices were not heard.

After Lee's execution, some of his families crossed the Colorado and moved into Arizona and New Mexico. It was better to get into a new country where their children would have an opportunity to succeed on their own merits. While some mothers never spoke of their ancestor at all, others passed on stories of his loyalty and courage, impressing their children with the idea that they must try to live worthy of such a heritage. They must make the Lee name honorable by their own achievements and demonstrate that a good tree brings forth good fruit.

John D. Lee claimed to have fifty-four living children at his death. Of these we have record of fifty, twenty-five girls and twenty-five boys, all of whom married and, with only two exceptions, had children. To show how widely spread they were even in the second generation we list the married names of the girls, arranged alphabetically: Anderson, Blair, Bliss, Clark, Cornelius, Cluff, Dalton, Darrow, Haley, Lamb, Maloney, Matthews, Morris, Mortensen, Norton, Pace, Prince, Schurtz, Smithson, Wood, and Young. Mrs. Manetta Henrie (695 North 3 East, Provo) has just printed a twelve-hundred page book of John D. Lee's family. It shows quite clearly that if Brigham Young ever did pronounce a curse upon them (and there is no documentary evidence yet found to show that he did), that was one time when he was mistaken, for among the group are leaders in many fields, financial, professional, cultural.

In the early 1900's some of his descendants began to collect affidavits from Lee's associates who still lived, giving their experiences with him. Though most of these were flattering, the document which affected his family profoundly was his own last message to them. Written in the prison at Fort Cameron, it was delivered to Sumner Howard on the field of execution minutes before the fatal shots. Howard was to copy it and send the original to Rachel, who was asked to make copies for each of the other wives. In 1950 it was printed and passed out to all who attended the Lee reunion that year. It reads:

CAMP CAMERON,   March 13th, 1877

Morning clear, still and pleasant. The guard, George Tracy informs me that Col Nelson and Judge Howard have gone. Since my confinement here, I have reflected much over my sentence, and as the time of my execution is drawing near, I feel composed, and as calm as the summer morning. I hope to meet my fate with manly courage. I declare my innocence. I have done nothing designedly wrong in that unfortunate and lamentable affair with which I have been implicated. I used my utmost endeavors to save them from their sad fate. I freely would have given worlds, were they at my command, to have averted that evil. I wept and mourned over them before and after, but words will not help them now it is done. My blood cannot help them, neither can it make the atonement required. Death to me has no terror. It is but a struggle, and all is over. I much regret to part with my loved ones here, especially under that odium of disgrace that will follow my name; that I cannot help.

I know that I have a reward in Heaven, and my conscience does not accuse me. This to me is a great consolation. I place more value upon it than I would upon an eulogy without merit. If my work is done here on earth, I ask my God in Heaven, in the name of His Son Jesus Christ, to receive my spirit, and allow me to meet my loved ones who have gone behind the vail. The bride of my youth and her faithful mother, my devoted friend and companion, N.A. [Nancy Armstrong], also my dearly beloved children, all of whom I parted from with sorrow, but shall meet them with joy — I bid you all an affectionate farewell. I have been treacherously betrayed and sacrificed in the most cowardly manner by those who should have been my friends, and whose will I have diligently striven to make my pleasure, for the last thirty years at least. In return for my faithfulness and fidelity to him and his cause, he has sacrificed me in a most shameful and cruel way. I leave them in the hands of the Lord to deal with them according to the merits of their crimes, in the final restitution of all things.

To the Mothers of My Children

I beg of you to teach them better things than to ever allow themselves to be let down so low as to be steeped in the vice, corruption and villainy that would allow them to sacrifice the meanest wretch on earth, much less a neighbor and a friend, as their father has been. Be kind and true to each other. Do not contend about my property. You know my mind concerning it. Live faithful and humble before God, that we may meet again in the mansions of bliss that God has prepared for His faithful servants. Remember the last words of your most true and devoted friend on earth, and let them sink deep into your tender aching hearts; many of you I may never see in this world again, but I leave my blessing with you. Farewell.

JOHN D. LEE

The publication of A Mormon Chronicle, the Diaries of John D. Lee (Henry E. Huntington Library, 1955) has given the family something more concrete upon which to base their evaluation of their ancestor, and other diaries still unprinted but circulated in typewritten form have helped to change the attitude of his family from one of apology to one of militant pride.

An example is a grandson who said recently, "I am going to the Mountain Meadows and shoot the words *as leader* off that plaque with my rifle. When I am apprehended and arrested, I shall plead guilty, but shall refuse to pay the fine upon the ground that the words are not true and should be taken off. That will force the case into court. In this, his third public trial, Lee will be acquitted."

For the fourth printing of my *Mountain Meadows Massacre*, I was asked to sketch changes which I would make if I were to do it over. The information is in a 15-page insert in the front of the book.

First, the massacre grew out of the war plans to keep out an invading army. The Indians, often called "The Battle-Ax of God," were important, as shown by an entry in the diary of Brigham Young, Sept. 1, 1857:

Kanosh the Pavaunt chief with several of his band visited me gave them some council and presents. A spirit seems to be takeing possession of the Indians to assist Israel. I can hardly restrain them from *exterminating* the Americans.

This from Brigham Young himself, added to the fact that Indians were brought from as far south as the lower Virgin, seems evidence that the Mormons had "started a fire they couldn't quench." "The Indians, we suppose, will do as they wish," written into two different letters lends credence to the plan of an Indian massacre.

Second, the number of people killed was less than the 123 given on the Marker. It could have been not more than 96; perhaps as few as 67. The train divided almost in half at Salt Lake City; at least three families remained there to come later. The twelve men, "The Missouri Wildcats," who caused the trouble, stopped only over-night at the Meadows, and learned of the massacre at San Bernardino.

Of the 18 children saved, 17 were returned to relatives. The infant, Nancy Cameron, daughter of William Cameron, was taken by Klingensmith to his wife who had a nursing baby, kept there until she was two years old, and then given to a childless couple at Cedar. She grew up a Mormon and was married in the Mormon Temple.

The third problem centers about the money which the Fancher train is supposed to have carried. At the Fancher family reunion held September 5, 1955, at Harrison, Arkansas, Judge Fancher from Florida told how the leader of the murdered train, Alexander Fancher, had crossed the continent in 1855, traveling over this same route both out and back, and was treated well by the Mormon settlers on both trips. He purchased a large tract of land in California, returned and persuaded his friends to sell out and go with him to colonize. According to Judge Fancher, they carried with them in a strong box $4,000.00 in gold coin to be the down payment on the ranch.

In a letter to the author from Mr. Frank Beckwith of Delta, Utah, shortly before his death, he stated in effect, "It is well known that

No. 17

ERECTED 1932

MOUNTAIN MEADOWS
A FAVORITE RECRUITING PLACE ON
THE OLD SPANISH TRAIL.

IN THIS VICINITY SEPTEMBER 7-11,1857 OCCURRED ONE
OF THE MOST LAMENTABLE TRAGEDIES IN THE ANNALS
OF THE WEST. A COMPANY OF ABOUT 140 ARKANSAS AND
MISSOURI EMIGRANTS LED BY CAPTAIN CHARLES FANCHER,
ENROUTE TO CALIFORNIA, WAS ATTACKED BY WHITE MEN AND
INDIANS. ALL BUT 17, BEING SMALL CHILDREN, WERE KILLED.
JOHN D. LEE, WHO CONFESSED PARTICIPATION AS LEADER,
WAS LEGALLY EXECUTED HERE MARCH 23,1877. MOST OF
THE EMIGRANTS WERE BURIED IN THEIR OWN DEFENSE PITS.

THIS MONUMENT WAS REVERENTLY DEDICATED SEPTEMBER 10, 1932
BY THE UTAH PIONEER TRAILS AND LANDMARKS ASSOCIATION AND
THE PEOPLE OF SOUTHERN UTAH.

PLAQUE ON THE MOUNTAIN MEADOWS MONUMENT
Photograph by Oliver Sigurdson, Los Angeles, California.

Extract from the Daily Diary of Amos Milton Musser
Courtesy of Burton W. Musser of Murray, Utah.

the emigrants carried with them $4,000.00 in gold coin, and it is also well known that the money was never found." He gave the cash as one of the motives for the massacre and reasoned that as soon as the troubles with the Indians began Captain Fancher would have buried the money within the enclosure and probably built a fire on the spot to mark it. He suggested that we go together to search for the buried treasure, using a device which he had secured — evidently a Geiger-counter — and promised that I should have half of what we found. I did not take this suggestion seriously, not even seriously enough to file his letter, but answered to remind him that since the floods of 1861 the place had been eroded so deeply and the gully cut was so large that whatever money might have been buried there in 1857 was likely somewhere between its original hiding place and the Gulf of Mexico, probably in the bottom of Lake Mead.

About a year ago, in going through the handwritten diary notebook of Amos Milton Musser, I came across the following entry:

"City Mon-Jan-17, /76
Returned this pm from Holden whence I hv been to receive & bring home *4000$ gold* coin the liberal donations as offering for Temple building purposes made by Father *Wm Stevens* now in 76 yr of age For a long time he has been anxious to make this disposition of this means & felt much relieved after placing it in my possession to convey it to this Cit [italics his].

The fact that this was the exact amount said to have been carried by the Fancher Train, and that it was in gold coin intrigued me greatly, as did the expression that *for a long time* Father William Stevens had wanted to give this money in to the church and that he *felt much relieved* after doing so. Amos Milton Musser was from 1858 until 1876 the "Traveling Bishop" of the church. The entry in his day-book which precedes the one quoted was of his going to Pioche to collect the rent on the telegraph line and gives a graphic picture of the mining activities there. In less than three months after the entry made above, Brother Musser was released from his position and sent on a mission to Pennsylvania.

I was so interested that I visited the town of Holden, located the old store, saw the fine brick homes built by the sons of William Stevens, and visited with two of his descendants. The first, a very intelligent, gracious lady who was a granddaughter-in-law, received me cordially. She was the family genealogist, she said, and was then writing a family history. She had heard a story to the effect that William Stevens had given to the church $5000.00 in gold, but considered it so incredible that she refused to include it in her story.

When I explained that I was not interested primarily in genealogy, but in history, she sent me to her sister-in-law who lived just around the corner.

Here also I was well received, and early in our conversation she volunteered, "My grandfather gave five thousand dollars in gold pieces to the church. He wrote a letter to President Young and told him about it. Brother Brigham didn't come after it himself, but he sent a man in a buggy who took it up to Salt Lake City and turned it in. It wasn't counted as tithing, either."

Here then is only the coincidence of the four thousand dollars in gold coin. I had been skeptical about the Fancher's company having it in the first place, and if they did have it, how could it have come into the hands of Father William Stevens? Any conjecture is farfetched — whether Fancher left it with Stevens when the first Indian shooting took place there at Holden; whether it was pulled out of the debris of a sand dune along the Virgin River bottom by Stevens as he searched for wood to make a fire — any guess is not more strange than the fact that he had the gold coin for a long time and was much relieved to be rid of it.

Thus it is that not only John D. Lee as a man, but the forces which were set into motion by the one tragedy in which he was an important actor, reach out and touch life and history from many angles, the last word of which remains to be said.

Through all the eighty-four years which have elapsed since the execution of John D. Lee, the dearest hope of his many descendants has been that his name should some day be cleared. An action taken on Thursday, April 20, 1961, has made that hope a reality for them.

On that day the First Presidency and Quorum of the Twelve of the Mormon Church met in a joint session and "It was the action of the Council after considering all the facts available that authorization be given for the re-instatement to membership and former blessings to John D. Lee."

On May 8 and 9 following, the necessary ordinances were performed in the Salt Lake Temple.

Appendix

THE WIVES OF
JOHN D. LEE

	children born	" dead by 1877
Aggatha Ann Woolsey	11	3
Nancy Bean	1	1
Louisa Free	1	1
Sarah Caroline Williams	11	2
Abigail Woolsey	0	
Rachel Andora Woolsey	8	1
Polly Ann Workman	0	
Martha Elizabeth Berry	5	1
Delethia Morris	0	
Nancy Ann Vance	1	
Emoline Vaughn Woolsey	0	
Nancy Gibbons Armstrong	0	
Mary Vance (Polly) Young	3	1
Lavina Young	3	
Mary Leah Groves	7	
Mary Ann Williams	0	
Emma Batchelor	7	1
Terressa Morse Chamberlain	0	
Ann Gordge	3	
Totals	60	10

Years of Marriage: 1835, 1840, 1845, 1850, 1855, 1860, 1865, 1870, 1875, 1877

* deceased

Aggatha Ann Woolsey, Abigail Woolsey, and Nancy Armstrong all died faithful
wives to John D. Lee. Five others remained faithful until his death.

Families of John D. Lee

1. JOHN DOYLE LEE, b. 6 Sept. 1812, Kaskaskia, Randolph County, Illinois; d. 23 March 1877, Mountain Meadows, Southern Utah; m. 24 July 1833: AGGATHA ANN WOOLSEY, b. 18 Jan. 1814, Lincoln County, Kentucky; d. 4 June 1866, New Harmony, Utah.
   CHILDREN:
   William Oliver, b. 3 July 1834, near Vandalia, Illinois; d. 5 Sept. 1835, Vandalia.
   Elizabeth Adoline, b. 8 April 1836, Vandalia; d. 16 Apr. 1838, Vandalia.
   Sarah Jane, b. 3 March 1837, Vandalia; d. 27 March 1915; m. Charles W. Dalton.
   John Alma, b. 26 Aug. 1840, Nauvoo, Ill.; d. 11 Sept. 1881; m. Mary Ann Williams.
   Mary Adoline, b. 24 Aug. 1842, Nauvoo, Ill.; d. 26 Dec. 1925; m. Don Carlos Shurtz; 2 m. Marcus Henry Darrow.
   Joseph Hyrum, b. 12 July 1844, Nauvoo, Ill.; d. 25 April 1932; m. Mary Elizabeth Woolsey.
   Heber John, b. 15 Aug. 1846, near Omaha, Neb.; d. 1847, Summer Quarters.
   John Willard, b. 11 Oct. 1849, Big Cottonwood, Utah; d. 7 Oct. 1923; m. Lucinda Margaret Clark.
   Louisa Evaline, b. 16 Oct. 1850, Big Cottonwood, Utah; d. 4 Sept. 1932; m. William Prince.
   Samuel Gulley, b. 26 May 1853, Harmony, Utah; d. 4 March 1897; m. Rebecca Ann Alexander.
   Ezra Taft, b. 14 May 1856, Fort Harmony, Utah; d. 19 Sept. 1925; m. Annie Hamblin.

2. John Doyle Lee [see above] m. Feb. 5, 1845, Nauvoo, Illinois: NANCY BEAN, b. 14 Dec. 1826, West Troy, Missouri; married later to Zachariah Decker.
   CHILD:
   Cornelia Lee, b. 15 January 1846, Nauvoo, Ill.; d. 26 Dec. 1937, Sanford, Colo.; m. Lars Mortensen, bore him twelve children.

3. John D. Lee, m. 19 April 1845, Nauvoo, Ill: LOUISA FREE (daughter of A. P. Free) b. Tennessee; divorced 12 May 1849; later the wife of Daniel H. Wells.

CHILD:

Heber John, b. winter 1845-6; died at the age of twelve, Salt Lake City.

4. John D. Lee, m. 19 April 1845, Nauvoo, Illinois: SARAH CAROLINE WILLIAMS, b. 24 Nov. 1830, Murfreesboro, Tennessee; d. 16 Feb. 1907, Torrey, Utah.

CHILDREN:

Harvey Parley, b. 1 Oct. 1852, Parowan, Utah; d. 4 Feb. 1927; m. Sarah Ellen Adams.

George Albert, b. 1855, Fort Harmony; d. 6 Feb. 1862 (falling wall).

Margaret Ann, b. 3 Jan. 1857, Fort Harmony; d. 6 Feb. 1862 (falling wall).

Rachel Olive, b. 6 Nov. 1858, Fort Harmony; d. 15 May 1924; m. Riley R. Norton.

Sarah Ann, b. 6 Nov. 1860, Fort Harmony; d. 21 Dec. 1920; m. John D. Young.

Charles William, b. 9 Aug. 1862, Fort Harmony; d. (?); m. Leah A. Young.

Mary Elizabeth, b. 1 April 1864, Fort Harmony; d. (?); m. Charles Lamb.

Robert Edmund, b. 2 Jan. 1866, Fort Harmony; d. 24 April 1928; m. Alpharetta R. Cluff.

Helen Josephine, b. 18 Jan. 1868, Fort Harmony; d. (?); m. Daniel Matthews.

Walter Brigham, b. 30 Sept. 1869, Fort Harmony; d. (?); m. Leah M. Phelps.

Ammon Doyle, b. 15 Jan. 1872, Kanab; d. 12 April 1940; m. Annie Maria Imlay.

5. John Doyle Lee, m. 3 May, 1845: ABIGAIL WOOLSEY, mother of his wives Aggatha Ann, Rachel, and Emoline. Lee always insisted that although she was sealed to him to be a member of his family, she was never a wife in fact. She died en route to Utah, 3 Sept. 1848.

6. John Doyle Lee, m. 3 May 1845, Nauvoo, Illinois: RACHEL ANDORA WOOLSEY, b. 5 Aug. 1825; d. 1912, Lebanon, Arizona.

CHILDREN:

Elizabeth Abigail, b. Dec. 1848, Big Cottonwood, Utah; d. age 5.

Nancy Emily, b. 22 Jan. 1850, Big Cottonwood; d. 1931; m. Heber Dalton.

Helen Rachel [Nellie], b. 29 July 1852, Parowan; d. (?); m. Joseph Woods.

Amorah, b. 29 March 1856, Harmony; d. July 1945; m. Lehi Smithson.

Ralph Doyle, b. 12 Feb. 1858, Harmony; d. 20 July 1918, Stafford, Ariz.; m. Mae McDonald.

John Amasa, b. 9 March 1860, Harmony; d. 29 April 1939, Lebanon, Ariz.; m. Mary Elvira Bigelow.

William Franklin, b. 5 Aug. 1863, Harmony; d. 14 June 1946; m. Clarabell Hamblin.

Joseph Willard, b. 9 Aug. 1868, Harmony; d. 30 Oct. 1916; Lebanon, Ariz.; m. Edith Kimball.

7. John D. Lee married during the fall of 1845 in Nauvoo: POLLY ANN WORKMAN. Of her we know little except that she was taken across the Mississippi River with Nancy Bean in the first of the Lee wagons to go, on February 12, 1846. There were misunderstandings between her and Lee, and on February 11, 1847, he sent her back to stay with her brother. She married a Mr. Bennett in Iowa and did not come to Utah.

8. John Doyle Lee married during the summer or fall of 1845 in Nauvoo: MARTHA ELIZABETH BERRY, b. 22 Nov. 1826, Lebanon, Tenn.; d. 18 June 1885, Kanosh, Utah.

CHILDREN:

Harriet Josephine, b. 16 Feb. 1850, Big Cottonwood, Utah; d. 24 Oct. 1922, Moab, Utah; m. Orley D. Bliss.

William Orson, b. 23 May 1852, Parowan, Utah; d. 1908, Kanosh, Utah; m. Elizabeth Riddle.

Armelia, b. 1854; died an infant.

Thurza Jane, b. 24 Oct. 1855, Palmyra, Utah Co.; d. 16 July 1894; m. Oscar A. Anderson.

Henrietta, b. 1858; died aged two years.

Martha Berry left John D. Lee in 1858 and was married to Dennis Dorrity as his third wife. By him she had six additional children, two of them died young. The family lived at Kanosh, Utah.

9. John Doyle Lee married during the fall or winter of 1845-46 in Nauvoo: DELETHIA MORRIS. Of her we have learned nothing except that while Lee was away on his trip to Santa Fe, New Mexico, she was married to a Mr. Miller, a trader.

10.   In the fall of 1845 Lee married Nancy Ann Vance, daughter of John Vance. She was born 29 Sept. 1824; baptized 1 Oct. 1839. Her daughter, Hannah, was born at Winter Quarters in 1846. At Summer Quarters on May 3, 1848, she received a letter from her father "togeather with $5.00 requesting her to act her pleasure about coming back." She returned to Winter Quarters, and later married William Shin Wordsworth by whom she had three additional children. The daughter, Hannah, adopted the Wordsworth name, and later married a Mr. Harris.

11.   John D. Lee married on December 21, 1846: EMOLINE VAUGHN WOOLSEY, younger sister of his wives Aggatha Ann and Rachel. During the summer of 1847 she left the home at Summer Quarters and went back with Charles Kennedy on a visit to Pisgah. Lee refused to accept her into his family again, an action which he later regretted. She remained in the mid-west and did not come to Utah.

12.   On February 27, 1847, in Winter Quarters, Lee had three women sealed to him in one ceremony. The first of these was one of his converts: NANCY GIBBONS ARMSTRONG, b. 7 Jan. 1799, at Knoxville, Tennessee. Thirteen years older than Lee, she had followed him out and asked to become a member of his family. She died at Summer Quarters in August, 1847.

13.   John D. Lee married on the same date, 27 February 1847, at Winter Quarters: MARY VANCE [POLLY] YOUNG, b. 10 Nov. 1817, in Jackson County, Tenn.; d. (?).
CHILDREN:
Elizabeth, b. 24 April 1851, Parowan, Utah; d. 17 June 1912; m. Wilson D. Pace.
James Young, b. 12 July 1852, Harmony, Utah; d. (?); m. Anna Pace.
John Doyle, b. 21 Feb. 1859, Harmony, Utah; died an infant.

14.   John D. Lee married in a common ceremony a sister of Polly Young: LAVINA YOUNG, b. 25 Sept. 1820, in Jackson County, Tenn.; d. 4 July 1883, at Nutrioso, Arizona.
CHILDREN:
John David, b. 19 March 1851, Parowan, Utah; d. 22 May 1922; m. Evelyn D. Clark; 2 m. Inez Hamblin.
Ellen, b. 11 Nov. 1852, Parowan, Utah; d. 12 June 1924, Cedar City, Utah; m. John Wesley Clark.
Sabina, b. 18 June 1855, Cedar City, Utah; d. 9 Feb. 1920; m. Hyrum Brown Clark.

15. Because the emigration records list a Mary Leah G. Lee with the same birth date, it would seem that there had been a sealing ceremony much earlier, but there is evidence that this girl did not join the Lee family until 1853. Married to John D. Lee as his fifteenth wife was: MARY LEAH GROVES, b. 30 Oct. 1836, Far West, Caldwell County, Mo.; d. 12 July 1912, at Virgin, Utah.

CHILDREN:

Erastus Franklin, b. 1 March 1854, Cedar City, Utah; d. 4 Nov. 1914; m. Harriet E. Stratton.

Miriam Leah, b. 14 April 1856, Harmony, Utah; d. 6 Jan. 1941, Virgin, Utah; m. Henry Cornelius.

Lucy Olive, b. 15 April 1858, Harmony, Utah; d. 30 Jan. 1922; m. Thomas Maloney.

John Hurd, b. 27 March 1860, Harmony, Utah; d. 20 Sept. 1938; m. Martha Titt.

Elisha Squire, b. 20 July 1862, Kanarra, Utah; d. 15 March 1937; m. Eliza Titt.

Mary Sarepta, b. 23 July 1865, Harmony; d. 23 Nov. 1897; m. William Bliss.

Jacob, b. 28 Oct. 1867, Toquerville; d. 1 Feb. 1947; m. Mary M. Morrey.

16. MARY ANN WILLIAMS, b. 11 Sept. 1844, Springfield, Illinois; d. 8 Feb. 1882, Panguitch, Utah.

In his *Confessions*, Lee said that he was "sealed" to Mary Ann Williams in 1856, which would indicate that she was an orphan child who lived in his home. In the *Mormon Chronicle* he gave evidence that she was not happy and when at last he learned that she was in love with his oldest son, Alma, he married them on January 18, 1859. They lived happily together and had a family of seven children.

17. John D. Lee married his seventeenth wife in Salt Lake City, 7 Jan. 1858: EMMA BATCHELOR, b. 21 April 1836, at Negkfield, England; d. 16 Nov. 1897, Winslow, Arizona.

CHILDREN:

John Henry, b. 30 June 1859, Harmony, Utah; d. 10 July 1859.

William James, b. 16 Dec. 1860, Harmony; d. 20 Nov. 1920, Holbrook, Ariz.; m. Clara Workman.

Isaac [Ike], b. 29 Nov. 1863; d. 9 Nov. 1892 (shot by Chas. C. Wagner); m. Bertha Avis Leevan.

Ann Eliza, b. 22 July 1866, Harmony; d. (?); m. Barney Haley.

Rachel Emma, b. 22 July 1866 (twin); d. (?); m. Frank Cliff.

Frances Dell, b. 17 Jan. 1872, Lonely Dell, Ariz.; d. (?); m. David Blair.

Victoria Elizabeth, b. 5 Nov. 1873, Lonely Dell, Ariz.; d. 8 April 1888, Winslow, Arizona; unmarried.

Lee's wife Emma's maiden name appears in various spellings. Two in Lee's diary are "Bachellor" and "Batchellor"; elsewhere as "Batcheller" and "Batchelder." However, LDS Church records and her family genealogist spell it "Batchelor."

18.   TERRESSA MORSE CHAMBERLAIN, b. 20 October 1813, Luzerne Co., Pa. Came with her husband, Solomon Chamberlain south to Parowan in John D. Lee's company in 1851, and in 1852 moved with the group to Fort Harmony. The census of 1850 gave the family as Solomon Chamberlain, aged 62 b. Conn.; Terressa, aged 30 b. Pa.; Charles, aged 17 b. Mo.; Robert, aged 16 b. Ohio; Louisa, aged 1 b. Deseret. When her husband moved north, Terressa refused to go, but remained to live in the Lee home. She was married to John D. Lee, 18 March 1859, by Amasa Lyman, and remained with Lee until 1870, when she joined a son in Provo.

19.   John D. Lee's last wife was ANN GORDGE, born 1848, in Adelaide, Australia. The date of the marriage has not been found; probably 1865.

CHILDREN:

Samuel James, b. 14 March 1867, Harmony, Utah; d. 7 Dec. 1937, Portland, Oregon; m. Mary Effie Savage.

Merabe Emma, b. 14 Oct. 1868, Harmony; d. 21 Nov. 1945; m. George L. Morris.

Albert Doyle, b. 1871.

Bibliographical Note

For this book I have drawn much from the writings of John D. Lee himself. From 1840 until the day of his death this man kept a faithful account of his activities, for he believed that he and his people were making significant history which should be recorded. Much of this has never been printed, but has been photostated and copied on the typewriter. It includes his mission diaries from 1840-1844 inclusive, a summary journal of 1844 and early 1845, as well as his diary of the winter of 1845-46. From February to September 1846 Lee was one of the official recorders and clerks of Brigham Young, so during this period he kept a careful account of the journey from the Mississippi River to Winter Quarters. This adds up to well over a hundred typewritten pages.

The next unpublished diary is a record of the trip made by Lee and Howard Egan from Winter Quarters west to Santa Fe to overtake the Mormon Battalion. This record is remarkable for its intimate, day-by-day account of the terrain, the plant and animal life, the general background of the area at that time. A part of it is retold with remarkable fidelity in his *Confessions* (St. Louis, 1877, and later reprints; title varies).

Lee returned from his Santa Fe trip on November 20, 1846. His next diary, beginning on the very next day, was found and published by Charles Kelly in 1938 under the title *Journals of John D. Lee* (Salt Lake City, 1938). It carries on the daily account until July 24, 1847. Since the edition was limited, this is now a rare book.

After a period of six months in which the diary has not been found, the *Mormon Chronicle* (2 vols., San Marino: The Huntington Library, 1955) opens on February 29, 1848, and continues without interruption until September of that year. During the next months entries are more brief and the original itself so faded and torn that parts are illegible, but the record continues until August 17, 1849.

Lee's diaries covering the call to settle at Parowan in Southern Utah, the journey there, and the establishment of the new community, cover the period from December 1850 to June 1851 and are published in the *Utah Historical Quarterly* for April, July, and October of 1952.

The Mormon Chronicle picks up the record on December 10, 1857, after a lapse of some six years, and except for another five year blank from 1861 to 1866, continues until 1876, just before Lee was released on bail to three months of freedom before his second trial.

From all this minutiae I have tried to reconstruct the life and character of John D. Lee, weighing it always against the general background of time and place and considering always the writings of contemporaries.

For background of his early life I used the large volume, *The Combined Histories of Randolph, Monroe, and Perry Counties, Illinois* (Philadelphia: J. L. McDonough & Company, 1833) which was compiled from the writings of many people who had pioneered the area around Kaskaskia, and from public records. *The Pioneer History of Illinois,* by John Reynolds (Chicago: Fergus, 1887) furnished other valuable material, while items from the National Archives and from the Wisconsin State Historical Society gave pertinent facts.

For conditions in Missouri in 1838, at the time of Lee's conversion to the Mormon Church, I used a number of the pamphlets of dissenters and apostates, among them the writings of Reed Peck "Mormons So Called," copied from the original manuscript by Dale L. Morgan; and *Mormonism Exposed* by William Swartzell (Pekin, Ohio: The Author, 1840). *The Life of David W. Patten* by Lycurgus A. Wilson (Salt Lake City: The Deseret News, 1900) represents the Mormon version of conditions, as do *A Comprehensive History of the Church* by B. H. Roberts (6 vols., Salt Lake City: Deseret Book Co., 1930) and other approved church writings. The diary of David Lewis gives a vivid story of the massacre at Haun's Mill.

Lee's own missionary diaries and his published reports in the *Times and Seasons* (Nauvoo, Illinois) furnish material for his own activities, while conditions in Nauvoo were pictured in the diaries of Hosea Stout, George Laub, Samuel Richards, Oliver B. Huntington, and Norton Jacob. The journal of James M. Monroe, who taught school in Nauvoo, is an illuminating document also. In spite of the many inaccuracies and misspelled names, William Hall's *The Abominations of Mormonism Exposed* (Cincinnati: I. Hart Co., 1852) gives a good idea of the excesses of both the Mormons and their neighbors, as do the writings of William Smith published in *The Illinois State Register* (Springfield) in *The Frontier Guardian* (Kanesville, Iowa).

The exodus from Nauvoo and the journey to Winter Quarters, the winter there, the season following during which most of the people remained while the pioneers made their way west to the valley of the Great Salt Lake is depicted by Hosea Stout, John Pulsipher, Mary Richards, and by Lee himself, as well as by the letters of Ursula Haskell. *The Women of Mormondom,* written largely by Eliza R.

Snow, but edited by Edward W. Tullidge (Salt Lake City, 1877) is also eloquent of life in a wagon or a temporary camp.

The last twenty-seven years of Lee's life were spent in Southern Utah and Arizona. Background for this period comes from James G. Bleak's "Annals of the Southern Mission," Books A and B, from the "Journal History of the Church," and from many personal records. These include Thomas D. Brown's "Journal of the Southern Indian Mission," diaries of Isaac C. Haight, Lorenzo Brown, George Laub, Charles L. Walker, John Pulsipher, George Washington Bean, George W. Brimhall's *Workers of Utah* (Provo City: Enquirer Co., 1889), Myron Abbott, Martha Cox, and Martha Spence Heywood. The military records of Iron and Washington counties are a rich source of material along with the original papers of William H. Dame, and the records of Indian Affairs from the National Archives.

Lee's own account of his trials is not available, but a complete transcript of the court record of both trials is on microfilm at the Henry E. Huntington Library and the Brigham Young University; this along with the official letters and orders, and the petitions which were circulated just before the execution, give a reliable account of Lee's last years. None, however, are more moving than his own day-by-day record of his life in the state penitentiary or his last message to his family.

The above mentioned sources represent specific materials used in this work, and are in addition to the bibliographical citations found in the author's *Mountain Meadows Massacre* (Stanford University Press, 1950).

The originals of John D. Lee's diaries, and copies of them, are now located as follows:

1840-1844: Mrs. Mozelle Bickley, Salt Lake City, Utah; typescript copy at the Utah State Historical Society.

1844-1845: Latter-day Saints Church Archives, Salt Lake City; typescript copy at the Utah State Historical Society.

1845/46 Winter: Later-day Saints Church Archives; typescript copy owned by Mrs. Manetta Henrie, Provo, Utah (use restricted).

1846 February to September: Latter-day Saints Church Archives; typescripts at the Utah State Historical Society, and at Brigham Young University.

1846, Santa Fe trip: Latter-day Saints Church Archives; typescripts at the Utah State Historical Society, and at Brigham Young University.

1846 November to 1847 July: Huntington Library, San Marino, California; published in Charles Kelly's *Journals of John D. Lee,* 1938.

1848 February to 1849 August: Huntington Library; published in *A Mormon Chronicle,* 1955.

1850 December to 1851 June: Latter-day Saints Church Archives; typescripts at Brigham Young University, and at the Utah State Historical Society; published in *Utah Historical Quarterly,* 1952.

1857 December to 1861, and 1866 to 1876: Huntington Library; published in *A Mormon Chronicle,* 1955.

Index